Words are the starting point. Without words, children can't talk about people, places, or things, about actions, relations, or states. Without words, children have no grammatical rules. Without words, there would be no sound structure, no word structure, and no syntax. The lexicon, then, is central in language, and in language acquisition.

Eve Clark's book argues for this centrality and for the general principles of conventionality and contrast at the core of language acquisition. She looks at the hypotheses children draw on about possible word meanings, and how they map their meanings onto forms. She starts with children's emerging knowledge of conventional words and their meanings – the ontological categories they rely on for early meanings and their strategies for mapping meanings onto forms. She then takes up their growing knowledge of word structure as reflected in their formation of new words, and shows that children learning different languages follow similar paths as they learn about words and word structure.

The lexicon in acquisition is unusual in dealing with data from a large variety of languages, in its emphasis on the general principles children rely on as they analyse complex word-forms (transparency of meaning, simplicity of form, and productivity), and in the broad perspective it takes on lexical acquisition.

CAMBRIDGE STUDIES IN LINGUISTICS

General Editors: J. BRESNAN, B. COMRIE, W. DRESSLER,
R. HUDDLESTON, R. LASS, D. LIGHTFOOT, J. LYONS,
P. H. MATTHEWS, R. POSNER, S. ROMAINE, N. V. SMITH,
N. VINCENT

The lexicon in acquisition

In this series

Supplementary volumes

Earlier issues not listed are also available

THE LEXICON
IN ACQUISITION

EVE V. CLARK

Stanford University

CAMBRIDGE
UNIVERSITY PRESS

Published by the Press Syndicate of the University of Cambridge
The Pitt Building, Trumpington Street, Cambridge CB2 1RP
40 West 20th Street, New York, NY 10011–4211, USA
10 Stamford Road, Oakleigh, Melbourne 3166, Australia

First published 1993
Reprinted 1994
First paperback edition 1995

Printed in Great Britain at the University Press, Cambridge

A catalogue record for this book is available from the British Library

Library of Congress cataloguing in publication data

Clark, Eve V.
The lexicon in acquisition / Eve V. Clark
    p.   cm. – (Cambridge studies in linguistics : 65)
Includes bibliographical references and index.
ISBN 0 521 44050 5
1. Language acquisition. 2. Vocabulary. I. Title. II. Series.
P118.C548   1993
401'.93–dc20   92–40122 CIP

ISBN 0 521 44050 5 hardback
ISBN 0 521 48464 2 paperback

Contents

Acknowledgments

This book has changed enormously since I began writing. The final version owes more than I can say to colleagues, friends, and students. I have benefited immeasurably from working with Ruth A. Berman, Kathie L. Carpenter, Sophia R. Cohen, Susan A. Gelman, Barbara F. Hecht, and Randa C. Mulford. Colleagues and friends have generously added to my collections of children's coinages over the years; and I am particularly grateful to Melissa Bowerman, Fortunée Kayra-Stuart, and Randa C. Mulford who have been more than generous in making data from their own records available to me. I also owe thanks to Elaine S. Andersen, Jean Berko Gleason, William Brewer, Michel Denis, Charles A. Ferguson, Uli Frauenfelder, Rochel Gelman, Diane Horgan, Peter Jordens, Aditi Lahiri, Philip Lieberman, Lise Menn, Marilyn M. Vihman, Jill G. de Villiers, and Jürgen Weissenborn for contributing comments, data, and references. I am specially indebted to Melissa Bowerman, Willem J. M. Levelt, and Dan I. Slobin for all their comments, insights, challenges, and discussion over the years.

Grateful thanks also to Margaret Amara, Center for Advanced Study in the Behavioral Sciences, Stanford, and to Karin Kastens, Max-Planck-Institut für Psycholinguistik, Nijmegen, for locating so many articles and books for me; to Laura Weeks and Susan Toumanoff for translating articles on Russian word-formation; and to Jens Allwood, Ruth A. Berman, Werner Deutsch, Barbara Kryk, Svenka Savić, Richard Schupbach, Magdalena Smoczyńska, Ragnhild Söderbergh, Stephen Wechsler, and Alessandro Zucchi for their willingness to help me with facts and data in German, Hebrew, Italian, Polish, Russian, Serbo-Croatian, and Swedish.

Herbert H. Clark, Lila R. Gleitman, and Dan I. Slobin made detailed comments on an earlier version of this book. I have incorporated many of their suggestions and I remain indebted to them for their enthusiasm and their encouragement.

My writing was supported in part by a Fellowship from the John Simon Guggenheim Memorial Foundation, and in part by the Max-Planck-Gesellschaft. My own research has been supported by the National Science Foundation (SOC75–17126, BNS80–07349), the National Institute of Child Health and Human Development (1-R01-HD18909), the Sloan Foundation, and The Spencer Foundation. I am particularly grateful to the Center for Advanced Study in the Behavioral Sciences at Stanford for support when I originally began this project, and to Willem J. M. Levelt and Wolfgang Klein for making it possible for me to complete the writing at the Max-Planck-Institut für Psycholinguistik, Nijmegen, The Netherlands.

Finally, I have special thanks for two people: Herb, long-time reader, critic, and friend, without whom this book might never have been written, and Damon, whose words I could not have done without. This book is for them both.

1 The lexicon: words old and new

Words make a language. They are used to talk about everything, from bee-keeping to bicycling, from navigation to international banking. They supply us with the means for everyday talk about our surroundings and activities, about people, objects, and places, about relations, properties, and states of being. We need them to communicate about events and ideas, technology, science, philosophy, and art. The stock of words speakers can draw on in a language is the lexicon. The present study is concerned with how children acquire a lexicon.

Words come first in language acquisition. Once children have some words, they begin to make generalizations about kinds of words – words for persons, places, and things, say, compared with words for actions and states. Children need words to instantiate syntactic categories, whether at the word level (noun, verb, adjective) or at the phrase level (noun phrase, verb phrase). And they must have words to realize grammatical relations like 'subject-of' or 'direct-object-of,' or mark such relations through agreement between subject and verb, say, for number and person. Without words, there would be no sound structure, no word structure, no syntax. The lexicon is central in language, and central in the acquisition of language.

The lexicon, as a result, offers a unique window on the process of acquisition for language as a whole. Although researchers have looked through this window at how children master the structure of sounds within words (the phonology of the language), and at the inflections on words (part of the morphology of a language), few have used this window to look at how children find out about, make use of, and build on words and word structure in lexical development. The present study makes such an attempt by focussing first on children's emerging knowledge of the conventional lexicon and then on their growing knowledge of word structure reflected in their formation of new words.

What do children have to learn when they learn the words of their

1

language? They must learn the word forms in use among the speakers around them, and they must the meanings those forms carry. More precisely, for each word, they need to store all sorts of information in memory. They must store the meanings for each word, the word class it belongs to (whether it is a noun or a verb, for example), its internal structure (whether it can be broken down into smaller parts), and how it is pronounced. Before we can look at how children acquire the lexicon, therefore, we must first look at what they have to learn. The focus of the present chapter is on the nature of the lexicon.

The lexicon

The lexicon of a language is the stock of established words speakers can draw on when they speak and have recourse to in understanding what they hear. This stock is stored in memory in such a way that speakers can locate the relevant units to use in both speaking and understanding. To do this, of course, speakers have to be able to identify words either by looking them up in memory (for comprehension) or by retrieving them as appropriate forms for conveying specific meanings (for production).

Words constitute the smallest semantic units that can move around in an utterance. They can move around to form new sequences with different meanings. Compare *The man chased the dog* with *The dog chased the man.* This mobility contrasts with the immobility of morphemes inside words. Morpheme order is fixed, as in the word *chased* versus the non-word **ed-chase*,[1] or *calmly* versus **ly-calm*. The grammatical category of a form may suggest that two (or more) words have the same form. Compare the verb *open* in *Rod opened the door* or *The door opened* with the adjective *open* in *The open window* or *The door is standing open.* Occasionally, even in the same grammatical setting, a word may have such distinct meanings that one posits two (or more) distinct words, for example *bank* in *He fished from the river bank* versus *That bank is a good example of art deco.*

These expressions must be stored in memory. But just what sort of information goes into memory with each one? How is this mental lexicon organized? One can think of this vast memory store as being organized like a dictionary – a mental list of lexical items together with detailed information about each one. The lexical items can be words (*cat, shell, rowan*) or idiomatic phrases (*cook someone's goose, do someone in, go to bat*

---

[1] An asterisk (*) is used to mark forms as ungrammatical.

for someone, blow one's own trumpet), each with its own "entry" in the mental lexicon.

Lexical entries

Lexical entries must include at least four kinds of information about each item: (a) the meaning, (b) the syntactic form, (c) the morphological structure, and (d) the phonological shape. The lexical entry for *skier*, for instance, might be outlined as follows:

SKIER:

(a)   meaning: 'one who skis'
(b)   syntax: category Noun, count
(c)   morphology: word root + -*er*
(d)   phonology: /skiər/

The information in (a) and (b) together comprise the LEMMA and the information in (c) and (d) the FORM for a word (Levelt 1989). So the lemma and form together make up the information associated with the lexical entry for each word or phrase in the lexicon.

The meaning in a lexical entry can be characterized broadly as the conceptual information that is tagged or pointed to by the lexical item in question. If we take the perspective of a speaker planning to talk, then the meaning may be a set of conceptual conditions that must hold for a particular word or phrase to be selected. In the case of a listener, the word points to a particular piece of conceptual knowledge. The meaning specified in the lexical entry is a shorthand for the pertinent conceptual information, as in the possible glosses offered for the meaning of *skier*: 'someone who skis' or 'someone who moves over snow by means of skis.' (Notice that glosses like these do not enlighten anyone who does not already know what skis or snow are.)

The meaning in a lexical entry is linked internally to other parts of the entry. It's closely linked to the set of syntactic properties, that is, to all the aspects of structure relevant to the possible syntactic environments. In the case of *skier*, this includes the syntactic category, namely NOUN, with the further specification that it is a count noun. The meaning portion of the entry is also linked to the morphology. The noun *skier* is built from the word *ski* combined with an affix, -*er*. This affix is further specified as indicating the agent of the action denoted by the verb root *ski*, and as attaching to a verb (or noun) to form a noun. Lastly, the meaning is linked to the phonological specification of the form in terms of the segments (/s-k-i-ə-r/), syllables (ski + er), and word stress (on the first syllable).

Lexical entries may also include information about the status of lexical items. They may indicate that an expression is dialectal, that is, not from the same dialect as the speaker's other vocabulary; that a term is characteristic of a special register or style of speech (baby talk, foreigner talk, formal speech, and so on); that it bears specific connotations, as in the differences between *statesman* and *politician*, *attempt* and *try*, or *skinny* and *slim* (Waldron 1979); or entries may contain information about usage, as for expressions like *break a leg, hello*, or *you're welcome*.

Lexical entries for verbs include more elaborate syntactic information than for most nouns. In addition to specifying the syntactic category as VERB, the entry also specifies the number of arguments. For a transitive verb, for example, there are two arguments, and these realize the grammatical relations of SUBJ (subject-of) and OBJ (direct-object-of). The lexical entry also indicates which roles are carried by the arguments (e.g., AGENT, PATIENT/THEME, LOCATION, and so on). So an intransitive verb like *run* would list a single argument (subject) in the syntactic portion of its entry, with the role of agent, as in *The boy runs*; transitive *read* would list two arguments, subject and direct object, with the roles agent and theme respectively, as in *The child read the book*; and transitive *put* would list three arguments (subject, direct object, and oblique) with the roles agent, theme, and location, as in *The woman put the flowers on the table*.

The morphological portion of the entry contains all the variant forms of each word. It identifies the root form (e.g., *run* or *give*), or the constituent parts of forms like *white-wash* or *compartmentalize*. In addition, for the verb *give*, it would include the forms *give*, *gives* (third singular, present tense), *gave* (past tense), and *given* (past participle). That is, this part of the lexical entry captures the intuition that the same *word* is involved in all uses of the verb *give* (*give, gives, giving, give, gave, given*); in all uses of the noun *horse* (*horse, horses*), or all uses of the pronoun *we* (*we, us, our, ours*). All the INFLECTED forms of a word belong to the same lexical entry.

Lexical items, then, are grouped into sets that link all the inflected forms of the same word within a single lexical entry. In a language like English, the inflections mark only the singular/plural distinction in nouns, and aspect, tense, and number in verbs. Case in English is marginal, and appears only in the subject and object forms of some pronouns (e.g., *I/me, he/him, she/her, they/them*). Adjectives in English can be inflected for degree, so forms like *red, redder, reddest* would belong in the same lexical entry. In other languages, nouns (and adjectives) may be inflected for case and gender in addition to number, and verbs may mark person, gender, and number in addition to tense and aspect. The range of distinctions in each of these inflectional categories varies across languages.

The inflected forms of a word are gathered into a single lexical entry. Words that are derived from a single form, though, are generally each sufficiently specialized in meaning to have their own lexical entries. For instance, *curious* and *curiosity* have separate entries, as do *eat, eater,* and *eatery;* or *act, active,* and *action.* For derived forms, both meaning and morphology interconnect all the lexical entries that contain a particular root (e.g., *paint* in *paint, painter, painting*). There are also interconnections among lexical entries that contain the same derivational affixes (e.g., all the words with *-er,* with *-tion,* with *-ity,* or with *-ness*). These interconnections link lexical entries through meaning (for each affix), syntax (the resultant syntactic category of the derived word), and morphology. But although word meanings in the lexical entries may be related through the root in each of the derived forms, the syntax often differs considerably (e.g., for nouns versus verbs, or for adjectives versus nouns).

At the same time, some lexical items with similar meanings may show parallels in their syntax and morphology. For example, syntactically, verbs with causative meanings (e.g., *bring, feed, break*) are all transitive and so have two arguments, assigned to the grammatical relations subject and object; these arguments mark the thematic roles of agent and theme or patient. Causativity itself may also be marked in the morphology with affixes like *-ify* and *-ize* (e.g., *causativize, nullify*). Similarly, nouns with the meaning 'state of being ADJ' may be marked by the affix *-ness* combined with an adjective (*green, silky*) as in *greenness, silkiness.* Affixes, then, mark part of speech and added meaning for the derived word in the lexical entry.

Some meaning units are larger than words. Idioms like *have a bee in one's bonnet* (be obsessed), *go west* (get lost), *be off one's rocker* (go crazy) require their own lexical entries. With each of these, the meaning of the whole (glossed in parentheses) differs from any meaning constructible from the parts (but see Wasow, Sag, and Nunberg 1983). Compare the idiom *kick the bucket* (meaning 'die') with the non-idiomatic phrase *kick the bucket* to describe an act of kicking. The idiomatic interpretation is often restricted syntactically compared with the non-idiomatic one. One can use the idiom in the simple present, future, and past tense, but not with progressive aspect (?*The old man's kicking the bucket*), and not in the passive (*The *bucket was kicked by the old man*). Syntactic restrictions on idioms vary from one idiom to another. Some are very restricted. *Break a leg*, for example, is only used in the imperative in its idiomatic sense, but *blow one's own trumpet* (with the sense 'boast'), provided it retains *own*, can occur in a much larger range of constructions (e.g., Fraser 1974).

Word formation and innovation

The kinds of lexical entries considered so far constitute the stock of established words and phrases speakers draw on. These established terms are conventional in that all speakers in a community agree on how to use such terms. But the lexical store is not fixed in size or unchanging in membership. Words get added and lost over time. Speakers coin new words to fill gaps in the established lexicon. These coinages may be used on only one occasion (nonce uses) or may answer some need common to a larger community and eventually be added to the established lexicon. Speakers typically choose the forms for such words from existing resources. The options they draw on fall into two major classes of word-formation – COMPOUNDING and DERIVATION.

Compounds are usually divided into types according to the syntactic class of the resultant word. In English, one finds compound nouns formed from combinations of roots only, and hence often called root compounds (e.g., established *sun-rise, push-chair, dog-sled*). One also finds compound verbs (e.g., *to white-wash, to side-step*), and compound adjectives (e.g., *gray-eyed*). Compounds may include affixes, as in the nouns *clock-mender* and *washing-machine*. These are sometimes called synthetic compounds (in contrast to root compounds). Compound nouns, like *snow-flake*, contain a head (*-flake*) and a modifying element (*snow-*), with the head carrying number agreement, and, in other languages, case and gender as well. In compound verbs, like *to dry-clean*, the head (*-clean*) carries aspect and tense as well as any agreement for person, number, and gender. In English, the head is the rightmost member of the compound (*-flake* in *snow-flake*), and compounds generally carry primary stress on the modifier and tertiary stress on the head.

Derivations are words formed with affixation added to a word or root. Affixes (prefixes, suffixes, or infixes) may maintain or change syntactic word class (e.g., *re-* with no change in *redraw* versus *-ize* for a noun to verb change in *hospitalize*). Derivational affixes can be divided into two classes: primary or Class I affixes which typically require some modification of the root they are added to, and secondary or Class II affixes which do not require changes in the form they are added to (Kiparsky 1982). In English, Class I affixes include *-ous*, *-ive*, *-ate*, *-ory* and *-ify*. Their addition may often shift the stress in the word, as in *elEctric* to *electrIcity*, change the pronunciation of the vowel from tense to lax, as in *opaque* to *opacity*, and palatalize /k/ to /s/ (*opacity*). Class II affixes have much less or no effect on the form they are added to. Members of this group include *-ness*, *-less*, *-er*, *-ize*, *-y*, and *-ish* (e.g., established *darkish, penniless, farmer, hybridize*). Class I affixes are always added to the root before any Class II affixes in words that contain both. For example, one finds *nationalize* with Class I *-al* followed by Class II *-ize*, but not **nationlessify* with Class II *-less* followed by Class I *-ify*.

In English, derivation may also occur without affixation, with a mere shift of syntactic form class, as in the move from verb to noun (e.g., from *to drop* to *a drop*), or from noun to verb (e.g., from *a captain* to *to captain*). This type of derivation is usually called either CONVERSION – to emphasize the change from one syntactic category to another – or ZERO-DERIVATION – to emphasize parallels with affixal derivation.

Compounding and derivation characterize many established words in the lexicon. They also offer a range of options for creating new words. Adult speakers interpret and coin such innovations every day. When they encounter a coinage, they may be unaware that they have never heard that particular meaning–form combination before. When they themselves coin a word, they are filling in where there is no ready-made word available. The formation of new words, then, offers a means for conveying new meanings. It thereby contributes to the continual evolution of the lexicon as a whole (see Adams 1973, Bauer 1983, Marchand 1969).

Meaning relations

Within the lexicon, there are systematic patterns of meaning relations that hold across many groups of lexical entries. Among them are inclusion or class membership (as in *A cat is a kind of mammal*), part/whole (as in *The hand is part of the arm*), incompatibility (as in *It's a dog, not a cat*), overlap (as in *That rat is a pet*), and identity.[2]

INCLUSION is common, for example, in hierarchical taxonomies. Lower level terms are included in all the levels above them. For example, a water spaniel is a member of the kind designated by the term *spaniel*, which in turn is a member of the kind designated by *dog*, and so on up through

---

[2] On semantic relations, see further Cruse 1986, Fillmore 1978, Lyons 1977, Miller 1978.

mammal and *animal*. The relation of *dog* to *mammal* here, or *spaniel* to *dog*, is one of HYPONYMY. That is, *dog* is a hyponym of *mammal*, and since *cat*, *cow*, *sheep* and *lion* bear the same relation to *mammal*, they are called co-hyponyms of the term above them.

Lexical hierarchies for plants and animals, for example, can contain terms at five levels:

(a)	unique beginner	(*plant*)
(b)	life form	(*bush*)
(c)	generic	(*rose*)
(d)	specific	(*hybrid tea* [*rose*])
(e)	varietal	(*hybrid tea Peace* [*rose*])

The most important of these is the generic level. It is the level of labels in everyday use. And terms at this level are likely to be morphologically simple in structure (root forms). They are generally also original, in the sense that they have not been borrowed by extension from another domain. The generic level is the level with the greatest number of terms. Below this level, words are often morphologically complex and compounds are frequent. Lexical hierarchies may be full of gaps in that they often lack terms at one or more levels. And many hierarchies end at the generic level and have no specific or varietal terms. Others may have such terms but they may not exist for every branch of the hierarchy. Still others lack life-form or unique-beginner terms. The generic level, then, is the level with the most extensive representation in the lexicon (Berlin, Breedlove, and Raven 1973).

The PART/WHOLE relation, sometimes called MERONYMY, can be seen in terms like *finger, hand, arm, body*; *second, minute, hour, day*, or *day, week, month, year*. It is the relation linking *handle* to *door*, *tail* to *dog*, and *sole* to *shoe*. One lexical item labels a part of the entity picked out by the other.

When two lexical entries are INCOMPATIBLE in meaning, the terms may have the same superordinate and be used syntactically in the same way. But use of the one entails exclusion of the other. For example, *That's a dog* is incompatible with saying of the same entity, *That's a cat*. Co-hyponyms are always incompatible. Other kinds of terms may also be incompatible: opposites like *alive* and *dead, win* and *lose, arrive* and *leave, deep* and *shallow*.

The relation of OVERLAP can be seen whenever the members of two groups have some properties in common, but each class has members not found in the other. For example, *dog* and *pet* overlap in that both terms may be considered subordinates, on occasion, of *animal*, but not all dogs are pets, and not all pets are dogs. Equally, the terms *father* and *policeman* may overlap, with *human males* as a superordinate, but fathers may not be policemen, and vice versa. Overlap is a common relation but, at times, a rather tenuous one.

Identity or SYNONYMY, where two terms have the same meaning, is said to hold when two utterances containing different terms have the same truth-value on a particular occasion. For instance, one could say *Jan's playing the fiddle tonight* or, with the same truth value, *Jan's playing the violin tonight*. Full or true synonymy is rarely if ever found, but it is very common to find lexical items with different degrees of overlap in meaning. In the case of *fiddle* and *violin*, for example, the two terms in fact differ considerably although they refer to the same instrument. *Fiddle* is typically used in talking about country music and country dance, while *violin* is more usual in the context of talk about orchestral or concert playing.

Semantic fields

A SEMANTIC FIELD is a set of lexical entries with shared core meanings. That is, it groups together lexical items whose meanings are all pertinent to a specific conceptual domain. Within such a field, the different items may exemplify a large range of semantic relations. Semantic fields offer a way of cutting up the lexicon along semantic lines to group together lexical items related to each other in a variety of ways. Take the field we might call "schooling": Some of its member terms are *teach, teacher, learn, student, school,* and *class*. Some terms may have lexical entries connected by meaning and morphology, but not syntax (e.g., *teach, teacher*); others are connected only by meaning (*teach, school*), others still by meaning and syntax: for example, *school, teacher, class,* and *student* are all nouns, while *teach, learn,* and *remember* are all verbs. Nouns like *teacher, pupil,* and *student* all have animate referents, while *school, classroom,* and *building* have locations as referents. And so on. Any one semantic field may be divided into subfields (schooling is a subfield of the broader education), or itself be included in yet larger fields (education might be included in a field like societal institutions, for example). The notion of semantic field is therefore a relative one. It allows us to capture some of the details of how lexical entries are related to and differ from one other within a specific domain (Trier 1934; also Lehrer 1974, Lyons 1977).

Each semantic field covers a conceptual domain, and the meaning relations that link all the lexical items in the field show how that conceptual domain is represented. The semantic field and its member terms might be thought of as a covering laid over the conceptual domain. Languages design their coverings differently with different numbers of terms in the designs, but all place the coverings as a whole over the same domain.

Conceptual organization and its component concepts are not the same as the meanings for the lexical items of a language. For example, English speakers typically make do with just one verb in talking about dressing, namely *put on*. This verb serves for all clothing, headgear, socks and shoes, jewelry, glasses, everything. Yet ask a group of English speakers to demonstrate, with gestures, how to put on a shoe, a glove, or a sweater, and they will offer clear and consistent actions based on their conceptual knowledge. They know more about dressing, in other words, than the one lexical item *put on* would suggest. And speakers of other languages in fact use a much more elaborate lexicon for talking about dressing. Japanese speakers use one verb for garments on the upper body, another for those on the lower body, yet another for garments on extremities like feet and hands, another for articles that go on the head, and another still for jewelry like earrings or a watch (Backhouse 1981, Kameyama 1983). At the conceptual level, though, these speakers will represent the same actions as speakers of English. Conceptual knowledge, in other words, is not identical to our knowledge about word meanings.

The terms in a semantic field may share some elements of meaning with all the members, and share others only with a few. In the field of motion, for example, the majority of items are verbs that share the core meaning of movement: *walk, trot, go, spin, carry*. Some of these incorporate differences in the manner of the motion involved (compare *walk, run, trot, jog, race*), some the manner of action that results in something else moving (*carry, tow, pull, drag, slide*), and some the direction of the movement (*come, leave, bring, rise, drop*). Manner may be added with an adverbial (*quickly, slowly, bouncily*) or prepositional phrase (*in haste, in a rush*), and so can direction (*up the hill, over the fence, through the rocks*). In English, verbs of motion often contain information about manner in their meanings; in French and Hebrew, such verbs are more likely to contain information about direction.

The relations among verbs can be further specified in terms of the argument types each can appear with. Compare *He pulled the sled* with *The skater is spinning*. Transitive *pull* has a subject and object (agent and theme respectively), but intransitive *spin* has only one argument, the subject in the role of agent. *Pull*, then, can be aligned with other transitive verbs of motion and *spin* with intransitive ones (Miller 1972, Talmy 1985). (*Spin*, of course, can also be transitive, as in *Will you spin that wool?* or *Spin me around.*) The syntax of each lexical entry offers additional information about meanings within a semantic field. So semantic and syntactic information must both be taken into account in considering meanings and meaning relations in the lexicon.

Polysemy and ambiguity

POLYSEMY occurs when a word form carries more than one meaning. It must be distinguished from homonymy, where two roots that were unrelated historically, 'ear of corn' and 'ear to hear with,' converge in form over time (Ullmann 1962). Some polysemous words are among the most frequent in the language, yet deciding which meaning is intended rarely seems to cause any difficulty. English has a very large stock of word forms, so its lexicon is relatively free of polysemy compared with many languages. Yet polysemy poses a potential problem: how does one make sure that the meaning intended is the one people access when they hear a polysemous word? Consider the word *line*: it appears as both a noun and a verb, and both have multiple meanings listed in the dictionary. Among the many noun meanings given are 'line of trees,' 'line of sight,' 'line of argument,' 'line of duty,' 'line of poetry,' 'line of rope,' and 'line of type.' When such uses of *line* are accompanied by their prepositional phrases, the intended meaning seems easy to discern. But how do we know that *line* in *Two lines are missing* is 'lines of type'; that in *They were behind the enemy lines*, it means 'line of battle'; and that in *He follows the party line*, it means 'line of argument'? That is, how are the meanings of polysemous words related? In the case of *line*, the range of meanings suggests that one can extend the initial meaning from concrete ('line of trees') to abstract ('line of argument') (Caramazza and Grober 1976).

For many instances of polysemy, syntactic information about part of speech may be enough to identify the pertinent meaning. For example, it will distinguish the noun *brush* from the verb *brush*, and the verb *drop* from the noun *drop*. This in turn suggests two additional bases for polysemic extension in English: words for objects can be extended to denote actions connected with the objects (e.g., *to carpet, to sled, to paper*); and words for actions may be extended to denote their results (e.g., *a fall, a break, a cut*). By one calculation, syntactic information about whether a term is a noun or verb, for example, can resolve between 60 percent and 70 percent of potential ambiguities (Kelly and Stone 1975). That still leaves many ambiguities to be resolved through some other means. In part, people probably rely on the domain of the ongoing conversation – are they talking about war, printing, or politics? – and select the meaning of *line*, say, that makes sense. How they do this on every occasion is something we know little about, but they must clearly draw on what they know given the preceding discourse and the knowledge shared with their interlocutors. The appropriate meaning may be computed from some core meaning, common to all the senses of *line*, for example, and then simply filled in with more detail in each context of use. Most polysemy arises from small extensions of existing meanings. So *line* may have some minimal, central meaning only, which is then supplemented in different ways. This supplementation, though, requires just as much reliance on discourse and mutual knowledge as selection from a large number of distinct meanings. Although many words have more than one meaning associated with them, this appears to cause few problems for the speakers of a language.

Another pervasive form of ambiguity speakers must deal with is that between "unit" and "type" meanings. Notice that in an utterance like *I hadn't seen this jacket before*, the speaker may be talking about the particular jacket being worn by her addressee on that occasion, or about the type of jacket being worn on that occasion. Moreover, the type interpretation may cover a large range of types, as when the grocer asks his customer, *Is this the fruit you mean*? The noun *fruit* on this occasion may pick out the variety of apple (a Macintosh, say), apples in general, fruit from a particular supplier, organically grown apples, and so on. The number of possible type-interpretations is limited only by the speaker's need to coordinate with her addressee (Cruse 1986, Nunberg 1979).

Taking a perspective

Many words can be used for talking about the same thing or the same event. For example, the owner of a collie might refer to it by name, *Nell*, or use *my collie, the dog, the guard, the growler* or *that animal*. The choice of one expression over another depends on the occasion, on what the speaker is trying to convey, and on what the addressee already knows. The need to refer successfully (that is, to make sure the addressee understands the reference intended) may set some limits on how specific a speaker is expected to be. For example, in attributing membership in some category for a referent already identified, speakers normally try to tell their addressees something new. So if Jan looks at a dog and asks *What's that*?, she expects to be told more than *It's a dog*. On an occasion like this, Bob would respond appropriately with, say, *It's a collie*. This is because it is already clear to both Jan and Bob that they're looking at a dog. The generic- or basic-level term *dog* therefore would not carry enough information here. But *dog* could be used provided it was modified, as in *It's a farm dog from up the hill.*

Speakers may sometimes use a term that carries less information than the generic-level *dog*. For example, Bob might say *I must take the animal for a walk now.* This again would only be appropriate, typically, if the addressee already knew he was talking about his dog. Under such circumstances, use of *animal* could then connote some degree of distance, or of irritation, depending on the occasion. It contrasts with the neutral or everyday word, *dog.* On every occasion, then, speakers should choose expressions that are specific enough for their addressees to understand the intended reference. The need to be specific enough may sometimes lead speakers to provide extensive detail, as in *the dark brown and white long-haired border collie* or *the dog with one torn ear and a black muzzle.*

By choosing one word or expression over another, speakers present different PERSPECTIVES on the object or event being talked about. The perspective may be a matter of the level of categorization, as in the choices of *border collie, collie, dog,* or *animal.* Or it may highlight one property or characteristic at the expense of others. For example, the same person might be referred to as *the clarinetist, the sailor, Justin's cousin,* or *the student.* Each expression picks out what is pertinent, in the speaker's judgment, on that occasion.

Overall, speakers have many different choices to make every time they talk. Many different words and expressions can be used to refer appropriately to the same entity or event. There is no one-to-one relation between words and the concepts they pick out.

Acquiring a lexicon

To give some idea of what a formidable task children face in acquiring a lexicon, consider the fact that adult speakers of English dispose of a production vocabulary of between 20,000 and 50,000 word forms, and a comprehension vocabulary that is considerably larger. In the case of young children, some estimates suggest that from the age of two on, children on average master around 10 new words a day to arrive at a vocabulary of about 14,000 words by age six. Growth in vocabulary from then on to about age seventeen averages at least 3,000 new words a year. From age ten or eleven, it has been estimated, children encounter about 10,000 new words a year; and, between nine and fifteen, they are exposed to some

85,000 distinct word-roots and at least 100,000 distinct word-meanings in their school textbooks alone.[3]

How, though, do children go about this task? To identify possible words of their language, they must isolate word forms. They must also identify candidate meanings. And they must link the two together in setting up lexical entries in their mental lexicon. This feat is a considerable one. Consider the complexity of mapping meanings onto forms. Children must deal with many kinds of ambiguity and sort out, for example, which meaning, or meanings, go with each form. They must also deal with speaker perspective, where the same entity or activity can be talked about on different occasions with different word-forms. They must identify semantic fields and the conceptual domains they cover. They must learn how meanings are organized in terms of such relations as inclusion, overlap, or incompatibility. They need to identify inflected forms of the same word and hence inflections, and to distinguish forms derived from the same root using different affixes. That is, they must identify both word-forms and parts of words, the inflections and derivational affixes. They must also learn how the semantic and morphological properties of words are linked to their syntactic properties. In short, acquiring the lexicon is a formidable task. Chapter 2 outlines the course of early lexical development: when children produce their first words, and what they use them for.

One of the first problems children take on is the MAPPING of meanings onto forms (Chapter 3). They must identify possible meanings, isolate possible forms, and then map the meanings onto the relevant forms. In doing this, they draw on their conceptual categories in identifying possible meanings. At the same time, they draw on the input – the language addressed to them – for possible word forms and also any clues to the meanings of those word forms. (These clues may come from the syntactic and morphological properties of a word form, and also from patterns of usage.) Children must then map the one onto the other. In doing this, they rely on certain assumptions or guiding principles, among them CON-VENTIONALITY and CONTRAST (Chapters 4 and 5). These two pragmatic

---

[3] Estimates rarely distinguish between comprehension and production, but production is typically a subset of comprehension (Clark and Hecht 1983). Templin 1957 computed that six-year-olds would know as many as 14,000 words (presumably in comprehension), and this total was the basis for Carey's 1978 calculation of a daily rate of acquisition. Vocabulary estimates for schoolchildren and their exposure to new words have been computed by Nagy and his colleagues (Nagy and Anderson 1984, Nagy and Herman 1987).

principles play a major role for adults as well as children. They regulate the relations between established words and innovations in the lexicon. And they constrain the choices children make as they first map meanings onto forms and accumulate knowledge about words and word structure.

I then take up two additional principles important to children's initial analyses of word structure and its use in the coining of words. The first is TRANSPARENCY OF MEANING. Compare the child form *tent-man* to the adult *camper*. The familiar component elements, *tent* and *man* will be relatively more transparent in meaning than *camper* to a child who has not yet analyzed the meaning of the suffix *-er*. If children rely on transparency, they should make use of more transparent options over less transparent ones early on. But what is transparent to children *changes* as they learn more about the structure and conventional meanings of words in the language. Transparency, then, should affect choices more in the earlier than in the later stages of acquisition. The second principle is SIMPLICITY OF FORM: Compare the child verb *to flat*, without a suffix, to adult *to flatten*, with a suffix, both from the English adjective *flat*. A form without a suffix, according to this principle, should be simpler to produce than one with a suffix, and so on. Essentially, this principle captures the fact that, at first, children tend to use as building blocks in forming new words only unadorned elements, with no affixes or changes that might render them more difficult to produce (Chapter 6).

One consequence of these two principles is widespread regularization. Compare the agentive forms *rider, reader, farmer, biker* (all alike in form and sharing the same suffix to express agentive meaning) with *bicyclist, cook, nurse,* and *musician*. Words with similar meanings that also have similar structures (here, the suffix *-er*) should be easier to learn than words with similar meanings (all agentive) but different structures. In fact, regular meaning–form correspondences give rise to paradigms for organizing whole segments of the lexicon.[4] And words that share elements of meaning but not form with members of a paradigm are liable to be regularized by children. For instance, *bicycler* often replaces *bicyclist*, and *cooker* replaces *cook* in young children's speech.

I then take up the principle of PRODUCTIVITY. This principle, unlike transparency and simplicity, is not a purely acquisitional one since it also affects adult choices. In acquisition, it captures the fact that productive forms appear to be more available to children in that adults use them more

---

[4] See Marle 1983, 1985 on the notion of paradigm, and Bybee and Pardo 1981 on regularization.

often. If frequency affects acquisition, more-productive forms should be acquired before less-productive ones. In English, for example, children should acquire the agentive ending in *-er* before the one in *-ist* for constructing new agent nouns: *-er* is the more productive of the two (Chapter 7). Transparency, simplicity, and productivity, in conjunction with conventionality and contrast, I argue, account for when and how children build up a repertoire of word-formation devices for extending their vocabulary.

In Part 2, I turn to case studies of young children's uses of WORD FORMATION, both in their spontaneous speech and in elicitation studies designed to tap what children know about using word formation to express novel meanings. These studies draw on spontaneous coinages from children acquiring a variety of languages, and are supplemented with elicited coinages from various word-games and tasks designed to explore children's knowledge of word formation. I first review studies of children's novel words for kinds of things (Chapters 8 and 9), and then, more specifically, novel words for agents and instruments (Chapter 10). Next I take up novel words for actions (Chapter 11), and for the undoing of earlier actions (Chapter 12). Each domain illustrates in a different way how the acquisitional principles interact with each other and with the options available in each language to give a general account of the order of acquisition.

Finally, in Part 3, I take up some of the implications of these findings for theories of word formation on the one hand, and theories of language acquisition on the other. Among the issues addressed are the relations between linguistic theories and acquisition data, between productivity and frequency, and between conventional and innovative words in the lexicon. I also take up how best to characterize the course of acquisition within the different domains discussed, the mechanisms we need to postulate in order to account for *change* during acquisition, and whether the facts of acquisition are compatible with models that have been proposed; and the relation between language typology, word-formation options, and the application of acquisitional principles.

Summary
The lexicon is very complex. In learning the lexicon of a language, children must learn about the forms of words – their pronunciation and their internal structure; the syntax of words – whether they are nouns or verbs, and the inflections that belong to each class; how to coin new words

through compounding and derivation; the semantic relations that link word meanings within and across semantic fields; the degrees of polysemy and ambiguity present in many words; and how word choice reveals the perspective taken by the speaker. In the next chapter, I take up some of the facts of early lexical acquisition.

1

LEXICAL ACQUISITION

The tutor names things in accordance with the semantic customs of the community. The player forms hypotheses about the categorical nature of the things named. He tests his hypotheses by trying to name new things correctly. The tutor compares the player's utterances with his own anticipations of such utterances and, in this way, checks the accuracy of fit between his own categories and those of the player. He improves the fit by correction.

We play this game as long as we continue to extend our vocabularies and that may be as long as we live.

Roger Brown 1958, p. 194

2 Early lexical development

Children utter their first recognizable word around age one. In the first few months, they tend to produce words one at a time, often with considerable effort, and with pauses in between. Early word productions may be hard to recognize because children take time to master adult pronunciation, even though they have as their targets the conventional adult forms they hear in input. In addition, the meanings they express do not always fully match the adult ones. As a result, the distinctions made by children may differ from adult usage. For example, a child who knows 3 animal terms will not use them in the same way as an older child with 25 terms, or an adult with 150 or more.

At first, children add new words for production rather slowly. Later, their repertoire grows more rapidly. From about age two, they add new words on a daily basis. They also go beyond the word itself to analyze word-internal structure and identify meanings carried by each component element. This can be seen in their analyses of familiar words, and in their spontaneous construction of new words to carry meanings not available in the everyday vocabulary they already know.

In this chapter, I sketch the course children follow in the early stages of building a vocabulary, and lay out some issues raised by early language production. I begin by taking up the rate of acquisition – the number of words added each week during the first months of language production. After a relatively slow start, children add words at an increasing rate during their second year, but they do not all go at the same pace or follow the same schedule in attempting longer utterances. Early words fall into a small number of semantic fields that are gradually elaborated as more words are added. Some early word meanings depart from adult use, as when children under- or over-extend relative to adult meanings, while others may coincide quite closely with adult meanings. As children learn more words, they make comments on their internal structure. They also coin new words. All these observa-

21

tions raise a number of issues that are taken up in detail in later chapters.

First words

After a slow start, children appear to absorb and produce new vocabulary at quite a rapid rate. They generally produce between 50 and 200 words by around age 1;6, and by age 2;0 may produce as many as 500 or 600 distinct, comprehensible words. During the period from age one to two, children steadily add new words to their stock of vocabulary. But the paths children follow may differ somewhat. Some children go through several months of producing only one word at a time, and do not attempt any multi-word utterances. Others appear to have less of a one-word stage, and produce multi-word utterances within a few weeks of the first words. From then on, they add new word combinations in parallel with the addition of new words. These two paths are illustrated in some detail with data from case studies of two children, Keren and Damon.

Two children

Keren, who acquired Hebrew as her first language, had a distinct one-word stage covering her first eight months of language production, from age 0;10 to 1;6 (Dromi 1987). In the first nine weeks, her rate of production for new words (types not produced before) was very slow, with between 1 and 5 words added each week. The rate then increased slightly, with three small peaks of 8 or 9 words. Then her rate roughly doubled (at age 1;3) for the next month just before a spurt of additions – 111 new words in three weeks, from 1;3,27 to 1;4,17. Her rate then declined again, to around 20 new words a week, for three weeks, and then dropped again in the final two weeks of the study. And in that last week, aged 1;5,16–1;5,23, Keren produced her first word-combinations. The number of new words she added each week is shown in Figure 2–1. During her first thirty-two weeks of talking, Keren acquired a cumulative production vocabulary of 337 words, as shown in Figure 2–2.

Damon, a child acquiring English, followed a different course.[1] His rate of producing new words is charted by week in Figure 2–3. After a relatively slow start, with additions of between 1 and 7 words a week up to the twelfth week (age 1;2,26) of production, his rate increased slightly with small peaks every few weeks, of 11 or 12 words, later rising to between 18 and 25 words, with lower rates in between. Over the course of forty-two weeks (up

[1] These data are from my unpublished diary of his language development.

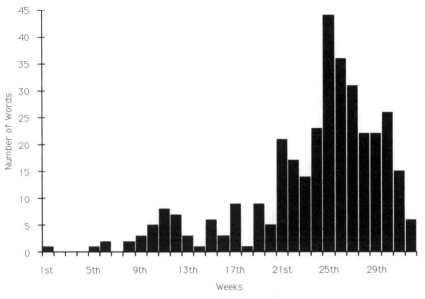

Figure 2–1 Keren: number of new words produced each week from 0;10,12 to 1;5,23 (up to 337 words) (Dromi 1987, p. 112)

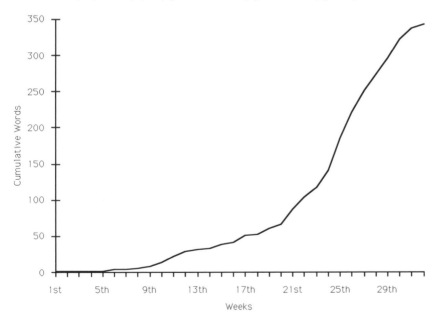

Figure 2–2 Keren: cumulative vocabulary 0;10,12 to 1;5,23 (n = 337) (Dromi 1987)

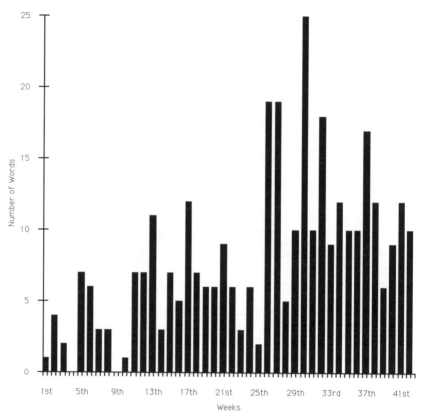

Figure 2–3 Damon: number of new words produced each week from
1;0,10 to 1;9,24 (up to 337 words) (Clark, diary data)

to age 1;9,24) when his vocabulary size equalled Keren's, he showed no
spurt of vocabulary production comparable with hers. (Nor did he produce
any spurt over the next six months, although his general rate of word
production increased.) Within a few weeks of producing his first words,
Damon also produced his first combinations (from 1;1,29 on). He used
only a few new ones each week for several weeks. (The only word
combinations counted for the present purpose were those with no
antecedent adult utterance that could have provided a model for imitation.
I also excluded any sequences that could have been picked up as a chunk,
from part of a routine, say, unless he gave independent evidence of having
both pieces independently. Only novel combinations for each week are
included here, i.e., combinations that had not been noted before in the
diary.) Then, from 1;6,29 on (week 29), Damon produced new combi-

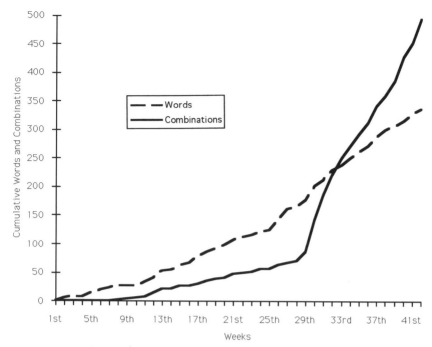

Figure 2–4 Damon: cumulative vocabulary 1;0,10 to 1;9,24 (n = 337) and multi-word utterances 1;1,29 to 1;9,24 (n = 495) (Clark, diary data)

nations with increasing frequency, and four weeks later, his new combination types overtook the new word types produced (at 1;7,22). Damon's cumulative vocabulary and cumulative word-combination types are shown in Figure 2–4. Over the next weeks and months, his combinations increased in both length and complexity.

Keren and Damon, then, followed rather different paths. Keren began slowly, adding only a few new words each week. Then she began to add new words in bursts, often with a pause in between, and then showed a large spurt followed by a pause just before she began to combine words after 32 weeks of using just one word at a time. Damon began in the same way, slowly, but after just eight weeks began to produce occasional combinations of words. His novel word-combinations increased steadily in number over time in parallel with a steady increase in the new words he produced. In the first 25 weeks, for example, he averaged 5 new words a week and just over 2 novel combinations a week; then in the next four weeks, he added an average of 13 new words and over 7 new combinations a week. His rate of adding new words, some 13 a week, then didn't change for the next eighteen weeks, but the number of novel combinations did, up to 31 a week. And in the last four weeks of his second year, his rate of word acquisition and his novel word-combinations increased again, to 22 new words and over 65 new combinations a week.

Other children may follow still other paths, with a vocabulary spurt like Keren's appearing earlier or later, and with word combinations appearing at different points relative to vocabulary size. They may even skip a one-word stage altogether either by targetting sequences longer than words, or by not talking until a later point. Some of these possible variations are likely to depend on how children tackle the sound system of their language. Some begin with words or word-like chunks, and aim for short combinations of specific sounds. These children typically produce recognizable approximations to adult words, much as Keren and Damon did, from early on. Others start by producing intonational contours over larger chunks or phrases, but these children are often harder to understand at first because they produce few or no recognizable sequences of segments (Peters 1983, 1985). Even if children do produce recognizable words early on, they do not necessarily follow the same path into language.[2]

Keren and Damon also differed in how they apportioned their time during the early stages of learning to produce words. Both started out with very imperfect versions of the adult words they were attempting to produce, so both had to work hard on improving their production to be recognizable to others. Over the eight-month period of her one-word stage (from 0;10,12 to 1;5,23), Keren made an increasing number of phonological changes in the forms of newly produced approximations to conventional words. In the third month of the study, for example, only 9 percent of Keren's new words were conventional in form, while 70 percent were approximations to the adult targets. (The remaining 21 percent were nursery or baby-talk forms.) By the eighth (and last) month of the study, these two proportions had changed to 45 and 55 percent respectively. (All nursery forms had been replaced by conventional words or approximations to them.) At the same time, the number of words undergoing phonological changes in Keren's pronunciations during the third month compared to the eighth month went from an average of 0.5 words to an average of 26. Finally, the work involved in changing the forms of new words was inversely related to new vocabulary acquisition: increases in intelligibility

---

[2] Not surprisingly, their routes are also affected by the amount of input they receive (Huttenlocher, Haight, Bryk, Seltzer, and Lyons 1991).

typically coincided with weeks where Keren added few or no new words. This is reflected in the pattern of adding words in spurts some weeks and then pausing in between, as shown by the numbers in Figure 2–1.

Damon's record of production shows little evidence of such spurts. His consolidation of word shapes as he moved his pronunciations closer to the conventional adult words proceeded at a steady rate throughout his second year, and appeared not to interact with the addition of new words to his vocabulary. But improvements in pronunciation were related to word combinations. These increased in number as more of his words became recognizable. This was particularly apparent in the last four weeks of his second year (1;11,5 to 2;0,2) when he began to produce many more, and longer, word combinations. During this period, for example, having mastered final nasals and final voiceless stops, Damon attempted voiced final stops for some months before managing to produce them (Clark and Bowerman 1986).

Motor development

Motor development may be a major factor in the one-word stage. This stage has often been regarded as the product of a cognitive-linguistic limit on what children can say, linked to their degree of knowledge about what language can be used for. But it is also partly a product of motor development. Children who take longer to set up articulatory programs for the words they are attempting are more likely to delay trying to produce two or more words in sequence because the motor coordination required is still too complicated for them.[3] These children prefer to try just one word at a time for up to several months until they perfect some of the necessary articulatory skills. Others whose articulatory plans get established more quickly can move on to longer sequences and so produce multi-word utterances sooner.

One phenomenon that may have a partial explanation in motor skill is the so-called "vocabulary spurt." This spurt has been defined in a variety of ways, all based on shifts in the relative numbers of new words added in production. It has often been regarded as evidence that children have grasped the point of language as a symbolic system. That is, that there are, potentially, words for everything around them. An alternative view is that

---

[3] See further on production Levelt 1989, Sternberg, Monsell, Knoll, and Wright 1980, Sternberg, Wright, Knoll, and Monsell 1980; also Norman and Rumelhart 1983, Rumelhart and Norman 1982; and on the acquisition of production skills, Elbers and Wijnen 1992, Kent 1992, and McCune 1992.

the vocabulary spurt reflects attainment of a certain level of mastery in articulatory plans for production.

Keren offers an example of such a vocabulary spurt. In week 25 of her one-word stage, she added 44 new words in production, followed by a further 36 and 31 in the next two weeks. Earlier, she typically added a few words over one or two weeks then added none in the next week before adding a few more. In the intervals, she practiced intensively to improve the production of the words she had produced up to that point (see Figure 2–1). The vocabulary spurt, then, could simply be spurred by her increasing articulatory skill. Indeed, when she began on multi-word utterances, she produced them in large numbers within the first week (Dromi 1987). This interpretation of vocabulary spurts could apply regardless of the varying definitions of what counts as a spurt – a rise from 2 words a week to 7 or 8, or the kind of dramatic jump in numbers that Keren displayed.

Early words and semantic fields

As they get older, children make their words sound more and more like the adult targets they are aiming for. But they do not always use these early words as an adult would. Although children may use some words to refer to the appropriate adult categories, they know much less about the world than any adult and they also know much less about their language than any adult. And children who can produce 100 distinct words will necessarily differ in their uses of these words from adults who can draw on 50,000 to 100,000 words. More words make for more detailed distinctions and hence more meanings to be understood or conveyed, within each domain. But learning all the meanings takes time.

The first 50 or so words English-speaking children produce today fall into much the same categories as the words of children learning English fifty or a hundred years ago.[4] What domains do they first use their words for? Like adults, they talk about the people, objects, and activities around them. They talk about people (e.g., *dada/papa, mama/mummy, baby*) and animals (e.g., *dog, cat/kitty, bird*). They talk about food (e.g., *juice, milk, cookie*), body parts (e.g., *eye, nose*), and clothing (e.g., *diaper/nappy, shoe, sock*); they talk about vehicles (e.g., *car, boat, train*), toys (e.g., *ball, block, doll*), and household items (e.g., *cup, spoon, bottle, light*). They talk about space and motion (e.g., *up, off, open*). Early on, they pick up a few terms for routines such as *bye-bye* for departures, accompanied by a parentally

---

[4] Clark 1979; see also Bates, Bretherton, and Snyder 1988, and Dale, Bates, Reznick, and Morisset 1989, Goldfield and Reznick 1990, Reznick and Goldsmith 1989.

Table 2–1 *Some general-purpose verb uses from a two-year-old*

Verb	Utterance	Context and gloss
DO	*I do it again.*	As he knocks over some blocks
	You … do … doing that.	As adult builds blocks into a tower
	You do do it, okay?	Asking adult to unroll some computer tape, after trying unsuccessfully to do it himself
	You do [ə] that!	Indicating which toy adult should take out
	The clown do!	Asking adult to make the toy clown "clown"
	Uh oh. I did.	As he turned off the tape-recorder by pushing a knob
MAKE	*Make name!*	Telling adult to write the child's name
	Make a dog.	Telling adult what to draw next
	Make [ə] that.	Asking adult to move the clock-hand
	I make a little doggie.	As he cut a dog-shape from playdough

Source: Clark 1978c.

guided handwave, or *peek-a-boo* as either parent or child conceals face or hand behind a cloth and then makes it suddenly re-appear. Children acquiring other languages build up a very similar early repertoire.[5]

Just as in the adult lexicon, children's labels for different kinds of objects outnumber labels for activities, states, and social routines (Gentner 1978, 1982, Goldin-Meadow, Seligman, and Gelman 1976). In the children's case, this may mean they have rather few options for talking about activities. Nonetheless, they do so from their earliest utterances on. For example, they use *gone* or *allgone* to comment on the disappearance or unexpected absence of an object; they talk about the consequences of an action, with *gone* or *down*, say, commenting on an object affected by their own prior act; they talk about success in an action, with *there* or *did-it*; about failure or disaster, with *uh-oh*, *oh dear*, or *no*; and about the recurrence of an action, with *more* or *again*. They also begin early to talk about motion in space, and may draw attention to a moving object with *there* or *look*; they focus on vertical displacement with *up* or *down*, and on containment or attachment with verb particles like *in*, *out*, *on*, and *off*

---

[5] Compare the early vocabularies recorded for French by Grégoire 1947 and Pavlovitch 1920; for German by Lindner 1898 and Stern and Stern 1928; for Hebrew by Dromi 1987, Dromi and Fishelzon 1986; for Hungarian by MacWhinney 1973; for Kaluli by Schieffelin 1985; for Polish by Szuman 1968; and for Russian by Gvozdev 1961.

(Farwell 1975, Gopnik 1988, Gopnik and Meltzoff 1986; also Bowerman 1989).

For talking about actions, they frequently rely at first on general-purpose verbs like *do, make, get,* and *go.* They use these verbs for talking about many different activities, as shown in Table 2–1. These verbs are gradually displaced as children add more specific verbs to their repertoire and use those instead. Initially, children tend to talk more about their own actions than those of others. They appear to do this earlier for action categories that map onto verbs for characteristic motion (e.g., *walk*) than for verbs that encode change (e.g., *break*) and may require inferences about causes, goals, or the internal states of other beings (Huttenlocher, Smiley, and Charney 1983). At the same time, they are more likely to talk about movement, which is directly observable, than about causes or goals. And their verbs of movement are the first to be extended to talking about the activities of others, followed only later by other kinds of verbs.[6]

Semantic fields

Although children talk about actions and the outcomes of actions from the start, over half their early words are words for objects. Even when their vocabulary amounts to no more than 50 or 100 words, they name or draw attention to people, to animals, to body parts, to vehicles, to clothes, to toys, to food and utensils, to social routines, and to a few properties of objects (Nelson 1973). But at this early a stage, children typically have only one or two words available in each of these domains.

As they add more words, they expand the size of each domain. For example, for animals, Damon began at 1;1,15 with *dog*; in the next week he added *bear*, then *bird*; three weeks later, he added *duck*, then *mouse*, and a week after that, *cat.* Over the next few weeks, he added further *chicken, horse, barking, turtle, fish, cow, rabbit, goose, animal, pig, monkey*, then *ant, bug, ladybug* all at once, followed by *frog, snake* and *alligator* all at once in two successive weeks. As children build up such domains, they often seem to add several new members all at once, sometimes even on the same day (Dromi and Fishelzon 1986, Smith 1973).

By the end of his second year, Damon had expanded some of his early semantic domains to a considerable size. Among them were:

PEOPLE: 18 terms (including proper names)
e.g., *baby, man, mummy, boy, girl, people*

---

[6] For early verbs, see Berman 1978b, Clark 1978b, 1978c, Dromi 1987, Edwards and Goodwin 1986, and Huttenlocher, Smiley, and Charney 1983, Tomasello 1992.

ANIMALS: 25 terms

    e.g., *cat, dog, rabbit, duck, mouse, zebra, animal*

VEHICLES: 18 terms

    e.g., *car, truck, train, bike, sled, fire-truck*

BODY PARTS: 14 terms

    e.g., *nose, toe, eye, head, finger, hand, knee*

CLOTHING: 14 terms

    e.g., *diaper, sock, jacket, shirt, button*

TOYS: 35 terms

    e.g., *block, ball, clown, doll, bus, slinky, toy*

FURNITURE: 12 terms

    e.g., *chair, cushion, table, rug, bed, bath*

HOUSEHOLD ITEMS AND UTENSILS: 39 terms

    e.g., *telephone, light, kettle, plug, clock, stairs*

FOOD: 31 terms

    e.g., *milk, juice, cheese, nut, egg, carrot, food, cereal*

FOOD UTENSILS: 11 terms

    e.g., *bottle, cup, spoon, plate, lid, bowl, glass*

PROPERTIES AND STATES: 24 terms

    e.g., *hot, big, stuck, wet, tight, shut, sleepy*

ACTIVITIES: 74 terms

    e.g., *get, put, go, do, up, out, fall, jump, drive*

Overall, in the week before his second birthday, Damon's production vocabulary amounted to 477 words. The majority (65 percent) were labels for object categories. There were also a number of terms for actions or the locations where actions ended (20 percent), and for states or properties of objects (6 percent). The remaining 9 percent was made up of deictic terms, routines, quantifiers (e.g., *more, two*), the terms *yes* and *no*, and a few phrases (see also Dromi 1987, Gentner 1982).

Elaborating semantic fields

As children add more words to their vocabulary, they also build up further domains. For instance, terms earlier grouped together for convenience as words for states or properties of objects begin to cluster in subgroups, e.g., words for temperature (*hot, warm, cold*), for color (*red, blue, pink*), for dimensionality (*big, little, long*), for surface texture (*wet, sticky, clean, soft*), and so develop into further semantic domains to which children add more words. Much the same happens with deictic terms, which, with additions, separate into subject (*I, me, you*), object (*me, you*), and possessive pronouns (*my, mine, your*) on the one hand, and terms for places (*here, there*), objects (*this, that*), and times (*now, yesterday*) on the other. The same expansion and then subdivision into separate subdomains takes place with both nominal terms and verbal terms.

Some semantic domains have been studied for patterns of use during development. Dimensional terms, for instance, have been examined to find out when children produce words for different dimensions (e.g., *big/small, tall/short, high/low*) and how they are applied. Are children equally willing to use terms for positive (e.g., *tall*) and negative extent (e.g., *short*)? Linguistically, the term for the positive end of a spatial dimension is unmarked. That is, it appears in neutral questions about the amount of a specific dimension, as in the neutral *How long is that board*? compared with the marked *How short is that board*? It also appears in measure phrases, as in *Three metres long* (compare the ungrammatical **Three metres short*). And it typically underlies the term for the whole dimension, here *length* (derived from unmarked *long*) in contrast to *shortness*, which designates length only relative to some standard.

Children typically produce the most general pair of adjectives first, namely *big* and *little*. They usually follow these by positive terms for various dimensions. But they rarely produce any negative dimensional terms. If necessary, they may substitute *little*, say, for *short* (length or height) as well as for a term like *narrow*. The asymmetry children exhibit in producing dimensional terms appears to be independent of the relatively greater frequency of positive over negative terms in the language at large. In a learning task with nonsense words, for instance, three- and four-year-olds found it easier to learn terms for the positive ends of dimensions than for the negative ones, even though both positive and negative were equally frequent. This suggests that the asymmetry observable in lexical acquisition is based on a conceptual asymmetry in how extent along a dimension is represented.[7]

First meanings

Children do not start out already knowing the meanings of the words they are attempting to pronounce and use. They must first assign some meaning to them, and that takes time. In fact, children's earliest mappings of meanings onto forms diverge from adult usage in a variety of ways.

[7] See further Clark 1972, Donaldson and Wales 1970, Wales and Campbell 1970; also Brewer and Stone 1975, Eilers, Oller, and Ellington 1974, Klatzky, Clark, and Macken 1973.

Situation-bound uses

Among the first 10–20 words children produce are some that are produced only in certain contexts. To some extent, they appear bound to specific situations much as adult uses of expressions like *hello, goodbye, oh, well,* and *peek-a-boo* or *uh-oh* are. One child may say *bye* only when someone leaves the room. Another may say *car* only upon catching sight of a car on the street below from a window, but not upon seeing toy cars, cars at street level, or cars in other settings (Barrett 1986, Barrett, Harris, and Chasin 1991, Bloom 1973, Bowerman 1978, Braunwald 1978, Dromi 1987). In general such uses do not simply involve analogues to adult terms that are situation-bound. They may also involve nouns and verbs in phrases that have yet to be analyzed.

Situation-bound words are typically few in number and appear only during the earliest part of the one-word stage. Some investigators have suggested these terms might be called "indexical signs" since they are used communicatively and pick out events as a whole. At the same time, they appear to have minimal lexical content and so probably do not yet serve as category labels.

The majority of early words in production are not situation-bound; they are applied flexibly to a range of appropriate instances. For example, the word *dog* may be produced for a real dog, for pictures of dogs, and for a toy dog; or the word *biscuit* may be produced for a biscuit tin, for a biscuit, and for pictures of biscuits (see further Harris, Yeeles, Chasin, and Oakley, 1993).

Under-extensions and over-extensions

Although many early word-uses coincide with the adult's, others diverge. Children may UNDER-EXTEND a word by using a category label, for instance, for only a subset of the members of the (adult) category (Bloom 1973, Reich 1976). In fact, this would account for some situation-bound uses. Children may also OVER-EXTEND a word by applying it to members of the adult category *and* to members of other categories that are perceptually similar. For example, they may use *ball* for balls of all kinds, and also for round hanging lampshades, doorknobs, and the moon. Or they may over-extend a term like *door* to corks, jar-lids, box-lids, and gates when wishing to have the relevant object opened or closed (Anglin 1977, Clark 1973a, Griffiths and Atkinson 1978, Thomson and Chapman 1977).

Children aged one and two typically produce both under- and over-extensions. These may involve up to one-third of their production vocabulary (between 30 and 60 words out of a vocabulary of 200, say). Under-extensions are commoner with more peripheral category-members: for instance, a child might readily use *dog* for any kinds of dogs that are central or prototypical (most dog-like), but not for a Chihuahua or a Pekingese (Kay and Anglin 1982).

Over-extensions fall into two main categories – over-inclusions, where children extend a term to other entities from the same taxonomy, e.g., *dada* used for both the father and mother, *baby* used for self-reference and all children, *apple* used for apples and for oranges; and analogical extensions where children use a term for objects from other taxonomies on the basis of perceptual similarity, e.g., *cotty-bars* (= bars of a cot) extended to an abacus on the wall and to a picture of a building with a columned façade, or *comb* extended to designate a centipede. Over-inclusions are marked both by perceptual similarity and conceptual contiguity. That is, the words being extended are applied to instances of other categories within the same or an adjacent conceptual domain. For example, a child may over-extend a term within the domain of animals, as when *horse* is applied to goats, cows, and sheep; or within the domain of vehicles, as when *truck* is applied to buses, tractors, and vans; or within the domain of clothing, as when *hat* is applied to a crown. Analogical extensions include mainly over-extensions where the child produces a single term for objects from two (or more) different domains where the objects in question are nonetheless similar in some way. For instance, when a child over-extends his word for "ball" to onions, doorknobs, and the moon, he is making an analogical over-extension since none of these objects belongs to the domain of balls (or toys).

True over-extensions need to be distinguished from re-categorizations, as when a child pretends one thing is in fact another. For example, a child may place a waste-basket on his head and then say *hat*. If an adult did this, it would be assumed that he was simply saying 'for current purposes, this is a hat by virtue of my calling it one,' just as one may call a tree-stump a table if it serves that function. The same logic applies to young children.

Over-extensions also have to be distinguished carefully from comments on ownership or location. These are utterances where children name, say, the possessor of the object under scrutiny, e.g., *mummy*, said as the child points at his mother's shoes, or *cup*, said as the child looks in the usual location for his cup which is not there. What do children intend by such utterances? They are clearly not trying to label the objects being pointed to. (On other occasions, these children show they can label the objects as *shoe* and *cup*.) Rather, they are predicating some property (this belongs to, this is where) of the object or place in question. These uses should not be regarded as labels at all, and hence not as any kind of over-extension (Rescorla 1980; also Greenfield and Smith 1976, Huttenlocher and Smiley 1987).

Terms from some domains seem to be more prone to over-extension than others. The first word for a letter or number is nearly always over-extended, as are some terms for vehicles, clothing, and, less often, animals. This observation seems to hold across languages, suggesting two things: first, some domains are of greater interest to children than others, and second, children make greater efforts to talk about what interests them. At a stage when they have only a small vocabulary, this could be what leads them to over-extend some of the words they already have.

This account is lent further support from the discrepancies between production and comprehension. Children who over-extend words in production typically do not over-extend them in comprehension. Instead, they restrict themselves to identifying an appropriate referent, as shown in Table 2–2. That is, children understand the words they over-extend in production. This would be consistent with over-extension being a communicative strategy: use the nearest word that seems appropriate.

Occasionally, children may under- and over-extend the same word. For example, a child may use *dog* of all large dogs, but not small ones, and also over-extend this term to sheep, calves, goats, and cows. Such instances are not common, and may be hard to distinguish from another subtype of over-extension that has been called "complexive." These appear to be made on the basis of a different shared characteristic on each occasion so the different referents have few features in common. For example, a child might use *moon* for the real moon, and then on the basis of such features as shape (round, crescent, half-moon), color, texture, contour, and so on, over-extend the word to different objects that share one or more features with the moon proper, but have little in common with each other. For example, one child extended *moon* to a half-grapefruit seen from below, to a lemon slice, to a dial on a dishwasher, to a shiny leaf, crescent-shaped paper, the inside of a lampshade, pictures of vegetables on the wall, circles on a wall-hanging, and so on (Bowerman 1978, Dromi 1987). Complexive word-uses like this, though, appear to be rare among over-extensions.

Over-extensions have a limited life-span. Children do not immediately over-extend new words: they usually do it only after using the words for some weeks apparently correctly, with adult-like extensions, to members of

Table 2–2 *Over-extension in production versus comprehension*

Production		Comprehension	
Word	Extensions and over-extensions	Word	Extensions and over-extensions
doggie	dogs	*doggie*	dogs
	bears		
	horses		
	cats		
	hippopotamus		
	rhinoceros		
	lamb		
	donkey		
	wolf		
	Cookie Monster		
apple	apple	*apple*	apple
	balls of soap		
	a rubber-ball		
	a ball-lamp		
	a tomato		
	cherries		
	peaches		
	strawberries		
	an orange		
	a pear		
	an onion		
	round biscuits		

Source: Thomson and Chapman 1977.

the appropriate (adult) categories. Diary studies suggest that children noticeably over-extend words only up to about age 2;0 or 2;6 (Clark 1973a; also Dromi 1987, Rescorla 1980).

Mismatches

Children occasionally come up with complete MISMATCHES to adult word-meanings. That is, they try to pronounce some word having assigned some meaning to it, but the adults around neither recognize the word being attempted, nor the meaning assigned to it. The children encounter only incomprehension whenever they use it, and, presumably for just that reason, give up on it after a few days or weeks. Instances of this type have only rarely been reported, probably because observers are unable to work out what the child is attempting to say and may not even recognize any consistency in the form being produced (Bloom 1973).

Adult usage

Even at this early stage, when children have only 100–200 words in their active vocabulary, they use some two-thirds of them much as an adult would. These terms appear to have adult-like extensions and consistently pick out members of the appropriate categories. This does not necessarily justify our assuming that children are *therefore* using their words just as an adult would, with adult-like meanings and contrasts. One problem is this: usage that appears to be correct offers little information about how children have arrived at the adult meaning. Children must make use of some highly efficient procedures if they can effect such a good match for more than half their earliest word uses. As they get older, divergences between child meanings and conventional (adult) meanings become even harder to detect. This suggests children become more skilled as they get older in making use of any principles they are relying on to assign meanings to unfamiliar words.

Multi-word utterances

Once children have assigned some meaning to a word, they must also consider how that word may combine with others. Many children begin to produce two-word utterances between age 1;6 and age 2;0. One view is that children go through a one-word stage in production, followed, 6 to 10 months later, by a two-word stage. The two-word stage is marked by the emergence of two-word utterances, which gradually give way some two to six months later to longer utterances (Bellugi and Brown 1964, Bloom 1970, Bowerman 1973, Braine 1976, Brown 1973, Slobin 1970). However, this general account needs to be modified because, as we have seen, not all children go through a distinct one-word stage. Some combine two or more words in their utterances within a few weeks of producing their first words. Compare Keren and Damon (Figures 2–2 and 2–4).

Longer utterances (two words or more) do not appear to mark any cognitive leap forward. In them, children generally talk about the same kinds of roles that they picked out with one word at a time (Braine 1976, Greenfield and Smith 1976). They talk about agents and their actions (*Daddy open, Timmy run* for ' Daddy's opening the door' and ' Timmy [self-reference] is running/wants to run'), agents and objects affected by their actions (*Mommy sock, Susan clock* for 'Mommy [is putting on my] sock' and 'Susan [is touching the] clock'), objects and locations (*Pillow bed, There book* for '[The] pillow [is on the] bed' and 'There [is the] book'), and so on. Across languages, children appear to express very similar relations when they combine two or more words in a single utterance (Bowerman 1973, Slobin 1970).

As children try to express more complex meanings, they must work out which word combinations are appropriate for what they wish to say. For instance, each verb licenses certain arguments. The verb *to open* can appear with three arguments in the roles of agent, object, and instrument, as in *The man opened the door with a key*. It can also appear with certain subsets of these arguments, as in *The door opened* (object alone), *The key opened the door* (instrument and object), but not *The man opened* (agent only) or *The key opened* (instrument only). Nouns also place certain requirements on the words they appear with. These specify, for example, whether they can occur with articles like *a* or *the*, and which types of adjectives they can co-occur with, as in *The orange pillow* but not usually *The bald pillow*. Different adjectives occur as attributes, predicates, or both, as in *The boy was faint* but not (with a similar meaning) *The faint boy* ... or *That utter fool* but not *That fool is utter*, compared with *The book is thick* and *The thick book*. That is, over and above the denotative meanings, knowing how to use words includes knowing how they can combine with each other syntactically.

Word class and word structure

Children's words can be identified as belonging to particular word classes only once children have begun to combine words and use them with some grammatical morphemes. In English, the article *the* or the plural morpheme *-s* signal nouns, for example, while the morphemes *-ing* or *-ed* signal verbs. Once children produce inflections and use two- or three-word utterances, it also becomes possible to identify novel words as nouns or verbs, even in the absence of affixes to mark word class. At earlier stages in production, word-class membership cannot be reliably assigned from children's utterances alone. For example, consider the following productions of *door* (Griffiths and Atkinson 1978, p. 313):

(1)   a.   ə door. (J 1;11,8)
        b.   Door, door please. (R 1;10,17)

The utterances in (1a) and (1b) at first glance appear to contain *door* functioning as a noun. But the child who produced utterance (1a) consistently used *door* where adults would use *open*. In other words, the utterance could be glossed either as 'That's a door' or as 'That's open.' The latter would also be consistent with the use in (1b), from another child who also produced *door* in contexts where adults would have used *open*. This utterance, then, is best glossed as 'Open [it], open [it] please.' Yet the adult term *door* is indisputably a noun. The point is a methodological one: children in the earlier stages of acquisition may not make the same assignments to word classes that adults do, so we cannot automatically assume adult-like assignments until children's terms appear with enough other grammatical information for the diagnosis to be certain (Dewey 1894, Stern and Stern 1928; also Griffiths and Atkinson 1978, Hutten-locher, Smiley, and Charney 1983).

The identification of word class is critical in the analysis of children's novel lexical items. Consider the utterances in (2) and (3):

(2)   Baby broom.
(3)   I broomed her. (S 2;7)

The production of *broom* in the hypothetical utterance in (2) could be picking out the entity designated by the conventional noun *broom*, and identifying it as the property of the baby or as the object affected by some action of the baby's. Or it could be picking out some kind of action one might perform with a broom, and indicating either that the baby was doing this, or that someone else was doing this to the baby. The status of *broom* here is indeterminate between noun and verb. The utterance in (3), though, offers four pieces of evidence for *broom* being a verb: it is marked inflectionally for past tense with the suffix -*ed*; it appears after a nominative pronoun *I*; it is followed by an accusative pronoun *her*; and the word order combined with pronoun-case marks *I* as the subject and *her* as the direct object. Grammatical cues like these are critical when there is no overt derivational marking of word class, especially in the analysis of lexical innovations.

Word structure

Children begin early to analyze the units – roots and affixes – that occur in the words they are learning. To do this, they must attend to the order of units within words and to possible combinations of such units of word structure. Only once they have identified the forms of roots and affixes can

Table 2–3 *Spontaneous analyses of word-parts from one child*

(1)	D (2;4,3, looking at toy car): *That a motor-car. It got a motor.*
(2)	Mo (pointing at picture of lady-bug): What's that?
	D (2;4,13): *A lady-bug! That like "lady."*
(3)	D (2;4,18, to Mo, of toy car painted white all over, including windows):
	Eve, this is a snow-car.
	Mo Why's that a snow-car?
	D *'Cause it's got lots of snow on it. I can't see the windows.*
(4)	D (2;6,20, to Fa, about a stick): *This is a running-stick.*
	Fa A running-stick?
	D *Yes, because I run with it.*
(5)	Fa (to D, in the bath): You're making a cake?
	D (2;7,1): *It's a water-cake.*
	Fa Why do you call it a water-cake?
	D *I made it in the water.*
(6)	D (2;9,10): *You know why this is a HIGH-chair? Because it is high.*
(7)	D (2;9,24): *Does cornflakes have corn in it?*
(8)	D (2;9,24): *Eve, you know what you do on runways? You run on them*
	because they start with "run."
(9)	D (2;10,23, offering a pretend present to Fa): *I bought you a tooth-brush*
	and a finger-brush.
	Fa What's a finger-brush?
	D *It's for cleaning your nails.*
(10)	D (2;11, in Safeway grocery store): *Is this where you get safe? 'Cause this*
	is Safeway and you get safe from the cold.
(11)	Mo We're going to a place called Sundance.
	D (2;11,0): *And you dance there. If there is music, we will dance there.*
(12)	D (2;11,2): *Windshield! Wind goes on it. That's why it's called a*
	windshield.
(13)	D (2;11,25, wearing a sun-hat): *I look like a little pony-kid.*
	Mo What's a pony-kid?
	D *A kid who rides ponies.*
(14)	D (2;11,25, asking about a road): *What's it called?*
	Mo King's Mountain Road.
	D *Do kings live in it?*
(15)	D (2;11,28, looking at flowering ice-plants): *What's that called?*
	Mo That's ice-plant.
	D *Does it grow ice?*
(16)	D (3;2,15): *I'm going to build a monster-building. A monster-building has*
	a lot of monsters in it.
(17)	D (3;2,15): *Egg-nog comes from egg!*
(18)	D (3;2,15): *Hey, "golden" begins with Goldilocks, in one of my books!*
(19)	D (3;2,20, as climbed into the car, holding both index fingers up to his*
	head): *D'you know what head-lights are?*

Table 2–3 (*Cont.*)

	Mo No.
	D *They're lights that go on in your head!*
(20)	D (3;2,28, of a toy airplane): *This is a shoot-plane because it shoots monsters!*
(21)	Fa (with D, looking at Zoo Guide from Durrell's Zoo in Jersey): And this is a wood-duck.
	D (3;3,30): *So he's made of wood!*
(22)	D (3;4,29): *You know what that is? It's a cannon-truck because it has cannons on it.*
(23)	D (3;4,29, playing at "cook"): *What would you like, sir?*
	Mo Could you make me some angel-cake?
	D *I don't have any angels.*
(24)	D (3;5,3, of cakes from a birthday treat at school): *They were candy-cupcakes because they had candy on top.*

Source: Clark, diary data.

they construct new forms to carry new meanings. And they construct them from units of word structure already identified. Their prior analyses allow them to add the pertinent inflections, for example, to newly learnt nouns and verbs, even where the result may not be the conventional form, as in noun plurals like **foots* or **sheeps*, or past tenses like **buyed* or **sitted*.

Children's own analyses of the internal structure of words are sometimes explicit in their spontaneous comments about word structure, as shown in Table 2–3. In these utterances, D spontaneously commented on similarities among morphemes. In both conventional words and innovations, the roots that bear stress (e.g., *motor-, snow-, corn-*) tend to be the elements commented on. In several instances, the child's recognition of a root inside a complex word offered the basis for jokes and teasing (see also Slobin 1978). One- and two-year-olds may spontaneously display some of what they have and haven't analyzed in this way.

Children also display what they know in their construction of new words when they build on ingredients already familiar to them. Consider the exchange in (4):

(4)   Noah (picking up a toy dog): *This is Woodstock.*
   (he bobs the toy in Adam's face)
   Adam: *Hey Woodstock, don't do that.*
   (Noah persists)
   Adam: *I'm going home so you won't Woodstock me.*

Here Adam (aged 3;7) coins a new verb, *to Woodstock*, to talk about the relevant action. He does so by taking the proper name Woodstock and, from it, forming a novel verb with the meaning, on this occasion, of 'push the toy called Woodstock into (my) face.' (Notice that *to Woodstock* could in fact have an indefinite number of meanings, depending on the contexts it is coined in.)[8] Or consider an example reported by James Sully a century ago, from another child the same age:

(5)   C (3;7,7) was looking forward to going to the circus; his father told him that he wouldn't be able to go if it rained, for nobody could drive away the rain. C instantly remarked: *The rainer can.* Asked by his father who this person was, C replied: *A man who lives in the forest – MY forest – and has to drive the rain away.* (Sully, 1896, p.454)

Here, C coins a novel agentive noun by adding the affix *-er* to the familiar word *rain*. Both types of coinages, verbs like *to Woodstock* and nouns like *rainer*, suggest that these children have analyzed similar uses in conventional words – noun/verb pairs in English like *button/to button*, *spoon/to spoon*, and agentive nouns like *farmer*, *rider*, *swimmer* alongside the verbs *farm*, *ride*, and *swim* – so, when they need to, they can extend the same patterns to new instances. Children coin new words alongside conventional ones as early as age two. They appear to coin them, though, only when they do not already have words available to express the requisite meanings. Their innovations complement the conventional words they are learning by filling gaps in their vocabulary.

Summary

Children begin to produce their first words around age one, and add steadily to their vocabularies over the next year. After some weeks or months of one word at a time, they graduate to longer utterances as they express more complex meanings. They soon add inflections to nouns and verbs, another way to elaborate their meanings. Their early words fall into several semantic fields, and these in turn are gradually expanded with the addition of more terms. Around age two, children can make explicit analyses of words into parts and begin to coin both nouns and verbs. But this story offers no account of how children identify possible meanings and map them onto word forms. I turn next to some of the factors that play a part in this mapping.

[8] I am indebted to Adam Gallistel for this example.

3 The mapping problem

Children acquiring words have a mapping problem. They must isolate the word-forms of their language; they must create potential meanings; and then they must map the meanings onto the forms. All three tasks are critical to the solution of the mapping problem in lexical acquisition. For present purposes, I presuppose that children can isolate the relevant forms.[1] The focus in this chapter is on the creation of meanings and their mapping onto word forms. The early meanings children map onto forms are based on what they already know about the world around them (Clark 1983, Gibson and Spelke 1983, Mandler 1983). I therefore look first at the stuff early meanings are made from – children's ontological categories of objects, actions, properties, and relations. I then turn to mapping itself. Children appear to map meanings onto forms rather swiftly given the large numbers of words acquired in the early years. A number of people have proposed that the mapping task is made easier by children's reliance on various assumptions about the relations of words to the categories they denote. I look first at conceptual constraints on mapping, and then turn to lexical constraints.

Ontological categories

When children create possible meanings to map onto word forms, they do so by drawing on two kinds of information. They draw on their own experience, and they draw on patterns of use for each form in the input language they hear. In their first few months of life, children come to distinguish certain kinds of objects, activities, and relations. By age one, they have built up a considerable repertoire of conceptual categories and have a good deal of information about them represented in memory.

---

[1] This task is not an easy one: it depends critically both on children's attention to adult language and on the way adults speak to very young children (Bernstein-Ratner 1987, Broen 1972, Fernald 1989, Garnica 1977). However, it will not be covered further in the present discussion.

What kinds of categories do the speakers of a language need? Which categories offer the necessary basis for meanings in language? In general, all languages offer ways to talk about objects and events, about activities and states, and about relations in space and time. Note that they do not offer speakers an exhaustive means of expression for talking about every detail of each object and event. They are selective in what receives lexical expression, so the connection between a conceptual category and its linguistic label is necessarily a somewhat indirect one. The label stands for the category the speaker wishes to denote, but the relation between category and label is a conventional one, and languages may carve up the same domain in different ways, as when speakers of English rely on one verb for talking about getting dressed while speakers of Japanese rely on several.

The major kinds of ontological categories that children begin to establish early on include OBJECTS, ACTIONS, EVENTS, RELATIONS, STATES, and PROPERTIES. These are the categories speakers make reference to when they speak, and these are the categories that underlie major word classes such as noun, verb, and adjective. Across languages, there is a strong correlation between word class and ontological category: nouns typically denote objects, verbs denote actions, and adjectives properties (Croft 1991).

Objects

The ontological categories children draw on in creating meanings for nouns must include kinds of individuals that are countable, and typically identified by shape. Children draw on kinds like these in creating meanings for count nouns like *woman, leaf, chair,* and *book*. They must include individuals picked out by proper names or pronouns such as *Kate* or *they*. In fact, from birth onwards, infants begin to extract and analyze information about the world around them. They attend particularly to shape and give evidence of forming object categories very early: they respond selectively to novel instances of schematic drawings, for example, distinguishing members from non-members for a category previously learnt. Their everyday responses to objects around them also offer strong evidence that prior to the production of any words, children have set up numerous categories of objects. They spontaneously touch like objects in sequence from age nine months on; and by twelve months, they also sort objects into groups on the basis of shape and can match pictures of like

Table 3–1 *Characteristic over-extensions from one- and two-year-olds*

Word	First referent	Successive over-extensions
bird	sparrows	cows, dogs, cats, any animal moving
titi	animals	pictures of animals, things that move
tee	cat	dogs, cows and sheep, horse
buti	ball	toy, radish, stone spheres at park entrance
tick-tock	watch	clocks, all clocks and watches, gas meter, fire-hose on spool, bath scale with round dial
ball	rubber-ball	apples
bébé	reflection of self	photo of self, all photos, all pictures, all books with pictures, all books
kotiba:s	bars of cot	large toy abacus, toast rack with parallel bars, picture of building with columns
fly	fly	specks of dirt, dust, all small insects, his own toes, crumbs of bread, toad
pin	pin	crumb, caterpillars
koko	cockerel crowing	tunes on violin, tunes on piano, tunes on accordion, tunes on phonograph, all music, merry-go-round
dany	sound of bell	clock, telephone, doorbells
cola	chocolate	sugar, tarts, grapes, figs, peaches
sizo	scissors	all metal objects
va	plush dog	muffler, cat, father's fur coat

Note: Commas separate successive over-extensions.
Source: Clark 1973a.

kinds of objects.[2] Above all, they are attentive to shape, the property perhaps most critical for the identification of object category members. This reliance on shape can be seen, for example, in children's early over-extensions of words, illustrated in Table 3–1. Children stretch their still limited vocabularies by over-extending many of their words to objects similar in shape to the original referents. In fact, shape provides the basis for the vast majority of such over-extensions, and presumably plays a major role in appropriate extensions too.[3]

But kinds and individuals are not the only relevant ontological categories

---

[2] See further Bornstein 1981, Cohen and Strauss 1979, Strauss 1979; Daehler, Lonardo, and Bukatko 1979, Ross 1979, Spelke 1990, Starkey 1979; Church 1966, Piaget 1951.
[3] See Clark 1973a, Anglin 1977 on over-extensions; also Au 1990, Baldwin 1989, Bornstein 1985, Landau, Smith, and Jones 1988, 1992, on reliance on shape in language learning.

here: Children must also draw on kinds that come as substances without individuation, as meanings for mass nouns like *earth, sand, water*, or *soup*. (They may draw on these kinds only later since there is no major cue such as shape for setting them up.) Children must also form categories based on one or more individuals linked by some activity, as in the events picked out by such nouns as *meal, circus*, or *revolution*. Again, these kinds would appear harder to place into categories than objects are, although, like other kinds, they are also picked out with count nouns. And ideas picked out by nouns like *honor, audacity*, or *glory* should take longer still. These give the range of ontological categories children draw on for possible noun-meanings.

Actions

Children also draw on their ontological categories when they create possible meanings for verbs. Here they must rely on their categories of kinds of activities and states. And here again, infants attend intensely to motion and to repetitive activities; they prefer moving objects over static ones, and they are very attentive to motion and noise combined – a bell ringing, a rattle shaking. By the age of eight months, there is evidence that infants are able to distinguish certain activities that result in a change of state from an ongoing process. For example, they attend differentially to displays of a ball rolling across a screen and a ball that rolls and hits a second object that then moves.[4] And by eighteen months, children have clear expectations about certain types of actions and their results: they are surprised, for instance, if an arch does not collapse when a supporting pillar is removed (Gelman, Bullock, and Meck 1980, Keil 1979). That is, infants clearly set up expectations about actions and results, and have some notions of causality. Whether they have categorized kinds of actions in much the way they have begun to categorize kinds of objects is unclear.

Categories of actions appear to be less coherent than categories of objects. Activities are relations that link an act and its participants, but each kind may apply to a large range within any one category. Consider the activities we group together as instances of 'holding.' These include a vase holding flowers; a hand holding a fork, cup, plate, pebble, or water; a father holding a baby; a truck holding sand or bricks; a rubber band holding hair; and so on. The range, largely determined by how an activity

---

[4] See further Leslie 1982, 1984, Lewis and Strauss 1986, Pieraut-Le Bonniec 1985, Roberts 1988, Younger 1985, Younger and Gotlieb 1988.

is adapted to each object it affects, may make it harder to set up categories of actions in the first place. This in turn may make it more difficult initially for children to create meanings for verbs than for some types of nouns.

Properties and relations

Children must also make use of their ontological categories when they create meanings for adjectives that pick out properties like shape, size, or color (e.g., *round, small, red*) and for prepositions that mark relations in space or time (e.g., *in, on, near,* or *above*). In their first year, infants often attend to small parts like buttons on clothes, and during their second year become particularly attentive to cracks (in plates, for example), broken or torn edges (e.g., on a newspaper or book page), or missing knobs. This suggests they can distinguish the normal or usual properties of many objects from abnormal (broken, torn, cracked) states.

Other properties mark relations. For example, the comparative size or height of objects is picked out by terms like *big* or *long* (e.g., *His stick is longer than mine*), and the relation of an object to a place is picked out by terms like *beside* or *on* (e.g., *The shovel is beside the back door*). Again, children's ontological categories are built on their growing knowledge about objects, their possible properties, and their placement in space or time.

In summary, before children begin to produce their first words, they have been exposed to at least a full year of experience with the world around them. This exposure allows them to set up ontological categories they can then draw on as they create possible meanings for word forms. In creating meanings, children respect the ontological types among conceptual categories. These types may offer a distinct helping hand to children in the acquisition of the relevant syntactic categories.

Bootstrapping and fast mapping

Although grammatical entities like Noun or Verb do not have semantic definitions, nouns and verbs typically refer to distinct, identifiable semantic classes in parental speech. That is, people and physical objects are referred to with nouns; activities and changes of state with verbs; properties and colors with adjectives, and so on (Croft 1991, Lyons 1966). Notions like physical object, agent, and action are therefore available to children in the input they hear. Adults talk about things, actions, and properties when they talk to small children. And when they use a noun, for example, they do so with the relevant formal information that goes with its syntactic word class. Nouns are accompanied by noun inflections (*a dog, two dogs, the dog's tail*) and verbs by verb inflections (*we give, he gives, they are giving, you gave, they have given*). That is, adult word-use is consistent with the correlation of conceptual category type and word class. Because of this, the input children hear offers a semantic route into syntax.

If children assume early on that there must be different word-classes on the basis of the meaning–form mappings of different ontological types, then they will be able to bootstrap themselves into the syntactic categories they will need for the clause- and sentence-level organization of words. Once they have a basic scaffolding of semantically induced information about word classes and lexical items belonging to these word classes, they are in a position to learn what else belongs in each by observing the distributions of unfamiliar terms within known structures. This semantic bootstrapping, it has been argued, offers children a *way in* to the syntactic categories needed for the acquisition of syntactic rules (Grimshaw 1981, Macnamara 1982, Pinker 1984, 1989).

Might children start from syntactic information instead, and use it to make inferences about certain aspects of meaning? That is, once children have begun to register that *dog* takes the plural ending, and that *jump* takes past tense *-ed*, can they use inflectional information to tell whether a new word is a verb or a noun, or whether a new noun is count or mass? While syntactic class does not yield particular noun and verb meanings, it does "suggest the general type of that meaning, whether action, object, substance, or whatever" (Brown 1957, p. 4). Young children make use of inflectional clues to distinguish nouns and adjectives, count and mass nouns, and proper names and common nouns.[5] They may rely on such syntactic bootstrapping in particular to assign preliminary meanings to new verbs. For example, they could use information about number of arguments and word order in deciding whether a new verb was transitive or not: compare *The boy patted the rabbit* and *The boy coughed*. Indeed, three-year-olds appear to do just that, for example, when translating unfamiliar words from a puppet language: they treat terms with two noun phrases as transitive verbs with an agentive first argument, and terms with one noun phrase as intransitives.[6] Clearly children must take advantage of

---

[5] On nouns and adjectives, see Taylor and Gelman 1988; on count and mass nouns, Gordon 1985, Soja 1992, Soja, Carey, and Spelke 1991; and on proper names, Gelman and Taylor 1984, Katz, Baker, and Macnamara 1974.

[6] See further Behrend 1990a, Dockrell and McShane 1990, Gleitman 1990, Gleitman and Gleitman 1992, Maratsos 1990, Naigles 1990.

all the clues to meaning available. But the verb meanings derivable from inflections, number of arguments, and word order alone are only part of the story. Children also have their ontological categories to draw on in assigning possible meanings. The structural clues presumably complement their use of ontological information. The extent to which children can bootstrap their way into syntax as a whole, though, is not yet clear.

Lastly, children appear to assign *some* meaning to a new form after only minimal exposure to use of the form. In one study, when three-year-olds heard an unfamiliar word form, *chromium*, alongside other words for color, for example, they assumed that it picked out a color. They did this on the basis of hearing the new word only once or twice (Carey 1978, Carey and Bartlett 1978, Heibeck and Markman 1987). This suggests that children may well try to map some chunk of meaning onto every form they isolate. Mapping even a partial meaning may help to make the word form itself more memorable, so that it is more easily recognized the next time it occurs in the input.

The meaning actually assigned with such fast mapping may comprise only a fraction of what must eventually be mapped onto the form in question. The working out of the full conventional meaning may take months or even years. At the same time, children often seem to map enough of the adult meaning for some of their own uses to be appropriate, and enough for them to recognize the same word-form on later occasions. Children's willingness to assign some meaning to a new word-form after hearing it only once or twice allows them to set up a large number of lexical entries (albeit incomplete ones) in a relatively short time. Once they have some entry in memory, children can continue to add or adjust information that seems pertinent, over a lifetime if need be.

Conceptual constraints

As children map their initial meanings onto word forms, they must make certain decisions. Does word *X* pick out an object or an action, a state or a property, a relation in space, an event with many participants? In making an initial decision, children presumably attend to their existing ontological categories, and pick out whatever is salient – an entity or action, say – for which they do not yet have any label, as their initial target. In doing this, children seem to observe certain constraints or assumptions. These appear to guide their mapping as they add new words to their lexicon. (The same constraints should also guide adults when *they* are faced with assigning a meaning to an unfamiliar form.) Researchers have identified several candidate constraints, but have paid most attention so far to their effects on labels for objects.

Assumptions about objects

In the case of object categories, children appear to assume that labels pick out the WHOLE OBJECT – not just a part or a property of the entity being talked about. For instance, eighteen-month-olds who are given labels for parts of an unfamiliar object assume that the part labels in fact pick out the whole object. Three-year-olds also make this assumption. When they hear a label for a part of an unfamiliar as-yet-unlabeled object, they too take the part label to be the label for the whole object. From an early age, then, children appear to expect that when they hear an unfamiliar label, they should find that it picks out some kind of object as a whole – and not just a part of it (Macnamara 1982, Markman and Wachtel 1988, Mervis and Long 1987, Woodward 1992). This whole object assumption for a first label is equivalent to what has been called the "shape bias" in acquisition – that children attend to shape and hence to whole objects, since shape is a salient defining characteristic for members of object categories (Landau, Smith, and Jones 1988, 1992, Landau and Stecker 1990).

The whole-object assumption, then, will lead children first to label categories of whole objects and later to label parts and relations pertinent to those categories. This presupposes that children already have an ontological category of object, such that kinds of objects are conceived of as whole entities distinct from their locations and distinct from specific relations they bear to other kinds of objects. Also presupposed is that children have some reason to assume that an adult is picking out an object on such occasions. And here, of course, children may make mistakes. They may start by mapping an activity meaning onto what for an adult speaker is a noun, or an object meaning onto an adult verb.

In doing this, children must also assume that words denote TYPES, and not individuals. This holds for words for objects, as here, words for actions, and words for properties. When speakers use words to refer, of course, they can use them either to refer to the type or to specific individuals belonging to the type. This specificity is typically marked in English by the definite article *the*, as in *the dog*. But even though the speaker here is talking about a specific individual, the term *dog* itself denotes the type.

The kinds of categories of whole objects one- and two-year-olds favor are often categories at what psychologists have identified as the BASIC LEVEL.[7] Conceptually, objects at this level turn out to be easier for adults to categorize than objects at levels either above or below this level. Members of a basic-level category typically have more parts in common with each other than with members of a higher-level category, and they are more easily distinguished from members of neighboring categories in the same domain than are instances of lower-level categories (Tversky and Hemenway 1984). Conceptually, then, basic-level categories are highly privileged: they cohere internally more than categories at other levels, so their members are readily perceived as clear members of their category, and, simultaneously, as non-members of neighboring categories. Children attend early to basic-level categories. The basic level is also privileged from a linguistic point of view: the labels assigned to basic-level categories are simpler in form than those assigned to lower levels, and are therefore easier to learn and remember. According to the whole-object assumption, they should also be easy to assign labels to.

When children start to attach labels to neighboring categories within the same conceptual domain, they may also look for EQUAL DETAIL in the alternatives they consider. A child who uses the label *dog* for dogs, say, will look for a category at the same level of specificity when trying to map the term *cat*, and is therefore more likely to attach it to the category of cats than just to Siamese cats or just to Persian cats, both *subkinds* of cats and therefore presenting more detailed points of comparison than are needed (Shipley and Kuhn 1983). If children mapped *dog* at first only onto 'spaniel,' they would have to exclude many instances very similar in details of head shape, eye color, and ear size, in addition to such properties as fur length and tail length. Although the initial mapping children make in such cases may depart from the adult one, it still overlaps with it in many respects. The input children hear will help them adjust the boundaries of their initial mapping.

If children look for roughly equal detail as they map terms within a single domain, they may try to maximize the number of labels they assign. If they assigned them to category instances on the basis of too many specific details, they would end up with narrower categories than would be useful given their small vocabularies. If they took account of too few details, they would allow a great deal of overlap among all their words. Children's tendency to aim for equal detail when they first assign labels

---

[7] This is the level in a taxonomy that linguists have called the *generic level* (e.g., Berlin *et al.* 1973).

should ensure that most categories labeled by one- and two-year-olds will be drawn from the same level of categorization. And this level will typically be the basic one, or something very close to it. Young children's basic categories may not always coincide with adult basic categories, but there is generally considerable overlap, so children can readily adjust their categories and labels with more experience (Mervis 1987, Mervis and Mervis 1982).

The level of categorization and of label assignment is important for what has been called the TAXONOMIC assumption – that labels pick out categories of objects rather than associated clusters of objects. That is, children assume that the word *dog* picks out dogs, and not dogs-and-bones, or dogs-chasing-cats, and a label like *swing* picks out swings and not swings-with-children-on-them, or swings-and-trees (Markman and Hutchinson 1984).

This point captures a general design feature of languages: most words pick out single categories with a certain internal coherence, and combinations of categories are then designated through the appropriate syntactic arrangements. For example, the word *dog* in the referring expression *the dog* designates the particular instance the speaker is concerned with on that occasion. If the speaker wishes to talk about the fact that the dog is lying down chewing a bone, then he must also choose the separate terms for the relevant activities and objects, perhaps *The dog's chewing a bone*. Notice that if *dog* instead designated a category of 'dog-R-bone' (where R marks some unspecified relation between the two), then one would also need separate words for dogs in relation to other objects such as leashes, children, lamp-posts, rugs, fires, food bowls, and kennels, as well as for dogs alone. The number of potential combinations of objects from different categories is both very large and, to a great extent, unpredictable, in the sense that novel combinations could arise every day. To base word meanings on such combinations, then, would be unparsimonious in the extreme. And no language does so, except perhaps in one or two terms for a distinctive and culturally important combination. The combinatorial work is done instead by combining words, as in *black dog*, *barking dog*, or *big dog*.

The assumptions that guide young children all pertain to what speakers can do with words for objects:

> *Whole-object assumption*: Speakers use words to pick out whole objects, not just a part or property of an object.

Type assumption: Speakers use words to denote types.

Basic-level assumption: Speakers use words to pick out objects in basic-level categories.

Equal-detail assumption: Speakers use words to pick out equally detailed instances of object categories from within a single domain.

These four assumptions constrain what children may count on when they create a potential meaning from a conceptual category. They are supplemented by one more:

Taxonomic assumption: Speakers use words to pick out coherent categories of objects.

This assumption explicitly supposes that object categories are coherent. One could have a category of 'pencils and my brother' or 'bricks and waterfalls,' but such categories are not internally coherent, and are thus unlikely candidates for single-word labels. Conceptual organization, then, has implications for what children assume about objects in connection with words.

Notice that all five assumptions must be over-ridden at certain points because of the nature of the lexicon itself. The whole-object assumption is violated by every noun for a part or property (e.g., *dog* versus *claw, fur, ear*); the basic-level assumption is violated by nouns for categories above or below the basic level (e.g., *dog* versus *mammal, animal; cocker spaniel, boxer*); and the equal-detail assumption is violated by the fact that nouns can convey different amounts of detail (e.g., *dog* versus *fox terrier*). Lastly, only a certain number of nouns label taxonomic categories; many label categories organized in other ways, such that the meanings of their labels may overlap (e.g., *comfort, softness, ease; nap, sleep, dream; sunlight, warmth*). In addition, pronouns and proper names only pick out individuals. Overall, then, this suggests that such assumptions offer firm guidelines for only the earliest stages in lexical acquisition. Ultimately, these assumptions must each be modified and restricted.

The assumptions considered so far pertain just to categories of objects. Is this the general default? Do children assume first that an unfamiliar label picks out an object category of some kind, and only when they find evidence to the contrary consider that it might pick out some other kind of category? Or do they make use of other ontological categories too? Opinion here is divided, and few studies are available (Behrend 1990b,

Woodward and Markman 1991, Soja, Carey, and Spelke 1991). But the nature of early vocabularies suggests it is reasonable to assume that children also create possible meanings using categories of actions, relations, and properties from the earliest stages of lexical acquisition on.

Assumptions about actions and events

How do the different levels line up from object to event categories? Do basic categories of events have the same kind of internal structure as categories of objects? For example, basic-level 'bird' has prototypical and non-prototypical members. Prototypical members are instances of birds with more of the characteristic properties of members of this category (robins, blackbirds, or pigeons). Less prototypical members have relatively fewer relevant properties, and some lie at the outer edge of the category (ostriches or penguins). This type of category structure is often called a "family-resemblance structure," since some members resemble each more than others (Rosch 1973, 1978, Rosch and Mervis 1975, Smith and Medin 1981, Tversky and Hemenway 1984). The extent to which action and event categories have a prototypical structure is unclear for two reasons: the lexicon for events and actions tends to be less elaborated than the lexicon for kinds of objects; and categories of actions differ from categories of objects in ways that may be critical for the kinds of categories people construct.

In adults, some categories of events are probably organized much as some domains of object categories are.[8] Events may consist of one action (*The leaf fell to the ground*) or a sequence of actions (*Duncan ran down the hill, jumped the stream, and vanished behind the trees*). Events, then, may generally be superordinate to actions. So categories of actions could make up the basic level. But the analyses available so far of how event and action categories are represented and stored still lack many details. What counts as a subtype of action versus a basic-level action? Are categories of actions organized internally with a family-resemblance structure, around proto-types, as object categories are? That is, in an action category like 'jump,' are some kinds of jumping better members of the category than others in the same way that a robin is a better bird than an ostrich?

Action categories differ from object categories in several ways: (1) Actions are always relational in structure. They link one or more

[8] See further Abbot, Black, and Smith 1985, John 1985, Rifkin 1985, Rosch 1978, Tversky and Hemenway 1984; also Barsalou and Sewell 1985, Fellbaum and Miller 1990, Pustejovsky 1991, and Rips and Conrad 1990, on properties of event categories.

participants to the activity, and there is no action without the pertinent participants to perform it or be affected by it. (Few object categories have a relational structure.) (2) Action categories have vaguer boundaries than object categories: it is difficult to decide, for instance, where an act of opening a door begins. Does it begin when the person approaches the door intending to open it? When she reaches out a hand? Grasps the doorknob? Turns the handle? Pushes the door away from the jamb? And when does the act of opening end? (3) The actual physical sequence of moves may differ considerably from one occasion of opening to another. Imagine opening a door, opening a can of sardines, opening a jar of marmalade, opening a zippered briefcase, opening a book, opening a box of chocolates. All these acts receive the same label in English: the verb *to open*. The same holds for acts of eating: one eats apples, blackberries, celery sticks, salmon, crab, steak, cucumber salad, and candy-floss – all with different actions, some with and some without utensils, yet all receive the same label in English: the verb *to eat*.

This diversity could make action categories harder to identify as categories initially, so children might take longer both to form categories and to attach labels to them (Clark 1978b, Gentner 1982, Maratsos 1990). This suggestion receives some support from the fact that children appear to be slower to learn labels for actions than for objects and rely on general-purpose verbs (usually *to do*, *to go*, *to get*, and *to put*) in their first year or so of talking about actions. This reliance on general-purpose verbs itself shows that they do distinguish actions as an ontological type distinct from that of objects. Children may begin by organizing their categories of actions and causality around prototypical events. These are taken to contain either common, distinctive intransitive actions such as walking, running, swimming, and climbing; or typical transitive causative actions where the agent of the action affects some other entity and possibly changes its state, as when someone breaks something, eats something, hits something, or makes one thing out of another (Slobin 1981, 1985c).

Here too children presumably rely on some guiding assumptions as they draw on categories of actions for meanings. For example, they should label whole actions, not just small parts of them. The verb *to somersault* in English, for instance, does not pick out just the curving of the back, or just the placing of the hands palm down on the ground, or just the pushing off with the feet. It picks out the whole action. So children may postulate a whole-action assumption in assigning possible meanings to word forms.

If categories of actions have a basic level, children would presumably rely on the basic-level assumption here, just as they do for objects. That is, basic-level actions should be more like each other, within a category, and more distinct from each other, across categories, than at other levels of categorization.[9] Actions of eating, for example, have in common the ingestion of food, so eating an apple and eating porridge should have more in common than eating an apple and holding a ball, where both use the hands, yet the goals are different – ingestion versus possession or transfer of the object to someone else. Yet there may be a greater range within action categories than within objects since categorization often involves not just the sequence of moves a person must make but also the goal aimed at and the kind of entity affected by the action.

The type assumption should apply just as forcibly to categories of actions as to objects. The equal-detail assumption would presumably also apply here. In one respect, children might even have an easier time with labels for actions than for objects: languages typically offer few lexical subcategorizations of actions below the basic level; they tend instead to rely on added qualifying phrases to mark such dimensions as manner, speed, direction, and purposefulness. Lastly, it is unclear whether there is an analogue here to the taxonomic assumption. Action categories are inherently relational, and always link one or more participants to the action. From one point of view, they therefore lack the kind of internal coherence characteristic of object categories.

Children's initial assumptions about how speakers use words for actions, then, in part parallel their assumptions about words for objects:

> *Whole-action assumption*: Speakers use words to pick out whole actions, and not just a part of an action.
>
> *Type assumption*: Speakers use words to denote types.
>
> *Basic-level assumption*: Speakers use words to pick out basic-level action categories.
>
> *Equal-detail assumption*: Speakers use words to pick out equally detailed instances of action categories.

Conceptual organization offers certain guidelines for children's creation of possible meanings. This holds as much for their preliminary mappings of meanings onto words for actions like *come*, *get up*, and *open*, as it does for their first meanings of words for objects like *horse*, *ball*, or *cup*.

---

[9] Young children's reliance on general-purpose verbs might appear incompatible with this assumption, but these verbs play the same role for actions as deictics like *that* do for objects. They serve to pick out specific actions in context.

Assumptions about relations

Categories of actions are relational. They link one or more participants to the activity being performed. The role of each participant may be marked grammatically by such devices as word order or case. In fact, the means children choose when initially marking participant roles like agent or location, for instance, may offer further clues to the kinds of conceptual categories children draw on. These categories may lead them to group certain kinds of participants in actions and events that are not necessarily grouped together in adult speech.

Young children often talk about the source or origin of motion in space, the agent of an action, the cause of some event, the standard in a comparison, or the possessor of an object. Whenever these entities are not in subject position, children, in every instance, will use similar means to indicate the role these entities bear. Although each conventionally calls for different linguistic expressions in English, children may initially mark them all with the same term, *from*, as shown in Table 3–2. That is, they appear to be marking a category of sources that may at first contain only places. They learn that locative sources can be indicated in English by means of the prepositions *from*, *out of*, or *off*. But *out of* and *off* are both restricted, with *out of* used only for three-dimensional sources and *off* for two-dimensional ones. As children add other kinds of sources to the conceptual category, they find a consistent marking for them all in *from*. They produce it first for sources that are places; then sources that are agents (conventionally marked with *by*); causes (conventionally marked with *because*); standards of comparison (conventionally marked with *than*), and possessors.

The generality of such uses is attested by an elicitation study carried out with two- to six-year-olds. The children were asked to repeat and repair sentences containing grammatical and ungrammatical uses of *from*, *by*, and *with*. Two-year-olds retained ungrammatical *from* for agents and natural forces in sentences like *Birds are scared from big cats* and *The tree blew down from the wind* 80 and 70 percent of the time respectively. They also substituted ungrammatical *from* for *by* 30 percent of the time in grammatical sentences like *The dog was patted by the little girl*. They substituted *from* for ungrammatical *with* used to introduce agents or natural forces (40 percent) and for ungrammatical *by* used to introduce natural forces (30 percent). From age three on, children showed less reliance on *from* to mark agent phrases and instead repaired ungrammatical *from* 40 percent of the time when it marked agents. Overall, two-year-olds assigned *from* to mark locative sources and chose *from* more

Table 3–2 *Source expressions marked by* from *in children's spontaneous speech*

PLACE:

    Eve (2;2, of a book): *It came from my book-box.*

    D (2;2,5, of a sock): *That came from my toe.*

    Shem (2;3,16): *An' it come from in the bathroom.*

TIME:

    Eve (2;2) *... and when I wake up from my nap.*

    Abe (2;8,22) *... back from fishing.*

    D (3;9,29): *I haven't noticed that from years.*

AGENT:

    Julia (2;2, recounting a visit to the doctor): *I took my temperature from the doctor.*

    D (2;2,3, looking at pieces of a sandwich he'd pushed off the edge of his plate): *These fall down from me.*

    Shem (3;0, explaining that he'd put a doll on the bed): *He comed from me.*

NATURAL FORCE:

    D (2;11,12, looking at a fallen tree): *Look at that knocked down tree from the wind.*

    D (4;6,9, catching his father up on a story): *Daddy, the pigs have been marooned from a flood.*

    Sarah (5;1): *The rainbow is getting higher from the rain.*

CAUSE:

    D (2;6,12, recalling an episode from three months earlier): *When grandma 'ancy was here, you go fetch Herb ⟨pause⟩ Then I cried a bit from you go get him.*

    Shem (2;8,7, explaining why his fire-engine was stuck on the roof of his toy garage): *That's fro- that's from I put a thing on it.*

    Adam (3;0): *I not tired from my games.*

POSSESSION:

    Shem (3;0,13, of a picture of someone patting a horse): *That's a finger from him.*

    Adam (3;0): *I see boats from Mommy.*

    D (3;7,5, assigning roles in a game): *You can be a mum from two babies.*

COMPARISON:

    D (2;8,15): *This seat is getting too small from me.*

    Abe (3;1,15, of a toy rabbit): *See? This ear is longer from the other ear.*

Source: Clark and Carpenter 1989a.

often than *by* to mark oblique agents. They chose *with* for instruments. Older children reserved *from* for locative sources, *with* for instruments, and *by* for agents not in subject position – the conventional assignments for English (Clark and Carpenter 1989a, 1989b). Children start with a single notion of source that they then elaborate or divide into different subkinds.

Source is a domain where children's conceptual categories guide their initial mapping of a meaning to a form. Where their mapping fails to agree with the conventional expressions in the language, they must eventually give up their early assignments and adopt the conventional term in use around them. That is, they use both the information provided by the conceptual categories they have set up and that provided by the input language they hear. In some cases, children's uses are remarkably accurate from an early age. In the case of *from*, some early uses may diverge considerably from the adult's since children extend *from* to mark sources that are conventionally marked by other terms and constructions.

Assumptions about space and time

Children also rely on their conceptual categories as a source of possible meanings in the domain of spatial relations. These include relations such as containment and support; relations tied to the orientation of reference objects – on top of, beside, or in front of; or to the dimensionality of the object being located – height, length, size; and to the deictic relations linking the speaker's location to objects, places, or direction of motion.

Children know a good deal about relations in space by the time they are ready to create meanings to map onto forms. Their conceptual categories at times may offer possible meanings that match the conventional word-meanings quite closely; at other times they don't. One example is children's early mapping of meanings onto topological spatial prepositions like English *in*, *on*, and *under*.

Take children who have amassed considerable information about containers – things in which one can place other things. This placement may combine several different relations: (1) contact with partial or complete concealment, e.g., a block inside a wooden box or inside a jar, supported on the inside bottom surface; (2) loose or tight fit between the object and the container, e.g., an apple in a fruit basket versus a geometric shape that has to be fitted into exactly the right hole in a shape box; and (3) the orientation of the container, normally with the opening facing up. The relation between container and content will be called "containment" for short. Infants learn early about such containers as cups, boxes, and drawers, and they spend a good deal of time placing things in containers. When given a choice between placing something in a container or on a surface, one- and two-year-olds at first always choose the container.

Imagine a child with a small toy mouse and a box on its side in front of her. She hears *Put the mouse in the box* or *Put the mouse on the box*, and has then to do something with the mouse. Or she has a small wooden block and a toy crib in front of her and hears *Put the block in the crib* or *Put the block under the crib*. In such settings, one-year-olds systematically place small objects *inside* containers; if there is no container present, they place them *on top of* flat surfaces like tables. Yet these children do not yet understand the meanings of *in*, *on*, and *under*. Instead, they are relying on two strategies for locative placements, ordered with the container strategy first:

> *Containers*: If the reference object is a container, place X inside.
> *Surfaces*: If the reference object is a supporting surface, place X on top.

What children do in many settings is compatible with the adult meanings of *in*, *on*, and *under*, as shown in Table 3–3. They draw on their conceptual categories of spatial relations and rely on those in acting on the objects to be placed (Clark 1973b, 1977, 1980).

These strategies for responding, then, coincide in some instances with the prototypical locative meanings of *in* and *on* and hence provide appropriate initial hypotheses about the meanings to map onto these forms.[10] Their conceptual category of containment, for example, coincides with prototypical English *in*, but not with prototypical *on* or *under*. And their category of support coincides with prototypical *on*.

How is children's mapping reflected in their production as they begin to talk about location in space? In English, they often first mark their awareness that there is some term needed where an adult would use a locative preposition by inserting a schwa, [ə], in the preposition slot, as in *sit* [ə] *chair* (D 1;9,13). Later, the schwa is replaced in many contexts by a syllabic /n/, which suggests that children are now aiming for *in* or *on*, as in an utterance like *I put sand 'n turtle* (D 1;11,17) (see also Peters and Menn 1991). Then children start to produce full prepositional forms, here *in* and

---

[10] The prototypical meaning of *in* is exemplified by *in the box*: containment and concealment. Other kinds of English *in* present a family-resemblance structure for this category of spatial relations. Compare *in the house*, *in his hand*, *in his eye*, *in the design*, *in a temper*, and *in two hours*. These are all conventional uses of *in*, but they all depart in various ways from the prototype. The same holds for *on*: compare *on the table*, *on the brink*, *on the wall*, *on the ceiling*, and *on April 4*.

Table 3–3 *Preferred placements of objects in response to*
instructions with in, on, *and* under *by one-and-a-half-year-olds*

Relation requested	Predominant interpretation
Put X in the box	in the box
Put X in the tunnel	in the tunnel
Put X in the crib	in the crib
Put X in the truck	in the truck
Put X on the box	in the box
Put X on the tunnel	in the tunnel
Put X on the table	on the table
Put X on the bridge	on the bridge
Put X under the crib	in the crib
Put X under the truck	in the truck
Put X under the table	on the table
Put X under the bridge	on the bridge

Note: X was a small block, toy mouse, or other small object.
Source: Clark 1973b.

on, as in *I put a clothes-peg in there* (D 1;11,27) or *Peter put sand on my head* (D 2;1,20).[11] By two to two-and-a-half, English-speaking children produce a large range of spatial prepositions in both spatial and non-spatial uses.

Children also know something fairly early about sequence in time, and they rely on this in coming up with meanings to map onto terms that link two events. In the case of temporal sequence, they assume that the first event described is the first to occur, and the second event described is the second to occur, and so on. Again, this leads to a situation in which their conceptual knowledge maps more closely onto some conjunctions than others.

When three-year-olds are asked to act out sequences of events with toys as props, they consistently respond as if the order of description mirrors order of occurrence. When they hear descriptions like *The boy patted the dog before he jumped the fence*, they act out the sequence correctly. But if they hear *The boy patted the dog after he jumped the fence*, they enact the events in the wrong order, with the patting preceding the jumping. For three-year-olds, this results in their getting the descriptions right whenever

[11] Although most early productions of the prepositions *in* and *on* are appropriate, children make occasional mistakes, as in D: *Orange-juice*. Mo: Okay. D: *On a bottle, baby-bottle* (1;11,28, *on* for *in*), or D: *A birdie in the ladder!* (2;7,1, *in* for *on*) (Clark, diary data).

the linguistic description is compatible with clause order, as in (1), and exactly wrong whenever the two are incompatible, as in (2):

(1)   a. The boy patted the dog before he jumped the fence.
       b. After the boy patted the dog, he jumped the fence.
(2)   a. Before the boy jumped the fence, he patted the dog.
       b. The boy jumped the fence after he patted the dog.

As they get older, children generally get the mapping correct for the conjunction *before* first, and so get descriptions like (1a) and (2a) correct, while continuing to make errors with *after*. This favoring of *before* may also result in part from a general preference for placing subordinate clauses in second position (Clark 1971, 1973c).

   In summary, children gather a great deal of knowledge about the way objects and events can be related to each other in space and time. This knowledge is a major source of the initial meanings they create to map onto new word-forms they encounter. Some of these hypotheses serve them well since they coincide quite closely with adult meanings. But others may result in serious mismatches, and children will eventually have to look for other meanings to map onto these forms.

Lexical constraints

Children make assumptions about conceptual categories as they assign meanings to word forms. They also make assumptions about the kinds of relations words bear to each other. These lexical assumptions affect how they use their words, and they typically have to be modified as children learn more about structure within the lexicon. Two quite prevalent assumptions are what I have called the SINGLE-LEVEL assumption and the NO-OVERLAP assumption. Both are reflected in children's early word uses (Clark 1987).

Single level

With the single-level assumption, children act as if all the words they produce at first apply at only one level of specificity, as if there were only one level in the lexicon, with no superordinate or subordinate levels at which one could group objects lexically:

> *Single-level assumption*: Speakers apply all words at a single level in the lexicon.

A term like *bird*, for example, will contrast on the same level with *duck* and *hen*, say, rather than being superordinate to them, and *dog* will contrast on the same level with *poodle* and *spaniel*. For adults, of course, this assumption holds only *within* any one level of a taxonomic hierarchy. That is, all the generic- or basic-level terms in a particular domain contrast at that level with each other, just as the terms at each superordinate or subordinate level do. So the single-level assumption is restricted to within-level application for adult speakers. Young children, though, may rely on it more widely.

The single-level assumption itself may stem from the importance of categories at the level where they receive basic labels, namely categories at that level. The properties of basic-level categories suggest they are more accessible as conceptual categories than some others may be. This in turn may be why they receive basic-level labels, where the basic level in lexical hierarchies is generally the one with the most labels available. In other words, basic-level categories are privileged conceptually, and this is reflected in the lexical items used to pick them out.

No overlap

With the no-overlap assumption, children do not allow overlaps in meaning among their early words.

> *No-overlap assumption*: Speakers do not let the meanings of any two words overlap.

This appears to be what leads them to occasionally reject such adult equations as *A dog is an animal* or *That bird is a sparrow*. Notice that inclusion is a crucial property of hierarchical taxonomies, where the terms at one level are included in the superordinate at the next level up. Overlap with inclusion appears in all taxonomic hierarchies, while overlap without inclusion is endemic in the lexicon. It holds wherever the meaning of one term is partially included in the meanings of others, as in the relations among *get*, *seize*, *grab*, and *take*. However, for adults, the no-overlap assumption holds only for terms within a single level of a hierarchical taxonomy. The lack of overlap within a lexical level in a hierarchy presumably stems directly from the nature of the conceptual categories children (and adults) draw on in such domains. Instances of the category 'dog,' for example, do not overlap with instances of the categories of 'cat' or 'horse.' The same object therefore cannot be called both *dog* and *cat*. So although no overlap is a lexical assumption, it seems to follow fairly directly from facts about the relevant conceptual categories.

Conventionality and contrast

Finally, children also rely on two pragmatic assumptions. They assume, first, that target word-forms are those *given* by the speakers around them. They rarely make up arbitrary phonological strings to confer meaning on. They take the conventional forms present in the language around them as their goal while they work on discovering which meanings to map onto each form. And they also seem to assume that each form contrasts in meaning with every other form. That is, an unfamiliar form signals use of some meaning other than those already mastered. Distinct forms are therefore assigned distinct meanings. One-year-olds who produce *dog* and *up*, for example, do not apply these words interchangeably: they act from the start as though the two have different meanings, and they follow the adult conventions, as best they can, on their use. Such uses, even where they diverge from the adult's, give evidence that young children are observing both conventionality and contrast.

> *Conventionality*: For certain meanings there is a form that speakers expect to be used in the language community.
>
> *Contrast*: Speakers take every difference in form to mark a difference in meaning.

Conventionality and contrast, combined with other assumptions, have several consequences for young children's word-use. For example, contrast, single level, and no overlap as a package make a number of predictions about mapping. Children should resist assigning the same meaning to two different forms (by contrast), and hence initially reject uses of hierarchically related terms such as *trout* and *fish* used to refer to the same object, as in *That fish is a trout*, because they appear to have the same meaning (by single level). They should also reject terms that clearly overlap in meaning, such as *pet* and *goldfish*, in *That goldfish is a pet* (by no overlap), and they should assume that unfamiliar word-forms have meanings that differ from any already known. For example, a child encountering the unfamiliar *lemur* alongside known animal terms like *zebra* and *cow* should assume that the meaning of *lemur* contrasts with the meanings of known animal-terms like *zebra* or *cow*.

This combination of assumptions is equivalent to a narrow version of MUTUAL EXCLUSIVITY (Markman 1984, 1987, 1989, Markman and Wachtel 1988). This predicts that children will initially assign only one label per category. That is, children will treat all labels as if they are mutually exclusive, contrasting with each other but all on a single level with no overlaps. But mutual exclusivity does not hold for adults. Once this assumption is broken down into contrast, single level, and no overlap, it is possible to see exactly what children must give up and what they should retain for assigning meanings to unfamiliar words. Contrast holds throughout the lexicon, for children and adults alike. Single level applies only at each level within a hierarchical taxonomy: *dog* and *cat* are at a single level, but *dog* and *animal* are at two distinct levels. So children's reliance on this assumption must be restricted. No overlap likewise applies only to terms within a single level of a hierarchy: *cat* does not overlap in meaning with *dog*, but *animal* does. No overlap must also be restricted. When an adult says *That dog is a spaniel*, children who assume contrast must give up both the single-level and no-overlap assumptions. Since these two have a place in lexical structure, children must find out where they do and don't apply. Contrast is different: it holds throughout the lexicon, and, along with conventionality, applies to every mapping children attempt.

The other assumptions hold in more limited domains, and so must be narrowed in their application as children find out more about conventional meanings and lexical structure. For example, children find out that many domains in the lexicon allow different types of overlap in meaning. Compare near-synonyms such as *slough, marsh,* and *bog*; hierarchically related terms such as *vehicle, car,* and *Volvo*; and simple overlaps such as *up* and *down*, where both terms designate 'vertical displacement,' or *walk* and *stroll* where both designate 'motion on foot', but nonetheless differ in meaning. That is, no overlap applies only to terms at the same level, and even there one has to specify what counts. *Dog* and *cat* share some meaning in that both designate a species of mammal, but they cannot be used to refer to the same entity. Similarly, single level applies, for adults, only within one level of a hierarchy.

Conventionality and contrast also interact with the conceptually based assumptions children rely on as they map meanings onto forms. Conceptually, children have formed a variety of ontological categories – categories of objects, properties (shape, texture, color), relations (location, orientation), activities, and events. These provide the basis for many of the initial hypotheses children make about meanings. But the meanings must ultimately conform to the conventions of the language community, and where they do not match children's early meanings, adult speakers play a decisive role in refining and shaping those meanings until they do conform. Children's usage is shaped by the input they hear from other speakers. To understand lexical development fully, we must take account of the joint influences of conceptual structure and language use. Together, these provide the starting point for the acquisition of the lexicon.

Summary

Children create meanings for words and then map them onto word forms. In creating meanings, they draw on their ontological categories of objects, actions, properties, and relations. And in mapping these meanings onto forms, they rely on a number of assumptions. These assumptions are of two types, conceptual and lexical. They govern meaning-to-concept and meaning-to-meaning relations respectively. These assumptions constrain how children map meanings onto forms, and thereby make mapping feasible. Among the constraints governing lexical structure are conventionality and contrast. I turn next to a more detailed account of these two pragmatic principles, and examine their role in the use of both established words and lexical innovations.

4 *Conventionality and contrast*

Speakers take for granted every day both that there *are* words for things and that words *differ* in meaning. We have assumed that the stock of words speakers draw on can be thought of as forming a mental dictionary. But it is more than that. Dictionaries list only words that are well established, but speakers can also construct new words, made just for the occasion. So the lexical resources speakers make use of must include both well-established terms, known to the speech community, and novel ones, coined for special occasions. In this chapter, I take up CONVENTIONALITY, that well-established words have conventional meanings, and CONTRAST, that words differ in meaning. These two together guide speakers in their use of the lexicon. The emphasis here is on their general consequences. In the next chapter, I explore their consequences for acquisition.

Conventionality

The principle of conventionality is the following: "For certain meanings, there is a form that speakers expect to be used in the language community." That is, if a conventional term expresses what they mean, speakers should use it. If they don't do so, or if they use a term in a non-conventional way, they are liable to be misunderstood.

But what makes something conventional? De Saussure (1916/1968) argued that "tout moyen d'expression reçu dans une société repose en principe sur une habitude collective ou, ce qui revient au même, sur la convention."[1] In other words, what makes terms conventional is that everyone in a speech community agrees with everyone else on which words

---

[1] "Every type of expression accepted in a community rests in principle on a collective habit or, what comes down to the same thing, on convention" (pp. 100–101). De Saussure's view of language as conventional has been widely followed since. Firth (1966, p. 113), for example, characterized it as "a network of binds and obligations." Wilhelm von Humboldt, a century earlier, argued that "nobody may speak to another person in a manner different from that in which the latter, under identical circumstances, would have spoken to him." (1836/1971, p. 28).

or expressions denote which kinds. For instance, speakers of English agree that the word *horse* generally designates members of the kind 'horse,' and *oak* members of the kind 'oak.' But things could have been otherwise. The relation between *oak*, say, and the specific kind of tree the word designates is quite arbitrary. For French speakers, horses are designated by *cheval* and oaks by *chêne*, and for Dutch speakers, by *paard* and *eik*. In learning a new language, then, speakers learn a new set of conventions. They may also have to learn new conventions in moving from one dialect area to another within the same language. Take the differences in the conventions governing the terms *suspender*, *vest*, or *elevator* in British versus American English (Moss 1986, Palmer 1981, Walmsley 1987). Conventionality, then, is characterized by the existence of collective agreements about language within a community of speakers.[2]

De Saussure's definition largely coincides with the view that a convention consists of a recognized regularity on the part of members of a group in situations where everyone expects everyone else to observe that regularity, and where everyone prefers to observe it as long as others do so too, in order to coordinate with them (Lewis 1969). For example, if everyone drives on the left in Country A, anyone getting into a car to drive will also drive on the left and expect to find everyone else doing so too. Not to drive on the left would, among other things, mark a failure in coordination, where coordination among the members of the community is essential to the maintenance of the convention. Or, to take another example, if four people meet regularly to play quartets, they will after a while assume they will meet next at the same time and place as before because each assumes that the others in the group assume likewise. For a convention to become established, therefore, it has to rest on mutual knowledge and coordination among the participants. If one member of the quartet is replaced, the new member will have to be informed of the convention about when and where the group meets, but need not be privy to the history of how that convention arose. A convention rests on the consistency over time of some joint solution for a problem – here the problem of when and where to meet (see further H. Clark, in press, Clark and Marshall 1981).

In language, the role of convention is central. For a language to serve as a means of communication in a speech community, members of the community must mutually agree on the conventional meaning (or meanings) of each established linguistic expression. To count as con-

---

[2] The community can be very large – speakers of American English, say – or very small -- devotees of Huysmans, for example (see Clark and Marshall 1981).

ventional, such meanings must be consistent from one occasion to the next. English speakers cannot, for instance, alternate from one day to the next in talking about oaks between the terms *oak* and *beech*, and expect to be understood. Conventionality in the lexicon, then, works in the same way as conventions elsewhere.

Contrast

The second pragmatic principle here is contrast, that use of a different word marks a difference in meaning. This can be stated more precisely as "Speakers take every difference in form to mark a difference in meaning." This principle has been assumed, either tacitly or explicitly, at least since Bréal (1897) and Paul (1898) in their work on historical change, as well as by de Saussure (1916/1968) in his synchronic analysis of language use. As Bréal pointed out:

> Ayant le sentiment que le langage est fait pour servir à l'échange des idées, à l'expression des sentiments, à la discussion des intérêts, [le peuple] se refuse à croire à une synonymie qui serait inutile et dangereuse. Or, comme il est tout à la fois le dépositaire et l'auteur du langage, son opinion qu'il n'y a pas de synonymes fait qu'en réalité les synonymes n'existent pas longtemps: ou bien ils se différencient, ou bien l'un des deux termes disparaît.[3]

This view motivated Bréal's law of differentiation ("répartition") – that a single meaning with several surface forms typically becomes associated with only *one* of those forms; the remainder take on other meanings. Some examples from English include the differentiation of *fox* and *vixen* (from two different dialects) for the male and female of the species; and, after the Norman invasion, the differentiation of French terms for many animals from their English counterparts by assigning the French terms the meaning 'meat of X' and the English terms 'X on the hoof,' as in *beef/cattle*, *veal/calf*, and *venison/deer* (see also Haiman 1980 and Horn 1989). Or as Bloomfield put it:

> If the forms [of words] are phonemically different, we suppose that their meanings also are different. (1933, p. 145)

For de Saussure, contrast was implicit in the notion of opposition: words have meaning by virtue of the oppositions they enter into with other words

---

[3] "Feeling that language is made to serve for exchanging ideas, expressing feelings, discussing interests, people refuse to accede to a synonymy that would be both useless and dangerous. Moreover, since people are at one and the same time the repository and the source of language, their assumption that there are no synonyms effectively results in synonyms being short-lived: either they are differentiated, or one of the two disappears." (1897, p. 30).

in the same domain, and in the lexicon as a whole. In English, for example, a term like *teach* enters into opposition with (and so contrasts with) many other terms from the same frame including *learn, absorb, read, educate; lesson, teaching; pupil, student, teacher; kindergarten, school,* and *university. Teach* also contrasts, ultimately, with all other terms in the English lexicon.

Notice that contrast should be distinguished carefully from its converse, the HOMONYMY assumption (Clark 1987). The latter assumption is that every two *meanings* contrast *in form.* Under this view, two different meanings should never be carried by the same form. But one need consider only a handful of examples to see that this assumption is violated all the time. Take the English nouns *bank* and *bat.* Each occurs with at least two very different meanings. *Bank* designates a river edge and also a financial institution; *bat* designates a small flying mammal or an instrument for hitting balls. The homonymy assumption doesn't hold for mature speakers as inspection of any dictionary quickly reveals. But homonymy occasionally causes speakers problems, and then they may act to eliminate it. For example, if two terms in the same semantic domain fall together over time, so that what were two distinct forms are collapsed into one, this could cause genuine confusion. In such cases, speakers typically introduce a second form to carry one of the meanings, hence eliminating confusion and homonymy at one blow (Bréal 1897, Gougenheim 1971, Orr 1962).

When homonymy is combined with contrast, it results in a "one form/one meaning" view of language. It has sometimes been assumed that this view is prevalent in young children. However, like adults, children accept homonymy quite readily, both in lexemes and in affixes. They take for granted that a single form may have several meanings, and they appear to experience no difficulty in English, for example, in learning plural and possessive forms on nouns (e.g., *dog-s* and *dog-'s*), or the third person singular present tense forms on verbs (e.g., *run-s*), all of which have the same form despite their differences in meaning.

Contrast, then, captures the insight that when speakers choose an expression, they do so because they mean something that they would not mean by choosing some alternative expression. Speaker choices in any domain mean what they do in part because they contrast with other options both in that domain and in the language as a whole. The major result of this is that speakers do not tolerate complete synonyms.

Conventionality and contrast work together through a general contract (Grice 1975) that takes roughly the following form: The speaker and addressee mutually assume that the speaker is trying to communicate some intended meaning to the addressee. So the addressee who hears the speaker use a familiar term in the course of a conversation about sailing will therefore reason as follows (where *I* is the addressee and *S* the speaker):

(a)   *S* used the term *sheet.*
(b)   Up to now people have been talking about boats and sailing.
(c)   I know that *S* knows as much about sailing as I do, and that *S* knows this too.
(d)   Therefore I assume *S* intends the term *sheet* in its nautical sense.
(e)   I therefore take *sheet* to contrast with *rope, stay,* etc.

That is, an addressee encountering a familiar term from a speaker can compute the appropriate meaning for it on that occasion in light of what else they both already know. The process is slightly different when the addressee is not familiar with the term used by the speaker, and, under those circumstances, the addressee may have to check up on what the speaker intends. That is, the speaker may not have taken full account of how little the addressee actually knows about sailing, so the addressee may instead reason as follows:

(a)   *S* used the term *sheet.*
(b)   Up to now people have been talking about boats and sailing.
(c)   I know that *S* knows much more about sailing than I do, but I'm not sure whether *S* knows this too.
(d)   Therefore I will assume *sheet* must have some nautical sense that I am unfamiliar with.

But by this point, if the addressee cannot work out what *sheet* might mean on the basis of other clues in the conversation (mention of *sails, tacking, rigging,* juxtaposition with terms like *stay* or *rope,* and so on), he can stop the speaker and check up, *Wait a minute, what's a sheet here?* or *I'm not sure what sheet means here.* On this occasion, the speaker has failed to take account of how little the addressee knows, and so has failed to some degree in making himself understood as he intended.

This reasoning exemplifies certain consequences of conventionality and contrast for language use. These consequences hold for established words in the lexicon whether familiar or unfamiliar to the addressee, and also for lexical innovations. And they hold, I shall argue, as much for children just learning their first language as for adult users. They can be couched in the form of predictions about general properties of the lexicon that result from what speakers do and don't assume as they observe these principles:

(1)   Words contrast in meaning.
(2)   Established words have priority.
(3)   Innovative words fill lexical gaps.

Support for each of these predictions comes from the overall structure of the established lexicon, and from what speakers do with established versus innovative expressions.

Words contrast in meaning

The established lexicon offers abundant evidence that words contrast in meaning. Within the lexicon, contrast works with conventionality on a variety of different planes. Differences in meaning are characteristic of the lexicon. The study of such differences, large and small, has traditionally been carried out within semantic fields where linguists have analyzed and characterized different patterns of contrast – in contrast sets (e.g., *tall/ short*, *young/old*; *cygnet/swan*, *fawn/deer*; *dead/alive*; *open/shut*); taxonomies (*vehicle*; *car*, *truck*, *van*; *Volvo*, *Ford*, *Austin*); meronymies or partonymies (*fingers*, *hand*, *arm*); paradigms (*go*, *goes*, *going*, *went*, *gone*); cycles (*spring*, *summer*, *autumn*, *winter*); chains (*Lieutenant*, *Captain*, *Admiral*); networks (*father*, *daughter*, *brother*, *aunt*), or the larger frames that index some conceptual or actional whole, as in 'commercial event.'[4] What characterizes such lexical domains is that all the member terms differ in meaning. The differences may be subtle, as in *oblige* versus *obligate*, or more tangible, as in *tiger* versus *horse*, or *sing* versus *run*. What such domains lack, as predicted, is terms that are complete synonyms. Their absence suggests that speakers not only have no need for them, but, as Bréal argued, actively work to get rid of them when they appear.

What then of any apparent synonyms observable in a language? Speakers are often familiar, for instance, with terms from two different dialects, or with terms from two different registers, that at first glance seem to have the same meaning. But in fact, within a single dialect, or within a single register, speakers are very consistent in observing contrast. Notice that sameness of reference in such cases does not make terms like *tap*, *spigot*, and *faucet* synonyms. Where one speaker uses *tap*, another on just those occasions uses *spigot*, and a third uses *faucet*. Since the three terms are from three different dialects, a single speaker would never use them

---

[4] See further Bierwisch 1967, Fillmore 1975, 1978, Kay 1971, Lehrer 1974, Lyons 1963, 1977, Trier 1934.

interchangeably. A speaker who uses one of them might, of course, on some occasions use a different one by way of adapting to his addressee. But this cannot be used to argue for synonymy either, since the *tap* user who produces *spigot* is thereby deferring to his addressee, and so does not have exactly the same meaning for *spigot* as for *tap* (Clark 1988, Giles 1984, Giles, Mulac, Bradac, and Johnson 1987).

The same argument holds for terms from different registers: terms like *policeman* and *cop*, *attempt* and *try*, *effluvium* and *smell*, or *sufficient* and *enough*. Different terms serve to mark formality versus informality, directness versus indirectness, pretentiousness versus bluntness, distance versus solidarity, politeness versus indifference or rudeness, and so on. The range of such dimensions is not clearcut, and it is important to note that the same choices may have different connotations on different occasions (Lakoff 1973, Nunberg 1978).

Yet other apparent synonyms differ in emotive coloring. Speakers may choose their terms to convey their attitudes towards what they are talking about. Consider the choice between *statesman* and *politician*: the former is laudatory and the latter not. Much the same contrast seems to underlie choices of *slim* versus *skinny*, *generous* versus *spendthrift*, *realistic* versus *unimaginative*, and *challenge* versus *attack* (Bolinger 1980, Lakoff and Johnson 1980, Orwell 1950). In short, sameness of reference no more makes for synonymy across dialects or registers than it does within or between languages.

Finally, a few languages have accumulated large sets of synonyms – and so appear to run counter to the prediction that speakers will not tolerate synonymy in language. However, closer examination of such cases shows that speakers typically make use of only one term out of a synonymous set. That is, the speakers do not make use, at any one time, of the range of synonyms actually available. In French thieves' argot, for example, speakers would use term **a** for a pickpocket, say, until that term began to become more widely known and to be recognized outside the group using the argot. At that point, argot users would introduce term **b** in lieu of **a** and relegate **a** to the attic. Over time, as **b** in its turn became more widely – too widely – known, argot speakers would replace it too, with term **c**, and so on. At some point, these speakers may come back to term **a**, by now forgotten by the larger French-speaking community, and return it to use again. So although an argot may accumulate many near-synonyms, speakers are consistent in observing contrast: they make use of only one term at any one time (Ullmann 1962, von Wartburg 1963).

Another analogous situation is the case of taboos on the names of people recently dead. In some Australian Aboriginal languages, such a taboo may extend not only to the names of the dead (people's names are drawn from the general lexicon) but also to words that sound like the name as well. One common strategy here is to substitute a near-synonym for the word in question. This substitute is then used for the relevant term by the kin or group that the dead person had belonged to. Only after some years do speakers in the pertinent group revert to the original term (Nash and Simpson 1981). So here too, despite the accrual of many near-synonyms over the years, speakers in any one group typically make use of only one of them during any one time. Just as in an argot, the existence of near-synonyms does not constitute a violation of contrast.

Established words have priority

When speakers plan their utterances, they look first in the mental lexicon to find words that fit the meanings they intend. And the words that are stored there are the words that are conventionally used to express particular meanings. In fluent speech, these words are produced in a smooth flow that confers on each established term the status of its being the right word for that occasion. But access to the mental lexicon is not always easy, and speakers sometimes have difficulty finding the right word. They may be sure it exists but be unable to find the precise form conventionally used to convey the meaning in question; or, as second-language learners, they may be a little uncertain about the exact form needed for their meaning; or it could even be that they are not yet entirely clear about the precise meaning they wish to convey on this occasion. In each case, speakers look first to the conventional lexicon and if it contains the expressions needed, those are what they use. This process appears straightforward when speakers find the words they need right away. Both speakers and addressees take for granted the use of conventional expressions. But what happens when speakers fail because they either come up with no appropriate word, or they come up with the wrong word? They rely on REPAIR to correct or adjust their initial utterances, and here again they have recourse first to the conventional lexicon.

Consider what happens when speakers fail in this way. First, they may signal explicitly that they are having trouble finding the right words. They may do this simply by pausing in mid-turn, or by using pauses and fillers (like *uh* or *er*). These devices serve to warn addressees that speakers are having some difficulty. The effect is to put addressees "on hold" by telling them that the speaker has not yet found the right word. Moreover, even when speakers then come up with a word, addressees who have witnessed the word search may remain to some extent on hold since they may not be entirely sure that a speaker has yet said just what he intended to say.

Repairs can be analyzed as occurring (a) where speakers have undertaken an overt word-search – a search that is visible to the addressees – so the repair is to the "gap" in the utterance being produced, and (b) where speakers initially retrieve the wrong word – one with a sense that doesn't match the meaning intended to be conveyed. Both types of repairs have been studied in some detail. The first type includes studies of the tip-of-the-tongue phenomenon: the speaker knows there is a conventional word for a particular meaning but has trouble accessing its precise form. In this situation, speakers can typically give quite detailed information about the final sound of the word, the number of syllables, and often about its initial sound and even its stress pattern (Brown and McNeill 1966, Kohn, Wingfield, Menn, Goodglass, Berko Gleason, and Hyde 1987, Levelt 1989). Word searches like this are often successful, with speakers retrieving the target word after two or three false starts. Some typical examples of repairs are given in Table 4–1.

Word searches, though, are not always successful. When speakers fail to find the word they are after, they may have to compromise. They can do this in several ways: (a) They can solicit help from their addressees. (b) They can come up with a circumlocution of some kind that describes the critical notion, as in 'lying flat on one's front' for *prone*, or 'curved sword used by the Saracens during the Crusades' for *scimitar*. That is, they may offer a phrase or fuller expression to cover the meaning conventionally expressed with a single lexical item. Or (c) they may settle on a momentary innovation as a make-shift expression – often with the right root morpheme in place, as in *sequencingly* for *sequentially*, *impartly* for *completely*, or *likeliness* for *likelihood*. Both circumlocutions and lexical innovations appear quite common following word searches by second-language speakers.[5] Speakers may sometimes underline the makeshift character of these forms by use of qualifications like *you know*. Or (d) speakers may make do with catch-all terms like English *whatchamacallit* or *thingamajig*, which signal explicitly that the sought-for word can't be

---

[5] For word searches, see Burke, Worthley, and Martin 1988, Clark and Schaefer 1989, Clark and Wilkes-Gibbs 1986, Fromkin 1973; and for second-language word-searches, Gaskill 1980, Poulisse 1989, Schwartz 1980.

Table 4–1 *Some typical self-repairs*

S.1.7, 1222–1223
Dave MOWAL is [ə:m], — is on the [op] is on the OPERATION side,
S.1.8, 167–168
  you want [ə:m] – something ROUND you when you think it . when you
    LOOK at it
S.1.8., 508–510
  if THIS had some more, COLOUR in it, . [ə:] that is the bottom
    FOREGROUND,
S.1.9, 341–344
  [jə] well he's a [gæl] he is the GALLIC . PERSON, YES, that's RIGHT,
    YES,
S.1.9, 387–388
  and I must get [ʌ] I've been MEANING to get hold of him, for a long TIME,
S.1.11, 119–124
  the ONLY one we've SEEN, . I'VE seen, — THIS time round, . YES, the
    only one YOU'VE seen this time round, – was one we missed last time, –
S.1.11, 128–133
  c I saw . the guy with the grave . what was his name . Bolz*mann*
  A *BOLZMANN*
  c Bolzmann
  A oh perhaps I HAD seen that before, — —
  c you know it had his sort of . scientific formula on his . on his headstone
  B oh YES, YES, I saw THAT one,

Note: The symbols in the table are to be interpreted as follows: CAPITALS =
heavy stress; *word* = overlapping speech; , = falling intonation (end of tone
group); . = brief pause (1 syllable); – = unit pause (1 beat).
Source: Svartvik and Quirk 1980.

found. This option may also function as a tacit request for offers of
candidate words from the addressee (see also Goodwin and Goodwin
1986).

In all these cases, speakers have filled a momentary gap in some way. But
if they then come up with the conventional form after all, they will still
repair the original utterance by interpolating the target form, regardless of
their current place in a new utterance. Such interpolations may occur just
a few words after the makeshift form, or as long as five minutes or more
later, whenever the right word "pops up" and becomes accessible.[6]

---

[6] On one occasion (12/12/90), I observed this happen a whole hour after the search for a
  name (McCann) had been abandoned: A speaker giving a lecture could not come up with
  the name of the author of a paper he was referring to. After using "what's-her-name," he

Whenever speakers make such repairs, they underline the priority accorded to the right word – the conventional expression for conveying a particular meaning. That is, speakers and addressees together go through roughly the following sequence of moves in resolving a difficult word-search:

(a)   S signals to A that a word search is in progress so A waits.

(b)   S looks for an established word and if there is one, produces it as soon as it is accessed.

(b')   S waits to find the right word and so pauses.

(c)   S fails, so makes do with temporary expedients:
   (i) a paraphrase or circumlocution
   OR (ii) a catch-all, general-purpose term
   OR (iii) a coinage designed to fill in.

(d)   S fails to use these options, so asks A to help in retrieving the right word.

(e)   S later retrieves the target form and so produces it as a repair to (c).

In other cases, the speakers' word searches may not be visible to the same degree. Speakers may initially produce a word and only then decide it isn't the one they wanted, and so repair it right away. This can occur regardless of fluency. And here again, speakers prefer to issue the repair themselves, typically in the very same turn in the conversation (Jefferson 1974, Levelt 1983, Schegloff, Jefferson, and Sacks 1977).[7] Speakers are also careful to mark where the repair occurs so addressees can adjust their interpretations appropriately, by discarding the first term produced and replacing it with the newly issued repair (Levelt 1983). This act of replacement leads addressees to put more weight on the term in the repair than on the original now discarded.

In filling a momentary gap or in getting closer to the intended meaning, speakers give evidence for both conventionality and contrast. They try to retrieve the right words for the meanings they intend to convey, and that requires accessing the appropriate conventional terms, provided they exist. If the conventional status of words and their meanings was unimportant, speakers would not bother to repair what they say, but would simply make do with whatever expression they had accessed first. (Though notice that

abandoned his search, and from then on alluded to "X and colleagues." An hour later, as he was answering a final question, the speaker came up with the name, McCann, and threw it in, in the middle of his answer.

[7] Second-language speakers may be more willing to accept other-repairs; see Gaskill 1980, Schwartz 1980.

even the assumption of "making do" suggests that the expression used is temporary and so not a legitimate expedient.) But speakers do repair their utterances: They try to express their intentions as precisely as possible, by choosing the exact word and not its near neighbor. If appropriateness (conventionality) and precision (contrast) played no role in speaking, there would be no need for certain repairs – those made to fill gaps or to refine an utterance already produced. Such repairs, then, whether immediate or delayed, point to the priority speakers grant to any conventional expressions for the meanings they intended.

Innovative words fill lexical gaps

Speakers of a language often need to convey meanings for which there is no ready-made, conventional expression. On such occasions, they turn to innovative lexical items – forms constructed to carry novel meanings interpretable in context, given the shared assumptions and mutual knowledge of speaker and addressee. Sometimes they may even make use of old forms with new meanings, provided these meanings are computable by the addressee. For example, after a speaker and addressee have been looking at sledges, each decorated in a different way, the speaker might coin *dog-sled* to mean 'sled decorated with small carved dogs,' a novel meaning that contrasts with the conventional one ('sled drawn by dogs'). But such a coinage is licensed only if the speaker makes sure his addressee can interpret it with the meaning intended.

With any lexical innovation, the speaker must make sure that his addressee can readily arrive at the intended meaning. This is done by mutual observance of a Gricean contract that takes roughly the following form (Clark and Clark 1979):

> In using an innovative expression sincerely, the speaker means to denote:

(a)   the kind of situation, object, relation, etc.
(b)   that he has good reason to believe
(c)   that on this occasion the addressee can readily compute
(d)   uniquely
(e)   on the basis of their mutual knowledge.

This contract applies to all lexical innovations that rely for their interpretation on the context – that is, on the mutual knowledge shared by speaker and addressee. In addition, each type of lexical innovation used adds a further condition to the contract specific to how that particular word-formation device is conventionally used. For example, in the case of an innovative denominal verb such as *to porch*, speaker and addressee must also agree on how to interpret such verbs, namely in such a way that the parent or source noun denotes one role in the relevant situation, while the surface arguments of the verb pick out the other roles. (*To porch* could mean 'to add a porch to X,' 'to place X in a porch,' 'to make X into a porch,' and so on, on different occasions.) Similar conditions go along with the devices used to form each type of novel verb, adjective, and noun.

If there is no lexical gap, the speaker cannot use a lexical innovation and expect to be understood. Notice what would happen if the speaker used an innovative verb, *to hospital*, with the intended meaning 'to put into a hospital.' By conditions (b)-(d), the speaker must have good reason to believe that the listener, here his addressee, can readily compute the intended sense uniquely. Thus his addressee would reason as follows:

> Suppose my interlocutor had intended to convey the sense 'put into a hospital.' If he had, he would have used the well-established verb *hospitalize*, which means precisely 'put into a hospital', because he would then have good reason to think I would compute the intended sense uniquely. Since he used *hospital*, he must have meant something distinct from 'put into a hospital', which I already know to be impossible. Thus I find *hospital* to be uninterpretable ...
>
> (Clark and Clark 1979, p. 798)

In many situations, there is a lexical gap, and then speakers are free to fill each one as needed. They may coin a new word because they find there is no established one that expresses just what they wish to convey on that occasion. They may need to fill a distinct gap, or just add some further nuance of meaning. And speakers take advantage every day of the fact that languages offer the means to do this. A television sports announcer at the 1988 Olympics, to underline the fact that a diver had already won a medal, coined the verb *to medal* meaning 'to win a medal,' when he said *Do you think Louganis is gonna medal in this event*? The Internal Revenue Service in the US, after recent changes in the tax laws, coined the term *assister* meaning 'a member of the Internal Revenue Service who helps the public with income tax forms.' Newspaper headlines frequently rely on novel compound nouns to express in succinct form rather complex meanings, as in the San Francisco *Chronicle*'s "Homeless hotel owners may get $1 million bill," where *homeless hotel owners* meant 'owners of hotels with rooms for homeless people.' Novel verbs, nouns, and adjectives can be

Table 4–2 *Pre-emption in the lexicon: nouns*

Source	Paradigm	Pre-empted	Pre-empter
curious	curiosity		
tenacious	tenacity		
glorious		*gloriosity	glory
furious		*furiosity	fury
blue	blueness		
happy	happiness		
true		*trueness	truth
prominent		*prominentness	prominence
to open	opener		
to polish	polisher		
to drill		*driller	drill_N
to whisk		*whisker	whisk_N
to drive	driver		
to ride	rider		
to cook		*cooker	cook_N
to spy		*spyer	spy_N
to apply		*applier	applicant
to inhabit		*inhabiter	inhabitant

heard every day, but their interpretation is usually so clear in context – speakers normally observe the Gricean contract with considerable care – that addressees may be unaware that they have just understood an entirely new noun or verb.[8]

Pre-emption

Established terms pre-empt any others that would be synonymous with them: "If a potential innovative expression would be precisely synonymous with a well-established expression, the innovation is normally pre-empted by the well-established term, and is therefore considered unacceptable" (Clark and Clark 1979, p. 798). In avoiding synonymy, speakers grant priority to established terms but still allow for innovations. And the condition on lexical innovations is that they must contrast in meaning with conventional lexical items. That is, speakers rely on

---

[8] See Clark and Clark 1979, Clark 1981a, H. Clark 1983, Clark and Gerrig 1983, and Gerrig 1989 for more on the conditions under which addressees can and can't arrive at the intended interpretations of lexical innovations.

conventionality and contrast as they use and expand the lexicon of their language. The contract they and their addressees rely on, for the interpretation of both established and innovative words, makes equal use of both principles.

There are several distinct kinds of PRE-EMPTION by synonymy.[9] In pre-emption by SUPPLETION, an existing form for a particular meaning blocks the use of an otherwise regular form. In the paradigm of *work/worked*, *jog/jogged*, *talk/talked*, etc., the past tense of *go* is not *goed* but *went*. The existence of *went*, with the requisite meaning, pre-empts use of the regular form built from verb root plus *-ed* (*goed*). One finds a similar type of suppletion among denominal verbs. The regular way of forming a verb that means 'go by [vehicle]' in English is to make a denominal verb from the bare name of the vehicle, as in the noun/verb paradigm *taxi/to taxi*, *canoe/to canoe*, *bicycle/to bicycle*, etc. Gaps in this list appear for *to car* and *to airplane*. These two denominal verbs are normally ruled out by the existence in English, with just the requisite meanings, of *to drive* and *to fly*. (If the meanings assigned to *to car* and *to airplane* contrast with *to drive* and *to fly*, they of course become perfectly acceptable.)

Pre-emption by ENTRENCHMENT occurs where an existing form, already derived from a particular root, prevents the formation of a second form from the same source with the same meaning. Among verbs in English, *to hospitalize*, built from the noun *hospital*, pre-empts **to hospital*, with the same meaning. And entrenched forms like *imprison*, *enthrone*, and *pollinate* pre-empt the formation of new denominal verbs from the same source nouns (*prison*, *throne*, and *pollen*) with the same meanings. Again, if the meanings of the two verbs differ, as in *to winter* versus *to winterize*, they may coexist. Among nouns, pre-emption by entrenchment accounts for the unacceptability of **applier* and **inhabiter*, pre-empted by *applicant* and *inhabitant*. Again, if the meanings of the two forms derived from the same root contrast, both are acceptable. Where they don't contrast, the entrenched one takes priority and pre-empts the other.

Pre-emption by ANCESTRY occurs when, for example, the source noun for a potential new verb has itself already been derived from a verb with the requisite meaning. *To baker the bread* is pre-empted by *to bake*, the verb that provides the source for the derived noun, *baker*; and **gloriosity* is pre-empted by *glory*, its source noun, when it would have the same meaning as

[9] Aronoff 1976, Clark and Clark 1979, Corbin 1976, Gruber 1976, Hofmann 1982, 1983, 1984, Kiparsky 1983, Rainer 1988, Scalise, Ceresa, Drigo, Gottardo, and Zannier 1983, Zwanenburg 1981, 1984.

Table 4–3 *Pre-emption in the lexicon: verbs*

Source	Paradigm	Pre-empted	Pre-empter
jet	to jet		
taxi	to taxi		
airplane		*to airplane	to fly
car		*to car	to drive
knee	to knee		
shoulder	to shoulder		
foot		*to foot	to kick
palm		*to palm	to slap
house	to house		
jail	to jail		
hospital		*to hospital	to hospitalize
prison		*to prison	to imprison
salt	to salt		
pollen		*to pollen	to pollinate
butcher	to butcher [meat]		
chauffeur	to chauffeur		
baker		*to baker [bread]	to bake
banker		*to banker [money]	to bank

glory. Again, if the new term contrasts in meaning with the ancestral one, it is acceptable, so *to farmer* with the meaning 'play at being a farmer' is accepted because it contrasts with *to farm*. Some examples of such pre-emptions, for nouns and verbs, are given in Tables 4–2 and 4–3.

These three types of pre-emption forestall the creation of complete synonyms, and point to the general applicability of conditions (b)-(d) of the Gricean contract between speakers and addressees. That is, whenever an expression might have a complete synonym, the speaker must have a good reason for selecting it over its alternative; and the addressee, to satisfy unique computability, will try to find such a reason. This achieves two things. It stops speakers from creating new expressions that are fully synonymous with old ones; and it forces them to add distinctions whenever they use one of two expressions that might otherwise be fully synonymous. Both prevent the creation of complete synonyms.

Summary

Conventionality and contrast together capture the fact that for a communication system to work, speakers must be *consistent* in the conventional meanings they assign from one occasion to the next, and they must maintain the *same* contrasts in meaning from one occasion to the next. By observing these two principles, speakers and their addressees always have at hand guidelines for when to use ready-made words and when to innovate.

In the next chapter, I take up acquisition. Conventionality, once recognized, should lead children to acquire the words they hear in the input around them. And contrast should lead them to avoid synonyms. But when do children recognize these pragmatic principles? Children must learn which meanings have a conventional expression, but, to begin with, they know so few words that they could easily produce illegitimate innovations. As they learn more conventional meaning–form pairings, they should give them priority over any innovations. These challenges for children are explored in detail in the next chapter.

5 Pragmatic principles and acquisition

If children observe conventionality, they should take the adult language – the input they hear addressed to them – as the target to aim for. If they observe contrast, they should assume that differences in form signal differences in meaning. I begin by looking at the earliest evidence for conventionality and contrast, and then turn to specific predictions these principles make about lexical acquisition.

Conventionality

What evidence is there that children observe conventionality? First, they target adult words from the start. They store in memory word-forms based on what they hear from adults. They must do this for two reasons. First, children who have not stored in memory something close to the adult sequence *cat*, for example, would have no basis for recognizing it and responding systematically upon hearing it in such adult utterances as *Look at the cat, Here's a cat, Find the cat, Get your cat*, or *Where's the cat*? In order to map any meaning onto a word form, children must store both the form and its possible meaning. And for them to treat any sequence of sounds (potential word-forms) systematically, they need to have stored that sequence in memory in a shape close enough to the adult version to allow for recognition on subsequent occasions. As they are exposed to more of the input language, they must add to their repertoires of stored forms (plus tentative meanings) since they will rely on those in recognizing words and processing further utterances from the speakers around them.

Second, children use such representations not only as targets for comprehension but also as targets for production. When they try to produce the words they have been hearing, they can use as guides any forms already stored in memory. The forms they store are unlikely at first to match adult targets exactly since young children at this stage are also working on the phonology of the language, and do not yet know which distinctions are systematic and which are not. For example, the distinction between an aspirated and an unaspirated /t/ (as in *teach* versus *stool*) in English is entirely predictable, so one need not represent aspiration in the forms being stored. The same goes, in many varieties of English, for the "light" versus "dark" /l/ (as in *like* versus *milk*) where the distribution of the two is again entirely predictable. But children do not yet know the full phonological system, and so may either store unnecessary detail, or fail to store critical detail. Their memory representations are presumably adjusted as they find out more (Peters 1983, Peters and Menn 1991). Their representations also have to allow for variation from one speaker to another so they can relate any particular instance in input to the forms they themselves have stored. Children attempt forms that match the adult pronunciations, and they try to use those forms according to the conventions they have observed in adult usage. While their early attempts at producing word forms may be fairly distant from the adult versions, they generally share sounds in common. This can readily be seen in the early attempts at words illustrated in Table 5–1.[1]

Children's earliest words often vary in pronunciation from one occasion to the next and diverge rather far from the intended targets. They have not yet had enough practice with the articulatory programs for specific words. Producing words takes practice, and children make many errors on the way: they omit unstressed syllables and attempt only stressed ones (e.g., *'fore* for *before*); they simplify consonant clusters by dropping fricatives (e.g., *too-too* for *choo-choo*), liquids (e.g., *tee* for *tree*), and nasals (e.g., *tet* for *tent*), and retain only the stops (sounds like /d/, /t/, /g/). They typically find some classes of sounds harder to produce than others: for example, fricatives like /f/ and /v/, and liquids like /r/, are usually harder for a two- or three-year-old than stops like /p/ or /d/. Finally, children show considerable individual variation in the specific sounds and sound classes that they master first (Ferguson and Farwell 1975, Ingram 1974a, Peters and Menn 1993).

The fis *phenomenon*

Children's reliance on adult-based representations stored in memory is attested by several kinds of evidence. One is the *fis* phenomenon: young children often reject their own pronunciations as wrong compared with the adult's. Although they themselves produce *fis*, they consistently favor the

---

[1] See further Ingram 1974a, Leonard, Fey, and Neuhoff 1981, Leonard, Schwartz, Folger, and Wilcox 1978, Leopold 1939–1949, Menn 1976, Schwartz and Leonard 1982, Smith 1973.

Table 5–1 *Early word forms and their adult targets: the earliest 20–25 word-forms produced by three children*

Jennika 1;3–1;4 Target and form(s)	Hildegard 0;10–1;1 Target and form(s)	Joan 0;10–1;7 Target and form(s)
blanket [ba, babi]	pretty [prəti]	up [ap]
bye-bye [ba, baba]	there [dɛ i, dɹi, de:]	bottle [ba]
daddy [da, dada, dadi]	pretty [prɪti]	bus [bas]
dot [dat, dati]	there [dɛ:]	put-on [baza]
hi [hai]	ticktock [tak]	that [za]
mommy [ma, mami, mama]	ball [ba]	down [da]
no [no]	Blumen [bu]	out [at]
see [si]	da [da:]	away [ba:'ba]
see that [siæt]	opa [pa]	pocket [bat]
that [da]	papa [pa-pa]	fuff [af, faf]
hot [hat]	piep [pi, pip]	put-on [bada']
hi [hai, haidi]	pretty [prti]	push [bus]
up [ap, api]	sch-sch [š-š]	dog [uf]
no [nodi, dodi, noni]	ticktock [tɪta tat-t]	pie [ba.]
	bimbam [bɪ]	duck [dat]
	da [da]	lamp [bap]
	Gertrude [dɛ:da, də:di]	M [am]
	kick [ti]	N [an]
	kritze [tɪtsə]	in [n]
		doll [da·]
		S [as]
		O [u·]
		R [a]
		nice [nas]

Note: Variant pronunciations are separated by commas.
Source: Ingram 1974a, Leopold 1939, Velten 1943

adult pronunciation, *fish*, just as they do *merry-go-round* over *mewwy-go-wound*, or *ostrich* over *osrich* (e.g., Berko and Brown 1960, Maccoby and Bee 1965, Smith 1973, Weir 1962, 1966). These observations of spontaneous speech have been corroborated experimentally. When three-year-olds hear their own (non-adult) pronunciations on tape, they can identify only 50 percent of the target words, compared to nearly 100 percent when they hear the same words pronounced by an unfamiliar adult (Dodd 1975).

Children also make accurate judgments about their own ability to pronounce words. From as young as age 2;6, they comment on the pronunciation of specific words, and from about 3;0, may explicitly announce mastery of words they were formerly unable to say in an adult fashion (Leopold 1939, Smith 1973, Weir 1966). Children, then, recognize newly achieved matches between the adult targets they have stored in memory and their own productions.

Spontaneous repairs

Further evidence that children rely on adult-based targets comes from their spontaneous repairs. First, they repair their own productions from their earliest words on. They repair pronunciation, word endings, prepositions, pronouns, articles, and word order, as well as other aspects of lexical choice and sentential structure. What they repair, of course, depends in part on what they already produce at any one stage, so repairs to pronunciation tend to predominate before age two. Once children have mastered much of the phonology of their language, their repairs tend to center on whichever part of the system they are currently acquiring. As they get older, they make more of their repairs to inflections, to verb forms marked for tense and agreement, for example, and to nouns marked for plurality or possession, as well as to the forms of grammatical morphemes like prepositions or articles. They also begin to repair word order in complex noun-phrases and predicates. Some typical early repairs are shown in Table 5–2 (Clark 1982b, Clark and Andersen 1979, Käsermann and Foppa 1981).

Children also make repairs when they practice words and utterances. For example, many young children rehearse episodes of the day, going over events in monologue form, and repeating what sound like mini language-drills (Kuczaj 1983, Scollon 1976, Weir 1962, 1966). In doing this, they continually repair and re-repair forms that do not yet match the adult target. By age 3;0 or 4;0, children often correct others, especially when younger siblings produce non-adult forms. Around the same age, they also start to comment on adult uses that diverge from the conventions of the speech community the children are most familiar with (Clark 1978a, Leopold 1949).

Finding the right word

The form of an adult word constitutes only part of the target children aim at. They also have to master the uses to which each form is put. That is, they have to learn the conventions that govern use, including the meanings usually carried by each term. Again, children's earliest uses typically bear

Table 5–2 *Some typical repairs from D*

(1)	D (1;4,6, greeting a familiar guest who'd been staying some days): *bye, -hi, hi,*
(2)	D (1;6,8, looking out of the car window as we passed a medium-sized van): *car -* TRUCK.
(3)	D (1;6,26, watching his father change, as the latter was about to put on a belt): *get down - get* ON,
(4)	D (1;7,5, climbing onto his mother's knee and pretending to go to sleep, after first announcing his intention): *get down, . up, sleep,*
(5)	D (1;8,23, talking about a figure from his puzzle): *animal broke,* Mo yes, but he's all fixed now. D *all fex - fix, all fix,*
(6)	D (1;9,12, as his mother got him into the car and began to take a towel off his car-seat): *I sit mine . Eve towel,*
(7)	D (1;10,24, addressing his grandmother's parakeet in its cage): *ge' out - get out, get out,*
(8)	D (1;11,4, correcting a final consonant in *roll*): *rown - roll,*
(9)	D (1;11,9, correcting his pronunciation of *Eve*): *ee doing . Eve doing?*
(10)	D (1;11,22, as he moved chairs in to the table): *I pu' [ə] chairs – – I push [ə] chairs,*
(11)	D (2;0,9, in the car): *Herb open [ə] window, make it hot, - make it Damon* NOT *get hot,*
(12)	D (2;0,14, noticing the open sunroof in the car): *Eve open [ə] window, Damon don't get hot – – Damon get hot. Damon get cool,*
(13)	D (2;2,4, at the table, D trying to correct misunderstandings): *where Herb cap?* Mo his cap? D *where Herb cape?* Mo his cape? d'you mean a rain-cape? D *where . where Herb gwass?* Mo oh, his glass - here it is,

Note: The symbols in the table should be read as follows: , = falling intonation (end of tone group); . = brief pause (1 syllable); - = pause (1 beat); SMALL CAPITALS = heavy stress.
Source: Clark, diary data.

some discernible relation to the adult conventions for the words in question. On the first occasion they hear a word, of course, children must make a guess at the meaning based on what is most salient on that occasion. After that, they can look for consistency in word uses over time in the speech around them. It is possible that recognition of consistencies is one prerequisite for "breaking in" to language. If children do not grasp this until around age one or so, then the idea of consistency itself, inherent in the principles of conventionality and contrast, may be one factor that places a lower bound on when children can start learning to talk. Until they recognize that there is consistency in the input they hear, they have no *way in* to the language around them.

Children pay a lot of attention to the words they use and they seem to try to chose the right word on each occasion for the meaning they are trying to convey. Evidence for this comes from the high proportion of lexical repairs they make. This amounts to as much as 40 percent of all repairs in the speech of children aged 2;0 to 3;6 (Clark 1982b). That is, children access one word and produce it, but then realize they've not conveyed exactly the meaning they had intended, so they repair it. Their lexical repairs, then, are further evidence that children are trying to produce the right word, the conventional one, for the meaning they wish to convey.

Early attention to conventionality is also demonstrated by children's deliberate elicitation of labels. Early in acquisition, when their spoken vocabulary is only around 20–50 words, children already point to things while producing a deictic term. It may be based on their version of *that*, for example, perhaps produced as *da* or even *eh*. As soon as the adult supplies a term, for example *That's a* CANDLE, with heavy stress on *candle* (Broen 1972, Snow and Ferguson 1977) or just stressed CANDLE alone, children stop pointing, point to something else, or turn away to some other activity. When they use a deictic word in conjunction with persistent pointing, they appear to be deliberately eliciting a label. This activity appears to be a direct precursor to the frequent questions children begin to ask around age 2;0. At that stage, the deictic term seems to be replaced by question forms like *What that?* or *'S that?* asked with great persistence and great frequency. Again, the questioners appear satisfied when the adult supplies labels or makes comments that contain labels. Children's explicit elicitation questions, along with their earlier deictic elicitations, strongly suggest that they assume that there are, potentially, terms for everything they wish to talk about (Clark 1973a, Leopold 1939–1949, Major 1906, Stern 1924).

The quest for labels is signaled around this time by two other changes in children's own word use. First, they begin refusing to name things for which they currently lack labels. Earlier, they would often simply over-extend a known word on such occasions, and so might call a horse a *dog* when they still lacked a word for horses, or an orange a *ball* when they lacked the word for oranges. But now, they refuse to over-extend known terms and instead try to elicit a label. Second, as children this age add new words to their vocabulary – *cat* and *moon*, say – they simultaneously stop over-extending old words to the domains covered by the new words. That is, they now use *cat* for cats in lieu of their earlier *dog*.

Summary

Reliance on stored target-forms – shown by children's choices of word-forms, their spontaneous repairs, and their requests for labels – offers evidence that children have recognized that language is conventional, and that uses of lexical expressions depend on the conventions associated with them. (Their grasp of the conventions at this stage, of course, is rather rudimentary.) This recognition of conventionality seems to emerge early in the second year. Logically, conventionality is not the only option children could assume. The conclusion that each word has a conventional meaning linked to the kind of object or action being picked out is by no means inevitable. They could in theory have assumed instead that each word has a different meaning on each occasion, such that each one simply picks out whatever is salient in each setting. That is, words in general could all be equivalent, in some sense, to demonstrative *that*. What is important for the present account is that the evidence strongly favors the view that children recognize conventionality (rather than some logical alternative to it) and it is that that allows them to start making use of language.

Contrast

Contrast in language is not easily disentangled from conventionality. When children take conventional forms as their targets, they typically observe contrast as well. Yet that leaves unanswered the question of what the antecedents of contrast itself might be. One possibility is that it develops with children's recognition of intentions as part of rational behavior. That is, they would first have to grasp that people do things intentionally: they pick things up on purpose; they move things from one place to another on purpose; and they carry out all sorts of actions on purpose. Among these actions is speaking. When people speak, children would then assume,[2] they have a reason for choosing one word, x, on a particular occasion, rather than another, y. From this it would follow that x could not be equivalent to y, and so must contrast with it in some way. This then would lead children to assign different meanings to words that differed in form (Clark 1988, 1990).

---

[2] This assumption, of course, is tacit rather than explicit, whether for an eight-month-old or an eighteen-month-old.

Intentions are recognized early on by children in themselves and in others. From the age of seven or eight months, infants will repeatedly attempt actions themselves (crawling to a particular place, manipulating a toy). They themselves both initiate and elicit exchanges in games like peek-a-boo, and they respond appropriately to initiations from others. A month or so later (0;9–0;10), they recognize and elicit more elaborate intentions: they can successfully get adults to do things for them – open boxes, doors, or purses; pick up fallen toys; or repeat games like pat-a-cake or peek-a-boo (Bates 1976, Escalona 1973, Piaget 1951). These acts all assume that adults have intentions, just as they must have intentions in uttering words, choosing now one form, x, and now another, y. The very notion of *speaker's meaning* is predicated directly on its being an attempt to get someone else (the addressee) to recognize the speaker's intention in producing a specific utterance on a specific occasion (Grice 1957, H. Clark 1985, in press). Yet precisely how good children are at relating their knowledge of intentions to language use, and exactly when they do so in their first twelve to twenty-four months, in detail and with proficiency, remains an open question.

For children to assume contrast offers considerable economy of effort in acquisition. As they work out the meaning of a new term, they can automatically eliminate consideration of the meanings of all the terms already known: they can start right away on working out *how*, not whether, the new word is different from each of the words they already know. Contrast, then, should make the overall task of acquiring meanings simpler. I turn next therefore to more detailed consideration of the role it plays as children acquire new word-meanings.

Contrast predicts that children will assume that differences in form mark differences in meaning. From this and conventionality it follows that in building up a vocabulary:

(1)   Words contrast in meaning.
(2)   Established words have priority.
(3)   Unfamiliar (new) words fill lexical gaps.
(4)   Innovative words fill lexical gaps.

These predictions essentially parallel those made for adult language-use. The difference is that children start from a very small vocabulary and very limited knowledge of the world. Their knowledge about categories – their ontogeny, history, and functions in the overall scheme of things within a specific culture – is necessarily limited by their experience. What a one-year-old can know is only a fraction of what a six-year-old knows, or of what a twenty-five-year-old knows. Children have to find out which possible contrasts in fact hold in their language, and at first they will not necessarily observe the same ones as adult speakers. They also have many more gaps in their vocabularies. They can fill these gaps with new words that they have heard used in contrast to familiar ones. They also fill them at times with innovative words coined just for the occasion.

Words contrast in meaning

Very young children, just like adults, act as if words contrast in meaning and they reject apparent synonyms. Evidence for this comes from several sources. Children narrow down over-extensions as they acquire new words; they build up lexical domains by adding contrasts with the addition of new terms; and they assign contrasting meanings to distinct words and morphemes.

Some of the earliest evidence that children assume contrast comes from their narrowing-down of lexical over-extensions. Take two-year-old Alan, who initially over-extends *dog* to cats, sheep, and other four-legged mammals in addition to dogs. When he acquires the term *cat*, a word for part of his domain for *dog*, he stops over-extending *dog* to cats. And when he acquires *sheep*, he stops over-extending *dog* to sheep. At this point, Alan relies on *cat* for picking out cats, *sheep* for sheep, and *dog* for dogs and other small mammals for which he still lacks words. This over-extension followed by narrowing has been widely observed in diary records of young children's speech (Grégoire 1948, Leopold 1948, Lewis 1951, Major 1906, Pavlovitch 1920, Stern and Stern 1928; also Clark 1987, 1991).

Narrowing the application of each word acquired would not be predicted by contrast alone, but it follows directly from the combination of contrast with the single-level and no-overlap assumptions. If Alan gave up the single-level assumption at this point, he could then assign *dog* to two distinct levels. It could function as a superordinate for the various animal terms he knows (much as *animal* does for adults), and it could function as a co-hyponym of *cat* and *sheep*. This pattern, in fact, is common from around age two to two-and-a-half. Children often use a term like *car*, for example, both as a superordinate for *truck*, *van*, etc., and as a co-hyponym of these terms. These children have already given up the single-level assumption for this part of their lexicon. Learning where in the lexicon there are multiple levels, and what patterns of overlap are found in specific domains takes time. So children probably give up the single-level and no-overlap assumptions on a needs-must basis, one domain or so at a time, as they learn more words and more about how they are organized.

Evidence for contrast also comes from children's assignments of non-conventional meanings to some forms. Some English-speaking two-year-olds, for example, take the nominative pronoun *I* to mark a relative absence of control over an activity, and *me* (the accusative form) to mark control on the child's part – compare *I want a cookie* with *Me throw ball* (Budwig 1989). Or children may assign non-grammatical meanings to case distinctions. For instance, some one-year-olds acquiring Hungarian use the nominative or citation forms of nouns when naming things, but the accusative forms of the same nouns when talking about what they want to have (MacWhinney 1985). And some French-speaking two- to three-year-olds assign partitive meaning to contracted forms of " *de* + article" (e.g., *du, des*) and possessive meaning to uncontracted forms of these (*de la*). This results in non-conventional partitives like the feminine **da neige* '(some) snow' alongside masculine *du pain* '(some) bread,' and non-conventional possessives like masculine **de le garçon* 'of the boy' alongside *de la fille* 'of the girl' (Vinson 1915–1916). When children encounter differences in form, they assume differences in meaning. They may be wrong, though, in which differences they assume and the resultant mappings they make of meaning to form.

Established words have priority

At the same time, children give priority to familiar, conventional words. They give up their own coinages, for example, in favor of the conventional terms used by adults: they eventually replace innovations like *to sand* (2;4,13, 'to grind into powder' [of pepper]) or *to crack out* (2;6,11, 'to crack a shell and get out' [of chicks]), with conventional *grind* and *hatch*, and they replace innovative nouns like *sleepers* (2;6) and *climber* (2;5,24) with conventional *pyjamas* and *ladder* (Clark 1987).

How long it takes well-established terms to pre-empt such innovations will depend on the circumstances. Take two-year-old Kate, who is looking for a word for the action one does with oars when rowing a dinghy. If she hasn't yet learnt the verb *to row*, she has to find some other means for talking about this activity, so she might coin *to oar*, as in *The man [is] oaring the boat*. This makes use of a common option where the term for the instrument provides the source for a verb for the associated activity. From now on, Kate may use *to oar* but she will also hear *to row* in the appropriate contexts from the adults around her, and she will hear it where she would have used *to oar*. Before she gives up *to oar*, she will first have to work out that the meanings of her verb and the adult verb are identical, and then, since conventional forms take priority, she should give up *to oar* in favor of *to row*.

How long before such pre-emption takes effect should vary with individual experience – the range of occasions on which children hear *to row* when they would have expected to hear *to oar* – and with the nature of the adult input. Some children may be told immediately after their coinage, *That's called rowing*; others may receive the same information less directly in the form of an expansion like *Yes, Stuart's rowing the boat, isn't he?* as a follow-up to the child's saying *He's oaring*. And others still may hear no direct juxtaposition of the two forms for a long time, and so take longer to adopt the conventional term. Some coinages, then, may be given up immediately in favor of the conventional term, while others may linger because children assume that a pair like *to oar* and *to row* differ in meaning, with the latter, for example, taken to be superordinate to the verbs *to oar*, *to paddle*, and *to sail*. By age four to five, children seem to be sensitive to the conventionality of many verbs when faced with a choice between conventional and innovative forms (Clark 1981a, Clark, Neel-Gordon, and Johnson 1993). What is critical is that children have first to recognize that the two terms have the same meaning. Only then can they choose to retain only one of them, the established conventional one.

Pre-emption by conventional terms sometimes causes problems for word-learning tasks. Werner and Kaplan (1952) examined the difficulties children had in inferring the meanings of nonsense words presented in a set of sentential contexts. The task proved so difficult that five-year-olds typically failed it, and only a few nine-year-olds did well. This finding appears incompatible with the observation that children add unfamiliar words to their vocabularies at a rapid rate, averaging some 9–10 words a day between age two and age six.

If children acquire real words so quickly, why did they have so much difficulty inferring the word meanings in a learning task? The answer is that the task itself dealt in synonyms, so it violated the assumption of contrast. In constructing each set of sentences, the researchers took an English word like *stick*, made up several sentences using it, and then replaced *stick* with a nonsense word, *corplum*, as in:

(a)   A corplum may be used for support.
(b)   Corplums may be used to close off an open space.

(c)   A corplum may be long or short, thick or thin, strong or weak.

(d)   A wet corplum does not burn.

So the children's task was to discover the meanings of nonsense words that were precisely synonymous with English words they already knew.

In a replication of this study, French-speaking children evinced the same difficulty. These children heard sets of four sentences with a nonsense word substituted for a familiar French noun, verb, or adjective. The children were told that the sentences had been produced by a second-language speaker who made mistakes, and that their task was to find what was wrong and correct it. Again, few of the younger children (under age seven) managed to supply the target word across all four sentences in each set. But when children heard a pause instead of a synonymous nonsense word, they found the task much easier. Now they simply had to fill in the missing word. The older children, aged eight, did very well at this, and even the younger ones (aged five and six) often succeeded. When they did not have to find synonyms, children could make use of the linguistic contexts to identify the missing words (Braun-Lamesch 1962). It is easier to fill gaps than places that are already taken. And finding existing words does not violate children's assumption of contrast.

Unfamiliar words fill gaps

Children assume contrast when they encounter unfamiliar words. This often occurs when they hear both familiar and unfamiliar words in the presence of objects, some of which they have words for and some not. From as young as 1;6 or 2;0, children readily assign unfamiliar terms to categories for which they lack labels, rather than to ones for which they already have labels. For example, when three- and four-year-olds are presented with a set of animals, three familiar (a pig, a cow, and a sheep) and one not (a tapir), and are asked to put each away in a box, they consistently assume that the unfamiliar word, *gombe*, picks out the unfamiliar animal (Dockrell 1981).

Two-year-olds also readily attach unfamiliar words to unfamiliar objects. For example, when they are presented with a series of unfamiliar objects mixed in with familiar ones to play with, and then hear both familiar and unfamiliar labels, they consistently choose an unfamiliar object as a referent for an unfamiliar word, alongside appropriate objects as referents for familiar words. Since all the objects had been played with and handled equally often, the children's assignments of labels cannot be attributed just to the salience of novel objects. In the same study, two-year-olds also readily extended the unfamiliar word to a new exemplar from the same category. And, when given a choice (through the introduction of a second unfamiliar word with further unfamiliar objects from a further category), these children preferred *not* to pair a second unfamiliar label with any object that had already been labeled. Instead, they assumed that the second unfamiliar word must refer to an as-yet-unnamed unfamiliar object.[3]

The setting influences these inferences. For example, children this age were given a set of solids of different colors, in two different linguistic contexts. In the shape context, they were asked for *the gombe one, not the square one or the round one*. In the color context, they were asked for *the gombe one, not the green one or the red one*. When the contrast was with known shapes, children consistently chose the only solid for which they lacked a name. When the contrast was with color, they generally chose solids of an unusual color or with some pattern, though some still preferred shape (Anglin 1977, Au 1990, Baldwin 1989, Clark 1973a, Dockrell 1981, Thomson and Chapman 1977).

Children make the same assumption in dealing with labels for actions. Many two-year-olds already know the conventional meaning of a verb like *to kick* and interpret it appropriately. So when they hear two verbs that call for use of the same body part – *to kick*, say, alongside the unfamiliar *to foot* – they assign different meanings to them, and do so consistently from as young as age two. For the verb *to foot*, for example, they regularly assign some other action involving the foot – standing on a ball or a pillow, touching something with the foot, and so on. Even those children who didn't yet have a conventional meaning for *to kick* assumed that the action associated with it must differ from the actions associated with other verbs (Clark, Neel-Gordon, and Johnson 1993).

When children already have a label for something and are given a new label, they may do one of several things: where possible, they assume it picks out some as-yet-unnamed category; or they treat it as a subordinate of the label already known, or they assign it some other relation to the known word such as superordinate; or they simply reject it because it appears synonymous with the word they already know.

---

[3] See Golinkoff, Hirsh-Pasek, Baduini, and Lavallee 1985, Golinkoff, Hirsh-Pasek, Bailey, and Wenger 1992, Lyamina 1960, Vincent-Smith, Bricker, and Bricker, 1974; also Markman and Wachtel 1988, Taylor and Gelman 1988, 1989, and Tomasello, Mannle, and Werdenschlag 1988.

In their spontaneous speech, two-year-olds do on occasion reject a label used or offered by the adult (François 1977, Macnamara 1982, Valentine 1942). Such rejections would appear to offer additional evidence that children observe contrast. That is, they should reject only terms that appear to be synonymous with words they already know. But their rejections in fact seem to fall into two classes: sometimes young children will reject one highly familiar label in favor of another one, also familiar, as in (1); at other times, they reject an unfamiliar label in favor of one already known, as in (2):

(1)   Fa (looking at a book): Look at those birds.
       D (aged 2; 2,20): *That's not birds, those* PARROTS.
(2)   Mo (at the fish-counter): That's a trout.
       D (aged 2; 5,1): *That's a* FISH. *That* NOT *a trout.*
       Mo: Well, a trout's a KIND of fish.
       D (pause, then pointing at a row of crabs): CRABS *are a kind of fish.*

Inspection of an estimated 4,000 diary entries for D between the ages of 1; 0 and 3; 0 revealed just 20 instances where he explicitly rejected an adult label. Most of the rejections (80 percent) occurred on occasions where he substituted a more specific familiar noun for the term rejected (e.g., *soup-spoon* for *spoon*, *parrot* for *bird*). In every instance, D already knew the more general rejected label and used it appropriately. On only 4 occasions did he reject unfamiliar labels (e.g., *fish* preferred to unfamiliar *trout*, *plane* to unfamiliar *flying fortress*). In these 4 instances, he was not familiar with the new (subordinate) term. The small number suggests that it may be quite rare for children to be *unable* to find some possible difference in meaning when they are faced with two terms in the same context. Overall, the rejections of adult labels seem to reflect a labeling preference on the child's part, rather than a rejection of synonymy. On other occasions, both superordinate and subordinate labels are used appropriately. For instance, *bird* was produced for flocks of birds, for mixed groups of birds where there were several kinds seen together, and simply in contrast to various animals (e.g., *bird* versus *dog*), while *parrot* was used for various kinds of parrots.

The type of rejection illustrated in (1) also makes clear that by their second birthday, children may know that many domains have at least two taxonomic levels, and be familiar with labels for some categories at both levels (Banigan and Mervis 1988, Berman and Clark 1989, Clark, Gelman, and Lane 1985, Clark and Svaib 1991, Gelman, Wilcox, and Clark 1989, Waxman and Gelman 1986, Waxman and Hatch 1992). This is consistent with the fact that from about age two on, children discover, first, that many lexical domains are organized hierarchically, with more than one level, and second, that the same term may serve at two different levels. By age two, then, children have already begun to give up any broad reliance on the single-level assumption and, between levels, on the no-overlap assumption.

It may be rare for children not to be able to come up with contrasting meanings for different forms. But one setting where they might have more difficulty is in learning two languages at once. In fact, an early solution chosen by very young bilinguals appears to be to produce a label for a particular category from only one of their two languages, despite exposure to labels from both. That is, these children may initially treat their production lexicon as a single system in which all the terms contrast. But implicit and explicit rejections of second labels in bilingual settings seem to occur at most for only a few months; it may cease when children have fewer than 50 words in production (Quay 1993). At that point, they begin to solicit doublets – equivalent terms from their two languages.

This shift may coincide with when young bilinguals distinguish one language from the other on phonological grounds. Early on, they may make use of a single sound-system (Vogel 1975) as well as a single lexicon. If they assume they are dealing with one language, their early rejections and avoidance of apparent synonyms would follow directly from contrast: different forms carry different meanings. These rejections should also emerge earlier than rejections from monolinguals because bilingual children should have a hard time discerning the grounds for a difference in meaning for translation equivalents (Ervin-Tripp 1974, Fantini 1976, Taeschner 1983; see also Au and Glusman 1990, Rosenblum and Pinker 1983). On the other hand, if bilinguals realize they are dealing with two languages from the start (De Houwer 1990, Lanza 1990, Mikeš 1990), their rejections are also more likely to reflect a labeling preference than a problem with potential synonyms.

As soon children realize they are dealing with two systems, they need only apply contrast within each language. They should therefore accumulate doublets freely, and show a high degree of overlap for words in the two languages. And they do. Consider Caitlin, acquiring Dutch and English from birth. By age 2;0, she produced at least 373 terms in Dutch and 388 in English.[4] Of these, 299 were doublets. She had English

---

[4] Caitlin's vocabulary was assessed within a few days of her second birthday with The MacArthur Communicative Development Inventory. I am grateful to Kerry Kilborn and Ann Cooreman for making these data available.

Table 5–3 *Typical innovative nouns*

(1) D (1;8,5, playing with spoon and cup, then put spoon in cup): *Orangejuice-spoon.*
(2) D (1;9,27, as Mo put an empty 1/2-pint cream carton on the table in front of a 1/2-gallon milk carton): *Baby-milk.*
(3) D (1;10,5, comparing cousin's towel with a face-cloth): *Justin towel.* Mo Yes, that's Justin's towel. D (pointing next at his face-cloth): *Baby-towel.*
(4) D (1;11,28, wanting to be read *Lion in the meadow*): *read* [ə] *lion-book.*
(5) D (1;11,30, removing *Pigs go oink*, open at a picture of ducks, from Mo's knee) *I read a Babar-book*, NOT [ə] *duck-book.*
(6) D (2;2,0, playing with a small and large strainer in the sink): *That* [ə] *tea-sieve.* Mo What? D *That* [ə] *tea-sieve.* (then pointing at the large one for vegetables): *That* [ə] *water-sieve.*
(7) D (2;3,0, rejecting a striped T-shirt): *I want my boat-shirt.*
(8) D (2;3,21, of a Duplo box that looked like a lion): *I'm going to put those toys back in the lion-box.*
(9) D (2;4,7, looking at a picture of a cake with candles): *That a candle-cake.* Mo What's it for? D *For a birthday.*
(10) D (2;5,11, successively labeling a car-carrier, a truck carrying cows, and an earth-mover with a power-shovel): *That a car-truck. A cow-truck. A shovel-truck.*
(11) D (2;5,26, as he reached across the counter in the kitchen, helping Fa cook): *I'm a big reacher.*
(12) D (2;6,6, wanting the nut-cracker): *Where's the crackener?*
(13) Mo (to D, 2;9,3, talking about the family car): It's a Volvo. D *A volvo-car?* Mo Yes, a Volvo. D *A volvo-car.*

Note: '-' between two terms in an innovative noun indicates compound stress, with primary stress on the first (modifier) noun; SMALL CAPITALS indicate emphatic stress.
Source: Clark, diary data.

equivalents for 80 percent of her Dutch vocabulary, and Dutch equivalents for 77 percent of her English vocabulary. These proportions are almost identical to those found for a bilingual child learning Estonian and English: at age 2;0, Raivo had a 76 percent overlap between his two vocabularies (Vihman 1985). Within twelve months of starting to talk, then, bilingual children may have doublets for the majority of the words they have acquired in their two languages.

Coinages fill gaps

Young children are often faced with gaps where they cannot find words. Their vocabulary is still very limited and they have yet to acquire the majority of conventional terms. One strategy here is to construct new words to carry the meanings needed. And they do construct new words. They begin to coin words to fill gaps around the beginning of their second year. They construct new nouns, new verbs, and new adjectives, and in doing so, make use of whatever they have learnt so far about the word forms and meanings in their language. Some typical examples of early coinages are shown in Tables 5–3, 5–4, and 5–5.

When children fill lexical gaps, they often do so where there is also a gap for the adult speaker. But they may also coin words where there is no gap for the adult. And these coinages, from the adult point of view, are illegitimate. Any existing words with those meanings pre-empt new words designed to take their place. So these innovations must eventually give way to established ones as children learn the conventional forms that carry those meanings.

The options children choose when they coin words vary with the type of language being learnt (e.g., Indo-European versus Semitic versus Uralic), the availability and productivity of different word-formation options (e.g., zero derivation, affixation, compounding), and individual lexical history (e.g., each child's existing vocabulary, its size, the number of terms in the relevant domain, and how close the child's meanings are to the conventional meanings). The choices children make also depend on principles they apply in analyzing and constructing word forms. The nature of these principles forms the topic of the next two chapters.

Summary

In summary, children give extensive evidence of observing both conventionality and contrast from very early, possibly from their earliest productions on. They take the adult language as their target in memory and in production; they repair their own forms to approximate adult ones; and they give priority to adult forms over others. In assuming contrast, they assign different meanings to different forms. This leads them on occasion to reject terms as potentially synonymous, both within and across

Table 5–4 *Typical innovative verbs*

(1)	D (2;4,13, grinding pepper onto the kitchen counter): *I'm sanding.* [= making sand]
(2)	D (2;6,11, pretending to be a chick hatching): *I'm gonna crack out.*
(3)	D (2;6,23, of two pencils, to Fa): *I sharped them.*
(4)	D (2;8,4, wanting to have some water left in the bottom of the shower so he could paddle): *Leave a puddle in there so I can water in it.* [= paddle in the water]
(5)	D (2;8,5, of some children playing and laughing): *Are they silling?* [= being silly]
(6)	D (2;8,20, of the hose in the garden, to Mo): *An' water the dirt off my stick.* [= wash off with water]
(7)	D (2;9,1, of a sock, to Mo): *And did you needle this?* [= mend with a needle]
(8)	D (2;9,10, after talking about seeing some boats): *And we might see a man oaring a boat with oars.* [= rowing]
(9)	D (2;9,10, of plastic shapes filled with sand): *I'm gonna shape 'em all out.* [= turn out all the shapes onto the sand]
(10)	D (2;9,24, of Pan Am badge on his shirt): *I was tighting it. I tighted my badge, and you should untight it.* [= tighten, loosen]
(11)	D (2;10,1, as Mo opened the car-window): *Not very wide, because it will wind.* [= the wind will blow]
(12)	D (2;10,13, explaining why peanut-butter was coming out round the edges of the sandwiches): *You flatted and flatted and flatted it and the peanut-butter came out.*
(13)	D (2;11,28, after he dropped a toy car on the floor, to Fa): *CAR me! I want my car.* [= give me the car]
(14)	D (3;0,21, Mo and D digging a hole at the beach and discussing whether it would have water at the bottom): *Will it wave in?* [= come in via waves]

Note: Square brackets contain glosses.
Source: Clark, diary data.

languages. It also causes them difficulty in tasks where the goal is to identify exact synonyms. Finding out that two words do not contrast can take a long time. This is also at issue when children have to give up their own coinages in favor of the conventional terms for those meanings: it is difficult to establish that their own form and the one used by adults have precisely the same meaning.

Table 5–5 *Typical Innovative Adjectives*

(1)	D (2;5,23, as Fa closed the trunk of the car, blowing a draft of air at D standing beside him): *It makes me windy.* [= blown by the wind]
(2)	D (2;6,8, after seeing a picture of a manhole): *At Anamaria's I saw a cracky hole.* [= a hole in a crack]
(3)	D (2;6,22, of the wet newspaper): *It's all soaky. The paper is soaky.* [= very wet, soaked]
(4)	D (2;7,5, driving home in the dark after dinner out): *It's very nighty.* [= pitch dark]
(5)	D (2;10,23, looking at some stone walls still standing in a ghost town): *There's a rocky house.* [= made of rocks]
(6)	D (2;11,8, looking up at crockery cupboard above the kitchen counter): *...bowls and plates white.* Mo Oh yes. They're white. D *An' spotty. When dogs have spots, they are called Dalmatians.* [= with spots on]
(7)	D (2;11,16, in response to overhearing part of a conversation): *But you can SKI down cliffs.* Mo Some you can. D *But not walky ones.* [= ones one can walk along]
(8)	D (3;0,5, going into a parking lot): *It's a bit crowdy in here. There are lots of cars here.* [= crowded]
(9)	D (3;1,1, objecting to Mo's removing a stick cut from a Diefenbakia stem): *No, it's not poisony.*
(10)	D (3;2,5, of a shop with balloons painted on the window, near D's school): *There's a balloony store.* [= for balloons, covered in balloons]

Note: Square brackets contain glosses.
Source: Clark, diary data.

Morphology and allomorphy

When children acquire irregular verbs in English (and in other languages), they appear to violate contrast when they replace conventional irregular forms by regularized ones with the same meaning. The problem is that, superficially, the past tense of an irregular verb like *to go*, for example, has the following order of acquisition (Brown 1973, Cazden 1968):

(a)   Children make use only of the bare root, *go*;

(b)   they make sporadic use of the conventional irregular past form, *went*;

(c)   they begin to produce a regularized form for the past, *goed*;

(d)   at some point several years later, they drop the regularized past *goed* in favor of *went*.

This is the traditional account, but it contains no explanation for why children would initially pick up the form *went* and then reject it in favor of regularized *goed*, a different form with apparently the same meaning. So is this really what happens?

One alternative is that regularized past-tense forms like *goed* reflect a failure to retrieve the appropriate form from memory for the meaning 'past time.' Children fail on irregular forms because they have to be learnt one by one, and this takes time. And when they fail, they have recourse to a regular rule that allows them to construct a past-tense form, namely *goed*, *bringed*, *sitted*, and so on (Marcus, Ullman, Pinker, Hollander, Rosen, and Xu 1992). This account argues that the correct irregular forms are in fact produced most of the time, and the over-regularized ones (*goed*, *bringed*) are produced only when children's memories fail. In favor of this account is the low overall rate (under 10 percent) of such regularizations between about age two and age five. However, some children show much higher rates of over-regularization for individual verbs at certain points in time; they also produce apparent double marking of the past, as in forms like *wented* and *broked*; and they occasionally add other inflections as well.

Another alternative, therefore, is that some children at stage (b) are not using *went* as a tensed form of *go* at all, though they may have assigned some motion-related meaning to it. So at stage (c), children who produce the form *goed* are simply constructing a past tense form on the regular model of *jump/jumped*, *work/worked*, and so on. That is, children do not follow the sequence: **go – went – goed – went**, but the sequence **go – goed – went**. Indeed, some children take irregular past forms to be verbs in their own right. For example, they take *went* to be just another verb root and, as a result, produce other inflected forms, *wents* and *wenting*, in the present, as well as the regular *wented* in the past (Clark 1990, Kuczaj 1978). Their occasional early uses of irregular past-tense forms are misleading, because they suggest children have already acquired the conventional adult meanings. The new developmental sequence proposed both accounts for the other inflected forms found on irregular pasts and is consistent with children's observing contrast.[5]

Eventually, children must come to realize that *go* and *went* are parts of

---

[5] This account makes no predictions about the frequency of over-regularizations, but is not incompatible with the finding that the more frequent a verb is in input, the lower the rate of over-regularization (Marcus *et al.* 1992). Greater exposure should make it easier for children to learn irregular forms and store them for retrieval when they themselves need to use them.

the same verb, so they will replace *goed* by *went*, the conventional past. But for *went* to pre-empt *goed*, children must establish that the two forms in fact have exactly the same meaning. This can take a long time, typically several years. Even when children realize that *went* carries the same core meaning as *go* and has to do with past time, they may continue to contrast the two. For example, some children assign to one form the meaning 'recent past' and to the other 'remote past' (Clark 1987). To get rid of *goed*, they must establish that *goed* and *went* have exactly the same meaning. This in turn requires that they establish that wherever they would have used *goed* (and *went*), adult speakers use only *went*.

The length of time children take to resolve such problems is in part a direct consequence of the difficulty they face in identifying violations of contrast. Violations only become apparent where children conclude that two forms have the *same* meaning. They then have to make a choice; they cannot retain both. The choice is determined by conventionality: the conventional, adult form wins. This eventual pre-emption of over-regularized forms by established ones has been widely attested, not only in English but in a wide range of other languages as well (Slobin 1985c).

Morphology also offers another apparent challenge for contrast. Grammatical morphemes may have several realizations or allomorphs, depending on the phonological shape of the root they are added to. In English, for instance, the plural morpheme takes one of three shapes: /-s/ as in *cats*, /-z/ as in *dogs*, or /-ɪz/ as in *houses*, depending on the final segment of the root, but the meaning is the same. In Finnish, back vowels and front vowels can never appear in the same word, so each suffix (and there are many) has one realization for roots with front vowels, and another for roots with back vowels. the meaning of each pair of front- and back-vowel realizations is the same. In other words, phonology, and not meaning, accounts for the variations in shape of certain morphemes. If contrast predicts that different forms differ in meaning, are these allomorphs the same or different forms?

When children hear two allomorphs of the same morpheme, as in English /-s/ and /-z/, they could follow one of two possible paths. On path A, they could hear the two as the same from the start, and so, in applying contrast, they would treat them as a single form with two realizations. On path B, children could hear the two allomorphs initially not as different realizations of a single morpheme, but as two different forms. On this path, they would look for differences in meaning that were not there. How children actually treat alternative realizations of the same morpheme is an empirical issue. If they do not have the right phonological rules by the time they start to identify the two allomorphs, they should find it harder to identify them as allomorphs. Contrast per se makes no prediction about which path children will follow, and the available evidence suggests they sometimes follow A and sometimes B.

Let's assume path A. To assign meanings to grammatical morphemes, children must be able to identify different realizations as the same form. This requires them to establish phonological rules that will account for different realizations. For English plurals, the rules will specify that final voiced segments call for the voiced /-z/, while voiceless segments call for the voiceless /-s/. (The allomorph /-ız/ requires a more complicated rule.) Although children hear both /-z/ and /-s/, they know they are realizations of the same morpheme. Contrast then applies as usual, to distinguish this morpheme from other grammatical morphemes.[6]

Some support for path A comes from children's early acquisition of simple phonological rules. Children acquiring English appear to make no errors in their choices of /-z/ versus /-s/ for plural nouns, which suggests that here they follow path A. They also seem to follow path A in their acquisition of the /-d/ and /-t/ allomorphs of the regular past tense in English, allomorphs that likewise depend on the voicing of the final segments in the verb root. Another example of where children follow path A comes from languages with vowel harmony such as Turkish, Hungarian, and Finnish. Children often master alternate realizations of each morpheme by age two or earlier (Aksu-Koç and Slobin 1985, MacWhinney 1973, 1978, Toivainen 1980, 1993). When they encounter an unfamiliar suffix containing a back vowel, they know it also has a front-vowel version. Phonological rules arrived at early on eliminate the differences of form among allomorphs for the purposes of contrast. At the same time, when children follow path A, it is difficult to find out what they do with the relevant forms *prior* to allomorphs being identified as being instances of the same form.

Path B offers a different scenario: here children would identify some forms as affixes before acquiring the necessary phonological rules. They should follow path B, then, where the phonological rules for allomorphs are complex and harder to analyze. In applying contrast under these

---

[6] In fact, this is a very general problem: children have to work out when any variants count, e.g., *dog* with and without a suffix, *go* with different intonations, or *road* pronounced with or without a diphthong. Intonation, stress, and dialect, for instance, all contribute potentially distinct forms of the same word.

circumstances, children would assume that allomorphs differ in meaning since they differ in form. This could be true for the /-ɪz/ allomorph of the English plural. It does not fit the initial phonological rule children use for the plural morpheme, so they could think it was a different form that contrasted with the plural. Equally, they could think that such words as *horse* or *rose* were already plural. The same holds for the /-ɪd/ allomorph of the regular past in English (e.g., *melted*). Like the plural allomorph, past tense /-ɪd/ could well be treated at first as a morpheme distinct from the allomorphs /-d/ and /-t/, and hence as having a different meaning (see also Bybee and Slobin 1982).

Where children follow path B, contrast predicts that they should try to set up different meanings for each allomorph. Do they? English-speaking children take much longer to work out the conditions for the /-ɪz/ plural than for /-z/ and /-s/; they also take much longer to work out the conditions for the /-ɪd/ past tense than for /-d/ and /-t/ (Anisfeld and Tucker 1968). This suggests that they could be following path B, but it is unclear what meanings they might have attributed to /-ɪz/ or /-ɪd/ in the meantime. (Notice that children should have still greater difficulty in identifying the past-tense forms of irregular verbs in English where the relation of present to past forms is even more complex, as in *bring/brought*, *sit/sat*, or *dig/dug*.) To find out whether children are following path B requires detailed analysis of their early systems in order to detect which non-conventional distinctions they may have made in first assigning meanings to the relevant forms (Budwig 1989, Gerhardt 1988).

When do children follow path A and when path B for particular morphemes? To answer this, one needs to pay more attention to the meanings children assign to each form they produce. Previous studies suffer from two defects: (a) most research on the acquisition of morphology has focussed on the production of forms with little or no study of the precise meanings children give them. And (b), when children produce adult-like forms, they are typically credited with the conventional adult meanings with no further ado. What is needed are studies that weigh meaning as heavily as form, and that take into account the role played by children's phonological rules (Peters and Menn 1993). In domains with simple rules, children will most likely follow path A and apply contrast to morphemes by treating different realizations (allomorphs) as instances of the *same* form. In domains with more complex rules, children will also apply contrast, but in following path B, they will begin by treating each allomorph as a different form. Once they acquire the phonological rules for these instances, though, they should treat allomorphs of a single morpheme as being the same (see also Slobin 1985c).

Essentially, adherence to the principle of contrast offers a way out of the so-called "no negative evidence" problem (Baker 1979, Bowerman 1987, Pinker 1986). During acquisition, children produce errors and are apparently given no corrections (i.e., no negative evidence). How then do they ever succeed in changing their language to eliminate these errors? Contrast supplies a possible mechanism: children who assume contrast have available a means for getting rid of over-regularizations of every type. But they can get rid of a form only if it doesn't differ in meaning from another form in their vocabulary, where the latter is the conventional one used by adult speakers. Establishing the absence of contrast should usually take a long time. It should also give rise to individual variations, across children and across words, since each case will depend on the specific occasions of adult use that children happen to be exposed to.

Innate versus learnt

To what extent can one ask whether conventionality and contrast are innate versus learnt? As we've already seen, if children observe conventionality, they should systematically take the adult language – the input they hear addressed to them from the people around them – as the target to aim for. And if they observe contrast, they should assume that differences in form signal differences in meaning. Children are in a position to observe language in action as soon as they realize both that adult vocalizations are purposeful and that they are often directed towards them, so they could very well arrive at some primitive form of these two principles during their first year, even before they themselves begin to produce any recognizable language. But this would assume that these principles are learnt rather than innate.

If conventionality and contrast hold for every language (and it's unclear how languages could function without them), one might wish to argue that conventionality and contrast are actually innate. If they are, it is presumably only to the extent that any other principles of societal organization and interaction can be said to be innate. That is, interaction and communication rely on certain conditions in order to work. The exact form of such conditions depends on the kind of interaction at issue – whether it is coordinating the players in an orchestra, say, or the participants in a conversation. It is unclear what it would mean to claim innateness for conventionality and contrast in particular, beyond a claim about willingness to observe societal agreements on word uses (conventionality) and utilization of cognitive-perceptual abilities to perceive differences among word forms and hence differences in meaning (contrast).

The way conventionality and contrast are used within a language community must presumably be discovered by very young children as they begin to learn about general conditions that prevail in language use. Whether innate or learnt, though, what is important is when and how children make use of such principles.

Summary
The principles of conventionality and contrast are fundamental to the functioning of language. Children appear to grasp these principles very early, and reveal their adherence to them in many different ways. The principles themselves make predictions about acquisition – that children who observe them should assume that words contrast in meaning, that established words pre-empt the use of others that would be synonymous with them, that unfamiliar words fill gaps, and that innovations can be coined when needed, again to fill gaps.

But to fill gaps with forms appropriate to the meanings being assigned, children must analyze the internal structure of familiar words into roots and affixes, and map the relevant meanings onto each one. I take up two factors that affect such analyses – transparency and simplicity – in the next chapter.

6 *Transparency and simplicity*

The word forms that children map meanings onto may be simple or complex. So far in this book, nearly all the word forms studied have been simple nouns like *dog* or *ball*, terms with various relational meanings like *uncle*, *top*, and *in*, and adjectives and quantifiers like *big*, *long*, and *more*. These are typically simple in form, without internal structure. How do children map meanings onto complex word-forms? They must map meanings onto both roots and affixes, as well as onto combinations of roots.

The premise of this chapter is that some complex words are easier for children to map onto because their word forms are transparent in meaning or simple in form. A complex word is transparent when children know the meanings of its elements (roots and affixes), and a word is simple when the elements to be combined require either no changes or minimal changes in form. After a brief look at the mapping of meaning onto form in complex words, I take up the roles of transparency and simplicity in lexical acquisition.

Complex words

The first complex word-forms children encounter are probably not recognized as such. Established compounds like *birthday* and *breakfast* are not amenable to analysis even by adult speakers of English (Berko 1958, Derwing 1976a, 1976b). Yet by age two children show that they do attend to the separate roots in complex word-forms. For example, they offer spontaneous analyses of established compounds like *lady-bug*, *high-chair*, *corn-flakes*, and *run-way* (see Chapter 2, Table 2–1). This suggests that they can and do recognize smaller units inside larger ones, for instance, the word *run* in *run-way*, and *gold* in *Goldilocks*. It would appear to be a necessary precursor to analysis of complex word-forms and the identification of possible root–affix and root–root combinations.[1]

Identifying a particular word-part as an affix may require exposure to several instances of that affix, or possibly only to one, provided the root is already familiar. When an affixal form has been isolated, children can map some meaning onto it. They may create possible meanings through comparison with the meanings of other words with the same affix. For example, if I hear *This road is muddy* and I know the word *mud*, I can infer that this instance of -*y* means 'having [mud] on it.' The affix then becomes available for use in the construction of new word-forms, as well as in the interpretation of unfamiliar words. In analyzing word forms, children must look for common elements in the meanings of all established words – adjectives in -*y*, for instance, or nouns in -*er*.

The meanings of unfamiliar words rarely consist just of a composition of the meanings of their parts. Complex words often become specialized over time, so children have to learn the specific meaning they carry over and above the meanings contributed by the parts. This can easily be illustrated for English compound nouns. The conventional meaning of *dog-sled*, for instance, can be glossed as 'sled pulled by dogs.' Notice, though, that the combination of *dog* and *sled* could have many other interpretations: a sled for dogs to ride on, a sled decorated with pictures of dogs, a sled that carries food for dogs, a sled that goes in last place, and so on. That is, the *relation* between parts like *dog* and *sled* in conventional words must be learnt as part of the conventional meaning of the whole. It is not predictable as a composition of the parts alone. The same holds for many affixes combined with roots. The conventional lexicon contains a plethora of specialized meanings associated with particular complex lexical items, and these meanings have to be learnt for each word.

Novel words might seem to offer a more purely compositional case, with the new meaning made up from the combination of root and affix meanings, or from the combination of two root meanings. But consider compound nouns again: the constituent nouns alone cannot specify what relation holds between the instances of the two categories denoted in a compound like *umbrella-man* or *Ferrari-woman*. Nothing in the noun meanings alone, or their combinations, would allow one to arrive at the meanings intended on their occasions of use, namely 'man with his head

[1] The analysis children do is not intended to be construed as metalinguistic reflection. Rather, it is a part of the segmentation of the speech stream necessary to identifying any potential units of form that might bear meaning.

entirely hidden by his umbrella' and 'woman whose will specified that she should be buried in her Ferrari.' Novel word-meanings are not conventional, but CONTEXTUAL in nature, so their further meaning is adduced on the basis of mutual knowledge shared by speaker and addressee (see Chapter 4). That is, the specific meaning the speaker intends must be accessible enough on the basis of mutual knowledge, given the context, to be computable by the addressee on the occasion of the utterance (Clark and Clark 1979, H. Clark 1983). When children map complex words, they may often need added help to identify specialized meanings in the conventional lexicon. When they themselves coin new words, they tacitly rely on their addressees' ability to go beyond a simple composition of the word parts. The adults they talk to typically know enough, on each occasion, to compute the intended meanings of novel word-forms.

Types of mapping

Are some kinds of meaning–form pairings easier for children to map than others? Languages differ, for instance, in the degree to which the meanings of roots can be modulated by grammatical morphemes such as noun or verb inflections. They also differ in which combinations of meanings are commonly lexicalized as single words, and in the range of derivational affixes available for word formation. We'll consider three different cases, from Turkish, Spanish, and Russian.

(a) In Turkish, each modulation on a word is typically carried by a separate affix added to the root (or root–affix combination). Each affix carries one meaning. With a noun like *el* 'hand,' each of the meanings 'plural,' 'first person possessive,' and 'locative,' for instance, can be added to the noun base as separate suffixes, singly, or in combination, as in:

el-ler	(PL)	'hands'
el-im	(1SG POSS)	'my hand'
el-ler-im	(PL + 1SG POSS)	'my hands'
el-im-de	(1SG POSS + LOC)	'in my hand'
el-ler-im-de	(PL + 1SG POSS + LOC)	'in my hands'

(b) In Spanish, in contrast, one affix often has several elements of meaning mapped on it at once, in a one-to-many fashion. Verb inflections simultaneously mark person (whether first, second, or third), number (singular or plural), and tense (present, past, future), as in:

camin-as	(2SG PRES)	'you're walking'
camin-a	(3SG PRES)	'he's walking'

| camin-an | (3PL PRES) | 'they're walking' |
| camin-ó | (3SG PAST) | 'he walked' |

(c) In Russian, several affixes may have some elements of meaning in common plus one or two that differ, for a many-to-many mapping. (These are not phonologically conditioned allomorphs.) There is therefore little consistency across nouns of different genders in the form of the affix that marks each grammatical case. Consider the singular forms for the nominative (subject), accusative (direct object), genitive (possessive), dative, and instrumental cases for the nouns for 'fairy tale' (first declension), 'leader,' and 'face' (both second declension) in Table 6–1.

Table 6–1 *Russian noun delensions*

	1st declension 'fairy tale' feminine	2nd declension 'leader' masculine	'face' neuter
NOM	skázk-a	vozhd′	lits-ó
ACC	skázk-u	vozhd-yá	lits-ó
GEN	skázk-y	vozhd-yá	lits-á
DAT	skázk-e	vozhd-yú	lits-ú
INST	skázk-oy	vozhd-yó	lits-óm

Most languages contain a mixture of such patterns in inflection and derivation. Some affixal meanings are mapped onto single forms, one-to-one, but many or most are mapped with a one-to-many, or many-to-many relation onto the forms they go with.

One proposal is that children should find it easier to map meanings onto forms where the mapping for affixes is one-to-one than where it is one-to-many or many-to-one (Slobin 1973, 1985b, 1985c). Support for this position has been adduced from bilingual children acquiring languages with different mappings for a specific semantic domain. In Hungarian, locative notions like 'in,' 'on,' 'into,' 'towards,' and so on, are each expressed by a single invariable suffix added to the pertinent noun-root. In Serbo-Croatian, the same notions are marked by case endings on the noun in combination with prepositions. Some of the prepositions take two different cases, with a different meaning attached to each combination. The same case-ending may co-occur with several prepositions, again with a different meaning for each combination. Hungarian, then, offers a one-to-one mapping for locative meanings and forms, and Serbo-Croatian, a many-to-many mapping. Which system is acquired earlier by Hungarian/ Serbo-Croatian bilinguals? When such children speak Hungarian, they produce many locative endings appropriately by age two. When the same two-year-olds switch to Serbo-Croatian, they omit the prepositions and make inconsistent use of case on locative nouns. The one-to-one mapping is acquired earlier (Mikeš 1967, Slobin 1973).

The major languages with extensive one-to-one mappings for affixes are typically agglutinating ones like Hungarian or Turkish. Children acquiring such languages produce many inflections appropriately at age two, and have little opportunity to produce over-regularization errors because the morphology of these languages is inherently regular.

Homonymy

The general vocabulary of a language – its nouns, verbs, and adjectives – rarely presents much one-to-one mapping, if only because over time, words tend to add extensions to their original meanings. This holds true for both agglutinating and non-agglutinating languages. As a result, the general lexicon of virtually every language contains mostly one form to many meanings in its mappings. This is even more evident in languages like French or Thai that, in addition, contain numerous homonyms – different words that sound the same (one form) but carry many unrelated meanings.

Although homonymy presents children with one-to-many mappings, it does not seem to cause them any difficulty in the lexicon at large. They seem to master the meanings of such homonyms as *night* and *knight*, *pair* and *pear*, *light* (illumination) and *light* (weight) without difficulty. There is no evidence that children avoid homonyms during acquisition. Rather, they appear to understand and use them from an early age. In English, even two-year-olds understand and produce many homonymous nouns and verbs, e.g., *bus, to bus*; *sled, to sled*; *truck, to truck*; *hand, to hand*, and so on. Homonymy also poses no problem for inflections. Children readily use homonymous inflections, again understanding and producing them with no apparent confusion (see Chapter 5).

Allomorphy

Another logical possibility, many-to-one mappings, with many forms for a single meaning, is in principle ruled out by contrast. In fact, its nearest equivalent is provided by phonologically conditioned allomorphy, where the form of nouns in the accusative case, say, may be determined solely by the phonological shape of the root. Learning each of the different forms in such systems becomes a matter of mastering word shapes, where these are governed in part by the sound sequences permissible for words of the language.

The commoner situation in allomorphy represents a many-to-many mapping where many forms are used to mark a particular case, for example, but their variety is actually determined by multiple factors in addition to phonological shape. One example of this, as we have seen, is the forms for each case in Russian which depend on the class of noun as well as on gender (masculine, feminine, neuter) and number (singular, plural). This is entirely consistent with the principle of contrast. When several apparently distinct forms appear to convey the same meaning, children do exhibit some difficulty as they map forms and meanings. Faced with several different forms all apparently used to mark case in nouns, they typically opt for just one form in production and use it, initially, to the exclusion of the others. For example, Russian-speaking children at first opt for the masculine and neuter -*om* and use it as the singular instrumental case on all nouns (Zakharova 1973). This outcome in the face of apparently synonymous case-markers is just what contrast would predict. By choosing only one form to mark a particular case on every noun, children avoid using apparent synonyms. Once they discover that the different forms do differ in meaning (they express, in addition to case, dimensions like gender and number), they can map the different forms and meanings according to the adult conventions for each noun type.

Regularization

Children appear to deal with some allomorphy initially by rejecting multiple forms in favor of just one to represent a particular case, say, or plural number. In doing this, they temporarily regularize the system. This results in what has been dubbed 'inflectional imperialism.' In English, for instance, children choose the regular past -*ed* to use on irregular and regular verb-roots alike, producing **taked*, **goed*, and **buyed* to parallel *jumped* and *walked*. They may also rely on a single means for marking plural, as in the regularized **mans*, **sheeps*, and **foots* beside *dogs* and *cats* (see Chapter 5). In French, children regularize verbs by assigning many in -*re* or -*oir* to the first conjugation in -*er*, as in **rier* (for *rire* 'to laugh'), **buver* (for *boire* 'to drink'), or **éteigner* (for *éteindre* 'to put out [a light]') (Clark 1985, Cohen 1969, Guillaume 1927). In Russian, children at first favor a single ending for each case and add it to all nouns, regardless of class or gender (Slobin 1966, 1973).

This solution to allomorphy, which results at times in the extensive over-regularization of certain paradigms, is one way of imposing contrast in the face of apparent synonymy among competing affixes. By selecting just one affix for a particular meaning, children also impose what looks like a one-to-one mapping. Once they analyze the input further, they realize that other distinctions are also encoded with the information about grammatical case: information about number (singular, plural, dual, collection), and gender (masculine, feminine, neuter) or noun class (human, animal, plant, material, etc.). As these dimensions are identified, children elaborate their inflectional system to add further forms that take account of number, say, or number and gender in combination, or number and case.

In summary, when children map meanings onto complex words, they have to identify all the affixes and roots. They presumably set up paradigms based on shared structures, and assign consistent meanings to suffixes and prefixes. (A single affix may carry more than one meaning.) At the same time, prior to full analysis, children may opt to produce only one of several allomorphs so as not to violate the principle of contrast. This in turn may make it look as if children favor a one-to-one mapping over many-to-one or many-to-many, but their tolerance for homonyms suggests that contrast rather than one-to-one mappings is what's at stake (see also Carstairs-McCarthy, in press). If children placed a premium on one-to-one mappings, they should not accept homonyms at this stage, but they do.

How do children deal with the mapping in complex words? Combinations in which the constituent parts are recognizable should be more *transparent* in that children can use the meanings of the parts in computing a meaning for the whole. But combinations that disguise the forms of the constituents in any way – with a shift in stress or a change in a vowel – should be harder to analyze or produce. Some of these operations may be *simpler* than others in the construction of complex words. We turn now to a more detailed characterization of TRANSPARENCY OF MEANING and SIMPLICITY OF FORM in children's interpretation and construction of complex words.

Transparency of meaning

When children coin new words, one factor that affects the forms they choose is transparency. The new meaning must be accessible in part from the elements making up the new word. Compare *pain-killer* and *analgesic*. They differ in register but otherwise express similar meanings. For speakers of English, *pain-killer* is the more transparent of the two. Its meaning is accessible from the two roots, *pain* and *kill*, and the suffix *-er*. In the same way, *kingly* is more transparent than *regal*, and *river-bank* more so than *riparian*. The more transparent of the two, in each case, is built out of familiar roots and affixes known from many other words.

The proposal here is that children rely on meaning–form mappings already known to them when they interpret unfamiliar combinations or coin new words. Once they map meanings onto more affixes, they can make use of these as well in constructing novel complex-words.

> *Transparency of meaning*: Speakers try to interpret and coin new words that are transparent in meaning – that is, words that are based on known roots and affixes.

Given this, it should not be surprising that children fail to detect the connections between pairs like *magic* and *magician* (less obvious in pronunciation than in spelling) or between *animal* and *veterinarian*. Instead they are likely to coin *magic-man* and *animal-doctor*, transparent versions of *magician* and *veterinarian*. Transparency increases when all the elements in a new word are already familiar.

What is familiar to children changes over time, so what is transparent also changes. Children are continually adding new words to their repertoires, increasing the number of roots and affixes they know. What is transparent to them at Time-2 may be very different from what was transparent to them at Time-1. The principle of transparency captures a dynamic factor in language acquisition. Children map massive numbers of word meanings onto word forms during their early years, and each new word analyzed adds to the stock potentially available when children construct innovative words themselves.

Coining words

Transparency predicts that children will at first rely on known roots for their coinages. Later, as they map meanings onto affixes too, they will use those as well. This suggests that they should coin words based on one or more bare roots alone before they coin any based on root and affix combinations. Evidence for this prediction comes from children's earliest coinages. Their novel verbs are all formed from known noun-roots, as in:[2]

> *to button* (2;4) for 'to press [the button on a calculator]'
> *to bow* (2;5) of a violin

---

[2] These examples are drawn from a large corpus of observations, many from my own data, others from data contributed by colleagues, and the remainder from published diaries and vocabulary studies.

to flag (2;5) for 'to wave like a flag'
to fire (2;6) for adult 'to light [a candle]'
to horn (2;6) for 'to touch with a horn'
to rug (2;8) for 'to vacuum the rug'
to bell (3;0) for adult 'to ring'
to cello (2;11) 'to play the cello'
to key (3;0) for 'put a key into'
to coastguard (3;1) for 'to make [a boat] act as a coastguard boat'
to gun (3;2) for adult 'to shoot'
to dust (3;4) 'to get dust on'

Here children rely on single roots. They use a known noun for an object involved in an activity to designate the activity itself.

Children's innovative nouns in English at this stage, as predicted, are nearly all compounds formed from two nouns linked with a primary-tertiary stress pattern. The constituent elements of such compounds are single nouns already present in the child's repertoire. Some typical examples with their intended meanings, are:

sky-car (1;6) 'airplane'
crow-bird (1;7) 'crow'
baby-bottle (1;11) 'bottle the child had used as a baby'
hole-sack (2;0) 'sack with holes in it'
cup-egg (2;0) 'boiled egg'
spear-page (2;1) 'picture of people with spears [in a book]'

Here too, children rely on roots only, in this case combinations of roots in noun–noun compounds, where the second noun designates the kind of object being talked about – a car, a bird, an egg. In fact, they often use the same head-noun in several compounds to denote members of the same category: for instance, a noun like *-man* for agents, as in: *rat-man* (2;0) 'man who works with rats [in a psychology lab],' *store-man* (2;5) 'clerk,' *firetruck-man* (2;8) 'fireman,' or *plant-man* (3;0) 'gardener.' Or a noun like *-car* for different kinds of cars, as in: *beach-car, taxi-car* (1;6); *-dog* for different kinds of dogs, as in *chow-dog, dalmatian-dog* (2;2), or *poodle-dog* (2;6), and *-bird* for different kinds of birds, as in *crow-bird* (1;6), *parrot-bird*, or *flamingo-bird* (2;7) (Clark 1981a, Clark, Gelman, and Lane 1985, Clark and Hecht 1982). That is, known words are used not only to construct new compound nouns but also to mark relations among the members of the same categories by using the same head-noun.

Using an affix

Further evidence for transparency comes from some early uses of affixes. The prediction here is that once children have mapped some meaning onto an affix, it becomes available for the construction of words with root and affix combinations. With a known root and known affix, such combinations will be transparent. In fact, when children first map meaning onto an affix, they sometimes then apply the affix, unnecessarily, to any words whose meanings make them candidates for use of that affix. For example, soon after age two, D began to add adjectival -*y* to all the adjectives already in his repertoire. Prior to this, he had produced several adjectives in adult form, e.g., *dark, wet, stuck, cold, nice*. Then at 2;2, within two weeks, he added -*y* to all the adjectives in his repertoire. As a result, he now produced forms like *dark-y, bright-y, nice-y, cold-y*, and *white-y*. Then, at 2;4, he began to construct novel adjectives by adding -*y* to known nouns like *crack* and *crumb*. That is, D first identified this suffix as carrying some adjectival meaning, and then used it to construct new adjectives from known roots.

Where a single affix carries more than one meaning, one of them may become known before the others. When this occurs, children may use that affix with just that meaning for some time before extending their uses to encompass the other meanings as well. An example comes from English-speaking children's early uses of the agentive and instrumental suffix -*er*. Young children often restrict innovative uses of -*er* to agents alone. D, for example, coined nouns like *brusher* (used of his mother brushing tea-leaves out of the sink with her hand), *climber, gunner* (of himself, having just announced that his block was a gun), and *cooker* (for real cooks and pictures of cooks) from the age of 2;0. Not until several months later, at 2;5, did he extend -*er* to mark instruments as well, as in the novel *hider* (for a wastepaper basket he inverted and put over his head), *sharper* (a pencil-sharpener), and *brakers* (for the brakes in the car). From then on, he used it for both agents and instruments.

Once children have mapped agentive meaning onto a suffix like -*er*, they can then make use of it in their own coinages while continuing to analyze other agentive and non-agentive uses. Eventually they will analyze -*er* as having both meanings and adjust their own usage accordingly. In addition, as they acquire the meanings of particular affixes, they may find that these compete with other ways of forming new words. For instance, where many two- and three-year-olds rely on compound nouns with -*man*, as in *fix-man* (2;9, 'mechanic') or *iron-man* (3;0, 'man who mends pots') for agents, older children may have a choice of options – compounds with -*man* or addition of *-er* to a verb or noun root. Both types of combination are now transparent. When faced with a choice, children should opt for the one more specialized for the meaning intended. If no one affix, say, is more specialized, they have to base their choice on some other factor.[3]

As children gain control over more roots, affixes, and compound patterns, the more transparent they will find any complex word they encounter. They will also have a larger repertoire of roots and affixes available. They presumably continue to make use of transparency whenever they coin words for meanings whose conventional expression they can't retrieve, as when one offers a paraphrase for the real thing (with tip-of-the-tongue difficulties), and on the many occasions where there is no conventional expression for the meaning intended. In the latter case, children and adults alike should normally opt for a more transparent one (*pain-killer*) over a less transparent one (*analgesic*), all other things being equal.

Transparency has an outcome of some import for language acquisition: although it is a property of individual words, it encourages the construction of paradigms – sets of like forms with related meanings – for example, all agent nouns formed with the suffix *-er*, all adjectives in *-y*, and so on.[4] Paradigms make up small or large groups of words related in form *and* meaning. They make explicit the *regularities* that are present in the lexicon. Paradigms in word formation provide templates for over-regularization analogous to that observable for inflectional systems.

Simplicity of form

When children produce their first words, they typically take as their target only one shape for each word, and use it on all occasions. In highly inflected languages like Finnish, Polish, or Russian, they may at first use a specific noun always in its accusative case form, and only after weeks or months contrast different case forms of the same noun in different contexts. In languages like Swedish and English, children use virtually no inflected roots in early production. This initial preference for bare words, or for roots with just one of many possible inflections, pervades the earliest stages of word production. It reflects a reliance on simplicity:

---

[3] How children (and adults) make such choices among transparent alternatives is taken up in the next chapter.

[4] Transparency also applies to root + inflection combinations: First, children have to analyze each inflection and map some meaning onto it. From then on, combinations of that inflection with different (known) roots will be transparent, just as root and affix combinations become transparent in word formation.

> *Simplicity of form*: Speakers find it easier to interpret and coin a
> new word the simpler it is in form – that is, the less its root
> changes in its construction.

The prediction here is that initially children will rely only on roots. These may be used alone, as in English-speaking children's innovative verbs from nouns and adjectives, for example: *to pillow* (2;6) 'to throw a pillow at,' *to monster* (2;8) 'to act like a monster towards' (hands like claws, roaring), *to dark* (2;8) 'to scribble over' (of a drawing), and *to flat* (2;10) 'to flatten'; or in combination, as in their early compound nouns like *sky-car* (1;6) 'airplane,' *hole-sack* (2;0) 'sack with holes,' or *cup-egg* (2;0) 'boiled-egg.' Here the prediction coincides with transparency, but this is not the case elsewhere.

Children acquiring other languages also hold to simplicity. In French and German, for example, they construct new verbs from bare nouns, again with no change in the shape of the root beyond the addition of verb inflections. In French, one hears verbs like *emboîter* (3;3, from *boîte* 'box' for adult *cacheter* [*une enveloppe*] 'to seal an envelope'), *poissonner* (3;10, from *poisson* 'fish,' for adult *pêcher* 'to fish'), or *pianer* (no age, for adult *jouer du piano* 'to play the piano'); and in German, verbs like *bildern* (1;10, from *Bild* 'picture,' meaning 'to turn over pages in a picture-book'), *leitern* (1;11, from *Leiter* 'ladder,' for adult *klettern* 'to climb a ladder'), or *flügeln* (2;4, from *Flügel* 'wing,' for talking about a cloth being shaken with an up-and-down motion). In both languages, such innovations typically take the verb endings from the largest and most regular verb conjugation (Clark 1982a, 1985; see further Chapter 11).

Children acquiring Hebrew also rely on zero-derivation, but to form nouns from verbs, again with no change in shape, as in established pairs like *shofet* '(a) judge' from the verb 'judges,' *menahel* '(a) manager' from the verb 'manages,' or *mocec* '(a) pacifier' from the verb 'sucks.' As in English, the change is a syntactic one, with new nouns marked by noun inflections. These bare forms appear in children's speech before novel nouns formed through a change in the internal vowels associated with the root consonants, and before nouns formed with suffixes or prefixes (Berman 1985, Clark and Berman 1984). The fact that children's earliest innovations all make use of bare roots only, without affixes, offers broad support for the influence of simplicity.

Simplicity also predicts that children will combine bare roots before they combine roots and affixes. And they do. Two-year-olds construct new root compounds like *plate-egg* (2;0) 'fried egg,' *car-smoke* (2;4) 'exhaust,' and *coffee-churn* (2;0) 'coffee-grinder.' Only around age five or older do they produce new compounds that combine roots and affixes, as in *wagon-puller* for 'someone who pulls a wagon/wagons' or *paper-cutting-machine* for 'machine for cutting paper' (both from five-year-olds) (Clark, Hecht, and Mulford 1986).

Measuring simplicity

Simplicity of form is relative to the typology of the language being acquired. What is simple in one language may not count as simple in another. Children grasp some typological properties early and build on them. They learn to express grammatical relations through inflections in some languages and through word order in others (Slobin and Bever 1982). For some languages, they learn that words consist of consonantal skeletons modified by vowels, as in Semitic, and for others that they consist of relatively invariant consonant–vowel sequences, as in Indo-European. For some languages, they learn that word-shapes do not vary, as in Chinese, and for others that they can be modulated with prefixes or suffixes, as in Indo-European or Uralic. In word formation too, what counts as simple can vary from one language to another. No change at all is the limiting case, but this option is not available in all languages.

Consider affixation. Affixes are typically classified as prefixes, suffixes, or infixes. From an extensive survey of the acquisition of inflectional systems, Slobin (1973) concluded that children found suffixes the easiest to master, prefixes the next easiest (definitely harder than suffixes), and infixes the hardest of all. But it is not always clear what counts as infixing. If the vowel-patterns intercalated with consonantal roots in Arabic or Hebrew are counted as infixes, then children acquiring these languages appear to find infixes easier than suffixes or prefixes (Badry 1982, 1983, Berman 1981, 1982, 1985). By age two to three, for example, Hebrew-speaking children rely on contrasting vowel-patterns combined with a consonant root to express past versus present tense. Either the infixing so characteristic of Semitic is not difficult after all, or the intercalation of vowels into consonant roots should not be considered as infixation.

There is a further lesson here: children adapt to the typological characteristics of the language they are exposed to very early. Given a language with suffixes and prefixes, children set to work on roots. Given a Semitic language like Hebrew where consonants combine with vowel patterns, they set to work on consonantal frames instead. Or consider vowel alternations: English-speaking children take some time to learn that for certain strong verbs, the past tense is distinguished from the present by a change in the vowel (e.g., *drink/drank, fall/fell*). They take even longer to learn the consonant alternations for derivational pairs like *electric* and *electricity* (Condry 1979, Moskowitz 1973, Myerson 1978).[5] Yet by age two, children acquiring Turkish or Hungarian show no difficulty with vowel harmony and readily change vowels in suffixes to make them compatible in height and frontness with root vowels (Aksu-Koç and Slobin 1985, MacWhinney 1973, 1978).

Simplicity of form may ultimately need to be assessed both absolutely across languages, and relatively within them. From an absolute point of view, no change should be simpler than some change in a form. Zero-derivation or conversion, wherever it is available, should count as the simplest option. Affixation comes next, but some affixes should be simpler than others. Those that leave the root fully visible, with no alterations, should be simpler than affixes that change the root. Suffixes should be simpler than prefixes, in part because the word being altered is readily identifiable from the sequence of segments that precedes the affix (Hawkins and Cutler 1988, Kuczaj 1979).[6] Both suffixes and prefixes should be simpler than infixes. This is because infixes make the root less readily identifiable than either prefixes or suffixes.

Each of these generalizations is also relative to the typology of the language being acquired. The morphological processes typical of each language will affect what counts as simple versus more complex as children learn more ways to change the form of a root to reflect a change in meaning. At present, little is known about how soon children identify the pervasive characteristics of their language, or how this may modify any general order of acquisition.

Compound constructions

Simplicity distinguishes compound types. First, compound nouns that require no adjustments in the form of either head or modifier are simpler than compounds where the head, for instance, is marked morphologically in some way as the head. (In Hebrew, for example, a word like *smixa* 'blanket' becomes *smixat-*, with a final *-t* when it appears as head of a compound.) This prediction is straightforward within a language like

---

[5] Latinate words like these are hardly used every day to two- or three-year-olds. The late acquisition of vowel alternations like that in *electric* versus *electricity* are therefore more likely attributable to the low frequency of such terms.

[6] See also Mithun 1989 on the acquisition of Mohawk, a prefixing language.

Hebrew (Clark and Berman 1987), but more difficult to apply across languages. Noun–noun compounds in English should be simpler than noun–noun compounds in Hebrew since Hebrew often requires a special bound form for the head noun. But is the addition of compound stress to two nouns (and compression of timing), as in English, a more or a less complicated change than a morphological adjustment to the head noun, as in Hebrew? Simplicity may be assessable within a language, but allows few direct comparisons across languages.

Second, both root and synthetic compounds always contain a head and a modifier. The noun *-rider* is the head in the synthetic compound *camel-rider*. In English, the head is always the rightmost noun. In other languages, the first or leftmost element may be the head. The modifier plus head ordering in compounds in some languages has the same order as in other constructions. In French, compounds like *casse-noisette* 'nut-cracker' have the same head and modifier order as constructions such as verb phrases, where the verb is the head, followed by the direct object as modifier (e.g., *il casse les noisettes* 'he cracks nuts') and noun phrases, where the noun is the head and any following adjective the modifier (e.g., *les enfants riants* 'the laughing children'). In French and in Hebrew, the order of head followed by modifier is consistent across most constructions. In English, children find less consistency: in some constructions, heads follow modifiers, as in compound nouns; in others, heads precede modifiers, as in verb phrases. The prediction here is that the consistency of such orderings is also a factor in the construction of complex words. In consistent languages, the order of head and modifier in synthetic compounds should be easier to master than in languages where this ordering is not consistent. And children coining synthetic compounds in Hebrew make no order errors, while children coining them in English make a large number of order errors (see further Chapter 8).

Finally, simplicity, like transparency, is dynamic. The changes in form required to mark a new meaning will become easier as children learn to produce complex words with different affixes and compound patterns. The effects of simplicity should therefore be most visible during the earlier stages of acquisition. It offers short-cuts to unskilled speakers. But as children learn more forms in their language, they will have less difficulty constructing new words with changes in root forms.

Simplicity versus transparency?

Simplicity and transparency often lead to the same predictions, but not always. They diverge in the acquisition of affixes. Consider simplicity: the simplest new words are those based on roots alone – uses of zero-derivation with roots and the construction of root compounds. The addition of affixes makes new words more complex. And further morphological adjustments such as vowel changes or stress shifts make them more complex still. Now for transparency: the most transparent new words are formed from known roots and affixes. The most transparent forms – zero-derived verbs from nouns, for example, and root compounds – are also simple forms. But with transparency, the next step is for children to add affixes, in order, to their repertoires. Once they know affix-1, any unfamiliar words that contain it become transparent. The same goes for affix-2, affix-3, and so on. That is, as each affix is acquired, any new words containing it or constructed with it become transparent. Transparency, but not simplicity, differentiates among root and affix combinations, depending on whether the affix is known. And affixes, within a language, are generally acquired in order. What is transparent, then, is not necessarily simple. But what is simple is transparent.

Some languages make more use of simple options than others. Children acquiring such languages should produce coinages at an early age. The simple options are also transparent. Other languages make much less use of simple options. There, children should produce few early coinages since it takes time for them to analyze the options that *are* available. In such languages, children must wait until they have acquired some of the available options so they can construct new words that are transparent. At the same time, they should also rely on simplicity, and so, for example, may add appropriate suffixes incorrectly, without the morphological changes needed.

Overall, simplicity should show up early in children's coinages provided the language offers simple options for constructing new words. Transparency also applies from the start, and predicts that children will always make use of transparent structures in their coinages. The two diverge where languages offer few simple options: there children must wait to master some affixes, for example, before they can construct new words. The typology of a language, then, affects how simplicity and transparency interact.

Summary

Transparency and simplicity often work together, but not always. Provided a complex word-form is simple and transparent, children should be able to produce it early. If it is not transparent but is simple, they should find it harder. And if it is transparent, but not simple, it should again be harder to produce. Overall, simplicity should take priority in those languages where simple forms are available options in word formation. These forms will become accessible early to children, e.g., the formation of verbs from bare nouns. In other languages, where affixation is commoner, transparency may take priority over simplicity. If no bare roots can be used for forming new words, children will at first produce few lexical innovations. They must wait until they have acquired some affixes. Coinages in these languages, then, should emerge only somewhat later than coinages in languages that offer simple forms.

Once children have assigned some meaning to a range of roots, affixes, and compound patterns, they are no longer limited by transparency per se in choosing which option to use on a particular occasion. All the possibilities are transparent. So they only have recourse to transparency upon encountering new complex word-forms. Equally, once children can produce all the different form-types in complex words, they need no longer limit their productions to forms that are simple.

One further factor affects children's choices when they coin new words: the accessibility of roots and affixes. What makes these accessible in part is the extent to which they are used by adults speaking to children. In the next chapter, I look at productivity, the degree to which adults have recourse to particular options when they coin new words.

7 Productivity

How do children discover the affixes and compounding patterns they need for coining words? First they need to isolate and identify the relevant building blocks. To do this, they must attend to recurrent elements in the speech around them, and to recurrent combination-types within words. By hearing many familiar roots all with the same added element, they can isolate an affix like -*ly* or -*er* and then assign some meaning to it. By hearing combinations of nouns with compound stress, they can identify combination types among compounds. Children must therefore hear enough examples of the relevant word-structures to isolate and store the relevant patterns. Access to such information depends critically on how productive each option is for constructing complex words. That is, the more productive an option is, the more accessible it should be and the earlier it should be acquired by young children.

What makes one form more productive than another? The speakers in a community have preferences in coining new words for particular meanings. They make active use of many word-formation devices. But some (like -*ness*) they use frequently, some (like -*ity*) only occasionally, and some (like the -*th* in *depth*) not at all. The ones they prefer for coinages and so use more frequently are productive. The first issue is how to identify speaker preferences and hence what is productive in word formation. In established words, usage reflects only what has become conventional. It does not tell one what a speaker would use in coining a word for a particular kind of meaning. Use in coinages must therefore be the criterion for productivity, since it is in coinages that speakers' preferences appear. The second issue is how children acquire these preferences: first, why do some elements of complex word-structure become accessible to children before others? And, second, how do children come to have the same preferences as adults in coining new words?

In this chapter, I will briefly consider several proposals for identifying productivity. They are all problematic because they are based on what is already in the conventional lexicon rather than on what speakers use in lexical innovations. An alternative is to use a composite measure based on contemporary preferences. This allows one to capture the information needed for assessing the role of productivity in acquisition. I will begin by looking at productivity characterized in terms of structure. The drawbacks to this approach lie in neglect of meaning, emphasis on conventional words already in the lexicon, and on frequencies that therefore reflect past, not present, productivity. I then take up two further proposals for identifying productivity: linguistic norms and usefulness. I then argue that productivity must be assessed from use in coinages. This criterion is central to the notion of productivity in word formation. Other proposals fail to the extent that they do not apply it. Finally, I consider how children might learn adult preferences in the coining of new words.

Structure-based models of productivity

Linguists have long focussed on word structure and the conditions that govern affixes. In inflections, productivity has generally been characterized as all-or-none: either an affix is productive (like past tense *-ed*) or it isn't (plural *-en*). Measures for inflections are typically based on existing forms in the lexicon. In word formation, however, productivity must be a matter of degree: some affixes can be attached to a larger number of roots than others and are therefore more productive (Anderson 1985, Schultink 1961). The negative adjective prefix *un-*, for example, attaches with few or no restrictions to past participles (e.g., *broken/unbroken, peeled/unpeeled*) and to adjectives ending in *-able* (e.g., *rideable/unrideable, openable/unopenable*), but not to monomorphemic adjective roots (e.g., *good/ *ungood, sad/*unsad, long/*unlong*). Its productivity is relative to the kind of root it can attach to (Zimmer 1964; see also Nida 1948).

Level-ordering

An all-or-none view of productivity is integral to recent analyses of level-ordering in morphology. Each affix and word-form type is assigned to one of three levels, based on its ordered combinatorial possibilities:

> Level 1 contains all irregular inflections, the primary (stress-changing) affixes (e.g., *-al, -ic, -ian, -ist, -ity, -ize*) and any semantically inconsistent forms (e.g., *business, wilderness, witness; capable, drinkable*).

Level 2 contains secondary affixes (e.g., *-er, -ness, -y, -able*) and all types of compounding.

Level 3 contains all regular inflections.

In this account, Level-3 members are regarded as more productive than Level-2 ones, and Level-2 members as more productive than Level-1 ones. For example, all Level-2 word-formation – the derivation of verbs from nouns (by zero-derivation, with no affix), nouns from adjectives with *-ness*, adjectives from nouns with *-y*, and all varieties of compounding – is considered more productive than any Level-1 word-formation – the derivation of nouns from verbs, verbs from adjectives with *-ize*, nouns from verbs with *-(a)tion*, nouns from adjectives with *-ity*, and adjectives formed with *-ic* or *-al* (Kiparsky 1982, 1983).

As an account of productivity, this model runs into difficulties because it ignores differences within levels. For instance, agentive *-ist* and *-ian* are both Level-1 affixes and hence not productive. Yet in technical domains, *-ist* is more productive, as demonstrated by speaker preferences, than both *-ian* (also Level 1) and *-er*, a Level-2 suffix that is thereby identified as productive. Or take another instance: all compounding is assigned to Level 2, yet compounding patterns in English vary greatly in their productivity. Some, of the type *chimney-sweep* and *bell-pull*, or *pick-pocket* and *turn-coat*, are no longer productive. Others, like *bottle-opener* or *waiting-room*, are highly productive in particular lexical domains (Adams 1973, Jespersen 1942, Marchand 1969, van Marle 1986, Quirk, Greenbaum, Leech, and Svartvik 1972). But in the level-ordering account, they are all considered productive to the same extent because they all belong in Level 2. Level-ordering does not distinguish differences in productivity within levels. A more general problem is that the analyses of levels are based on established, conventional words already in the lexicon, and so liable to display all the idiosyncrasies of forms and meanings that accrue over time.

Form and productivity

One attempt to consider lexical innovations comes from studies of potentially available forms – roots that could be used with specific affixes. Consider English *-ness* and *-ity*: *-ness* typically attaches to adjectives in *-ive* (e.g., *perceptive/perceptiveness*), and *-ity* to those in *-ile* (e.g., *servile/servility*). English also contains some *-ive* adjectives with nouns in *-ity* and some *-ile* adjectives with nouns in *-ness* (Walker 1936). Given the proportions of nominal forms in *-ness* and *-ity* for each adjective-type,

-ness can be adjudged the more productive of the two since it has been applied to a larger proportion of the available input roots. Its word-formation rule is more productive than the one for *-ity* (Aronoff 1976).

Are these frequencies in the established lexicon paralleled by people's preferences for one form over the other in novel words? Judgment studies show that people more often choose the suffixes identified, on the basis of existing words, as more productive (Aronoff 1980, Aronoff and Schvaneveldt 1978). These judgments were based on forms alone, on the assumption that the suffixes were synonymous. But English contains a number of word pairs where the same root occurs with *-ness* and *-ity*, to mark different meanings. Just as *variety* and *variousness* differ in meaning, so do newer pairs like *ethnicity* and *ethnicness* (Riddle 1985, Romaine 1980, 1983). Preferences for form alone offer an incomplete account. Measures of productivity must also take account of meaning.

Meaning and productivity

Meaning has been taken into account in a few studies of word-formation, typically through a minimal characterization of the meaning(s) associated with a word-formation rule or pattern: "Where one is dealing with a clearly productive morphological process, a simple statement of the semantic content of the process in question ... seems to be as much as can or should be expected" (Zimmer 1964, p. 32).[1] An affix should add the same constant meaning to any root, so the resultant combination is a composition of the meanings of root and affix. Form and meaning together, then, contribute to productive paradigms in word formation (Jackendoff 1975, Thompson 1975).

But some meaning-slots in paradigms are filled by irregular forms. The lexicon is made up of partially regular paradigms, and many, if not most, have some of their slots filled by forms that pre-empt the regular form that would otherwise have filled the relevant slot (e.g., the noun *cook* in lieu of *cooker*). Historical factors therefore affect productivity by pre-empting regular forms with predictable meanings. If such forms are used, they must be used with a meaning that contrasts with existing meanings. Their meanings generally violate compositional regularities in specific paradigms. For instance, the adjective *deep* has as its noun the irregular but conventional *depth*, instead of *deepness*. *Depth* pre-empts the use of

---

[1] See also Aronoff 1976, p. 45: "productivity goes hand in hand with semantic coherence."

deepness for the meaning carried by *depth*. With another meaning, *deepness* would be eminently acceptable. By the same token, if one root occurs with two or more affixes, the resultant combinations must contrast in meaning. Two or more verbs derived from the same root must differ, as in *to winter* ('to spend the winter') versus *to winterize* ('to make winter-proof'), or *to farm* ('to cultivate land/livestock') versus *to farmer* ('to act the farmer') (Clark and Clark 1979). Similarly, two or more nouns or adjectives derived from the same root must contrast in meaning, as in the established pairs *notoriousness/notoriety, official/officious*, or *ceremonial/ceremonious*. This is all predicted by contrast (Chapter 4). But if an established form is irregular for the meaning it carries, that will affect the productivity of the form that, other things being equal, would have carried the pertinent meaning.

Frequency and existing words

Many structural accounts of productivity rely on frequency to measure productivity. But most assess productivity from existing words, with greater frequency (counted on types) taken to indicate greater productivity in lexical innovations. This is problematic. At best, the forms listed in a dictionary can reflect only what *has been* productive in a language, not what is productive now. What has been productive will have been widely used in lexical innovations and should therefore appear in words coined earlier and adopted by the speech community. These words are what is counted when a dictionary is used to assess, say, the relative frequencies of suffixes. But what is productive for speakers changes over time. Witness the demise of English *-th* and French *-esse* as nominal suffixes (e.g., Broselow 1977). Many affixes and compound patterns that appear frequently in the conventional lexicon are no longer among those favored in contemporary coinages.

Dictionaries in general present an amalgam of past periods of productivity for different word-formation patterns. By their very nature, they cannot offer a measure of what is productive in lexical innovations today (see also Bauer 1979, Chmura-Klekotowa 1964). But they can be revealing about changes in productivity. Dubois (1962), for example, showed that there had been changes in which French suffixes were favored, by showing shifts from 1906 to 1961. Changes in established usage, and hence in productivity, were measured for each derivational suffix by looking at the words added from 1906 to 1961, the words dropped over the same period, and the words retained, in the relevant editions of the dictionary *Le Petit Larousse*. Dubois' measure of productivity, though, necessarily reflects past, not present, usage.

Although text-based word counts can tally relative frequencies (Carroll, Davies, and Richman 1971, Kučera and Francis 1967, Thorndike and Lorge 1944), these too may bear little relation to current productivity. For example, the distributions of certain affixes in the 5,000 most frequent words of English do not correlate at all with the distributions of the same suffixes in appropriate innovative uses elicited from eleven-year-olds (Sterling 1983). This suggests that measures of productivity based on frequencies in established words may have little connection with the productivity measured by lexical innovations.

A third problem associated with reliance on the frequencies of established words is that many sources – dictionaries and text counts – *exclude* innovative uses. Yet lexical innovations offer the primary evidence for productivity. Even if one could make an inventory of possible, though non-occurring word-*forms*, it is not possible to make a similar inventory of all the possible *meanings* such forms might carry. The meanings are in principle not denumerable. This is because speakers could coin the same form on different occasions with very different meanings, and those meanings cannot be predicted or listed in advance (Clark and Clark 1979, H. Clark 1983, Clark and Gerrig 1983). Any forms that can be listed in their entirety, for instance all the English nouns in -*th*, are thereby marked as *not* being part of a productive word-formation pattern, regardless of their actual number in the dictionary (Karcevski 1932, Kastovky 1986, Schultink 1961). Counts of established, conventional words, then, and structural analyses based on such counts, do not offer an adequate tool either in principle or in fact for measuring what is and what is not productive in contemporary lexical innovations.

Another approach, still based on existing words, is to look at the distributions of affixes in a spoken corpus. The argument is that well-established forms with suffixes like -*er* or -*ness*, say, will occur frequently, with many tokens of a single root–affix combination. If a suffix is truly productive, it will also occur just once each on a large range of different roots (e.g., *richness, blackness, stateliness, sadness, gladness*). That is, the more instances of a suffix on different roots in the corpus (*rich-, black-, stateli-, sad-, glad-*), the more productive it is. This ratio of type-ranges over single tokens, then, measures productivity based on spoken words. It also allows for comparisons of productivity within different semantic domains (Baayen 1991, Baayen and Lieber 1991; also Frauenfelder and Schreuder 1991). One drawback is that spoken corpora are as yet available for very few languages. The other is that this predicts productivity but does not base the measure on what speakers actually use in their innovations.[2]

In summary, structured-based accounts of productivity have focussed primarily on the structural conditions for use of specific affixes on words *already in* the lexicon. Could children learn adult preferences in coinage from knowing such conditions? Take level-ordering. The division of affixes into productive and unproductive would not allow them to discriminate the relative productivity of different compounding patterns, nor account for the differences by semantic domain in uses of *-er* versus *-ist* (see Clark and Cohen 1984). If mastering speaker-preferences in coinage was a matter of acquiring rules, we could expect children to acquire them on the basis of the relevant structural information. But children in fact acquire preferences not accounted for by structural theories (Clark and Berman 1984). Structural information alone, then, is unlikely to prove an adequate guide for the learning of adult preferences.

Norm-based models of productivity

Many countries set norms for language use, both in speaking and writing. Such norms, for speaking, are typically based on a prestige dialect, and for writing, on the literary tradition of the culture. The norms are usually set by the members of language academies established for the purpose of maintaining the purity of the language, and protecting it from too much foreign influence, for example, from borrowed words. Language academies often set their standards by appeal to literature and the written language rather than current spoken usage, and this tends to make them conservative guardians of linguistic form. The question is whether attention to such norms could lead children to adopt adult preferences in word coinage.

Norms are disseminated from language academies to schools, in the form of grammars, recommended word-lists, lists of new, acceptable words (e.g., in a new technical domain), and tests of language proficiency (e.g., in school-leaving examinations). They are disseminated to the public at large through official publications, usage in government documents, newspaper articles, published lists of official new vocabulary, radio presentation and discussion, and so on. Norms, then, not only provide guidelines for the

---

[2] Spoken corpora will, of course, contain some lexical innovations along with all the conventional words used, but the numbers do not permit any separate analysis of innovations.

construction of new words but also offer a measure of productivity in word formation. For each option, the normative recommendations about use would set productivity a priori. But how much do speakers observe such norms in their everyday speech? Many suffixes in French, for example, are specialized for scientific or technical meanings and so rarely appear in everyday innovations. There may be differences between the constituent elements in neologisms deliberately designed for new technologies in agriculture or genetic biology, say, and the nonce formations people coin for everyday use.

Normative recommendations are often based on an idealized analysis of past usage that makes it even more distant from contemporary speech. French and Hebrew, for instance, both rely on norms from the written language, while Swedish relies more on analyses of spoken sources.[3] As a result, in Swedish, planned innovations in technological domains tend to make use of everyday options in word formation. The greater the gap between norms and current usage, the less likely normative recommendations are to be effective. Speakers' natural preferences and shifts in preferences over time may diverge from official norms (Berman 1987, Clark and Berman 1984). In short, productivity can't be legislated. And if norms do not reflect speaker preferences, they seem like an unlikely source of information about productivity for children.

Function-based models of productivity

Speakers, one might argue, need ways to coin certain kinds of words. That is, some kinds of word-formation devices are more *useful* than others for filling gaps, and are therefore more productive. For example, if one particular paradigm-type is more useful than others, speakers will have recourse to it more often in coining words, and it will become very productive (Karcevski 1932). But usefulness is relative to each system in a language, and may well not be uniform across either languages or cultures. It may be useful, for example, in a society whose language has a large stock of nouns but few verbs, to have a device for forming nouns into verbs. Equally, it may be useful in a language with a large stock of verbs but few adverbial modifiers, to have a device for making fine distinctions among different kinds of actions. For acquisition, the question here is whether children could rely on this in order to find out what is productive.

---

[3] For French, see the Conseil International de la Langue Française (CILF), de Bessé 1980, Lodge 1991, Robertson 1910, Schlieben-Lange 1971; for Hebrew, Alloni Fainberg 1974, Blanc 1957, Morag 1959, Nir 1978, 1982, Rabin 1983; and for Swedish, Selander 1980.

If usefulness has some universal measure, it must first be assessed for each language against what is *already in* the conventional lexicon. But what is useful for filling lexical gaps may change over time, with cultural, sociological, and technological developments. Some forms will be more useful in that they are needed more often to fill gaps in the available vocabulary. For example, in English, one could plausibly argue that the agentive suffix *-er* is more useful than the borrowed agentive *-nik*, and this in turn would partially explain why *-er* is so much more productive than *-nik*. Or one might make more global comparisons among such affixes as *un-*, *-er*, and *-ly* on the one hand – all useful and hence productive – and *-cade*, *-(a)thon*, or *-kin* on the other – less useful and hence less productive.

This approach, though, is difficult to maintain. Let me take up three problems. First, usefulness might account for the presence of certain categories of word-formation devices, but some languages may lack devices for particular lexical categories that in other languages are widely used. English, for example, has no locative or collective affix for nouns. But what a language loses in word formation is typically made up in syntax (and vice versa). So the absence of particular word-formation devices may not be crucial after all. English makes up in part for the lack of a collective affix by relying on a set of pseudo-classifiers such as *a bunch of*, *a flock of*, or *a herd of*. Dutch makes up for the lack of a verb inflection equivalent to English *-ing* (with the meaning of limited duration) with no less than three syntactic constructions designed to express allied notions: compare English *He's waiting* with Dutch *Hij is aan 't wachten*, *Hij staat te wachten*, and *Hij is bezig te wachten*.[4] Such trade-offs are probably common, although there has been little systematic study of the issue (but see Anderson 1985, Talmy 1985).

A second problem is that roughly the same meaning is often expressed by several different devices. If productivity is a reflection of the usefulness of a specific device in filling gaps, one needs a principled way of selecting among affixes with closely related meanings, or among different compounding patterns. One solution might be a finer-grained analysis of usefulness that would take into account (a) structural constraints on root and affix combinations, (b) differences in register (e.g., speaking to children versus adults, friends versus strangers), and (c) differences in semantic domain (e.g., general versus technical, specific professional or technical fields). More detailed analyses of usefulness along a variety of dimensions

---

[4] These three constructions differ subtly in meaning but are all translatable into English with *-ing* (Donaldson 1981).

might predict where word-formation devices will be needed, and the meanings they should carry. But such an analysis would require unusual foresight about social and technical change, not only in a specific society but also in the world at large.

A third problem arises from the actual measurement of productivity. What should be counted? Are lexical gaps and categories of gaps identifiable a priori? What gets counted if some gaps are filled with a syntactic construction instead of an innovative word-form? What proportion of gaps would one expect to be filled through lexical versus syntactic options? The gaps that need filling where whole new technologies have developed, as in twentieth-century aviation or computers, should be easy to identify, after the fact. But what might prove most useful for filling gaps in the everyday language of conversation, argument, and daily interaction appears impossible to analyze. One would need to be able to enumerate all potential meanings a priori, a feat that is impossible. Function, then, as a basis for productivity, appears to raise more questions than it can usefully answer.

Function, like structure and norm, is inadequate as a source for learning adult preferences. While children are continually trying to fill gaps, they know much less about the conventional lexicon than adult speakers. It should therefore be even harder for them than for adults to anticipate the kinds of meanings that might be needed. Effectively, function-based accounts of productivity offer no form of measure that children could use as a guide for acquisition.

Contemporary preferences

Productivity reflects collective conventional preferences. It can't be equated in any simple way with word structure, frequency, norm, or function, even though these factors all play some role in shaping speakers' preferences for particular combinations of meanings and forms in the coining of new words. These preferences mirror their current perceptions of the meaning–form relations possible and available for use in coinage. And, I will argue, children can use these preferences as a guide in their coinages.

What factors do speakers draw on in forming such preferences? First, they should select from structurally possible options in their language, and not try to coin words that violate these. Second, they should make use of construction types that are easily analyzable and hence transparent

(Chapter 6). They should use forms in which the roots and affixes are identifiable so the meaning of the the new combination is largely predictable (Dubois 1962, Uhlenbeck 1977).

If both root and affix are to be easily recognized, then affixes that involve shifts in word stress, vowel change, or other adjustments should be less favored for coinages than affixes that make no changes in the root they are attached to. Does this distinction coincide with that between Kiparsky's Level-1 affixes, which often change the roots they are attached to, and his Level-2 affixes, which do not? The answer, perhaps surprisingly, is no. Level-ordering distinctions among affixes make no difference as long as the suffix does not deform the root. Provided this is the case, speakers show no preference in judging word form for Level-2 *-ness* over Level-1 *-ity*, for example, or for Level-2 *-ish* over Level-1 *-ial* (Cutler 1980).[5] The preference for unchanged roots, regardless of affix type, suggests that they are always more accessible in complex words than roots that have changed shape. Speakers presumably show a similar preference in their own coinages.

Third, speakers should take into account the usefulness of particular word-formation options available. If there is an affix with the right meaning available, it should be more useful in the pertinent semantic domain than related affixes with slightly different connotations from other semantic domains or even from other eras. This factor, like the others, is only part of what determines the precise nature of the coinage preferences in evidence at any one time in a speech community.

In the approach I will take, productivity is established by a complex of factors – structural conditions on affixes, accessibility of roots (in effect, transparency of meaning), and the usefulness of some option for that specific occasion. These collective preferences are captured by the notion of productivity:

> *Productivity*: In forming new words, speakers rely on the most productive option with the appropriate meaning.

Speakers' preferences for coinage have multiple causes, so the best measure of productivity lies in the actual word-types favored in lexical innovations.[6]

---

[5] The absence of a preference for Level-2 over Level-1 affixes goes counter to another study where adults showed a clear preference for Level-2 affixes (Aronoff and Schvaneveldt 1978; also Anshen and Aronoff 1988). However, all the Level-1 affixes in the latter required some change in the form of the root so no comparison was possible between accessible (unchanged) and inaccessible roots.

[6] Notice that speaker preferences must in each case reflect what any other speaker in the community would have chosen in like circumstances. That is, within a community, speakers share these preferences for coinages in common. They are conventional.

There are no ready-made measures of the coinage preferences among speakers of English, so these have to be determined empirically. Speakers can be asked to coin new words to convey novel meanings not already represented in the lexicon. They can also be asked to make judgments about which of two or more word-forms best convey a particular (novel) meaning (Berman 1987, Clark and Berman 1984). Such elicitations yield an index of the relative frequency for each form type used in coining words. The forms that appear more frequently in coinages are thereby considered the most productive of the options available. Judgments among alternative forms for a specific meaning should yield a similar ranking of preferences, with the form produced most often being the one chosen most frequently in judgment tasks. Such measures, applied both within and across lexical domains, can be used to determine speakers' current preferences within a speech community (Berman 1987). Those elements used most often in the speech community will constitute the pattern of preferences to which children receive the most exposure.

Productivity in acquisition

The forms children use in their innovations may not initially coincide with adult preferences. There are two reasons for this. First, children start out not knowing what is regular in meaning–form mappings within the lexicon as a whole. They only gradually analyze those elements that occur and recur in many different words. Second, they start out not knowing, for the words they hear, which are innovative and which conventional. Before they can acquire adult preferences, therefore, they have to analyze many word-forms for their semantic coherence – the consistency of meaning–form pairings – as they gradually set up a vocabulary, for themselves, of conventional lexical items. Neither an appreciation of regularity nor some knowledge of the conventional lexicon will necessarily lead children to use productive word-formation options.

How, then, might children come to match adult preferences in their own coinages? One possibility is that children keep tallies and use them to form their own preferences. Since coinage preferences are reflected in the frequency with which adults use particular word-formation options, children would need to do two things: First, they must attend to analyzable words and store them. The more frequently they hear a form, the earlier it should be analyzed. Second, children must set up a scale of preferences, derived from tracking input forms. This tracking will take account of all the forms children hear in a day, say, and add them to earlier tallies. The higher a form is on the scale, the more often (all other things being equal) it will be used. And within any domain, the highest tally can shift from one form to another as a result of shifts in the input.

Is such a tally based on type frequency or token frequency? Children should be tallying types for word formation. Evidence that they do comes from regularizations of inflections and from coinages. In inflections, for example, over 90 percent of French verbs belong to the highly regular first-conjugation (*-er*), but many of the verbs used most frequently to young children are irregular, third-conjugation members (*-re*). Which do children learn first, regular first-conjugation verbs or irregular third-conjugation ones? Inspection of their verb uses shows that they consistently regularize third-conjugation (*-re*) verbs (e.g., *prendre* 'to take') by placing them in the first (*-er*) conjugation, despite the fact that they produce and presumably hear many more *tokens* of third-conjugation than tokens of first-conjugation verbs. First-conjugation verbs, though, make up 76 percent of the *types* children produced, but only 36 percent of the tokens. The first conjugation, in fact, provides the basis for nearly all children's initial over-regularization errors in French verbs (Guillaume 1927; also Clark 1985). In word formation, both French- and Polish-speaking children rely most often on the suffixes favored by adults, and their preferences shift along with adult preferences. Children in the 1890s, for example, favored French *-ier* in novel agentive nouns, while children nowadays prefer *-eur* (Compayré 1896, Egger 1887, versus Aimard 1975, Grégoire 1947, Seidler 1988). The same reflection of adult productivity over time appears in Polish children's innovations, again with a shift in the specific affixes favored in the 1890s compared with 1960 onwards (Baudouin de Courtenay 1974 versus Chmura-Klekotowa 1964, 1972; see also van Marle 1988).

Type frequency should be more informative to children because of analyzability. The larger the range of types children hear, the easier it should be to extract an affix and assign it some coherent meaning relative to the root it has been added to. Compare the effects of hearing 100 tokens of a single type of agentive noun, say the word *rider*, with hearing five tokens each of 20 types – *rider, jumper, walker, builder, singer,* and so on. The latter set, with the larger type-range offers children more material from which to identify and analyze *-er* as an affix, and so to map onto it some meaning (see also Baayen 1991). Types, then, and not tokens, should be the most informative product of a tally. This information is presumably stored alongside information about meaning and form, semantic domain, register, and any structural conditions associated with options for constructing complex words. Such tallies must be kept not only by children, but also by adults. Productivity is a factor in word formation for all speakers of a language.

Another way that children could arrive at adult preferences would be via analogy. If children knew the word *ride* and wished to come up with an agentive form for it, they could simply search for another agentive word with a verb root, *walker* say, then substitute the root *ride* for *walk* to arrive at *rider* (MacWhinney 1978). This approach would incorporate information about adult usage by postulating that children would first search for the largest available target paradigm, i.e., agentive forms, and then use a member from that paradigm in constructing the new word needed.

In either case, children would have to take account of certain conditionalities. They would tag each form by context so as to take account of differences in domain or register for productivity. Speaker-preferences for one semantic domain need not match those for another. They would also have to track which kinds of meaning–form combinations can occur and which not (constraints on the meanings expressible), and which kinds of root–affix or root–root constructions are represented in the language (constraints on the structures of word forms). The combination of such information provides a route for learning the preferences exhibited by adults in the speech community.

The tally-based view and the analogy-based one both offer possible accounts of how children might master the coinage preferences of the speech community. Essentially, they offer two different ways of looking at the same data. There could be other accounts too. What all of them must contain is some mechanism for combining several kinds of information simultaneously so as to select the appropriate productive option for each coinage.

Finally, productivity depends on transparency, but not the reverse. To be productive, a complex word-form must be transparent (Chapter 6). But not all transparent forms are productive. Productivity is the factor that leads children to choose from among two or more transparent forms, which to use on a particular occasion. Unless there is some reason to do otherwise, children, like adults, should pick the more productive of the options available. But first, all the pertinent options must be transparent.

Summary

Speakers have preferences in coining words. Their preferred forms are the productive options for word formation within a speech community. Children must learn adult preferences as part of what they know about word formation. Traditionally, lexical productivity has been measured in terms of structural constraints on forms, or in terms of norms or function. The present approach is to consider speaker preferences. Actual coinages then become the criterion for measuring productivity. This measure shows that children acquire first those complex word-forms that are most accessible from input. And once two or more options are transparent, children choose which to use on the basis of productivity.

The next five chapters take up the effects of productivity, transparency, and simplicity, across several languages, in children's lexical innovations. Chapters 8 and 9 focus on the kinds of complex words children coin for things. Chapter 10 looks at a more specific domain – words for agents and instruments – with emphasis on elicited production-data from English, Icelandic, Hebrew, French, and Italian. Chapters 11 and 12 look at innovative words for actions. Chapter 11 focusses on how children form new verbs, typically from nouns. The data come mainly from spontaneous speech, again from several languages. Chapter 12 takes up a more specific domain – verbs for the undoing of actions. The data here are from spontaneous and elicited innovations in two closely related languages, English and German, that differ in the options available. They are compared with spontaneous innovations from other languages.

Together these five chapters present an overview of the kinds of spontaneous innovations children produce. These are supplemented by elicitation data that allow for more precise comparisons across languages. Systematic trends in spontaneous coinages first suggested that children apply general acquisitional principles in word formation. These studies offer a preliminary evaluation of the principles, and show how they interact with each other and with the typology of the language being acquired.

2

CASE STUDIES OF LEXICAL INNOVATION

Words are not coined in order to extract the meanings of their elements and compile a new meaning from them. The new meaning is there FIRST, and the coiner is looking for the best way to express it without going to too much trouble.

Dwight Bolinger 1975, p. 109

8 *Words for things*

Young children often wish to talk about things they have no words for. When this happens, they can fill the gap by coining a word just for the occasion. Such coinages form the topic of this and the next chapter. Children acquiring English coin many nouns, mostly words for things. The forms they produce and the order in which they master different forms are the topic of this chapter. I focus first on data from English and other Germanic languages, and then, in the next chapter, take up similar data from children acquiring other types of languages. Where possible, I have drawn on languages for which there are both diary observations and vocabulary records. For a few, there is also systematic elicitation of novel word-forms. All the data are drawn primarily from children under six. For each language, I take up predictions from transparency, simplicity, and productivity, and test them against the data available. I also consider how language typology affects and is affected by children's reliance on these factors.

English

As we saw in Chapter 1, English has two major options for forming new words: COMPOUNDING and DERIVATION. Derivation can be either with or without affixes. With compounding, nouns are formed from two or more nouns (as in *egg-plant* or *house-key*), known as root compounds, or from one or more nouns combined with a verb (as in *push-chair* or *marathon-runner*), known as synthetic compounds. The criteria for identifying compounds as compounds are phonological, structural, and semantic. Phonologically, most compound nouns have a main stress on the first, modifier, element, and weaker stress on the second, head one. Novel compounds almost invariably carry this stress pattern, but a few well-established ones do not (Adams 1973, Bauer 1983). Structurally, compound nouns act like single words. They can be preceded by articles and adjectival modifiers, and are followed by verbs that agree with them in

143

number. Semantically, they have meanings that are related to, but not fully inferable from, the meanings of their parts: a *dark-room* is not a dark room, but a room for photographic processing that can be made dark. The relation between the parts of a compound has to be learnt for well-established ones such as *dog-sled* ('a sled pulled by dogs') or *horse-box* ('trailer for conveying horses'), and it has to be computable for novel ones (Clark and Clark 1979, H. Clark 1983, Downing 1977). Root compounds, along with several types of synthetic compounds (exemplified by the types in *washing-machine, day-dreaming, baby-sitter,* and *home-work*) are all relatively productive in modern English (Adams 1973, Quirk, Greenbaum, Leech, and Svartvik 1972).

With derivation, English makes use of both prefixes and suffixes. Prefixes are few in number and rarely change the word class or the lexical class of a root. Productive prefixes include *un-*, used as a negative prefix on both verbs and adjectives in English, and on their associated derived nouns, e.g., *unhappiness, uncertainty,* and *re-*, used on verbs and their associated nouns, to indicate repetition or return to a particular state, e.g., *return, relocation.*

Suffixes, unlike prefixes, often alter the word class of the root. They can be classified by the end-product – whether they form a noun or a verb, for instance – and by the roots they apply to. For example, *-er* and *-ing* both generally form nouns from verbs (*mover, washing*), while *-ness* forms nouns from adjectives (*loudness*). Many of the nominalizing suffixes available in English are quite productive in specific lexical domains (Marchand 1969, Quirk *et al.* 1972).

In derivation without affixes (also called conversion), a word may change syntactic class with no added affix. This type of derivation is widespread in English where, for instance, many nouns can be made into verbs (*to trumpet, to launderette*), and certain verbs into nouns (*a wrench, an attempt*). With verb-into-noun, it can be used for talking about single instances of events involving the activity named, as in *a jump* meaning 'an act of jumping,' or some object used in the activity, as in *a jump* that one jumps over. This way of deriving nouns from verbs competes with such affixes as *-er, -ist, -ian, -ness, -ity, -tion,* or *-ism,* all also used to form nouns. This may be one reason why zero-derivation for noun formation has always been less productive than for verb formation.

Predictions

Transparency predicts first that children will form new nouns from known elements (typically, from whole words to begin with). Second, they will rely on zero-derivation before they combine roots with affixes. This is because they must learn the meanings of affixes before they can make use of them (Chapter 6).

Simplicity predicts children will make the fewest changes possible in constructing a new word. Since the least change is no change at all, they should rely on zero-derivation early if it is available. If they rely on compounding, they should construct bare-root compounds before synthetic ones with affixes. In compounds with a verb, simplicity predicts children will at first omit affixes. Later, they should add affixes to the head of the compound regardless of word order. It also predicts that children will use affixes that require no change in the root before affixes that require changes (Chapter 6).

Productivity makes two predictions. First, greater frequency in input will lead children to pick out more productive (more frequent) options before less productive ones. Second, when making a choice between transparent options, children will follow adult preferences and choose the most productive option for the intended meaning (Chapter 7).

These predictions will be assessed against innovative nouns for things. The data come from two sources: First, the detailed diary study of D's language development (Chapter 2), from which I have extracted a corpus of all his lexical innovations. For example, between the ages of 1;8 and 5;11, D produced 1,351 innovative nouns. This amounts to nearly one new noun a day over the four-year-period analyzed here. (He also produced numerous innovative verbs and adjectives, for an overall average of two new terms a day.)

This corpus is supplemented by a further 276 innovative nouns produced by a number of English-speaking children aged two to six. These come from three sources: (a) less systematic observations by myself of other children; (b) examples from published diary and vocabulary studies,[1] and (c) occasional observations supplied by colleagues. Each entry in the corpus consists of a child coinage, its context of use together with the apparent intended meaning, and notes on any conventional term with that

---

[1] Sources for this corpus include the vocabulary lists recorded by Bateman 1914, 1915, Bohn 1914, Boyd 1914, Brandenburg 1915, Chamberlain and Chamberlain 1904, Gale and Gale 1902, Grant 1915, Grey 1925, Langenbeck 1915, Mateer 1908, Moore 1896, Nice 1915, 1919, O'Shea 1907, Pelsma 1910, Snyder 1914, and Sully 1896.

same meaning; the child's age; and, where available, information on how often this coinage was used to express that meaning. (I draw on similar data for the other languages considered both here and in Chapter 9.) Observational data are supplemented where possible by data from elicitation studies focussed on specific aspects of children's word-formation.

Damon's innovative nouns

Analysis of the word forms D used at each age showed that he initially favored compounding in innovative nominals. Before age 2;0, compounding accounted for all his innovative nouns, and from 2;0 to 4;11, it accounted for over 70 percent of them. All the earliest compounds (before age 2;0) consisted of noun–noun combinations, where the second noun names the category type being talked about. From age 2;0 on, this type accounted for a decreasing proportion of his innovative compounds, from 74 percent at 2;0, about 60 percent at 3;0 and 4;0, down to 46 percent at age 5;0. Bare verbs combined with nouns made up only a small proportion of these compounds at any age (averaging 11 percent from age 3;0 to age 5;11), but verb–noun combinations with an affix added to the verb root accounted for an increasing proportion, rising from 25 percent at age 2;0 and 3;0, to 31 percent at age 4;0, and then to 44 percent at age 5;0. That is, from 5;0 to 5;11, he produced equal numbers of root and synthetic compounds. In his synthetic compounds, he used only -er (agents and instruments) and -ing (mainly instruments and affected objects).

Derived nouns with affixes made up about 20 percent of his innovative nouns between age 2;0 and age 4;11, with a rise to 34 percent in the following year. Over time, there was a gradual increase in the number of different affixes produced. At age 2;0, he used only -er (mainly for agents, with a few instruments), -ie (diminutive), and -ing (activities). At 3;0, he began to use the suffix -ness (states) as well, and at 4;0, he added -ist (specialized agents) and -ment (events). Finally, noun derivation *without* affixes was rare, and accounted for only 4 percent of his nominals from age 2;0 on. These data are summarized in Table 8–1.

Transparency predicts that children will make use of known forms in constructing new nouns. Initially, all D's compounds consisted only of bare nouns (or a bare noun and verb), but as he got older, he added affixes like -er or -ing as well. This paralleled the emergence of affixes in his derived nouns. He produced few affixes with any frequency in his innovations before age 3;0 – only a scatter of forms with -ie (diminutive), -er (usually

Table 8–1 *Innovative nominal types for D* 1;6–5;11 [*n* = 1,351]

	1;6–1;11	2;0–2;11	3;0–3;11	4;0–4;11	5;0–5;11
Compounds	100	75	76	73	62
Derived (+ affix)	–	22	19	22	34
Derived (– affix)	–	3	5	5	4
N =	[18]	[379]	[408]	[355]	[191]

Note: Percentages are based on the total innovations for each age.
Source: Clark, diary data

agentive), and *-ing* (activity). After age 3;0, there was an increase in the number of affixes used, as well as in their frequency. If children observe simplicity, they will opt for unchanged word-forms in coinages – words without affixes and compounds from bare roots. As predicted, D favored compounding. This is apparently the simplest option available for English-speaking children since zero-derivation isn't productive for noun formation.

Productivity predicts that children will first adopt the word-formation patterns that they have been exposed to, and second that they will choose more-productive over less-productive options. The affixes D produced first are among the most productive in English: *-er*, *-ie*, *-ing*, and *-ness*. Less-productive affixes, often with more specialized meanings, began to emerge only after age 4;0, e.g., *-ist* and *-ment*. Among D's compounds, the noun–noun pattern for objects affected by activities – a very productive one in English – emerged early. It was also used early on for some agents, as in *soccer-man* (2;5,18) or *money-man* (2;6,23), but the suffix *-er* became the primary marker for agency from age 3;0 onwards, in both compound and derived nouns.

Overall, D's spontaneous innovations offer evidence that simplicity is influential early on, but the choice of a simple form also depends on productivity – which forms the child is exposed to. As D analyzed more affixes, they too became available for use. Once he had acquired several affixes in a domain, he appeared to favor the most productive option, e.g., *-er* for agents, unless there was some reason for another choice, e.g., *-ist* for types of musician, as in the novel *drummist* and *flutist* (both at 4;6,27).

Table 8–2 *Innovative nominal types in vocabulary studies* [$n = 274$]

	2;0–3;11	4;0–6;0	Mean
Compounds	80	63	70
Derived (+ affix)	13	26	21
Derived (− affix)	7	11	9
N =	[207]	[67]	

Note: Percentages are based on the total innovations for each age.
Source: Corpus from vocabulary studies.

Other children

Analysis of the second corpus of spontaneous innovations showed almost identical patterns. Compounds accounted for 70 percent of the innovative nouns overall, zero-derivation accounted for 9 percent, and derivation with affixes for 21 percent. When the children were divided by age, the younger ones – under age four – relied on compounds 80 percent of the time, on zero-derived forms 7 percent of the time, and on suffixes just 13 percent of the time. Older children relied on compounds somewhat less often (63 percent), and on suffixes rather more (26 percent) than younger children, as shown in Table 8–2. The shift from compounding to a larger proportion of affixation with age offers further support for the predictions of both transparency and simplicity.

The prevalence of compounding in young children's speech is also attested in experimental studies designed to elicit labels for as yet unnamed objects from two- and three-year-olds (Clark, Gelman, and Lane 1985, Gelman, Wilcox, and Clark 1989). When asked to name things, they often rely on compound nouns to differentiate objects within categories, e.g., *cup-tree* versus a *pencil-tree* (for two pictures of trees with cups and pencils respectively, in place of leaves). This contrastive function of noun–noun combinations is also present in adult speech, as in the attested innovations *moon-flag* versus *star-flag* (for flags decorated with moons and stars respectively), or in the established *law-man* and *air-man* (Clark *et al.* 1985, Downing 1977). In another elicitation study that asked children for labels for the agents of unfamiliar actions, three-year-olds relied on compound nouns 28 percent of the time, but older children relied almost entirely on derived nouns with the suffix *-er* instead (Clark and Hecht 1982; see further Chapter 10).

English-speaking children make use of only a few affixes in their spontaneous innovations. They often use *-er* on verb roots, for agents and instruments, as in *cooker* (2;4,18) for a cook, *teaser* (3;1,20) for someone who fools around and teases, or *presser* (3;0,5) for a button that has to be pressed to let water run out, and *lockers* (3;4,26) for locks; they also make occasional use of the diminutive *-ie*, as in *cattie* 'little cat' (2;2) or *forky* '(little) fork' (2;0), and, from about age four on, some instances of *-ness*, as in *angriness* (4;8) for 'anger' or *strongness* (5;6) for 'strength.' Affixes appear in children's innovations later than compounding, as predicted by both transparency and simplicity.

Some suffixes are simpler in form than others: *-er*, for instance, is merely added to the end of the pertinent root, as in *jump* to *jumper*, with no change in the form of the vowel or adjacent consonants of the root, but *-ist* is typically added only to Latin or Greek roots; and, unlike *-er*, it also functions as an adjectival suffix. Other suffixes, like *-ity* or *-(a)tion*, may require one or more of the following operations as well: changing the vowel of the root, as in *clear/clarity*, *metre/metrical*; shifting stress, as in *method/methodical*; and changing the final consonant in the root, as in the shift from /t/ to /š/ in *distort/distortion*. These adjustments are acquired late, typically some time after children have begun to read (Condry 1979, Moskowitz 1973, Myerson 1978; see also Cutler 1980, Jaeger 1984, Steinberg and Krohn 1975).

The data from both spontaneous and elicited innovations, then, show that compounding is heavily favored over derivation for noun-formation in two- and three-year-olds. Older children make greater use of affixes in their construction of new nouns. This shift with age appears in both spontaneous and elicited innovations.

Compounding with noun–noun combinations is very productive in English, as attested by both adult and child coinages. Among the innovative compounds in various diary and vocabulary studies, 89 percent from children up to age four were bare noun–noun combinations. This figure is matched by 86 percent of those from children over four. Compound nouns containing a bare verb are much less productive, and this is also reflected in children's spontaneous coinages: only 12 percent of their compounds contained verb roots. Many of these are ungrammatical because they lack affixes. Synthetic compounds in English often require an affix on the verb root, as in the established *washing-machine* or *hair-drier*.

Table 8–3 *Stages in the acquisition of compounds with verb roots*

Stage	Compound form	Example
1	*Verb + Noun$_{head}$	*wash-man, open-man*
2	*Verb + Noun$_{object}$	*hug-kid, break-bottle*
	*Verb-*ing* + Noun$_{object}$	*moving-box, throwing-ball*
	*Verb-*er* + Noun$_{object}$	*cutter-grass, puller-wagon*
3	Noun$_{object}$ + Verb-*er*	*water-drinker, well-builder*

Source: Clark, Hecht, and Mulford 1986

When children were asked to form compound nouns with verb roots in an elicitation task, the younger children (aged three) used the bare verb as a modifier with such familiar head nouns as -*man*, -*thing*, or whatever term designated the kind of category being talked about, as in *a pull-man* or *a open-thing*, in Table 8–3. At the next stage, they began to form the compound directly from the verb phrases given in the elicitation task. For example, in responding to a question like *What could you call a girl who pulls wagons?* they extracted the verb phrase (*pulls wagons*), stripped it of affixes, and formed a compound with compound stress, namely *a pull-wagon*. In such compounds, they correctly treat the verb root as the head: when they add an affix like -*er*, they attach it to the head, the leftmost element, as in *a puller-wagon*. Only around age five to six do they master the order in these compounds and place the head in the rightmost slot (Clark, Hecht, and Mulford 1986).

Lastly, nouns formed via zero-derivation, without affixes – the simplest option among those for constructing new nouns – appeared only rarely, 7 percent of the time among innovations from under fours and 11 percent of the time from over fours. This relative lack of reliance on zero-derived forms reflects the unproductive nature of this option. But children did form new nouns this way some of the time: one meaning associated with such nouns is that of an instrument pertinent to the activity denoted by the verb. And instrument meanings accounted for 63 percent of children's zero-derived nouns overall, with the proportion of such uses doubling with age, from under to over age four. Where zero-derivation is the major option, with few competitors, young children rely on it more (see Chapter 11).

Other Germanic Languages

The major word-formation options in other Germanic languages are similar to those in English, although there are differences of degree in the relative productivity of the options available. For example, English relies to a greater extent than other Germanic languages on zero-derivation in verb formation because it possesses few verb-forming affixes with this option compared with the other Germanic languages. But overall, the options available are rather similar across such languages as Dutch and German, Swedish and Icelandic. General lexical and acquisitional principles therefore predict a developmental story for these languages similar to that for English.

Dutch

In Dutch, as in English, new words can be formed through compounding and derivation. Compounding in Dutch is very productive, and serves as a major source of new nouns, both from bare noun–noun combinations and from combinations with a linking form (*-en*) on the first noun (e.g., *grasperken-scheerder* 'lawn-mower' or *astronauten-schoenen* 'astronaut-shoes'). Much as in English, primary stress is placed on the first, modifier, element in Dutch compounds (Booij 1977). The derivational options for forming nouns are mainly suffixal, as when verbs are made into agent nouns with *-er* or its less frequent allomorph *-aar* (e.g., *fietsen/fietser* 'to bicycle/bicyclist,' *leren/leraar* 'to teach/teacher'); or adjectives into nouns with suffixes like *-e*, *-heid*, and *-te* (e.g., *goed/het goede* 'good/the good(ness),' *rijk/de rijke* 'rich/the rich [man]'; *waarheid* 'truth,' *vrijheid* 'freedom'; *hoogte* 'height,' *flauwte* 'faintness.' Nouns can also be formed from verbs via zero-derivation, with either activity meanings, from verb infinitives (e.g., *het eten* 'eating, food,' *het geven* '(act of) giving'), or product meanings, from bare verbs (e.g., *de lach* 'the laugh,' from *lachen* 'to laugh'; *de loop* 'the walk, gait,' from *lopen* 'to walk'). This is less productive in Dutch than compounding (Baayen 1989, Booij 1977, 1979, Donaldson 1981, Rijpma and Schuringa 1969, Toorn 1976).

Overall, simplicity of form predicts early reliance on compound nouns formed from noun roots, and only later from noun and verb combinations. Among affixes, children should opt for suffixes before prefixes, and for the most frequent among the available affixes in a particular domain before less frequent ones. Other things being equal, this is the initial effect of productivity. Transparency of meaning likewise predicts that children should begin with compounding, using as head nouns ones that designate

Table 8–4 *Typical innovative nouns from Dutch-speaking children*

Age three and under

(1)   (2;6) *koppie-tafel* 'coffee-table' (for adult *teetafel*)
(2)   (3;0) *water-man* 'man who distributes water'
(3)   (3;0) *trem-boeken* 'tram-books' [= books of tram tickets]
(4)   (3;0) *sport-hond* 'sport-dog' [= dachshund]
(5)   (2;7) *hoffer* 'someone who works at court' (from *hof* 'court'/adult *hoveling* 'courtier')
(6)   (2;7) *snijter* 'cutter' (from *snijden* 'to cut'/adult *mes* 'knife')
(7)   (2;6) *timmer* 'hitter' (from *timmeren* 'to hammer')
(8)   (2;7) *een snijt* 'a cut' (from *snijden* 'to cut'/adult *mes* 'knife')

Age four and over

(9)   (4;3) *zakdoek-boek* 'handkerchief-book' (a book with a handkerchief between the pages)
(10)   (4;4) *pijltjes-waterpistool* 'arrow-waterpistol' (for a waterpistol that could shoot little arrows)
(11)   (4;7) *herfst-appel* 'autumn-apple' (pointing at an apple that was red and yellow)
(12)   (4;8) *maan-nootjes* 'moon-nuts' (for adult *cashewnoten* 'cashew nuts')
(13)   (5;9) *watervliegtuig-veld* 'waterplane-field' (looking at a picture of a seaplane about to land)
(14)   (6;4) *winter-juffrouwtje* 'winter-miss' (for a girl in a white coat)
(15)   (4;3) *vrouwen-maker* 'women-maker' (for a person who can make boys into women, so they won't have to grow a beard)
(16)   (4;4) *steek-mond* 'stab-mouth' (making the handle of a spoon protrude from his mouth)
(17)   (4;6) *stop-voeten* 'stop-feet' (for adult *karteltjes* 'notches,' the serrated edge on a skate blade)
(18)   (5;0) *strooi-wagen* 'sprinkle-wagon' (for adult *straat-reiniger* 'street-cleaner')
(19)   (c. 5;0) *eet-winkel* 'eat-shop' (for adult *restauratie* 'restaurant')
(20)   (5;9) *steel-jongen* 'steal-boy' (for adult *dief* 'thief')

Source: Elbers 1988, Kaper 1959, Schaerlakens 1980, Tinbergen 1919, de Vooys 1916

the kinds of category being talked about, e.g., *-man* '-man' for agents, say, and category labels like *-hond* '-dog' for affected objects. Productivity further predicts that, within lexical domains, older children will rely more on the most productive device among the options available.

The analysis of Dutch is based on a corpus of 103 innovative nouns. These were drawn from several diary studies, short reports of novel word-formation, and one elicitation study with elementary school children (Elbers 1988, Kaper 1959, Schaerlaekens 1980, Smedts 1979, Tinbergen 1919, de Vooys 1916). Overall, the data offer a much less detailed picture than that available for English. The corpus is made up of 75 percent compound nouns and 25 percent derived ones. These percentages show little change with age: children three and under produced compounds 77 percent of the time, mostly noun–noun combinations, as illustrated in Table 8–4. Their derived forms rely heavily on agentive or instrumental -*er*, as in *een hoffer* (2;5) for someone who works in *een hof* 'a court,' or *een timmer* (3;6) 'a hitter' (from *timmeren* 'to hammer') for a drummer or a carpenter, and on the diminutive suffix, usually -*je* (and its allomorphs), as in *zingetjes* (5;0) 'little songs' (for adult *liedjes*). Children also produced some nouns derived without any suffix from a verb, as in *een snijt* 'a cut' (for adult *mes* 'a knife,' 2;7) or *een spring* 'a leap, jump' (for adult *sprong*, 6;0).

Children over four still rely on extensive compounding (73 percent of the novel nouns counted), and use both root compounds and synthetic ones, as shown in Table 8–4. A number of these compounds appear to be used with a contrastive function, as in such pairs as *bromhoed* '(motor)cycle-hat' (for adult *valhelm* 'crash helmet') versus *zwemhoed* 'swim-hat' (for adult *badmuts* 'bathing-cap').

Children appear not to use verb roots at all in their early compound nouns. When they do use them, there is some tendency, as in English, to combine the verb root and the noun for the object affected in verb–object order, as in the following examples noted by parents, all from children under age six:[2] *een stop-kinderen* 'a stop-children' (for a school-crossing guard/adult *verkeersbrigadiertje*), *huil-knoopjes* 'cry-drops' (for tears/adult *tranen*), *krak-doosje* 'break-box' (for an egg-shell/adult *eierschaal*), and *rij-voeten* 'ride-feet' (for rollerskates/adult *rolschaatsen*). Even twelve-year-olds sometimes retain verb–object order in their compounds, as in *een mix-soep* 'a mix-soup,' coined as a term for a machine that mixed soup in lieu of *soepmixer* 'soup-mixer,' the preferred form (Smedts 1979).

In summary, Dutch-speaking children rely largely on compounding, initially with noun roots only, to form new nouns. From three or so on, they also construct compounds with verb roots, and they begin to use suffixes. As in English, they make little use of verbs with zero-derivation when they form new nouns.

---

[2] These examples are drawn from the occasional reports published in *Libelle*, from 1973 to 1975. I am grateful to Guus Extra for bringing them to my attention.

German

The word-formation options in German, and the predictions made by simplicity of form, transparency of meaning, and productivity, are virtually identical to those made for Dutch. What varies somewhat, of course, across such closely related languages, is which options are the most productive in particular semantic domains (Brekle 1978, Curme 1964, Dressler 1985). Again, the data from children's spontaneous innovations appear very similar to those in English and Dutch.

German-speaking children rely heavily on compounding from the start. In a corpus of 128 innovative nouns extracted from diary data, 80 percent of the nouns from children under three are compounds, and virtually all are constructed with two bare nouns, as shown in Table 8–5.[3] Many compounds noted in the diaries mark an explicit or implicit contrast between two subcategories, as in *Fenster-haus* 'window-house' (for a house made of building blocks with several windows, 2;9) and *Lantern-haus* 'lantern-house' (for a house with a glass-roofed balcony, 2;9), both subkinds of house, or the trio of compounds from a four-year-old: *Schnee-berge* 'snow-mountains,' *Felsen-berge* 'rock-mountains,' and *Woll-berge* 'wool-mountains' (for snow-covered mountains, rocky crags, and heavily wooded slopes, respectively). The remaining innovations are split between the *-er* and *-e* suffixes, both used to derive nouns from verbs. The *-er* nouns generally denote agents rather than instruments (in a ratio of 3:1). In contrast, almost all the *-e* nouns recorded denote instruments (see Table 8–5).

Older children use proportionately fewer compounds and more derived nouns among their innovations. The percentage of compounds decreases somewhat, to 66 percent, with a concomitant rise in use of the suffix *-er*, to 24 percent. (The data contain many more instances of each noun type for the older children than the younger ones, by ratios of 3:2 for compounds, 4:1 for *-er*, and 2:1 for *-e*.)

When the older children construct compounds, they use both noun and verb roots. As in English and Dutch, the earliest verb roots in compounds appear with the bare verb as a modifier, as in *Schiess-männer* (2;11) 'shoot-men' (from *schiessen* 'to shoot,' for adult *Zinnsoldaten* 'tin-soldiers'). Four-year-olds also use bare verbs as modifiers in compounds for objects affected, as in *Dreh-schraube* (4;1,15) 'wind-screw' (from *drehen* 'to wind,'

---

[3]   The German corpus was compiled from innovations listed in Stern and Stern 1928, with additional data from Neugebauer-Kostenblut 1914, 1916, 1917, and from Augst 1984a, 1984b, Augst, Bauer, and Stein 1977, Panagl 1977, and Plank 1976.

Table 8–5 *Typical innovative nouns from German-speaking children*

Age three and under

(1) (2;7) *Korb-wagen* 'basket-wagon' (for a small doll's pram of woven straw)

(2) (2;9) *Löchern-teller* 'holes-plate' (for a glass table mat with metal filigree work on it)

(3) (3;4) *Wiege-uhr* 'cradle-clock' (for a kitchen-scales dial)

(4) (3;6) *Frisier-mann* 'cut-man' (from *frisieren* 'to cut (hair)'/adult *Friseur* 'barber')

(5) (3;9) *Bau-mann* 'build-man' (from *bauen* 'to build'/adult *Maurer* 'mason')

(6) (3;9,15) *Bauer* 'builder' (from *bauen* 'to build'/adult *Baumeister*)

(7) (2;10) *der Wurster* 'the sausager' (from *Wurst* 'sausage'/adult *Fleischer* 'butcher')

(8) (3;11) *ein Klingler* 'a ringer' (from *klingeln* 'to ring', for someone who mends bells)

(9) (3;11) *ein Musik-macher* 'a music-maker' (for an elephant seen playing a barrel-organ)

(10) (2;9,15) *die Schneide* 'the cut' (from *schneiden* 'to cut'/adult *Schere* 'scissors')

(11) (2;10) *die Kloppe* 'the beat' (from *klopfen* 'to beat'/adult *Fleischkopfer* 'meat chopper')

(12) (3;6) *die Schliesse* 'the shut' (from *schliessen* 'to shut'/adult *Klinke* 'latch')

Age four and over

(13) (4;8, comparing types of mountains) *Schnee-berge* 'snow-mountains,' *Felsen-berge* 'rock-mountains,' *Woll-berge* 'wool-mountains' [= covered in trees]

(14) (5;8) *Cowboy-dings* 'cowboy-things' (for adult *Lasso* 'lasso')

(15) (5;11) *Welt-buch* 'world-book' (for adult *Atlas* 'atlas')

(16) (4;1,15) *Kellner-haus* 'waiter-house' (for a place where the family had stopped for refreshments)

(17) (4;4) *der Fischler* 'the fisher' (for adult *Angler* 'fisherman')

(18) (4;5) *der Stehler* 'the stealer' (from *stehlen* 'to steal'/adult *Dieb* 'thief')

(19) (4;5,15) *der Senser* 'the scyther' (from *sensen* 'to scythe', for a person scything)

Source: Augst *et al.* 1977, Brekle 1978, Panagl 1977, Stern and Stern 1928.

for adult *Fruchtpresse* 'fruit-press'). The verb roots in these compounds are stripped of inflections and lack any nominal suffixes. But it is unclear whether German-speaking children at any stage produce compounds with a verb–noun order in their synthetic compounds, where the noun refers to the object-affected, as English and Dutch children do.

Finally, a study of the active vocabulary of German children about to enter school also tallied the numbers of lexical innovations present. Parents and friends noted all the words used by ten upper-middle-class children (from age 5;8 to age 6;0). On average, these children used innovative words 10.5 percent of the time. In individual children, however, the proportion of lexical innovations was sometimes as high as 19 percent. For one child, 87 percent of the novel nouns were compound in form, and 13 percent derived by means of a suffix only. The most favored word-formation patterns were two- and three-element root compounds, where all elements were generally nouns (Augst, Bauer, and Stein 1977; also Augst 1984a, 1984b).

In summary, children acquiring German favor compounding in their novel nouns, as predicted by both simplicity and transparency. As in English and Dutch, compounding emerges before any affixation, and it remains the dominant option for new nouns even for five- and six-year-olds. The first derivational suffixes appear between age 2;6 and age 3;0, and are typically used to derive agent and instrument nouns from verbs. Reliance on affixation, mainly suffixes, increases with age.

Icelandic and Swedish

These two languages rely extensively on compounding, but they also possess a large stock of derivational suffixes. In Icelandic particularly, speakers rely on a variety of ways of forming nouns through modification of the vowels in a verb root.[4] Icelandic also uses derivational suffixes used to form nouns from verbs and adjectives, e.g., *-ari* and *-andi* for agent nouns from verbs; *-ð/-d/-t* to form feminine state nouns from adjectives; *-(n)aður/-(n)uður* for masculine activity nouns from verbs, and so on. Compounding is common, with the order modifier followed by head. The head and modifier may be bare roots, or be linked with a connecting vowel or genitive case-marking (Einarsson 1945, Friðjónsson 1978, Kiefer 1970, Mulford 1980). Swedish is very similar to Icelandic. It too makes extensive

---

[4] Icelandic is the most conservative of the Germanic languages and has retained some word-formation options now lost to other Germanic languages.

use of compounding, but relies rather less on vowel changes for derivation (Kiefer 1970, Söderbergh 1968, Thorell 1981).

Simplicity of form and transparency of meaning predict that children should rely on compounding before derivation. In Icelandic and in Swedish, children should therefore rely early on bare noun–noun compounds. Simplicity predicts they should also rely on zero-derived nouns. The latter is a more productive option in Icelandic than in either German or English. Once children begin to acquire affixes, they should first identify those used most frequently, and later opt for the most productive option unless there is some semantic reason not to.

The data on Icelandic show that young children, as predicted, rely extensively on compounding to form new nouns. One Icelandic child recorded monthly from 2;0 to 3;6 produced novel compound-nouns at each session.[5] Most consisted of two nouns combined (92 percent), and only six compounds (7 percent) contained a bare verb root in the initial modifier slot. As predicted, most of the child's compounds combined two nouns with no linking vowel or case marking. And as in English, many of the child's compounds named subcategories of familiar basic categories, and were thus implicitly or explicitly contrastive, e.g., *fólsvagna-bíll* 'Volkswagen-car' and *fíata-bíll* 'Fiat-car' (2;4,12), *kubba-bíll* 'block-car' (for a car made of blocks), and *flösk-bíll* 'bottles-car' (for a milk-truck, both at 2;4,25), or *sjónvarp-maður* 'television-man' (for a picture of man carrying a television), and *flugvél-maður* 'airplane-man' (for a pilot, both at 3;3,4). Compounding evidently has the same contrastive function in Icelandic as in other Germanic languages (see Clark *et al.* 1985, Berman and Clark 1989).

Children also make use of zero-derived forms for nouns at an early age. When Icelandic-speaking three-year-olds were given a simple elicitation task, they made use of zero-derived nouns (identical in form to the verb infinitive) for 23 percent of agentive nouns and for 34 percent of instrument nouns. They also made considerable use of the *-ari* suffix, used for 57 percent of their agents and for 43 percent of their instruments. They made relatively little use of compounds in this task (6 percent) or any other derivational affixes (4 percent). By age six, though, they relied almost entirely on the productive suffix *-ari* for both agents (98 percent) and instruments (78 percent) (see Chapter 10). These findings are consistent with the predictions of simplicity and transparency.

---

[5] I am indebted to Randa C. Mulford for letting me cite from unpublished longitudinal data on the acquisition of Icelandic.

Harder to assess is the effect of productivity since no adult data were collected in the elicitation task. However, a count of the agent and instrument nouns in the Icelandic translation of Richard Scarry's *What do people do all day?* shows that *-ari* is the most frequently used agentive and instrumental suffix. Moreover, zero-derived nouns made up the largest category of derived nouns used for instruments. The role of productivity in Icelandic acquisition, though, cannot be fully assessed until data are available, for each lexical domain, on adult innovations.

Swedish is very similar to Icelandic in the major word-formation options used today. Some of the possible patterns of derivation from roots with changes in the vowel, though, are no longer productive and would not be used by modern speakers. The predictions about Swedish, then, parallel those for Icelandic rather closely.

The data for Swedish are drawn from a study of seven three-year-olds, all observed for four weeks by their parents, who noted all the lexical innovations they heard their children use, together with glosses of the apparent meanings. This corpus contains 42 innovative nominals (Gustafsson 1979). Inspection of these innovations shows that 69 percent are compounds and 31 percent derived nominals. Most compounds were constructed by combining two elements in noun–noun or verb–noun forms, as in *finger-deg* 'finger-dough' (for playdough with finger prints marked on it), versus *hjälpings-gubbar* 'helping-old men,' with a linking *s* (for old men who help one find one's way in the fog). The majority of these compounds were made up of two nouns, but the children also used bare verbs 24 percent of the time in the leftmost (modifier) slot, e.g., *riv-katt* 'scratch-cat' (for adult *lokatt* 'lynx'). This compounding pattern, combining a bare verb and a noun, is increasingly productive in modern Swedish.

The commonest derivational affix was *-are*, used with agentive and, more commonly from these children, instrumental meaning, e.g., *bakare* 'baker' (for adult *kavel* 'rolling-pin'), *borrare* 'driller' (for adult *borr* 'drill'), or *klingare* 'ringer' (for adult *bjällra* 'bell'). Other agentive uses include, for example, from a child aged 3;8: *Du slösar sa med dina tvalar. Du är en riktig tval-slösare* 'You are wasting a lot of soap. You are a real soap-waster'; and from one aged 5;5: *bussklivpåare* 'bus-climb-on-er' (for 'someone who climbs onto a bus,' from *kliva på buss(en)* 'to climb on a bus/busses') (Söderbergh 1979). The other derived nouns coined by the three-year-olds were from verb roots, e.g., *skara* '(a) cut' (for adult *kniv* 'knife'), *ontet* 'hurt-the' (for adult *värken* 'ache'). Four of the five were formed by zero derivation from a verb root and one from a past participle (Gustafsson 1979).

As in other Germanic languages, many of the children's compound nouns were designed to carry explicit contrasts among subcategories. For example, Gustav (3;6) contrasted *trapp-käpp* 'stair-stick,' with *golv-käpp* 'floor-stick,' for two different kinds of sticks he used; Christian (3;6) did a similar thing with such compounds as *land-bil* 'land-car' (a flying car that can land on water, from *landa* 'to land') versus *sim-bil* 'swim-car' (a car that can swim in water, from *simma* 'to swim'), or *jobb-bilar* 'work-cars' (kinds of cars that work, i.e., trucks, tractors, etc., from *jobba* 'to work'). Similar contrastive uses of compounds have been reported for other Swedish-speaking children, e.g., from a child aged 2;6: *filmjölks-bil* 'sour(ed)-milk-truck' and *yoghurts-bil* 'yoghourt-truck' (cf. adult *mjölkbil* 'milk-truck'), for different kinds of trucks; or, for a special kind of room, from a child aged 3;2: *kläd-rummet* 'clothes-room-the' for a clothes closet (adult *klädscåp* 'wardrobe') (Söderbergh 1979).

Summary

Children acquiring Germanic languages make use of compounding very early in coining nouns. These compounds consist of noun–noun combinations, and appear to fit what are productive paradigms for adults although they may lack some adjustments in form required in the adult language. Later, they use verb roots in such compounds as well, at first with the verb in the leftmost (modifier) slot. Next they may combine verb roots with object nouns, in that order, and even add affixes to the verb root as head of the combination, without changing surface word-order. Later still, they realize that all compound-noun heads belong in the rightmost slot.

Children use some derivational suffixes to form new nouns too, mainly suffixes for agents and instruments. The data available suggest that children are sensitive to adult productivity: they tend to master first those options used more frequently by adults, and they continue to rely more heavily on those once they themselves reach the stage of being able to choose among several transparent possibilities.

In the next chapter, I look at data from some other language types to see whether the general predictions made by transparency, simplicity, and productivity are supported there too.

9 *More words for things*

To what extent do children acquiring other languages rely on transparency, simplicity, and productivity? To what extent are the predictions of these principles affected by the typology of the language? For example, if a language makes little or no use of compounding, that option will not be available. This in turn will affect children's reliance on simplicity, transparency, and productivity. This chapter surveys data from some Romance and some Slavic languages, as well as from Hungarian (Finno-Ugric) and Hebrew (Semitic). For each language, I evaluate the predictions of each principle against the kinds of novel nouns children construct.

Romance

The Romance languages, unlike Germanic, rely far more on derivation than compounding for word formation. New nouns are usually formed with suffixes. In French, for example, nouns for things can be formed with suffixes like *-eau* or *-on*, as in the established *rouleau* 'roller, bearing' or *jeton* 'token, chip'; nouns for agents and instruments with *-eur*, as in *chanteur* 'singer'; nouns for activities or states with *-age*, *-esse*, or *-ment*, as in *séchage* '(activity of) drying,' *sagesse* 'goodness, wisdom,' and *changement* 'change.' While French-speakers rely heavily on derivation with affixes, they also make some use of zero-derivation: nouns can be formed from verb infinitives, as in *le tomber* 'the fall/the action of falling' or *le jeter* 'the action of throwing/the throw.'

Compounding does occur in Romance, but is not very productive, and today appears more often in written French (e.g., advertisements) than in everyday speech. When compounds are used, it is typically for instruments, as in the well-established *abat-jour* 'lampshade, awning' and *tire-bouchon* 'corkscrew,' or for contrasting subcategories, as in *phrase-clé* 'key sentence' versus *nom-clé* 'key word,' or the innovative *déjeuner-concert* 'lunch accompanied by a concert' versus *dîner-concert* 'dinner accompanied by a concert.'[1] Overall, compounding is rare in colloquial Romance compared with Germanic.

French

For French, transparency of meaning predicts children will construct new nouns from known roots and affixes. Simplicity predicts that children will make the fewest changes possible in constructing new nouns. Children might therefore follow one of two routes: (a) they could rely initially on zero-derivation for new nouns and only later use affixes to form new nouns. But since zero-derived nouns more often denote activities than objects, (b) they might instead wait until they acquire some affixes before constructing novel nouns. That is, the relative unavailability of simple forms for nouns (zero-derived or compound) would mean that children simply have to wait until they have learnt some affixes before they can construct novel nouns. At that point, transparency and simplicity alike predict that affixes that require no changes in the root will be acquired before affixes that require changes. Productivity makes the same predictions here as for Germanic: more-productive forms will be more accessible and so among the first to be learnt, and once several complex word-types are transparent, children will show the same preferences as adults.

What kinds of novel nouns do French-speaking children coin? The data here come primarily from children acquiring French, with some additional observations from Spanish and Portuguese. In French, I draw on a corpus of 91 innovative nouns. These come from classic diary studies as well as on some more recent studies of acquisition (Aimard 1974, 1975, Cohen 1969, Compayré 1896, Decroly 1932, Descoeudres 1922, Deville 1891, Egger 1887, François 1977, Grégoire 1939, 1947, Guillaume 1927, Taulelle 1984). Very young French-speaking children produce few innovative nouns. Those they do coin rely on zero-derivation from verbs, as in *une roule* (1;10, from the verb *rouler* 'to roll,' for adult *une balle* 'ball') or *du pleuré* (3;0, from the past participle of *pleurer* 'to cry,' for adult *des gouttes* 'drops [of water]'). As predicted, they use no derivational suffixes at first, but by age four to five, they can use as many as 18 different noun suffixes.

Their suffixes fall, semantically, into three groups:

(a)   AGENTIVE AND INSTRUMENTAL SUFFIXES such as *-eur*, *-ier*, or *-euse*: these appeared with 41 percent of children's innovative nouns.

[1] The latter examples are drawn from innovative compounds noted in the Saarbrücken corpus. See also Dubois 1962, Grevisse 1964, Guilbert 1965, 1971, 1975.

The suffix *-eur* appears on both verb and noun roots, as in innovative *le dormeur* (3;8,14) 'the sleeper' (from *dormir* 'to sleep'), *le crêmeur* (3;8,14) for a person who eats cream (from *crême* 'cream'), *un salisseur* (3;11) for someone who dirties things (from *salir* 'to dirty'), *le fermeur* (5;6,10) for the one who shuts things, in a game (from *fermer* 'to shut'); *un montagneur* (4;6) for someone who likes climbing (from *montagne* 'mountain'), used in contrast to the conventional *montagnard* for someone who lives in the mountains, or *un mensongeur* (6;6) for a liar (from *une mensonge* 'a lie'), in lieu of adult *menteur* from the verb *mentir* 'to lie' (see further Chapter 10);

(b)   OBJECT SUFFIXES such as *-eau*, *-age*, or *-ure*: these accounted for a further 39 percent of their novel nouns, e.g., *un rouleau* (3;0) for a billiard ball (from *rouler* 'to roll'/adult *une bille* (*de billard*)), *une saignure* (3;4,2) for a cut on one's finger (from *saigner* 'to bleed'/adult *une coupure*), or *le racontage* (4;10,6) for a story (from *raconter* 'to tell (a story)'/adult *le récit*);

(c)   ACTIVITY SUFFIXES like *-ette* and *-ment* accounted for most of the remaining nominal innovations, e.g., *une petite lavette* (3;3) 'a little wash,' *tes brûlements* (3;9) 'your burnings' for the activity of burning weeds, or *le peignement* (3;11) 'the (activity of) combing.'

French-speaking children, overall, appear to produce fewer novel nouns early on than those acquiring Germanic languages, but, by age four and five, they construct complex words with a wide range of affixes.

The delay in novel noun-formation relative to Germanic seems attributable to the unproductive nature of both zero-derivation and compounding in French. Children have to learn the meanings of affixes before they can coin nouns. Among the earliest suffixes acquired are agent and instrument forms, used by all the children represented in the present corpus. In fact, these coinages accounted for two-fifths of the novel nouns produced by four- and five-year-olds. As predicted by simplicity, the suffixes used most often are those added to a verb with no changes in the root, as in the derived *sauteur* 'jumper' from the verb *sauter* 'to jump,' or *batteur* 'hitter' from *battre* 'to hit' (often regularized to *batter*), and so on. An agentive suffix like *-eur* (or its feminine counterpart *-euse*, often used for instruments as well as agents) should be learnt earlier than *-iste* or *-ien* with adjectival as well as nominal uses. In fact, the relatively greater transparency of *-eur* is attested in part by its greater frequency in innovative agent nouns, by 16:1, over -*iste*. French-speaking children also coin nouns for events from the verbs for the relevant activity, as in *la séchade* (3;3) 'the (activity of) drying' that follows a bath, or *la parlation* (4;2) 'the activity of talking' used of a discussion programme on television. Novel nouns of this type appear to be rare in the Germanic data. This may be because suffixes with this meaning are less productive than in Romance.[2]

Finally, the suffixes children favor most, the ones that have been reported most frequently in the spontaneous coinage of nouns of different types, appear to be those that are the most productive in adult speech. The measure for this, though, is an indirect one. For example, there has been a shift, since the beginning of the century, from -*ier* as the suffix favored for agency to -*eur*. Children observed in recent studies strongly favor -*eur*, whereas data from the end of the last century and beginning of this reported only instances of -*ier* for novel agentive nouns, as in *cerceaunier* [sic] (3;0, from *cerceau* 'hoop,' for 'a mender of hoops'), *un poutrier* (no age given, from *poutre* 'beam'/adult *charpentier* 'carpenter'), or *marronier* (no age, from *marron* '[eating] chestnut,' for 'a man who sells chestnuts'). More recently, the majority of children's agentive innovations carry the suffix -*eur*, as in *le crêmeur* (3;8,14, from *crême* 'cream,' for 'an eater of cream'), *le regardeur* (4;0, from *regarder* 'to look,' for 'person who looks at something'), or *un montagneur* (4;6, from *montagne* 'mountain,' for 'someone who likes climbing'/adult *alpiniste*).

In summary, French children in their innovations rely primarily on derivation with suffixes. But since they have to work out what each affix means first, they make little use of suffixes and produce few novel nouns before age three to four. The occasional innovation produced earlier, as simplicity predicts, is formed through zero-derivation. Once children have analyzed some suffixes, they coin nouns in profusion for a variety of semantic types. These data strongly support the view that children are sensitive early on to what is available in their language, and that affects their dependence on simplicity and transparency. Older children are further influenced by productivity: they choose productive suffixes over less productive ones. Finally, French-speaking children produce virtually no novel compounds before age four to five.

---

[2] The incidence of innovative event-nouns may be under-estimated in Germanic: for example, in English, activity nouns can be formed from any verb with the addition of nominal -*ing*. But unless children use an article with the V-ing form, it is hard to distinguish such nominals from verb forms marked for aspect.

Portuguese and Spanish

Portuguese and Spanish also rely heavily on affixal derivation and make little use of compounding. The predictions here, then, are the same as for French. But the data available are sparse, and come primarily from three elicitation studies supplemented by a small number of spontaneous innovations.

When four- to eight-year-old Portuguese speakers are asked to construct novel agent-nouns from a nonsense verb, they do best with the suffix *-dor*. That is, they supply this suffix 68 percent of the time in the form *-edor* on a second-conjugation nonsense root, but do less well on first- and third-conjugation nonsense roots where they supply *-idor* only 36 percent of the time (Costa 1976; see also Mediano 1976). Overall, children strongly preferred *-dor* as an agentive suffix, but, on occasion, also produced *-eiro* and *-ista*. What is not known is the relative productivity of each suffix for adults, and whether there were any changes with age in what children used.

The only data on spontaneous innovations come from a diary study that reports some coinages (Figueira 1977, 1979). These include an innovative agent noun in *-eira*, *sou ajudadeira* (4;0,19) 'his helper' (in lieu of adult *sou ajudado*). Others are coinages for objects intrinsic to or resulting from an activity. These were derived from verb roots, e.g., *esta pinto* (3;7) 'picture, design, drawing' (from *pintar* 'to paint'); *o dirigi* (3;10) 'steering wheel' (from *diriger* 'to drive'/adult *o volante*); and *um penteado* (4;10) for a comb case (from *pentear* 'to comb'/adult *um estojo de pente* 'a comb case'). Much as for French-speaking children, there is little or no novel derivation recorded before 3;6 or 4;0, and no instances of compounding.

For Spanish, the observations are similar. Elicitation tasks show that the four- to seven-year-olds add the suffix *-ador* to a first-conjugation nonsense root 67 percent of the time for a new agent-noun; older children, 11;0–12;0, do so 93 percent of the time. With a second-conjugation root, younger children add *-ero* 40 percent of the time, compared with 77 percent for the older ones (Kernan and Blount 1968). This suggests that *-(a)dor* may be more productive than *-ero*. However, the choice of suffix depends in part on the conjugation of the verb root. Unfortunately, the task was not designed to elicit a full range of noun forms, agentive or otherwise. As in Portuguese, no data were collected from children below age four.

Children produce novel agent-nouns, as in *yerbero* (3;7) for someone who pulls up weeds (from *yerba* 'grass, weed'), *ojero* (4;3) 'oculist' (from *ojo* 'eye'/adult *oculista*); nouns for locations, like *la ollera* (3;2) for the place where pots were kept (from *olla* 'pot, jar'); and nouns for objects affected, but their choice of suffix is not always correct, as in some uses of *-ura* (a suffix for effect or outcome), e.g., *quemaúra* (4;9) for a bonfire (from *quemar* 'to burn'/adult *hoguera*) (Montes Giraldo 1976). These observations are consistent with those from Portuguese and French, both in the types of nouns observed – mainly words for objects and agents – and in the ages at which such coinages appear, from three or so on. What is unclear is the range of noun suffixes Spanish-speaking children control by age three to four.

In summary, the data from children acquiring Romance languages show the same general pattern of very little noun innovation before age three, followed by increasing reliance on derivation with suffixes. They are sensitive to the productivity of derivation versus compounding, and make no use of the latter, unlike children learning Germanic languages.

Slavic

Slavic speakers can draw on a large repertoire of derivational affixes to form new nouns, mostly through the addition of a suffix to a noun, verb, or adjective root. There is some zero-derivation (e.g., in Russian, in forming masculine activity nouns from verbs), but this is less prevalent than affixation. Lastly, some compounding is possible, but it is relatively unproductive in Slavic.[3]

The predictions are similar to those for Romance: both simplicity of form and transparency of meaning predict that children will favor suffixes that require no modifications of roots, so the roots remain readily identifiable. Since children have to learn affix meanings first, it may be some time before they can construct novel nouns. Productivity predicts children will first master options that are frequent in input, and later prefer more productive over less productive affixes. The general pattern of acquisition should parallel Romance rather than Germanic. The data here come from Polish, Russian, and Serbo-Croatian. Most of the observations are drawn from longitudinal records of children between about 1;6 and 5;0. For Polish, the data on spontaneous innovations are supplemented by elicitation of new words for objects, agents, instruments, and places.

---

[3] See Fisiak, Lipińska-Grzegorek, and Zabrocki 1978, Schenker 1967, 1973, and Smoczyńska 1985 for Polish, and Forbes 1964, Schupbach 1973, 1984, and Unbegaun 1957 for Russian.

Polish

The data available for Polish consist of extensive longitudinal observations complemented by elicitation studies of children between 2;0 and 12;0. The bulk of this research was carried out by Chmura-Klekotowa, who based her work on Baudouin de Courtenay's diaries of his own children between 1887 and 1904 and on records of a further ten children observed in the 1950s and 1960s; she also drew on experimental data. Her elicitation tasks were designed to find out which derivational options children aged 3;0 to 7;0 favored when they were asked to construct words for unfamiliar objects and actions (Baudouin de Courtenay 1974, Chmura-Klekotowa 1964, 1970, 1971).

Of the 4,800 innovations analyzed for Polish, 50 percent were novel nouns. Half were derived from other nouns, 40 percent from verbs, 8 percent from adjectives, a handful from whole phrases, and a very few from combinations of two nouns used to form compounds (Chmura-Klekotowa 1971). Among the novel nouns were terms for activities or events, for states of being, for agents and instruments, and for objects. The first type, activity and state nouns, as in *wieżowanie* (from *wieża* '(a) tower') for the 'building of a tower,' or *gniewość* (from *gniewać się* 'to be angry') for 'anger,' were rare. The largest category of innovative nouns was that of agents and instruments – 26 percent of all the novel nouns used, with the most frequently used suffix (38 percent) being the highly productive *-acz* (feminine *-aczka*), as in *plakacz* (from *plakać* 'to cry') for 'someone who cries,' or *stlukacz* (from *stluć* 'to break') for 'someone who breaks things.' This suffix appeared more often on agent than on instrument nouns by nearly 4:1. Children also used other agentive suffixes. Some of these were favored more for agents than instruments, for example: *-ak* (8 percent) and *-ik* (*-iczek*), *-nik* (*-niczek*), *-niczka* (*-owniczka*), *-nica* (together 14 percent), both by 2:1.

Children favored other suffixes for instruments: *-ek*, *-ka*, *-ko* (21 percent), by 2:1; *-ec* (11 percent), by 4:1; and *-dlo* (5 percent), by 9:1. They also used some zero-derivation forms (4 percent), again more for instruments than agents, by 4:1. All these nouns (441 instances) were derived from verb roots. Children also derived some agent and instrument terms from noun roots – from nouns for places, as in *biżuteriarz* (from *biżuteria* 'jewelry'/adult *jubiler* 'jeweller'), *kopalnik* (from *kopalna* 'mine'/adult *górnik* 'miner'); from nouns in phrases: *zagranista* (from *za granicę* 'beyond the frontier, abroad') for 'someone who goes abroad'; and from nouns for objects: *pieniążyczka* (from *pieniądze* 'money'/adult *portmonetka* 'purse').

Children often used the same suffixes in new words for affected objects as in words for places. (Affected object uses were more frequent.) Among the suffixes children favored were *-anka*, *-anie*, *-enie*, and *-ek*, as in *podkręcanka* (from *podkręcać* 'to move something around'/adult *karuzela* 'merry-go-round'); *narysowanie* (from *narysować* 'to draw'/adult *rysunek* 'drawing'); or *piski* (from *pisać* 'to write'/adult *literki* 'letters'). They used a few suffixes primarily for locations, e.g., the productive *-arnia* in *biletarnia* (from *bilet* 'ticket'/adult *kasa* 'ticket-office'), but these uses were rare.

Among all the novel nouns coined, children produced only a handful of compounds. For the most part, these were agentive, e.g., *oknalaz* (from *okno* 'window' + *lazić* 'to wander, hang around') for 'someone who works on windows,' *mlekojad* (from *mleko* 'milk' + *jadać* 'to eat [habitual]') for 'someone who eats (drinks) milk,' or *herbatomocnik* (from *herbatą* 'tea' + *mocną* 'strong' + *-ik* '[agentive]') for 'someone who likes strong tea.'

Finally, children's innovations observed in the 1890s can be compared with those observed in the 1950s and 1960s. Overall, there were several shifts in the suffixes preferred by children, shifts that parallel shifts in adult preferences over the same period (Chmura-Klekotowa 1970, 1971). For example, agentive suffixes like *-an*, as in *brykan* (from the verb 'to frisk') for 'a horse that was frisking,' or *-owiec*, as in *marnowiec bulek* ('waster-roll') for 'someone who wastes rolls,' common in Baudouin de Courtenay's notes, by the 1950s had given way to the now highly productive *-acz*, *-aczka*, as in *brykacz* for 'someone or something that's frisking,' or *marnowacz* for 'someone who wastes things.' In fact, *-acz* was twice as frequent in modern coinages as it was at the beginning of the century. And where *-sk-* used to be the preferred option for forming adjectives from nouns (as in *Bulgarski* from *Bulgaria* for 'Bulgarian'), in modern Polish, speakers – including children – favor *-ow* instead, as in *pracownicny* 'belonging to the workers' (from *praca* 'work'). Overall, both adult and child speakers of Polish nowadays tend to avoid root changes in word formation, and the most productive suffixes are those that require none. Adults as well as children, therefore, appear to place a premium on transparency in word formation.

In summary, children begin to use suffixes between age two and three, and by four draw on an extensive repertoire. Their innovative nouns are formed from verb, noun, and adjective roots. Their commonest coinages, up to age four, are nouns for objects, agents, instruments, and, on occasion, places. Only the older children produce novel nouns for events and states. Children used a large range of derivational suffixes and some zero-derivation in their coinages, but hardly ever used compounding. Finally, the suffixes they relied on most frequently are those preferred by adult speakers.

Russian

Children begin to coin novel nouns in Russian between age two and three, and by four use a range of different affixes. As one diarist noted, "guided by meaning, the child freely creates forms on the basis of meaningful elements" (Gvozdev 1961, pt. 2, p. 187). Diminutive suffixes appear from age two onwards,[4] but productive noun-forming suffixes appear only from age three on (El'konin 1973). Between 3;6 and 4;0, children begin to construct agentive nouns with suffixes like *-shchik*, *-nik*, *-ec*, and *-tel'*. They also form some novel nouns by zero-derivation from verb roots. Not until age six or so do they coin any nouns for states or events, e.g., with the suffix *-ost'* (analogous to English *-ness*). These nouns remain rare, much as in Polish (see also Chukovskiy 1966, Ushakova 1969, 1976). Rarer still are novel compound-nouns. Children make little or no use of compounding in Russian until after age six.

Serbo-Croatian

The Serbo-Croatian data come primarily from a survey of research on Slavic that tried to establish, for Serbo-Croatian, some developmental stages in children's word-formation. The data consist of innovations from the spontaneous speech of three pairs of twins and three singletons from age two to four, with some examples from children as old as seven.[5]

By age three, Serbo-Croatian children produce a variety of novel nouns. They coin them for affected objects and for agents, as in *gasač* 'someone who turns out the light' (from *gasiti* 'to light'), *ležač* 'someone who lies down' (from *ležati* 'to lie'), or *sudovica* 'a woman who washes dishes' (from *sudovi*-NOM-PL 'dishes'). They also produce numerous diminutives

---

[4] The early emergence of diminutive suffixes is supported by elicitation data. Five- and six-year-olds are very proficient at adding diminutive and augmentative suffixes to mark relative size, although they still make mistakes about which diminutive suffixes can be added to which root type (Bogoyavlenskiy 1973, Ushakova 1970).

[5] Savić 1982 based her account on 950 forms, but she included in these novel case-assignment and novel uses of familiar words. She gave no breakdown by category for innovations; nor any ages for the examples she cited.

for familiar nouns.[6] But one thing Serbo-Croatian children do not do is coin any compound nouns. The compounding so prevalent for children acquiring Germanic is absent from the coinages of children acquiring Serbo-Croatian in particular, and Slavic in general. When compounding is used in Serbo-Croatian, it is more characteristic of written, bureaucratic language; it is rare in colloquial speech.

In summary, children acquiring Slavic languages show marked preferences for coining new nouns through derivation rather than compounding. Their first affixes are used to form diminutives, from as young as age two. From around three on, they begin to use a wide repertoire of nominal affixes, coining nouns for objects, agents, and instruments, from both verb and noun roots. Later, around age five to six, they start to coin novel nouns for activities and states. The options favored in each lexical domain appear to be those preferred in adult speech.

Two more languages

The last two languages considered here are non-Indo-European: Hungarian, a Finno-Ugric language, and Hebrew, a Semitic one. Structurally, these languages differ both from the languages considered so far and from each other. They offer further data on how sensitive children are to typological properties that affect their options for word formation.

Hungarian is an agglutinative language that forms new words through derivation and compounding. New words are usually formed through derivation, generally but not always with affixes added to verb or adjective roots. They can also be formed through compounding, through the combination of two or more roots, with or without affixes. Compounds carry primary stress on the modifier, in initial position, and weaker stress on the head, in second position, much as in English. Both derivation and compounding are major sources of new words for adult speakers.

Hebrew relies primarily on the combination of triconsonantal roots with intercalated vowel-patterns to construct new words. There are about 80 noun patterns (*miškalim*), some of which combine with a derivational suffix, or prefix, or both. Hebrew compounds place the head noun in initial position. Many nouns, when used as heads in compounds, have a special bound form. Overall, compounding is less productive in spoken than written Hebrew.

For both languages, I draw on records of children's spontaneous

---

[6] See Gvozdev 1961 and Pačesová 1976 for similar data on Russian and Czech.

coinages for comparison with the data summarized so far on Germanic Romance, and Slavic. The data for Hungarian come from diaries and reports on vocabulary development. The data for Hebrew are drawn from a few studies done in the 1930s, combined with recent diary and elicitation data.

Hungarian

Hungarian relies both on derivation with affixes and on compounding. For example, the noun *hir* 'news, message' provides the basis for derived verbs – *hirdet* 'to announce,' *hirlik* 'to be reported' – and nouns – *hirnök* 'herald,' *hirdetés* 'classified advertisement,' *hirdetgetés* 'the publication of classified advertisements,' *hirdetmény* 'notice, announcement' – as well as for compounds like *hiradás* 'broadcasting service [on the radio]' (from *hir* + *adás* 'service'), *hirlap* 'newspaper' (from *hir* + *lap* 'page'), *hirlapiro* 'journalist' (also from *hir* + *lap* + suffix), or *hirlapolvasó* 'newspaper reader,' and *hirlapszerkesztö* '[newspaper] editor.'

Compounding is common and typically requires only simple juxtaposition of two roots. This combination may then have an affix added, or be used as part of a further compound. Suffixal derivation is equally common in the coining of words. Diminutive suffixes are added freely to nouns, especially proper names. Verbs and adjectives are the source of numerous new nouns for objects (with suffixes like -*ó*, -*at*, or -*és*), for agent and instruments (with the suffixes -*os* or -*ó*), places (with -*oda*), states (with -*ság*), and activities (with -*és*). The choice of suffix within a domain is sometimes governed by the shape of the root, but where two different suffixes could appear on the same root, speakers have typically opted for specializations in meaning that maintain contrasts between them (Sauvageot 1951, 1971).

Transparency predicts that Hungarian-speaking children will rely on familiar words in zero-derivation and compounding to form new nouns until they acquire some affixes. Once derived words become as transparent as compounds, they should then choose the more productive option wherever they have a choice. Simplicity also predicts that children will rely first on compounding and zero-derivation, and only later on derivational affixes for coining new nouns.

The corpus of 92 innovative nouns analyzed here is drawn from diary and vocabulary studies published since the 1890s. These nouns were all coined by children between 1;8 and 5;6 (MacWhinney 1973; also Balassa 1893, Barcsai 1921, Csapodi 1905, Kardos 1896, Kenyeres 1928, Ponori

1905, Simonyi 1881, 1906, Zsidó 1928, 1931). Their novel nouns fall into three groups:

(a) 40 percent are derived with a suffix added to a noun, verb, or adjective root;
(b) 16 percent are derived with no affixation; and
(c) 44 percent are formed through compounding.

As children get older, they depend more on affixation (mainly suffixes) and compounding than on zero-derivation to form new nouns. Below age three, nearly half the innovative nouns observed were constructed without affixes (47 percent); a third with suffixes (30 percent), and the remainder were compounds (23 percent). Above age three, only 16 percent of the novel nouns were constructed without affixes. Nearly half were formed with suffixes through derivation, and half through compounding.

Children coined nouns for objects affected by or resulting from an action as early as age two, often with zero derivation, as in *savanyú* (1;9,9) 'sour' (used for a grape/adult *szõlõ*), or *farag* (2;3,11) 'carve' (used for a knife/adult *kés*). They also produced frequent diminutives from noun roots, again from as young as two years, but sometimes added the wrong form, e.g., *kockaka* (1;10,27) [block + dim.] 'little block' (adult *kockácska*), or *vödörke* (2;1,7) [bucket + dim.] 'little bucket' (adult *vödröcske*).

Hungarian children produce novel compounds from an early age, as predicted, e.g., *jegy + bácsi* (1;10,27) 'ticket-man' (adult *kalauz* 'conductor'); *motor + bácsi* (3;3,18) 'motorcycle-man' (adult *motoros bácsi* 'motorcyclist'), *csont + ember* (3;5) 'bone-man' (adult *csontváz* 'skeleton'), or *utazó + ház* (4;0) 'traveller-house' (adult *palyaház* 'station'). As in the Germanic languages, children use compounds for contrasts within categories; these are sometimes explicit, as in *lent + ágy* 'down-bed' versus *fent + ágy* 'up-bed' (for a bed that was downstairs versus one that was upstairs), and at other times implicit, as in *szem + tükör* (3;6) 'eye-mirror' (adult *szemüveg* 'eye-glass'), or *utca + ház* 'street-house' (for a house with a passage-way through it/adult *átjáróház*).

Lastly, in constructing such compounds, children make some errors. They make word-order errors, placing the verb root before, instead of after, the noun for the object affected, as in *mosó + fog* (3;1,10) 'washer-tooth' (in lieu of adult *fogkefe* 'toothbrush'). They also form some compounds with adverbs, as in *mindig + be* (4;2) 'always-in' (adult *csigavonal* 'spiral'); and they form compounds with negative modifiers, as in *nem + béka* 'none-frog' for that part of a violin without a frog grip.

They produce derived nouns from age three on, from verbs, as in agentive *pillogó* (3;3,7) 'blinker,' *csináló* (4;0,12) 'doer' for someone who does something, and *segitó* (4;0,12) 'helper' for someone who helps; and from nouns, as in *parancsolatos* (5;0) 'orderer' (adult *katonatiszt* 'soldier'). They also produce instrument nouns, as in *kötő* (3;3,7) 'binder, tier' (adult *zsinor* 'cord, string'), or *füstölő* (3;3,18) 'smoker' (adult *kémény* 'chimney'). From age four to five on, they also produce a few novel nouns for states, as in *aranyság* 'goldness' (for adult *drágaság* 'luxury').

These data show that Hungarian children, as predicted, rely first on simple forms, with most of their early innovative nouns formed through zero-derivation or compounding. Their reliance on zero-derivation declines after age two as they rely increasingly on affixes. From age four or so on, they rely almost equally on derivation with affixes and on compounding. Finally, the affixes children use, mainly suffixes, are among the more productive ones in adult speech. That is, they are those preferred by adults in *their* coinages (MacWhinney 1976).

Hebrew

Hebrew, like other Semitic languages, relies primarily on derivation with affixation for word formation. The main word-formation device in modern Hebrew is the association of consonantal roots with patterns of vowel infixes, plus prefixes or suffixes. For example, the root *g-d-l* 'grow' has given rise to established nouns like *gidul* 'growth, tumor,' *gódel* 'size,' *gdila* 'growing, growth,' *gdula* 'greatness,' *migdal* 'tower,' and *hagdala* 'enlargement,' while the root *k-t-b* has given rise to *ktav* 'script,' *ktiv* 'orthography,' *katav* 'reporter,' *ktiva* 'writing,' *któvet* 'address,' *mixtav* 'letter, missive,' and *haxtava* 'dictation' (Berman 1978a, Ravid 1978). Modern Hebrew also forms new words with suffixes added to stems (consonantal roots plus vowel patterns). For example, the stem *yald-* (from *y-l-d* 'bear, give birth to') appears with different suffixes in *yaldut* 'childhood,' *yaldutiy* 'childish,' and *yaldutiyut* 'childishness.' Similarly, the noun *nagar* 'carpenter' takes further suffixes to form *nagarut* 'carpentry' and *nagariya* 'carpenter's shop.'

Hebrew makes use of both zero-derivation and compounding. Zero-derivation occurs mainly with present tense verbs (the participial or *beynoni* 'intermediate' forms) used as nouns, e.g., *šofet* 'judges; a judge,' *mocec* 'sucks; a pacifier.' Compound nouns, with the head followed by the modifier, are quite common, but many types of head nouns require some modification since they must appear in bound form in compounds. For example, the free form *mexona* 'machine,' when in a compound, is modified to *mxonat-*, as in *mxonat-ktiva* 'type-writer.' And the full form *bayit* 'house' appears as *bet-* in compounds like *bet-séfer* 'school.' Compounding is more prevalent in written than in spoken Hebrew, and many loan translations introduced into Hebrew as compounds have since been replaced by single words formed with affixes (Kutscher 1982). Simplicity predicts that children acquiring Hebrew will rely first on zero-derivation for noun formation. But should vowel patterns intercalated with consonantal roots be acquired before stem–affix combinations in acquisition, or after? The problem is one of typology: since intercalation is a major option for both inflection and derivation, it is presumably simpler, overall, than affixation. Transparency predicts that once children analyze affixes, derived words should be just as transparent as zero-derived forms. Noun patterns with vowels intercalated with root consonants will emerge later than zero-derivation, since like affixes, each pattern must first be acquired (Berman 1985, Clark and Berman 1984). Productivity predicts that the options favored by adult speakers should be the preferred choices of children too, as they get older. Because these options are more frequent in the input, they will also be more accessible and so identified earlier than other options.

Hebrew-speaking children rely heavily on derivation in their spontaneous coinages (Berman and Sagi 1981). Most of their innovative nouns are marked by affixes (87 percent), either a suffix alone (e.g., *-an*, *-iya*, *-ut*), a suffix combined with a noun-forming pattern (e.g., CaCCan),[7] or a prefix and suffix forming part of a noun pattern (e.g., ma-CCeC-a). This compares with only 13 percent of novel nouns formed with an internal vowel pattern alone, with no external affix. Children produce diminutives from about 2;6 onwards, typically forming them with the suffixes *-i*, *-it*, or *-on*, as in *gamádi* (2;2, from *gamad* 'dwarf, smurf'), *lecáni* (2;5, from *lecan* 'clown'), *mazlegit* (4;9, from *mazleg* 'fork'), or *eglon* (2;6, from *egel* 'calf') (see also Dromi and Berman 1982). But only from age three to four on do they coin new nouns formed with affixes and combinations of noun pattern and external affix.[8]

Hebrew-speaking children's spontaneous coinages fall into several

---

[7] Noun patterns or *miškalim* in Hebrew are traditionally identified by the number of consonants (each designated with a capital C) and the vowel pattern they combine with (e.g., -i-u-, -a-a-), as in CiCuC or CaCCan. Verb patterns or *binyanim* are identified here by P1, P2, etc. (Berman 1978a).

[8] Nearly all the instances of novel nouns with affixes cited by Rivka'i 1938, for instance, come from children aged 4;4 or older.

categories. Aside from diminutives (18 percent overall), the largest is agent and instrument nouns (54 percent). Among the agent nouns, over 70 percent are formed with the *-an* suffix or the CaCCan pattern, e.g., *šeonan* 'watch-fixer, repairer' (from *šeon* 'clock'), *banyan* 'builder' (for adult *banay*, from P1 *bone* 'to build'), or *xalman* 'dreamer' (from P1 *xolem* 'to dream'), all from four- and five-year-olds. The remaining agents were split between the *-ai* suffix, usually added to nouns, as in *xalonai* 'glazier' (from *xalon* 'window', for adult *cagag*), and the CaCaC pattern without any affix, as in *coref* for a person who makes huts (from *crif* 'hut'), both from six-year-olds.[9]

Among instrument nouns, half were formed with the maCCeCa pattern, with a prefix, *ma-*, and suffix, *-a*, as in *mašketa* (3;2) 'waterer' for a sprinkler (from P5 *lehaškot* 'to water'/adult *mamtera* 'sprinkler'), or *maclema* (6;2) for 'camera' (from P3 *lecalem* 'to photograph'/adult *calmaniya*). The form *maclema* is now the conventional term for 'camera' in Hebrew, but that wasn't the case in the 1930s when it was noted as an innovation from a six-year-old (Rivka'i 1938). The rest were split almost equally between the maCCeC and the CaCCan patterns, as in *mahalix* (4;7) for 'the thing that makes the sun move' (from P1 *holex* 'to go'; this child was answering a question about what made the sun move) and *šorkan* (4+) 'a whistle' (from P1 *šorek* 'to whistle'/adult *mašrukit*). Most uses of maCCeC and maCCeCa, the two instrument patterns, come from observations made in the 1930s; children nowadays appear to rely instead on the suffix *-an* or the CaCCan pattern for new instrument nouns (Clark and Berman 1984).

Other novel nouns include terms for places or collections (9 percent), with the suffix *-iya*, as in *cdafiya* 'a collection of shells' (from *cdafim* 'shells') or *šomraniya* 'a jar one keeps sand in' (from P1 *šomer* 'to keep'); terms for states (14 percent), mainly from adjectives with the suffix *-ut*, e.g., *cmi'ut* (5;0) 'thirstiness' (in lieu of adult *cima'on* 'thirst'), or *hitvakxut* (5;0) 'argument' (from the verb *le-hitvakeax* 'to argue, quarrel'/ adult *vikuax* 'debate, argument') or *hišta'alut* (4;0) (from *le-hišta'el* 'to cough'/adult *ši'ul* 'coughing'); and a few abstract nouns in the CóCVC pattern (5 percent) usually for talking about dimensions, as in *róxak* (5;10) for 'distance' (from *raxok* 'far'/adult *merxak*), or *sórax* (6;10) 'smelliness' (from P5 *masréax* 'to stink'/adult *siraxon* 'smell, stink'). Most spontaneous coinages, then, are terms for affected objects, agents, and instruments.

---

[9] Adult *coref* means 'goldsmith.'

The noun patterns children prefer typically have either a suffix, or a prefix and suffix, in addition to any noun pattern. This finding holds both for spontaneous and elicited innovations from children. In one elicitation task where five- to eight-year-olds were asked to coin new words, the patterns most favored at every age all carried external affixes (Walden 1982). For new agent nouns, children favored the CaCCan form, with the suffix -*an*; for places, the suffix -*iya*; and for instruments (where they showed any preference at all), the maCCeCa pattern with both prefix (*ma-*) and suffix (-*a*). They made no use of noun patterns alone, such as the CaCaC pattern for agentive or attributive nouns where the vowel pattern, -a-a-, is intercalated with the root.

In summary, although the most typically Semitic word-formation option in Hebrew is the association, through intercalation, of a vowel pattern with a consonantal root, children make relatively little use of this option before age five or six. Instead, they choose patterns with derivational affixes, and make virtually no use of compounding (Berman and Clark 1989, Clark and Berman 1984, 1987, Walden 1982).

Reliance on affixes emerges around age four, much as in languages where derivational affixes are preferred for constructing new nouns. Once affixes are transparent, children rely on them extensively. What is less clear is what counts as simple. Hebrew-speaking children make little spontaneous use of zero-derivation for new nouns, though they do rely on it to some extent around age three when asked to coin agent nouns (see Chapter 10). Simplicity also plays a role when Hebrew-speaking children start to produce compound nouns: they rely first on forms with no change, and then learn to make successively greater changes to produce bound head-nouns (Berman and Clark 1989, Clark and Berman 1987).

The choices of both zero-derivation and compounding without changes both allow children to maintain familiar word-forms intact when they coin new words. But simplicity here is offset by lack of productivity. Neither zero-derivation nor compounding is very productive in spoken Hebrew. But most of the affixes and pattern plus affix combinations children use are productive in adult speech.

Summary

Simplicity, transparency, and productivity make predictions about the options children will begin with as they construct complex words, and about changes in their choices with age. Overall, their innovative nouns show striking parallels within language families as well as across language types. Children acquiring Germanic make extensive use of compounding from as early as age two. Compounding in those languages is both simple in form and transparent in meaning. In languages where affixal derivation is used almost to the exclusion of compounding, children rely almost entirely on derivation. They also show strong similarities across languages in the ages at which they begin to make use of affixes to form new nouns, rarely doing so before age three to four, typically a year after the emergence of compounding in Germanic. Learning the meaning of an affix takes time, and affixes are not put to use until they are known, so the construction will be transparent. At the same time, children appear sensitive from the start to the productivity of compounding and derivation, with and without affixes. They make use primarily of devices licensed by the input, so children learning languages that make little or no use of compounding do not produce innovative compounds. And as they get older and have to choose among different options, they favor those affixes and compounding patterns preferred by the adult speakers around them.

The data from two non-Indo-European languages offer further support for this account. Hungarian children rely on derivation and compounding, options that are productive in Hungarian. Hebrew-speaking children make extensive use of affixation, but only from about age three to four onwards. That is, children start to make use of derivational affixes at much the same age regardless of language.

Acquisitional principles in word formation are affected in how they apply by the typology of a language and hence by the range of word-formation devices available for acquisition. Whether a language makes use of compounding, or compounding and affixation, versus affixation alone, appears to mark a major dimension along which children acquiring different languages vary. Acquisitional principles are also affected by the lexical domain, whether children are constructing new words for objects, agents, or states, for instance, so the options available in each of those domains is important. In the next chapter, I look in more detail at these principles by focussing on a single domain – that of agent and instrument nouns – across several languages.

10 *Words for agents and instruments*

Agents of actions are typically animate instigators of the activity denoted by the verb. Instruments, in contrast, are typically inanimate, but like agents they play an essential role in effecting an action. Moreover, agent and instrument nouns are common in children's spontaneous coinages (Chapters 8 and 9), so the notions of agent and instrument are clearly accessible to children from an early point in acquisition. This chapter focusses, then, on a single semantic domain in order to compare elicited coinages from English with directly comparable data from Icelandic, Hebrew, French, and Italian. This will allow further evaluation of simplicity, transparency, and productivity in the acquisition of word formation.

Within a language, terms for agents and instruments often share one or more forms in common, and a single affix may serve in coining both noun types. In English, for example, the form *pointer* could designate a person who points at whoever gets the next turn, or an instrument that points at defective rivets. More specialized devices are available too, ones that serve only for agents, or only for instruments. Compounds with a head noun like *-man* appear in some established agent nouns (*milkman*) alongside instrument compounds with *-machine* (*washing-machine*). The suffixes *-ist* and *-ian* are used only for agent nouns, as in *chemist*, *librarian*, while zero-derivation is generally used only for instruments, as in *a drill* or *a whisk*. In English, then, there is one suffix common to both agents and instruments (*-er*), and several other more specialized options.

Icelandic, also a Germanic language, makes use of similar resources for forming novel agent and instrument nouns. It has several affixes for constructing agent and instrument nouns – the suffix *-ari*, as in *leikari* 'actor' or *leitari* 'view-finder' (on a camera), *-ir*, as in *laeknir* 'doctor' or *frystir* 'freezer,' *-andi*, as in the agentive *kaupandi* 'buyer,' and *-i*, as in agentive *loftfari* 'aeronaut.' It can also form instrument nouns through zero-derivation from verb infinitives, as in *lyfta* 'elevator' from *lyfta* 'to lift.' And like English, it has some established compounds for agents, with the head nouns *-maður* '-man' (e.g., *blaðamadur* 'reporter,' *kaupmaður* 'grocer'), and for instruments with *-taeki* or *-vél* 'machine, instrument' (e.g., *senditaeki* 'transmitter,' *sléttuvél* 'lawnmower'). Compounding is common, but not really productive for forming new agent and instrument nouns.

Hebrew represents a marked contrast to English and Icelandic. Four common options exist for constructing new agent and instrument nouns. (All four are more frequent with agents than instruments in the established lexicon.) The first is zero-derivation from a verb (the third person present form), as in the established *šomer* 'watchman' or *mocec* 'pacifier [for a baby].' The second is the intercalation of vowel patterns into consonantal roots, e.g., /-a-a-/ as in *cayar* 'painter,' or /-e-e-/ in *dévek* 'glue.' The third is use of the CaCCan pattern, as in *rakdan* 'dancer' or *šadxan* 'stapler.' This pattern is echoed in the suffix *-an* used to form agents, as in *yecu-an* 'exporter,' and instruments, as in *potx-an* 'opener.' Finally, there are two common patterns with the prefix *ma-* used mainly for instruments, maCCeC and maCCeCa, as in *masrek* 'comb' and *mamtera* 'sprinkler.'

The findings from these languages will be compared with data from French and Italian, where the primary means of forming new agent and instrument nouns is through derivation. In both languages, a suffix is added to a verb or noun, for example French *eur-* or *-ier* in such established nouns as *vendeur* 'seller,' *tailleur* 'tailor,' or *charpentier* 'carpenter,' and Italian *-aio*, *-(t)ore*, or *-ista* in such established nouns as *fioraio* 'florist,' *cacciatore* 'hunter,' or *autista* 'driver.' In each language, the data elicited are used to test predictions made by transparency, simplicity, and productivity.

English

To elicit novel agent and instrument nouns in English, children were asked to help find names for people and machines that did various actions denoted by familiar verbs. For example, the experimenter might say *I've got a picture here of someone who burns things. What could we call someone who burns things? Someone who burns things is a ——*. The children heard simple descriptions (all the verbs used were known to three-year-olds) and had to come up with a name for the agent or instrument described. The children were aged three to six; all understood the questions put to them and, except for the youngest group, consistently produced labels in response to almost all the questions. Data on the elicitation task were also collected from adults (who relied exclusively on *-er*) to provide a partial measure of productivity.

Analyzing novel word forms

To make sure the children had already analyzed *-er* and assigned it some meaning, they were asked to provide possible meanings for novel words constructed with this suffix. That is, they had to show they were able to segment novel complex words into a root and affix in order to come up with an appropriate definition. The experimenter might say, for instance, for a novel agent noun: *I've got a picture here of a kicker. What does a kicker do?*; or, for a novel instrument: *I've got a picture here of a breaker. What's a breaker used for?* (The novel words presented for analysis always contained different verbs from those in the elicitation task; see Clark and Hecht 1982.)

In answering such questions, all the children showed understanding of the meaning of the verb-root-plus-suffix combinations. In their answers, they consistently removed the *-er* suffix from the verb root and then added an inflection to it along with a pronoun subject or a direct object, or both, as in (for agents) *He kicks, He kicks things, He's kicking, Kicks things*, or (for instruments) *For breaking (with), It breaks things*, and so on. Even the children who did not produce *-er* when coining words, or who did so only occasionally, were able to interpret it appropriately. No children did the reverse – producing *-er* but being unable to interpret it.

Similar patterns in children's ability to analyze versus produce particular word-forms hold for the other languages investigated as well. The Icelandic children (like the English ones) did consistently better, especially in the younger age-groups, on analyzing novel forms with the suffix *-ari* than they did in producing them (Mulford 1983). The same held true for Hebrew, where children were asked to analyze several different forms for both agents and instruments (Clark and Berman 1984). (The children in the French and Italian studies were not asked to analyze novel words.)

In summary, the analysis data show that children are familiar with the pertinent word-form types and their meanings before they attempt to produce them for themselves.

Predictions

Transparency predicts that children will rely on *known* elements, roots or affixes, in constructing new words. In choosing forms, they should also be sensitive to what is available for agent and instrument meanings. For agent nouns, they may begin with roots only, in noun compounds if they do not yet know suffixes like *-er* or *-ist*. For instruments, they may begin with roots in either zero-derived or compound forms. Simplicity makes similar predictions for the first stage of agent and instrument noun formation: bare roots, alone or in compounds, are simpler than root–affix or compound–affix combinations. Once children acquire the suffix *-er*, they need to choose among different transparent forms designed to express the same meaning, e.g., *cut-man* or *scissor-man* versus *cutter*. At this point, they should opt for the most productive option, the one preferred by adults.

Producing novel agents and instruments

Children readily produce innovative word forms for both agent and instrument meanings, and with age, the forms they use become closer in usage to the preferences adults exhibit in the same task. In English, they favored *-er*, and used it more frequently the older they were. When they didn't rely on *-er*, the younger children used compound nouns for agents, and, to some extent, familiar words for instruments. In doing this, they typically opted for a known word for an instrument associated in some way with the action denoted by the verb, e.g., *spade* for *dig*, *hand* for *hit*, or *knife* for *cut* (Clark and Hecht 1982). The remaining responses consisted of repetitions of a verb or noun used by the experimenter (often in uninflected, root form), irrelevant comments, and 'Don't know's.[1] The percentages for each kind of response elicited are summarized in Table 10–1.

Transparency and simplicity both predicted that younger children would rely on compounds while older ones would use *-er*, and they did. As Table 10–1 shows, three-year-olds used compounds 21 percent of the time for agent nouns. This is consistent with spontaneous innovations where compounds are the only form used by two-year-olds for innovative agents (Chapter 8). Older children hardly ever produced them.

Productivity predicted children should identify *-er* as having agentive meaning before other less productive suffixes such as *-ist*, and again the findings are consistent with this prediction. First, adults doing this task produced only nouns with *-er*. This is consistent with *-er* being the most productive option for coining agent and instrument nouns. Second, in a

---

[1] Although zero-derivation is very common in English, especially for forming new verbs from nouns, it is rare for forming instrument nouns from the appropriate verbs. Most such nouns denote the product of the relevant action, as in *a jump*, *a cut*. Further analysis of the 'Other' responses in Table 10–1 showed that bare verb-forms accounted for only 2 percent of these responses. Adults never used this option in English.

Table 10–1 *Agent (A) and instrument (I) forms produced in English*

	-er		Compounds		Established		Other	
	A	I	A	I	A	I	A	I
3;0–3;8	55	42	21	6	3	28	21	24
3;9–4;5	90	71	5	2	2	8	3	19
4;6–5;2	76	70	5	3	10	10	9	17
5;3–6;0	91	72	2	10	3	6	4	12
Adults	100	100	0	0	0	0	0	0

Note: Each percentage is based on 120 responses.
Source: Clark and Hecht 1982.

separate memory task, four- and five-year-olds made consistent errors that favored more-productive over less-productive agentive suffixes. For example, they often substituted more-productive -er for less-productive -ist and -ian (Clark and Cohen 1984). Once compounds and -er have become equally transparent, productivity predicts that children should prefer nouns in -er, a conventional device for marking agent and instrument, over root compounds.[2] And, again, they did.

Finally, a number of children produced -er with only one of its meanings,

Table 10–2 *Consistency in producing agent and instrument nouns*

	Consistent on neither	Consistent only on		Consistent on both
		agents	instruments	
3;0–3;8	6	4	0	2
3;9–4;5	0	4	2	6
4;6–5;2	2	3	0	7
5;3–6;0	1	3	1	7
Total	9	14	3	22

Note: Each age group contained 12 children. Consistent children were those using the same form in at least 8 out of 10 responses for agents and instruments, respectively.
Source: Clark and Hecht 1982.

[2] Note that root compounds are common for constructing new nouns in English, but they are not productive for agent and instrument meanings.

typically that of agency. This can be seen from the two center columns of Table 10–2. Fourteen children consistently used *-er* only in its agentive meaning. Three others were consistent only in the forms they used for instruments: two relied on compounds and one on *-er*. These 17 children (mean age 4;5) were reliably younger than the 22 who used *-er* consistently for both agents and instruments (4;9). These findings offer strong support for reliance on contrast during the acquisition of *-er*. When children initially assign a meaning to *-er*, typically its agentive one, they often contrast the suffix with another form to which they have assigned an instrument meaning. Only later do they extend *-er* to both agent and instrument.

Icelandic

The Icelandic study was carried out by Randa Mulford using virtually the same materials and techniques as those devised for English, with two variations: (1) no data were collected from adults; and (2) the instructions to elicit novel nouns always contained the verb base in infinitival form (e.g., Icelandic *ad klippa* 'to cut') rather than in a third person inflected form as in English. In the case of 'to cut,' for example, the experimenter said, *Núna er ég med mynd af manni sem er ad klippa. Hvad getum vid kallad svona mann?*[3] In answer, children typically produced some form of derived or compound innovation, e.g., *klippari* 'cutter,' *klippamaður* 'cut-man.' As in the English study, children received two sets of questions, one about agents and one about instruments. In each set, they had to answer questions that tapped their comprehension of derived nouns with *-ari*, and their ability to produce appropriate word-forms. The age range was identical to that in the English study.

Predictions

Icelandic is quite close to English in the options its speakers exploit: compounding is common, but not productive for agent or instrument meanings despite well-established agent and instrument compounds with *-maður* ('-man') and *-vél* ('-machine') as heads. Affixation is also common, and Icelandic disposes of several suffixes for deriving agent and instrument nouns, including *-ari*, *-i*, and *-andi*. Another option for instrument nouns is the weak feminine noun in *-a*, zero-derived from the verb infinitive.

[3]   Equivalent to: 'Now I have a picture of a man who is cutting. What could we call that kind of man?' (Note that the English translation does not allow retention of an infinitival form of the verb 'to cut.')

Transparency predicts that Icelandic children will rely on known elements for constructing new words. Given the structural similarities between Icelandic and English, children should produce compound nouns before derived ones. Simplicity predicts that children will use zero-derivation and compounding before affixes. Productivity predicts children will adopt adult preferences as soon as they have more than one transparent form available for a specific meaning. In Icelandic, these were assessed only indirectly, from a compilation of the relative frequencies of agent and instrument nouns in a widely read children's book, an Icelandic translation of Richard Scarry's *What do people do all day*? These do not necessarily reflect contemporary preferences in word formation.

Producing novel agents and instruments

Data from children's spontaneous coinages in Icelandic suggest they begin by relying on compounding for new agent and instrument nouns. Typical examples of innovative agent-nouns appeared from age two in the speech of one child followed longitudinally, e.g., *jarn-menn* (2;4) 'rail-men,' *saelgaetis-maður* (2;9) 'candy-man' for someone who eats a lot of candy, *sjonvarp-maður* (3;3) 'television-man' for a picture of someone carrying a television set, and *sirkus-maður* (3;3) 'circus-man' for a lion-tamer. The same child also coined some novel compounds for instruments, but did this less often than for agents. Icelandic children also use *-ari* in their spontaneous innovations to mark both agents and instruments. For example, after turning on the light, one little girl (3;10) remarked *Mamma, ég er kveikjari. Eg er alltaf ad kveikja* 'Mama, I'm a lighter. I'm always turning on the light'; and a little boy (2;9), who had momentarily forgotten the word for toaster (*bradrist*), called it *ristari* (from the verb *ad rista* 'to toast') (Mulford 1983, unpublished data).

Icelandic children willingly produce word forms for both agents and instruments. In the elicitation task, they favored the suffix *-ari*, with older children using it more often than younger ones. They also relied on other means: all the children produced other derivational suffixes besides *-ari* (mainly *-i*); the younger ones used zero-derivation and some compounding, and also relied on some existing words, as shown in Table 10–3.

As predicted by transparency, the youngest children made some use of compounds (8 percent of agent forms for three- and four-year-olds), but these uses were overshadowed by their reliance on zero-derived nouns, with no change in form. These responses, predicted by simplicity, accounted for 23 percent of the agent nouns and 34 percent of the

Table 10–3 *Agent (A) and instrument (I) forms produced in Icelandic*

	-ari		Comps		No formal change		Other Derived		Establ		Other	
	A	I	A	I	A	I	A	I	A	I	A	I
3;0–3;8	57	43	8	3	23	34	5	4	5	8	2	8
3;9–4;5	83	49	8	1	7	41	1	5	0	1	1	3
4;6–5;2	87	80	1	3	4	11	7	4	2	0	0	2
5;3–6;0	98	78	1	3	1	8	0	6	0	2	0	3

Note: Each percentage is based on 120 responses.
Source: Mulford 1983.

instrument ones for three-year-olds. For four-year-olds, only 7 percent of the agents took this form, versus 41 percent of the instruments. By age four children respond to the conventionality of this form for instruments (versus agents).

As in English, children should produce *-ari* with just one of its meanings initially and only later with both. This prediction too was supported. This can be seen in Table 10–4: of the 13 children who consistently used a single form for agents, 11 used the suffix *-ari*, one used compounds with *-maður*

Table 10–4 *Consistency in producing agent and instrument nouns in Icelandic*

	Consistent on neither	Consistent only on		Consistent on both, with patterns	
		agents	instruments	different	same
3;0–3;8	2	4	2	0	3
3;9–4;5	0	3	1	4	4
4;6–5;2	0	3	1	1	7
5;3–6;0	0	3	0	0	9
Total	2	13	4	5	23

Note: Each age group contained 12 children. Consistent children were those using the same form in at least 8 out of 10 responses for agents and instruments, respectively.
Source: Mulford 1983.

('-man') as the head noun, and one used zero-derived nouns. Of the 4 using a single form for instruments, 1 used *-ari*, and the remaining 3 used zero-derived forms. Finally, of the 5 children using two consistent forms, one for agents and one for instruments, 4 used *-ari* for agents versus zero derivation for instruments, and 1 used compounds with *-maður* for agents versus zero-derivation for instruments. These data strongly suggest that children initially contrast different options and use them on the assumption that different forms have different meanings. This leads them to use some options with a meaning narrower than the conventional one. Just as for English, children who used *-ari* consistently with only one meaning were reliably younger than those who used it with both (4;5,12 versus 4;9,27). When children used the same consistent pattern for both, they always used *-ari*.

Icelandic and English compared

Icelandic children strongly resemble their English-speaking peers in the coining of agent and instrument nouns. The predictions for the two languages are similar, as are the kinds of word forms produced (compare Tables 10–1 and 10–3). Differences between Icelandic and English stem from specific properties of the two languages, and are predicted by the applicability of each acquisitional principle. From the point of view of simplicity, zero-derivation is simple in English, but only for instrument-noun formation, and it is not productive. But in Icelandic, instrument nouns are commonly derived from verbs with no change in form, as in *ad dirla* 'to twirl' > *dirla* 'helicopter.' As predicted, Icelandic children made use of this option, especially in the youngest age group (Table 10–3). Yet since the infinitive verb was used in each instruction in the production task, it's also possible the children simply repeated the verb used by the experimenter. Without articles to indicate nominal status, it is hard to distinguish verbs from instrument nouns. Two kinds of evidence suggest that these responses were nouns: (a) from age four on, children made reliably more use of such forms for instruments than for agents; (b) when children made consistent use of this form, in all but one case, they used it only for instruments (Mulford 1983).

The presence of a formally simple device – nouns derived from verbs with no change in form – may also account for the small number of compounds produced by Icelandic children compared with English-speaking ones. Icelandic children, given the option of using a maximally

Table 10–5 *Comparison of word types produced for agents and instruments in English and Icelandic*

	Agents		Instruments	
	English	Icelandic	English	Icelandic
-er/-ari	78	81	64	62
Compounds	8	4	5	3
No formal change	2	9	3	23
Other derived	0	3	0	5
Other responses	12	3	28	7

Note: Each percentage is based on 480 responses.
Source: Clark and Hecht 1982, Mulford 1983.

simple form, could take advantage of it until they learnt more about other possibilities. Overall, English and Icelandic elicit similar patterns of word formation in young children (Table 10–5), but differences in what is productive and therefore available, lead to different outcomes. This is most evident for simplicity in terms of the options that are available, in particular compounding and zero-derivation, in the earliest stages of constructing novel nouns for agents and instruments.

Hebrew

The Hebrew data come from a replication and extension of the original study in English using similar materials, with some minor changes: (1) the production task was separated from the comprehension task and always given first; (2) children analyzed three different word forms for agents and three for instruments (rather than just one form for both as in English and Icelandic); (3) the verbs were taken from the four active verb *binyanim* (form types); and (4) the instructions were worded so the pertinent verb form in the production task was always in the infinitive, a form that contrasts structurally with any nominal form children might try to produce. Change (4) allowed the identification of zero-derived nouns with greater certainty than in Icelandic. To elicit an agent noun from the infinitive *li-srof* 'to burn,' for instance, the experimenter would say *yesh li kan tmuna*

shel yéled she'ohev li-srof. ha'avoda shel hayéled haze, hi li-srof kol hazman.
ex efshar likro leyéled she'ohev li-srof? hu kol hazman roce li-srof. ex kor'im
lo?[4] To label someone whose job was to burn things, children could in
principle use any of several options – a noun pattern (with vowels
intercalated in the root consonants), a suffix added to a word form or noun
pattern, a zero-derived form, or a compound.

The children received two sets of questions, one to elicit production of
novel nouns, and the other to elicit analyses of novel nouns. The age range
was extended to include seven- and eleven-year-olds in addition to the
younger children and adults. All were second generation speakers of
Hebrew.[5]

Predictions

In word formation, Hebrew relies primarily on associations of consonantal
roots with patterns of vowel infixes. It also makes use of derivation, with
suffixes added to word stems, much as in English, and of zero-derivation
for verbs made into nouns. Hebrew also makes use of some compounding,
with the order head–modifier, as in *naaley-báyit* 'shoes-house, = slippers.'
Zero-derivation and compounding are rare in spoken Hebrew compared
with affixation or noun patterns intercalated with consonantal roots
(Berman 1978a, 1987, Ravid 1978).

Transparency predicts that children will use familiar elements to
construct new words. Of the three major options available for coining
agent nouns, the nominal pattern CaCCan and the -*an* suffix added to a
stem, both specialized in the established vocabulary for agentive meaning,
should be acquired earlier than the other agentive noun pattern, CaCaC.
Zero-derived nouns may be acquired earlier still but this option is not very
productive for agents. For instruments, transparency predicted that the
more specialized forms, carrying only instrumental meaning, should be
acquired first – namely the maCCeC pattern and its feminine counterpart,
maCCeCa. (The maCCeCa form may be slightly less transparent because
it is used at times, in error, for place nouns as well.) Next should come zero-
derived nouns, but since these also function as present-tense verbs, they
may be less transparent than noun patterns or affixal forms.

---

[4] Equivalent to: 'I have a picture here of a boy that likes to burn. The boy's (kid's) work is
to burn all the time. What can we call a boy that likes to burn? He wants to burn all the
time. What's he called?' (See Clark and Berman 1984.)

[5] As in English and Icelandic, children acquiring Hebrew were able to offer appropriate
meanings for novel word forms they were given to analyze before they produced them
themselves. Some forms they understood but never produced.

Here, the predictions made by transparency and simplicity do not coincide. For agents, zero-derived nouns should be the simplest, followed by forms with suffixes such as *-an* (whether as a suffix alone or as part of the CaCCan pattern), followed by noun patterns such as CaCaC. For instruments, zero-derived forms should again be the simplest, followed by suffixal forms like *-an*, followed by the prefixal maCCeC and maCCeCa patterns, with the latter considered more complex since it has both a prefix and suffix.

Productivity was measured here by analysis of contemporary adult preferences in the pertinent lexical domains (Berman 1987, Clark and Berman 1984). Once children find several options are transparent, they should follow adult preferences, namely CaCCan or *-an* suffixation for novel agents and for novel instruments.

Producing novel agents and instruments

The form children favored most, overall, for both agents and instruments, was the suffix *-an*, either as part of the CaCCan pattern or attached to a word stem. Older children used it more often than the younger ones. When they didn't use *-an*, they relied on several other means. The youngest (aged three) relied most on zero-derived nouns (31 percent of agent forms and 18 percent of instrument ones). This is consistent with the prediction from simplicity. Five-, seven- and eleven-year-olds also made some use of compounds for agents (on average, 13 percent) and, rather more often, for instruments (23 percent). The remaining responses consisted of other noun patterns, existing words, and 'Don't know's. These data are summarized in Table 10–6.

Simplicity and transparency converged in predicting reliance on zero-derived nouns for agents. The youngest children tested made greater use of this option than of any other for both agents and instruments. But, from age four on, once they acquired the *-an* suffix, children relied on that. In choosing between two transparent options – zero-derivation versus *-an* suffixation – they shifted almost entirely to the option preferred by adults, namely *-an*.

Children appeared to assume that each option contrasted in meaning with the others. This can be seen in the analysis made of the responses given by each child: Table 10–7 shows the number of children making inconsistent responses, consistent responses for agent or instrument forms, and consistent responses for both (using either the same or different

Table 10–6 *Agent (A) and instrument (I) forms produced in Hebrew*

	-an		Beynoni		Comps		Other noun patterns		Establ		Other	
	A	I	A	I	A	I	A	I	A	I	A	I
3;1–3;11	15	10	31	18	5	5	4	1	5	33	38	33
4;2–4;9	62	43	3	5	8	8	3	8	7	26	18	11
5;0–5;9	77	34	2	1	8	18	3	3	5	38	6	7
7;3–8;0	65	36	3	10	22	30	8	6	1	16	3	4
11;0–12;0	63	54	6	8	18	20	4	5	9	4	0	1
Adults	76	53	12	15	3	2	3	22	7	8	0	1

Note: Each percentage is based on 120 responses.
Source: Clark and Berman 1984.

options). As children get older, they show greater consistency in their choices of forms. This is particularly apparent for agent nouns, less so for instrument ones.[6]

Table 10–7 *Consistency in producing agent and instrument nouns in Hebrew*

	Consistent on neither	Consistent on only agent	Consistent on only instrument	Consistent on both
3;1–3;11	7	4	0	1
4;2–4;9	4	5	0	3
5;0–5;9	4	6	0	2
7;3–8;0	1	9	1	1
11;0–12;0	4	3	5	0
Total	20	27	6	7

Note: Each age group contained 12 children. Consistent children were those using the same form in at least 8 out of 10 responses for agents and instruments, respectively.
Source: Clark and Berman 1984.

[6] In Hebrew, the options in current use for instruments are more diverse than those for agents. This fact may account for the relatively small increase with age in the number of children consistent on both types of novel nouns. If the criterion applied in the consistency analysis is relaxed from 8 out of 10 to 7 out of 10 uses of the same form, two children move

Despite differences of typology between Hebrew on the one hand, and English and Icelandic on the other, Hebrew-speaking children appear to rely on the same principles (simplicity, transparency, and productivity) as children acquiring English and Icelandic. Across languages, children all show some delay in producing derivational affixes, so they at first favor zero-derivation or compounding (where these are available) and only later, between age three and age four, turn to derivational forms with suffixes. As soon as children had two or more transparent forms to choose from, they favored the most productive option of those available, the one preferred by adults.

French and Italian

The data on French and Italian are drawn from two studies based in part on Clark and Hecht's research on English. The French study looked at production data from five- and six-year-olds, and at both judgment and production data from adults (Seidler 1988). It did not include any comprehension data, nor did it elicit coinages from younger children. The questions given to the children contained the relevant verbs in third-person singular present form, e.g., *cache* in *Comment pourrait-on appeler un homme qui cache de l'argent?* to elicit a novel agent-noun, and *démolit* in *Comment pourrait-on appeler une machine qui démolit des chaises?* to elicit a novel instrument-noun.[7] In answer, the children typically produced a derived noun from a verb stem plus suffix. As in English, children received two sets of elicitation questions, one about agents and one about instruments. The age range was from 4;7 to 6;8 (Seidler 1988).

Predictions for French

French relies primarily on suffixation to form new agent and instrument nouns. The commonest are *-eur* (and its feminine counterpart *-euse*), *-ateur/-atrice*, *-ier*, and *-iste*, for agents; and *-ail/aille*, *-oir/-oire*, and *-eur/-euse* for instruments (Guilbert 1971). French also makes use of compounds for instruments, as in the well-established *tire-bouchon* 'corkscrew.' But in general, compounding is not productive, and young French-speaking children make no use of it in their spontaneous coinages (Chapter 9).

from the first column to the second, one moves to the third, and three move from the second to the 'Both' column in Table 10–7.
[7] These questions are equivalent to: 'What could you call a man who hides money?' and 'What could you call a machine that destroys chairs?', respectively; see further Seidler 1988.

Transparency predicts that children will build new words from familiar elements. In the case of French, that suggests that they must wait until they acquire one or more agentive suffixes before they will coin novel agent-nouns. The most productive suffix, and hence the one children are most likely to have been exposed to, is *-eur/-euse*. This suffix is the one preferred by adults, and the one most favored by children in spontaneous coinages. If children distinguish agent from instrument forms, they might either pick another suffix for the latter (*-oir/-oire*, say) or rely on compounding.

Simplicity predicts that children may first opt for root compounds, especially for instruments, since these require little change. (Zero-derivation for agents and instruments is not an option in French.) The addition of a suffix to a stem demands more of children since they have to decide which stem to attach it to. The verbs in the elicitation questions were drawn from all three conjugations: 10 from the first in *-er*, 6 from the second in *-ir*, and 6 from the third, with the largest number of irregular forms, in *-re*. For all three conjugations, the stem for derivation is the one that appears in first- (and second-) person plural present forms. For *-er* verbs, this stem is identical to that in the infinitive (e.g., *donner*-INF versus *donnons*-.1PL: both stems *donn-*), but for the other two, the infinitival and first person plural stems are different, as in *finir*-INF versus *finissons*-.1PL, with stems *fin-* and *finiss-*; and *prendre*-INF versus *prenons*-.1PL, with stems *prend-* and *pren-*. Since over 90 percent of French verbs belong to the first conjugation (in *-er*), children's initial choices of stems could be erroneous, especially if they assume that the first-conjugation stem is the infinitival one. With first-conjugation verbs, this makes no difference, but with second- and third-conjugation verbs, this results in wrong stem choices. Lastly, productivity predicts that children should rely on those forms most favored by adult speakers, namely the suffix *-eur/-euse*.

Producing novel agents and instruments

French-speaking five- and six-year-olds rely primarily on derivation to coin new agent and instrument nouns, as shown in Table 10–8. (There were no age differences for the range tested by Seidler.) As predicted by transparency, children tended to rely on a single suffix for agents and used it on 90 percent or more of their coinages. And, just as in English, Icelandic, and Hebrew, they typically relied on the same suffix for both agents and instruments, namely *-eur* and its feminine counterpart *-euse*. They made significantly more use, overall, of derivation than compounding (88 percent versus 4 percent), but when they did use compounding, they

Table 10–8 *Agent and instrument forms produced in French*

	Agents				Instruments			
	-eur	Other affix	Compound	Establ	*-eur*	Other affix	Compound	Establ
4;7–5;11	90	3	4	0	84	2	7	0.3
6;3–6;8	93	2	2	0	87	3	4	2

Note: Each percentage is based on 264 responses.
Source: Seidler 1988.

relied on it more often for instruments (6 percent) than for agents (3 percent). They were highly consistent in the suffixes they produced,[8] and there were no differences with age. Nine of the 12 from each age group were consistent on both types and used the same suffix on both. Among the fives, 2 were inconsistent, and 1 consistent only on instruments; among the sixes, 1 was inconsistent, and 2 were consistent on one type only (1 on agents and 1 on instruments).

As predicted by simplicity, French-speaking children evinced considerable difficulty in making the appropriate stem-choices when they constructed nouns with second- or third-conjugation verbs, shown in Table 10–9. For first-conjugation verbs, they produced appropriate stems 83 percent of the time, but for second-conjugation verbs, their stems were appropriate only 56 percent of the time, and for third-conjugation ones, only 42 percent of the time. Children's main error was reliance on infinitival stems in both second- and third-conjugation forms. Five-year-olds used the wrong stems more than half the time with second- and third-conjugation verbs, while six-year-olds produced a consistently higher number of appropriate stems.

Productivity predicted that children would rely on the options most favored by adults in the same community. This was supported by the parallels between children's forms and adult preferences in an analogous production task as well in judgments of novel forms.[9] Adult speakers overall preferred the suffix *-eur* (with less frequent use of feminine forms

---

[8] Consistent children were those using the same affix (except for gender) in at least 18 out of 22 responses to agents and instruments respectively.

[9] In the judgment task, for example, adults had to choose among the suffixes *-eur* and *-iste*, a verb–object compound, and the suffix *-ant*, as in *casseur de tasses, cassiste de tasses, casse-tasses*, and *cassant de tasses* (all for 'someone who breaks cups').

Table 10–9 *Appropriate stem-choices in French*

	Agents			Instruments		
	-er	-ir	-re	-er	-ir	re
4;7–5;11	79	42	47	78	51	30
6;3–6;8	87	69	61	85	60	29
Mean	83	56	53	82	56	30

Note: Each percentage is based on 120 responses for -*er* verbs, and on 72 responses each for -*ir* and -*re* verbs.

in -*euse*) for both agent and instrument nouns, but they showed greater unanimity, both in their judgments and their productions, on agent than on instrument forms.

Like adult speakers, children chose a single form for new agent-nouns, and relied on that in the vast majority of their coinages. And, like adults, they relied on the *same* suffix almost as often for new instrument-nouns. Children made use of few other suffixes for either agents or instruments, and made little use of compounds, although, again consistent with adult usage, they produced more compounds for instruments than for agents.

Predictions for Italian

For Italian, comparable data on agentive noun forms come from a corpus of spontaneous innovations as well as elicitation data from children aged 3;3 to 7;10 (Lo Duca 1990). In Italian, children must chose from among several suffixes that all mark agency. But these often have other functions too: some mark instruments as well as agents; others mark locations in addition to agents; and some have an adjectival use, and may also carry ameliorative or pejorative connotations in addition to agency. The suffix is added to the past participial stem of the verb[10] or to the stem of the noun. That is, an agentive suffix is typically both transparent and relatively simple in form. In addition to suffixation, Italian children could also make use of root compounds (with verb–noun form) for agents. But in Italian, compounds are not necessarily simpler than suffixal forms since, to decide

---

[10] This holds for the addition of agentive affixes to second- and third-conjugation verbs, e.g., the stem *lett-* in *lettore* 'reader' from second-conjugation *leggere* 'to read'; in the first conjugation, the stem for agentive nouns could be analyzed as present, e.g., *porta-* from *portare* 'to carry,' provided the affix is analyzed as -*tore*. Alternatively, the stem for first-conjugation derivations could also be taken to be the past participial one, i.e., *portat-*, with the suffix -*ore* added for agentive *portatore*.

on the form of the verb, children must know which conjugation it belongs to – the first in -*are* with -*a*, or second in -*ere* and third in -*ire*, both with -*e*. In Italian, both affixation and compounding require knowledge of verb conjugation for the necessary stems.

These options differ in productivity: compounds are not very productive for agent nouns, but they may be simpler for younger children since they do not require them to have identified an agentive suffix. In addition, agentive suffixes on nouns and verbs differ in form and in productivity. For example, -*ista* is the most productive agentive affix on noun stems, and -*ore* the most productive on verbs. The measure of productivity here is based on the number of new formations with each suffix recorded in Cortelazzo and Cardinale (1986) and Devoto and Oli (1985). (Lo Duca did not collect data from adults on the task she used with children.) Young children should acquire first the suffixes they have had most exposure to, and these should also be preferred once they have several transparent forms to choose among.

Producing novel agent nouns

In their spontaneous coinages, Italian children appear to favor the suffix -*aio* early on, but by age five or so they make equal use of -*aio* and -*ista* in their spontaneous innovations.[11] (Both these suffixes make agent nouns from nouns.) Children make occasional errors in their choice of affix for the stem type, e.g., a noun-stem affix added to a verb, as in *cucinaio* from the verb *cucinare* 'to cook,' for adult *cuoco*, or a verb-stem affix added to a noun, as in *librore*, for adult *libraio* 'librarian.' They also make some errors in verb conjugation when they construct novel compounds, as in *venda-palloncini* (from second-conjugation *vendere* 'to sell') for *vende-palloncini* 'balloon-seller.'

In the elicitation task, children between 3;3 and 7;10 were asked a series of questions about the agents responsible for various activities. The instructions in Italian took the general form of *Como si chiama quello che fa le pizze?*[12] The percentage of derived and compound innovations elicited from each age group is shown in Table 10–10, with the total number elicited given in the last column. The youngest group (three-year-olds)

---

[11] Lo Duca's 1990 corpus consists of 126 innovative agent nouns from 27 children between 2;4 and 10;3. The majority were collected from her daughter V, aged 5;8 to 8;2 (n = 76); some from another child, Al, from 4;0 to 6;4 (n = 14); and the remaining 36 examples from other children (1990, p. 103).

[12] Equivalent to: 'What could one call the person who makes pizza?' Each child heard 20 different verbs, some of them in several different questions; see further Lo Duca 1990, pp. 192–193.

Table 10–10 *Agent word forms produced in Italian*

| | Percentage | | Total |
	derived	compound	innovations
3;7	29	71	96
5;1	87	13	245
6;9	98	2	182
7;8	98	2	137

Source: Lo Duca 1990.

produced compound forms over two-thirds of the time and used only a few derivational affixes. The children in the three older groups used a larger range, but most of their uses were accounted for by the more productive suffixes added to nouns or verbs.

The range of suffixes produced on derived forms is shown in Table 10–11. For three-year-olds, *-aio* and *-tore* accounted for 61 percent of the derived innovations, but they were produced by only two children. By age

Table 10–11 *Agentive suffixes produced in Italian*

| | Age | | | |
Suffix	3;7	5;1	6;9	7;8
-aio	32	36	42	20
-ista	0	30	25	35
-tore	29	16	11	26
-iere	0	4	13	11
-ario	7	3	3	1
-ore	0	5	2	1
-one	4	2	2	1
-ino	4	2	1	1
-aiolo	0	1	0	2
-nte	4	1	1	1
Other	21	0	0	0
N =	[28]	[212]	[179]	[134]

Note: Each percentage is based on the total number of innovations in the age group tested.
Source: Lo Duca 1990.

five, the number of compounds produced was halved, and derived forms accounted for the vast majority of innovative agent-nouns. Of the suffixes used, -*aio* was produced by all 12 children, -*ista* by 6, and -*tore* by 8. Together, these three suffixes accounted for 82 percent of the innovative derived forms produced. Among six-year-olds, 10 used -*aio*, 8 -*ista*, 9 -*tore*, and 8 -*iere*. Altogether, these four suffixes accounted for 91 percent of the derived innovations. Finally, among seven-year-olds, 8 used -*aio*, 11 -*ista*, 9 -*tore*, and 9 -*iere*; their uses accounted for 92 percent of the derived innovations. The remaining suffixes were used by only 4 children or fewer in the three older groups.

In summary, children acquiring French and Italian exhibit similar tendencies when they coin words for agents. (There are no Italian data on instrument nouns.) In both languages, from at least age five and up, children rely mainly on suffixes to mark agency, with a strong preference for those suffixes productive in adult speech. However, before that point, young Italian children relied on novel compounds to talk about agents; whether three- or four-year-old French speakers would use compounds is unclear. Neither French nor Italian children produce compounds in their spontaneous coinages. In French, six-year-olds still have difficulty in producing the appropriate verb-stem for suffixation, especially for second- and third-conjugation verbs (see Table 10–9). In both French and Italian, the typical error is to choose a first-conjugation form as the paradigm for the derivational stem. French-speaking children relied mostly on the suffix -*eur* (or its feminine counterpart -*euse*) while Italian children produced a larger range in their coinages. Children from both languages favored more-productive over less-productive suffixes.

Summary

Children acquiring the means to form new agent and instrument nouns are sensitive to the typology of the language they are learning. They make heavy use of compounding from as young as age two on in languages where compounding is a common option, as in English or Icelandic. But children acquiring Hebrew, French, and Italian make virtually no spontaneous use of this option. Instead, they rely extensively on affixation and construct new agents and instruments by adding the appropriate suffixes to roots or stems.

Children follow similar routes in different languages. First, they consistently demonstrate their ability to interpret new noun-forms before they can produce such forms on demand. When presented with novel agentive nouns, they can identify the pertinent stem and the meaning of the suffix. They demonstrate this in the glosses they offer of possible meanings for novel words (Clark and Berman 1984, Clark and Hecht 1982, Mulford 1983). They are also sensitive to the productivity of the devices available in each language. Among suffixes, the first ones produced tend to be among the most frequent in adult speech. These are usually also the most productive, as measured by the numbers of innovations that have made their way into dictionaries (an indirect measure) or by the preferences exhibited by adult speakers. By age seven or so, children appear to rely primarily on the more productive among the options available, and show considerable consistency in their own usage.

Another general finding is that children (and adults) typically prefer a single suffix for both the agent and instrument meanings of new nouns. That is, they appear to recognize some conceptual unity in this semantic domain – a unity underlined by reliance on the same device for both kinds of meaning. At the same time, the notion of agency seems to have some priority in that children usually produce the chosen suffix first to mark new agent nouns, and only later to mark instruments as well.

Finally, although each language presented children with somewhat different issues in terms of which forms were most accessible and readily made use of, children appear consistent in holding to simplicity and transparency in their earliest coinages, with transparency taking over once they analyze the relevant affixes. Productivity both points children to the forms they should analyze first (the most frequent ones in the the input) and then guides them as they choose among transparent forms for a particular meaning.

To conclude, when children coin new words – whether spontaneously, or in response to a request for a label – they make use of what they already know about forms in the lexicon. They opt initially for the simplest forms available among those already known to them. And once they can choose among transparent options, they pick more-productive over less-pro-ductive word-forms.

In the next chapter, I take up children's coining of words for actions rather than things and then, in Chapter 12, I consider one aspect of this general domain in detail – the coining of verbs for talking about reversals of actions.

11 *Words for actions*

Young children don't only talk about things; they also talk about actions, and here too they coin new words. But where do new labels for actions come from? In many languages, perhaps most, the major source is nouns. Speakers can use the label for an object involved in the action to designate the activity itself, provided, of course, there is no established verb with just that meaning already available. In some languages, forming a new verb is also very simple, through zero-derivation; in others, the noun base requires an affix to mark its change of word class. Languages also differ in the extent to which such coining of verbs is productive: in some, it is highly productive, in others less so.

Factors like transparency, simplicity, and productivity should play the same roles in novel verb-formation as they do in noun formation, The extent to which this appears true is explored in the present chapter. I look first at innovative verbs produced in English and other Germanic languages, where noun into verb is generally productive, then turn to Romance and Slavic, and finally look at Hungarian and Hebrew. A before, I draw primarily from published records of longitudinal observations, supplemented by some cross-sectional studies of children's word formation. For English, these data are supplemented by my own observations of spontaneous and elicited forms. For the other languages as before, I have drawn on published diaries, reports of vocabulary development, and the occasional elicitation study.

New verbs in English

English, like most languages, offers several options for coining new verbs The most productive is the formation of verbs from nouns through zero derivation. This option has been available for several centuries and continues to be the most widely used source for new verbs entering the language. Adult speakers of English make extensive use of it, subject only to pragmatic constraints on lexical innovation: New verbs and their intended meanings must be interpretable for the addressee, and their intended meanings must contrast with meanings already represented in the established lexicon (Clark and Clark 1979).

Other options for coining verbs involve adding a suffix such as *-ate*, *-ify*, or *-ize* to a base, usually an adjective or noun, as in *complex/complexify* and *gentry/gentrify*. These suffixes appear mainly in technical domains, where speakers rely more on Latinate stems. They are all relatively unproductive compared with zero derivation for everyday additions to the lexicon of verbs (Adams 1973, Marchand 1969, Quirk, Greenbaum, Leech, and Svartvik 1972; also Ljung 1974).

Predictions

What predictions do the different principles make about the formation of new verbs from nouns? Transparency of meaning predicts that children should coin verbs from nouns already familiar to them. These nouns should be clearly connected to the intended meaning of the verb, and so, for example, should name entities directly implicated in the activities being designated. Simplicity of form predicts that new words formed from roots without affixation should be easier than those formed with affixation. Zero-derivation – here used to form new verbs from nouns – should be used before affixation (e.g., forming verbs from adjectives with the suffix *-ate*). Transparency and simplicity coincide here: what is simple in form is also transparent in meaning.

The accessibility to children of any word-formation option depends also on productivity in adult speech. Zero-derivation in English offers a highly productive means for forming new verbs from nouns. It is widely used for nonce formations, and it has also been the major source of new additions to the established lexicon of verbs for centuries (Clark and Clark 1979, Kiparsky 1982, 1983, Marchand 1969). The few suffixes available in English for verb formation are less productive than the zero option, and are generally restricted to technical domains. They should therefore be acquired later than zero-derived forms.

Producing innovative verbs in English

Children acquiring English begin to coin verbs as early as age two. The onset of such coinages appears to coincide with their discovery of other properties of verbs, notably that they can be used for talking about events

Table 11–1 *Typical innovative verbs from D*

(1)	D (2;4,13, grinding pepper onto the kitchen counter): *I'm sanding.* (a few moments later, looking at the pepper grains) *Look at the sand.*
(2)	Mo (to D, who was pretending he needed gas for his car): You want to try Herb's pump this time?
	D (2;7,22): *Herb, pump my car.* [= fill with gas from the pump]
(3)	D (2;8,4, to Mo in the shower): *Leave a puddle in there so I can water in it.* [= paddle in the water]
(4)	Mo (turning off hose in the garden): Oh, there's a bit too much water here.
	D (2;8,20, wanting Mo to wash dirt off his stick with water from the hose): *An' water the dirt off my stick.*
(5)	D (2;9,1, of sock): *And did you needle this?* [= mend with a needle]
(6)	D (2;9,10, after mention of boats): *And we might see a man oaring a boat with oars.*
(7)	Mo (unpacking a construction toy): And here's a wrench for undoing them.
	D (3;0,8): *How do you wrench them?*
(8)	D (3;1,6, to Mo who's carrying a stick for him): *It's meant to touch the ground.* Mo Oh.
	D *Let* ME *stick it hard.* (touches ground with it, firmly)
(9)	D (3;2,9, picking up Cuisinart blade Mo had left in the sink):
	Mo You shouldn't take that. It's VERY sharp.
	D *But I didn't blade myself.* [= cut with the blade]
(10)	D (3;3,8, putting blocks, pretend pieces of candy, on Mo's lap): *And you can marble them all.* [= roll like marbles]
(11)	D (3;3,25, after a visitor had mentioned a burglary): *When I get home I want to torch with the torch-light to see if anyone's taking things in my room.* [= turn on torch and look around]
(12)	D (3;4,5, handing Mo a small yoyo): *Eve, will you wind this up for me so I can yoyo it down?*
(13)	D (3;4,28, talking with Fa about a storm expected that night):
	Fa Very very windy and very very rainy.
	D *And it will wind* ALL *the toys away!*
(14)	D (3;5,17, after Mo said his toy plane was too noisy on the kitchen floor; holding it up in the air): *I'll wheel it like this.* [= make its wheels turn]
(15)	D (3;9,1, playing with two interlocked plastic rings at the pool): *I know what – I'll frisbee this. I'll frisbee this into the water.* [= throw like a frisbee]
(16)	D (3;9,20, tapping on the car-window with a tiny plastic axe): *I'm axing this, look: ax, ax, ax.*
(17)	D (4;0,17, playing with a small figure holding a scythe, just after Mo told him what a scythe was called): *I'm going to make him scythe.*
(18)	D (4;2,6, looking at a new carton of apple-juice, opened by cutting off one corner with scissors): *How do you know where to … to scissor it?* [= open with scissors]
(19)	D (4;3,15, assembling playmobile pirate-ship): *Mom, we need a bit of string so we can string down to the hold and then I'll string things out of the hold.* [= take out via the string]
(20)	D (4;4,0, Fa reading him Hans Anderson's 'Tinderbox Soldier'): *I think he could have sworded the door ə pieces.*

Note: Glosses are given in square brackets.
Source: Clark, diary data.

that involve only one participant, typically the actor (intransitive uses), or two, typically the agent and the patient (transitive uses). At around this time, they begin to use the same verb-form to talk about both action types, with intransitive to transitive/causative shifts in *He disappeared/He disappeared the rabbit* ('made the rabbit disappear'), and transitive to intransitive in *She threw the ball/The ball threw down* ('got thrown down'). Also, during the same period, children begin to use *make* and *get* periphrastically to express causation.[1] The discovery of the connections between intransitive and transitive causative pairs like *open* (*The door opened/He opened the door*), and of periphrastic expressions of causation, coincides with a general expansion in the forms children use to talk about specific actions (see Bowerman 1974, 1982a, Lord 1979).

When children coin new verbs in English, they do so mainly by taking a noun for one of the entities involved and using that as a verb, with zero-derivation. In D's speech, for example, the first innovative verb appeared at 1;10.[2] The majority of his innovative verbs were verbs coined from nouns (72 percent), with a smaller number coined from adjectives (19 percent). D also coined a few verbs from exclamations (e.g., *pow, ow*), and prepositions (e.g., *down*), mostly before age three. Together, these accounted for 9 percent of verb coinages. Some typical examples are shown in Table 11-1, from D, and in Table 11-2, from other children in the same age range.

English-speaking children produce many novel verbs from nouns. But up to age five (and possibly till even later), they never construct innovative verbs with the verbalizing suffixes *-ize*, *-ify*, or *-ate*. Even when they construct verbs from adjectives (prime candidates for using these suffixes), children rely almost entirely on zero-derivation as in *I'm talling* (1;9) for 'getting taller'; *It's still soring* (2;6) 'still feeling sore'(said of a scrape); *I'm darking the letters* (2;8), as the child scribbled over a drawing; *I pinking things* (2;10,1) 'making things look pink,' as the child looked through a transparent piece of pink plastic; or, while watching another child swinging

---

[1] In English, as in other languages, transitive causative verbs that are single lexemes are taken to express direct causation (Shibatani 1976). When periphrastic verbs are used (e.g., *make ... build*), they must contrast in meaning with the corresponding single-lexeme causatives, so they are typically assigned meanings of indirect causation. This holds for innovative as well as established verbs.

[2] Clark, diary data. The innovative verbs discussed here include all D's coinages from a noun or adjective base, but exclude established verbs where there is simply a change in transitivity, as when a child makes the intransitive verb *come* into a transitive causative one (*He comed it here*). Verb coinages in the diary record are less common than noun coinages, amounting to about one a week between age two and age five.

202   *Words for actions*

Table 11–2 *Innovative verbs from other English-speaking children*

Two-year-olds
(1)   (1;10, playing with some blocks): *I noised.* [= made a noise]
(2)   (2;3): *Mummy trousers me.* [= puts my trousers on)
(3)   (2;4, of a calculator): *I can button it.* [= press the buttons]
(4)   (2;4, resisting having his hair brushed): *Don't hair me.*
(5)   (2;4, of some cheese): *You have to scale it first.* [= weigh it]
(6)   (2;4, explaining a band-aid on her hand): *I stoved it.*
(7)   (2;5, waving a toy animal): *It's flagging around.* [= waving]
(8)   (2;6): *Can I fire the candle?* [= light]
(9)   (2;7, having hit smaller sister with a toy broom): *I broomed her.*
(10)   (2;7, pretending to play with a floor-sander): *I'm gonna sander.*
(11)   (2;9, as pushed parent in the stomach): *I'll stomach you.*

Three-year-olds
(12)   (3;0, looking at a doorbell): *Make it bell.* [= ring]
(13)   (3;0, wanting to light a candle): *I'm gonna match this.*
(14)   (3;1, designating a toy boat as a coastguard boat): *Can I coastguard the boat?*
(15)   (3;1, watching the revolving back of a cement truck): *That truck is cementing.* [= making cement]
(16)   (3;2, watching a flag spread out in the wind): *That flag is flagging.*
(17)   (3;3, fantasizing): *A fire, a fire! A fire is coming. Our house is firing.* [= getting on fire, burning]
(18)   (3;5, of a prayer book): *He prayers with it.*
(19)   (3;10, holding tongs for spaghetti): *I'm gonna pliers this out.*
(20)   (3;11, making dots over a drawing): *It's snowflaking so hard you can't even see this person.*

2 Age four and older
(21)   (4;0, rejecting some paper she'd previously cut herself on): *I don't think I'll have it because it papers me.* [= cuts]
(22)   (4;5, putting different objects into playdough she was kneading): *I think I'll bead it. I think I'll rubberband it.* [= put a bead in, put a rubber band in]
(23)   (4;6, pretending to nurse her doll against her chest): *Do you want to see how I milk Vicky?*
(24)   (4;9): *Can I typewriter on your typewriter or Daddy's?*
(25)   (4;11, of the Christmas tree): *We already decorationed our tree.*
(26)   (5;0, threatening to pour lemonade on someone): *I'm going to lemonade you!*
(27)   (5;1, watching a dancer): *She's ballerining.*
(28)   (5;3, wanting her hair fastened back): *Barrette my hair back.*
(29)   (5;7, hitting a ball with a stick): *I'm sticking it and that makes it go really fast.*
(30)   (5;9, wanting to push small cousin in the stroller): *Can I stroller Damon?*
(31)   (6;0, giving mother two walnuts to crack): *Will you nut these?*
(32)   (6;0, wanting to cut the deck of playing cards): *It's my turn to deck the cards.*
(33)   (9;0, watching a TV film of an Everest climb): *Who camera-ed that?*

Note: Glosses are given in square brackets.
Source: Bowerman 1982b, Clark 1978a, 1982a, Kuczaj 1977.

a jump-rope, *She is rounding the rope* (3;0). Children occasionally add the suffix *-en* to adjectives to form new verbs, as in D's (2;8,9) use of *fasten up* (from the adjective *fast*), meaning 'to go faster.' This use was also noted for SM (3;11,14) as in *Why do the cars fasten up when they get to Chestnut*

Street?, a use that persisted for several months. This child also produced inceptive *-en* on the adjectives *long* (*This lace needs longening* [4;2]) and *strong* (*strongen* for 'strengthen' [4;2,14]).[3]

Many innovative verbs are causatives. They begin to appear at about the same time that children discover how to express causation with established verbs, either through addition of the appropriate surface-argument to the configuration of noun phrases for a particular verb, or through use of the appropriate configuration with a periphrastic verb like *make, let,* or *get.* The generalizations children make from around age two about verbs already in their repertoires are also applied to their novel denominal verbs. So once the pertinent nouns have been made into verbs, they are used as causatives or intransitives depending on the meaning to be conveyed.

The verbs coined at different ages show no differences in simplicity of form. All the examples in the records for English-speaking children are produced through zero-derivation. The majority of such verbs fall into the same semantic classes as innovative verbs formed by adults. That is, children rely on the same kinds of relations between objects and activities in coining such verbs as adults do. As far as transparency is concerned, denominal verbs in English can be classified in terms of the relation of the referent of the source noun to the activity, as instrument verbs, e.g., *to broom* 'to hit with a broom' (where the source noun names the instrument used in the action); as locatum verbs, e.g., *to bead* 'to put a bead into' (where the noun names the object being placed somewhere); as locations, e.g., *to funnel* 'to put into a funnel' (where the noun names the place where something is put); as agents, e.g., *to ballerina* 'to do what a ballerina does' (where the noun names the actor) and so on (Clark and Clark 1979, Clark 1982a).[4]

Children not only produce innovative causative verbs, they are also able to interpret them appropriately from at least as young as age three. When given a sentence with a novel causative verb such as *Bert is pencilling the tree* and asked to match it to one of three pictures, three- and four-year-olds reliably chose appropriate referent scenes for causative verbs (Ammon 1980, 1981; see also Bushnell and Maratsos 1984). And when presented with innovative verbs based on body-part terms, in instructions acted out with dolls and props, two-year-olds reliably treat verbs like *to foot* or *to*

---

[3] I'm indebted to Lise Menn for the observations of SM.

[4] The one exception is a group of verbs used by young children to talk about the characteristic activity of the entity named by the noun, e.g., *That flag is flagging,* said of a flag by a two-year-old as the flag was blown out by the wind. This category is absent from adult innovations among verbs (see Clark 1982a).

knee in instructions like *Make the doll foot the radio* or *Make the doll knee the ball* as denoting transitive causative actions (Clark, Neel-Gordon, and Johnson 1993).

The innovative verbs children construct from nouns appear to have no constraints on valence. Many are causative, appearing with a surface subject and a direct object, e.g.,

> *I broomed her* (2;7, for 'hit her with a broom')
>
> *Mommy nippled Anna* (2;11, for 'nursed Anna')
>
> *He's keying the door* (3;0,21, for 'putting the key into the door')
>
> *I'm gonna lawnmower you* (3;6, for 'run over you with the lawnmower [= a push-toy]')
>
> *I'm gonna fork this* (3;7, for 'pick it up with a fork [= some food on his plate]')
>
> *Don't fire my foot* (3;10, for 'set fire to my foot,' as the child watched her mother sterilize a needle for removing splinters)
>
> *It can blade your finger if you do it real fast* (4;0, for 'hit with the blade [of a toy propeller]')
>
> *And syrup it* (4;5, for 'put syrup on it [= bread]')
>
> *You axed the wood and I didn't ax it* (5;0, complaining, for 'cut the wood with an ax')
>
> *I'm shirting my man* (5;7, for 'putting a shirt on my man [a doll]')

(See Bowerman 1974, 1977, 1982a, Clark 1982a, Lord 1979, and Maratsos, Gudeman, Gerard-Ngo, and DeHart 1987.)

Children also produce innovative intransitives based on a similar range of source nouns. For example, from two-year-olds, one finds:

> *I'm souping* (2;4) for 'eating soup'
>
> *It bows* (2;5), in answer to *How does a violin go?*
>
> *I'm lawning* (2;9), for mowing the lawn with a toy mower

and from older children:

> *It's teaing* (3;0) 'making tea', said of a tea-bag put into hot water
>
> *The puppets are warring* (3;0) for 'fighting a war'
>
> *Robin's pianoing* (3;0), said by a child of his sister
>
> *I guess she magicked* (3;3), said of a doll that disappeared
>
> *It will [rain] because it's dropping* (3;11) for 'coming down in drops'
>
> *Maybe it rained or fogged yesterday* (4;0)

It's only enough for one to milk (4;6, meaning only enough room for one piglet to nurse)
Don't vacuum-cleaner in the backyard (5;3)

Available records of children's spontaneous innovations do list fewer intransitive than transitive verbs, but this could be an accident of sampling (Bowerman 1982a, Lord 1979) or even of the conversational context (e.g., Braine, Brody, Fisch, Weisberger, and Blum 1990). There appear to be no syntactic factors associated with transitivity that place restrictions on the kinds of innovative verbs children will produce. Rather, the meaning a child wishes to express appears to determine the syntactic form, transitive or intransitive, of each novel verb.

Coining new verbs from nouns offers one of the most productive options available to speakers of English. It is an option exploited by children and adults alike. It is an option that is simple in form. Such verbs require no affixes and no change in the base used. They are also relatively transparent in meaning. These three factors combined make the formation of new verbs from nouns a particularly accessible option for young children acquiring English.

Other Germanic languages

Children acquiring other Germanic languages follow a route very similar to that of children acquiring English. When they lack words for talking about actions, they rely on general-purpose verbs or they coin verbs from nouns that refer to some object integral to the activity in question. I draw here on data from three other Germanic languages: Dutch, German, and Swedish. There have been only a few diary records kept on children acquiring Dutch, but several observers have recorded verbs formed from nouns. The language with the most extensive data is German, and there the data strongly resemble those for English. The data on Swedish are more limited, but three- and four-year-olds seem to use nouns as verbs in much the same way as their English counterparts.

Dutch

As in English, Dutch children coin new verbs from nouns for instruments, as in *otoën* (4;0) 'to car' (for adult *rijden* 'to drive, to go in a car'); from nouns for the object being placed somewhere (the locatum), as in *een kindje melken* (4;6) 'to milk a baby' (from *melk* 'milk,' in lieu of adult *een kind de borst geven* 'to give a baby the breast'), or *het zandt* (4;1) 'it's sanding' (from *zand* 'sand,' as the wind blew sand into the child's face); and from nouns for the goal or outcome of the activity, as in *moppen* (4;10) from *mop* 'joke' (adult *een mop/een grapje uithalen* 'to play a joke on'), or *silhouetten* (9;6) meaning 'to draw silhouettes' (in lieu of adult *silhouetten tekenen*) (Schaerlaekens 1980, Smedts 1979, de Vooys 1916).

Dutch children also coin some verbs from adjectives (e.g., *frissen* (4;6) from *fris* 'fresh,' for adult *zich fris maken* 'to refresh oneself'), but, as in English, this seems to be rare. In fact, even middle-school children (ten- to twelve-year-olds) often preferred constructions with general-purpose *maken* 'to make' or *worden* 'to become' when asked to make verbs from nouns and adjectives (Smedts 1979). When they used the noun or adjective as a verb, they did better with nouns than adjectives. But they often added a prefix like *be-* to the noun in forming a novel verb, as in *beplanten* 'to plant' (from *plant* 'plant'), and *bemuren* 'to surround with walls' (from *muur* 'wall'). The *be-* on Dutch denominal verbs adds a sense of 'X is at or in a place,' much as in German *be-* prefixation (Wunderlich 1987). Such verbs, then, appear to be typical locatum verbs (Clark and Clark 1979).

The available records for Dutch acquisition are too sparse for any real conclusions. The recorded innovations tend to be from children aged three or older, and they are few in number compared with the English data. Forming new verbs from nouns may not be as productive in Dutch as it is in English.

German

The extensive diary data available on the acquisition of German suggest that children acquiring this language coin verbs in much the same way for the same sorts of activities as children acquiring English (see Augst, Bauer and Stein 1977, Neugebauer-Kostenblut 1914, 1916, Stern and Stern 1928). The majority of German innovative verbs are formed from nouns that denote objects integral to the activity being talked about. And, as in English, children begin to coin such verbs as early as age two. Some typical examples are listed in Table 11–3. Again, as in English, children form both transitive (usually causative) and intransitive verbs from nouns. The kind of activities such verbs are used to talk about parallel the uses observed in English. In German, forming new verbs from nouns appears to offer a productive and widely used option to children who still lack many conventional words for specific actions.

Table 11–3 *Typical innovative verbs in German*

Two-year-olds

1) (1;10) *bildern* 'to picture' (from *Bild* 'picture'/adult *blättern im Bilderbuche* 'to turn pages in a picture book')

2) (1;11) *leitern* 'to ladder' (from *Leiter* 'ladder'/adult *erklimmen, besteigen* 'to scale, climb (a ladder)')

3) (2;2, using tongs to pick up things): *Mutter, was kann ich noch zangen?* 'what can I tong now?' (from *Zange* 'tongs')

4) (2;2) *messen* 'to knife' (from *Messer* 'knife'/adult *schneiden* 'to cut')

5) (2;6) *slachten* 'to battle' (from *Schlacht* 'battle'/adult *schlagen, bekäupten* 'to fight')

6) (2;8, watching adult wipe his nose): *Du näselt.* 'you're nosing' (from *Nase* 'nose'/adult *wischen* 'to wipe')

7) (2;9) *stökeln* 'to stick' (from *Stock* 'stick', meaning 'to run the stick over some stones')

8) (2;9, of piano playing): *Fertig klaviert.* 'done pianoing' (from *Klavier* 'piano'/adult *spielen* 'to play (the piano)')

Three-year-olds

9) (3;0, having drunk some milk): *Hab enug emilcht.* '(I)'ve milked enough' (from *Milch* 'milk'/adult *trinken* 'to drink')

10) (3;2) *handtucheln* 'to towel' (from *Handtuch* 'towel'/adult *einem nassen Umschlag machen* 'to apply a wet bandage')

11) (3;8, watching her mother drum her fingers on the table): *Warum klaviert du denn dort?* 'why are you pianoing there then?' (from *Klavier* 'piano')

12) (3;9) *metern* 'to ruler' (from *Meter* 'ruler'/adult *messen, abmessen* 'to measure')

13) (3;9,15) *maschinen* 'to machine' (from *(Näh)maschine* '(sewing)machine'/adult *nähen* 'to sew (with a sewing-machine)')

14) (3;11) *musiken* 'to music' (from *Musik* 'music'/adult *spielen* 'to play (music)')

15) (3;11, talking of splinters): *Ich splittre mich nicht.* 'I don't splinter myself' (from *Splitter* 'splinter')

16) (3;11) *vererden* 'to earth' (from *Erde* 'earth'/ adult *in die Erde begraben* 'to bury in the earth')

Four and older

17) (4;0, of the wind blowing): *Es windet.* 'it's winding' (from *Wind* 'wind'/adult *wehen* 'to blow')

18) (4;2, talking about a broom): *Best.* '(it) brooms' (from *Besen* 'broom'/adult *fegen* 'to sweep')

19) (4;4) *dieben* 'to thief' (from *Dieb* 'thief'/adult *stehlen* 'to steal')

20) (4;11,15, of bells): *Die könnten jeden Tag glocken.* 'they could bell every day' (from *Glocke* 'bell'/adult *Glockenläuten* 'to ring bells')

21) (5;7) *runterwellen* 'to wave down' (from *Welle* 'wave'+*runter* 'down', of waves in the sea)

22) (6;6, of someone blinking): *Du wimperst ja so schnell.* 'you're eye-lashing so quickly' (from *(Augen)wimper* '(eye)lash'/adult *blinken* 'to blink')

Source: Augst et al. 1977, Stern and Stern 1928.

Swedish

The data from Swedish on verb coinage are more limited, and come primarily from observations of three- and four-year-olds (Cederschiöld 1944, Gustafsson 1979, and Söderbergh 1979). Children this age form

Table 11–4 *Typical innovative verbs in Swedish*

(1)	*krita* 'to chalk' (from *krita* 'chalk'/adult *rita med krita* 'to write with chalk')
(2)	*fota* 'to foot' (from *fot* 'foot'/adult *sparka* 'to kick')
(3)	*pensla* 'to paint-brush' (from *pensel* 'paint brush'/adult *måla med pens* 'to paint')
(4)	*bensina* 'to petrol' (from *bensin* 'petrol, gas'/adult *fylla bensin* 'to fill with petrol/gas')
(5)	*osta* 'to cheese' (from *ost* 'cheese'/adult *hyvla ost* 'to cut cheese')
(6)	*mortla* 'to mortar' (from *mortel* 'mortar'/adult *stöta i mortel* 'to crush a mortar')
(7)	*våga* 'to scale' (from *våg* 'scales'/adult *väga* 'to weigh')
(8)	*tanda sig* 'to tooth oneself' (from *tand* 'tooth' + *sig* 'self'/adult *borsta tanderna* 'to brush one's teeth')

Note: All these coinages are from three-year-olds.
Source: Gustafsson 1979.

verbs from nouns in much the same way and for the same purpose
children acquiring English and German. Some typical examples are list
in Table 11–4. Swedish children coin both transitive and intransitive ver
and, as in English and German, these fall into several categories, t
commonest being instruments, as in *krita* 'to chalk' (for adult *rita m*
krita 'to write with chalk'); objects being placed somewhere, or locata,
in *bensina* 'to gas/put gas into' (for adult *fylla bensin* 'to put gas into/
with gas'); and locations, as in *mortla* 'to mortar' (for adult *stöta i mor*
'to crush in a mortar').

In summary, children acquiring Dutch, German, and Swedish all ma
use of nouns to form new verbs. And in doing so, they choose nouns for t
pertinent instruments, objects affected, or places where the activity is bei
carried out. This option is both available and exploited by children as th
try to talk about specific activities. As in English, zero-derivation requi
no change in the noun base chosen beyond the addition of verb inflectio
and so is simpler in form than any means that requires the addition of
affix for verb formation. At the same time, this means of forming verb
semantically transparent for the speaker, and, in context, for the addres
too. Finally, this option appears to be productive in all the langua
considered.

Romance and Slavic

Children acquiring Romance and Slavic languages also coin new verbs on occasion, but the incidence attested in diary and vocabulary studies, and the ages at which they appear, suggest that the options here may be less productive than in Germanic languages.

Romance

Any new verb in French (or in any of the other Romance languages) has to be assigned to one of the verb conjugations. In French, this is generally the first conjugation, in *-er*. This conjugation is the one to which the majority of conventional denominal verbs belong (Grevisse 1964) and to which borrowings from other languages are assigned. Verbs formed from nouns are simple in form in French: the noun root has verb inflections added to it, and, in the infinitive, appears with *-er*, as in the conventional *boutonner* 'to button,' from the noun *bouton*. Such verbs are also highly transparent when formed with nouns already known. But the option of forming verbs from nouns appears to be less productive in French than in English or German, and so less available for acquisition at a young age.

French-speaking children do coin new verbs from nouns, and they assign these verbs to the first conjugation, but they coin verbs relatively infrequently (Aimard 1975, Cohen 1969, Descoeudres 1922, Deville 1891, François, François, Sabeau-Jouannet, and Sourdot 1977, Grégoire 1947, Vinson 1915–1916). Diaries list a few instances from children as young as two or three up to age 13;0, but innovative verbs from nouns are very rare before age four. These verbs fall into categories similar to those already noted: for example, instrument verbs like *pincer* 'to brush' (from *pince* 'paintbrush,'/adult *peindre* 'to paint') or *mètrer* 'to metre' (from *mètre* 'ruler, tape-measure,'/adult *mesurer* 'to measure'); and locatum verbs like *pantoufler* 'to slipper' meaning 'to put slippers on' (from *pantoufle* 'slipper'), or *ensiroper* 'to syrup' meaning 'to put syrup on' (from *sirop* 'syrup'). Typical examples are listed in Table 11–5. French-speaking children seem to produce many fewer such verbs than their English or German counterparts.

One reason French-speaking children rely less on coining verbs from nouns may be that they make greater use instead of a common periphrastic option, where the verb *faire* 'to make, to do' is combined with a noun phrase. This is common during the early stages of acquisition (Cohen 1969, Grégoire 1947, Guillaume 1927), and remains widely used by six-year-olds. For instance, one hears *faire les tentes* ('to do tents') for *dessiner les tentes*

Table 11–5 *Innovative verbs in French*

Three- and four-year-olds	
(1)	(3;10) *poissonner* 'to fish' (from *poisson* 'fish'/ adult *faire de la pêche à la ligne* 'to go fishing')
(2)	(4;1) *beurrer* 'to butter' (from *beurre* 'butter'/adult *mettre du beurre* 'to put butter on')
(3)	(4;5) *pantoufler* 'to slipper' (from *pantoufle* 'slipper'/adult *mettre les pantoufles* 'to put on slippers')
(4)	(4;6) *joyer* 'to joy' (from *joie* 'joy', meaning 'to be cheerful')
(5)	(4;7,6) *rater* 'to rake' (from *rateau* 'rake'/adult *ratisser*)
(6)	(4;8,15) *piper* 'to pipe' (from *pipe* 'pipe'/adult *fumer* 'to smoke')
Five and older	
(7)	(5;8) *s'ensoldater* 'to en-soldier oneself' (from *soldat* 'soldier'/adult *s'armer* 'to arm oneself')
(8)	(6;0) *galocher* 'to clog' (from *galoche* 'clog, overshoe'/adult *marcher en portant des galoches* 'to walk around in clogs')
(9)	(6;3,17) *grelonner* 'to hail-stone' (from *grêlon* 'hail-stone'/adult *grêler* 'to hail')
(10)	(11;0) *argiler* 'to clay' (from *argile* 'clay,' meaning 'to play with clay')
(11)	(13;0) *microscoper* 'to microscope' (from *microscope* 'microscope,' meaning 'to play with a microscope')

Source: Aimard 1975, Descoeudres 1922, Grégoire 1947.

('to draw tents'), *faire de la peinture* ('to do painting') for *peindre* ('to paint'), *faire les jardins* ('to do gardens') for *jardiner* ('to garden'), *faire l circulation* ('to do the traffic') for *régler la circulation* ('to direct traffic' and *faire la marche* ('to do walking') for *marcher* ('to walk'), all from six year-olds (Méresse-Polaert 1969). Children acquiring Italian, Portuguese and Spanish appear to rely on the analogous periphrastic verbs, *fare, faze* and *hacer* respectively (e.g., Clark 1985, Figueira 1984). The extent t which they also coin new verbs from nouns is unclear.

Slavic
In Slavic languages, as in Romance, it is possible to form new verbs fro nouns. This appears to be a productive option that children resort t frequently. The diary data on Polish and Russian record examples of nov denominal verbs from children as young as two. From age three on, suc coinages appear widespread in both languages (Chmura-Klekotowa 197 1972; El'konin 1973, Gvozdev 1961, Ushakova 1969).

In Polish, one finds utterances like *zasoczyło tu się* (2;1,28) meani 'to spill lentil (juice) on oneself' (with the verb formed from the noun *soczewica* 'lentil'); *bo ja się tu popokrzywię* (2;7,15) meaning 'fall into a nettle-patch' (with the verb formed from the noun *pokrzywa* 'nettle'); or *ja zakluczyłem jarka w sypialni, teraz odkluczyłem* (3;5) meaning (successively) 'having a key, keyed' (with the prefix *za-*) and 'lacking a key, unkeyed' (with the prefix *od-*, both with the verb formed from the noun *klucz* 'key').

In Russian, one finds novel verbs like *raskrylilcja* (2;9,11) meaning '(she) flew', from the noun *kryl* 'wing'; *provesnuet* (3;5) '(it) will spring' (from the noun *vesnu* 'spring'/adult *prozhivet vesnu* 'will spend the spring'); *u menja kurica okurilas'* (3;9,25) 'my chick has chicked' probably meaning 'laid, hatched an egg' (from the noun *kurica* 'chick, chicken'); or *korova ne bodaet a rogaet* 'a cow doesn't gore, it horns' (from the noun *roga* 'horn').

Similar instances have been recorded in Serbo-Croatian, for instance, *hoćuda kredim* (3;0) meaning 'I want to write with chalk' (from the noun *kred* 'chalk'); or *munjiti* (3;10) 'to lightning' (from the noun *munja* 'lightning'/adult verb *sevati* 'to strike' [of lightning]) (Savić 1982).

In both Polish and Russian, diary data suggest that children construct a variety of innovative verbs, beginning in their third year, with quite extensive innovation from age 3;0 onwards. In Polish, many innovative verbs are formed from nouns, with some from adjectives. Chmura-Klekotowa (1971) noted that one-third of the 4,800 innovations she analyzed were verbs.[5] In Russian, new verb-formations also appear to be very frequent around age 3;0–4;0. Languages that are closely related may nonetheless differ in the productivity of this option. For instance, the Polish data contain many more denominal verbs than the Russian or Serbo-Croatian data. This may simply reflect differences in sampling, and, in the diaries, in the amount of attention paid to lexical innovations, or it may reflect a real difference in productivity.

The types of denominal verbs formed by Polish children between age two and seven are similar to those observed in other languages. Some typical examples are given in Table 11–6. Polish children coin verbs from nouns for things (locata), locations, and instruments, as well as agents and goals. The Polish data suggest that coining new verbs from nouns is a

---

[5] She included as innovations forms that filled aspectual gaps, e.g., novel imperfective or perfective prefix uses, as well as verb forms where the root was taken from a noun or adjective for the derivation of a new verb. Gvozdev, for Russian, and Savić, for Serbo-Croatian, also counted novel uses of aspectual prefixes as forming new verbs.

Table 11–6 *Typical innovative verbs in Polish*

(1)	*doktorować* 'to doctor' (from *doktor* 'doctor,' meaning 'to treat')
(2)	*kelnerować* 'to waiter' (from *kelner* 'waiter,' meaning 'to serve')
(3)	*magikować* 'to magic' (from *magik* 'magician,' meaning 'to do magic')
(4)	*papugować* 'to parrot' (from *papuga* 'parrot,' meaning 'to copy')
(5)	*sekretować* 'to secretary' (from *sekretarz* 'secretary'/adult *być sekretarzem* 'to act as secretary')
(6)	*stolarować* 'to carpenter' (from *stolarz* 'carpenter,' meaning 'to do carpentry')
(7)	*poszmatkować* 'to rag (from *szmatka* 'rag'/adult *trochę poczyścić szmatką* 'to wipe clean with a rag')
(8)	*plugować* 'to plough' (from *plug* 'plough'/adult *orać*)
(9)	*smokować* 'to dragon' (from *smok* 'dragon'/adult *odkurzać* "*smokiem*", tj. *elektroluksem* 'to clean with a vacuum cleaner' [called 'a dragon'])
(10)	*obsać* 'to penholder' (from *obsadk* 'penholder'/adult *robić coś obsadką* 'to act as a penholder')
(11)	*wachlarzyć* 'to fan' (from *wachlarz* 'fan'/adult *wachlować*)
(12)	*nawalkować* 'to roller' (from *walek* 'roller'/adult *naciąganąć wody walkiem, tj. korbą* 'to draw water up with a crank')
(13)	*maslować* 'to butter' (from *maslo* 'butter'/adult *robić coś maslem* 'to spread with butter')
(14)	*pooliwkować* 'to olive' (from *oliwka* 'olive,' meaning 'to collect olives')
(15)	*bibliotekować* 'to library' (from *biblioteka* 'library'/adult *pracować w bibliotece* 'to work in a library')
(16)	*obhutować* 'to foundry' (from *huta* 'foundry, steel-works,' meaning 'to work in a steelworks')
(17)	*bazgrotkować* 'to cave' (from *grotka* 'cave,' meaning 'to make into a cave')
(18)	*gzmotać* 'to thunder' (from *gzmot* 'thunder')
(19)	*glosić się* 'to voice' (from *glos* 'voice'/adult *wydawać glos* 'to make a noise')
(20)	*pokolońskować* 'to cologne' (from *kolonska* 'cologne'/adult *pokropić wodą kolonska* 'to make into eau de cologne')
(21)	*sokować* 'to juice' (from *sok* 'juice'/adult *wyciskać sok*; *wydzielać sok* 'to squeeze, secrete juice')

Note: All coinages are from children aged between 2;0 and 7;0.
Source: Chmura-Klekotowa 1971.

productive as well as a transparent and simple option for young children. Whether this option is as accessible to children acquiring other Slavic languages awaits further investigation.

Two more languages
Children acquiring non-Indo-European languages also coin new verbs for talking about actions. And they too rely on nouns to form these verbs. The data here again come from Hungarian and Hebrew. In both languages, such coinages seem to first appear around age two, and in both, the coinages seem designed to fill lexical gaps.

Hungarian
Hungarian contains a number of suffixes that form new verbs from nouns and adjectives. The meanings of such verbs cover the same kinds of categories as in English. The most productive of the verb-forming suffixes appears to be -(*o*)*zik* and its variants, -*azik* and -*ezik*. This is the earliest suffix Hungarian children produce to form new verbs, used from age two onwards, and it appears on 70 percent of the 74 innovative denominal verbs compiled from studies of children acquiring Hungarian (MacWhinney 1973). This suffix, with an intransitive or middle meaning, is very productive in adult speech. For example, it can be used on the nouns for any vehicles to coin verbs for different means of transport, as in adult *autozik* 'to go by car', from the noun *auto*. Typical examples of children's innovative verbs are given in Table 11–7.

Another suffix children use is intransitive *ol*(*ik*) (with its variants -*elik*, -*ölik*, and -*l*), as in *vasutol* (2;4) 'to train' (from the noun *vona* 'train'/adult *jár mint egy vonat* 'to go like a train') or *darázsolik* (2;11) 'to wasp' (from the noun *darázs* 'wasp'/adult *úgy csip, mint egy darázs* 'to sting like a wasp'). This suffix accounted for 23 percent of the denominal verbs in the corpus, and, like -(*o*)*zik*, emerged soon after age two. Children also made occasional use of the transitive suffix -*ít* (5 percent), from age three on. When added to a noun, this suffix conveys the sense of the product of the action. Such uses were rare compared with intransitive coinages. Finally, the causative suffix -(*t*)*at* was rarely used in any innovative verb. When children coin new verbs in Hungarian, they appear to prefer them in middle or intransitive form. This is in rather marked contrast to other languages where children appear to show no preference in their coinages for a particular valence or transitivity pattern. At the same time, data from other languages do point to some preference for causativization over intransi-

Table 11–7 *Typical innovative verbs in Hungarian*

Two-year-olds

(1) (2;6) *szappanbuborékozik* 'to soap bubble' (from *szappanbuborék* 'soap bubbles'/adult *szappanuborékokkal játszik* 'to play with soap bubbles')

(2) (2;6) *cirkuszozik* 'to circus' (from *cirkusz* 'circus'/adult *ugrik mint a cirkuszló* 'to jump like a circus horse')

(3) (2;7,5) *lefoltozik* 'to spot' (from *folt* 'spot'/adult *leönt tintaval* 'to make an inkstain on')

(4) (2;9,9) *becédulál* 'to tag' (from *cédula* 'tag'/adult *cédulat ráragaszt* 'to stick a tag on')

(5) (2;11,5) *kerekszik* 'to wheel' (from *kerék* 'wheel'/adult *forog mint a kerék* 'to turn like a wheel')

(6) (2;11,25) *krétál* 'to chalk' (from *kréta* 'chalk'/adult *krétával rajzol* 'to draw with chalk')

Three-year-olds

(7) (3;0) *vödörít* 'to bucket' (from *vödör* 'bucket'/adult *vödörrel merít* 'to dip out with a bucket')

(8) (3;0) *malacozik* 'to pig' (from *malac* 'pig'/adult *úgy viselkedik mint a malac* 'to act like a pig')

(9) (3;1) *kardol* 'to sword' (from *kard* 'sword'/adult *karddol vív* 'to use a sword')

(10) (3;2,23) *egérezik* 'to mouse' (from *egér* 'mouse,' meaning 'to act like a mouse')

(11) (3;3) *kulcsol* 'to key' (from *kulcs* 'key'/adult *zörög a kulcsokkal* 'to rattle keys')

(12) (3;5,20) *kulcsoz* 'to key' (from *kulcs* 'key'/adult *bezár* 'to lock')

(13) (3;10,9) *pénzezik* 'to money' (from *pénz* 'money'/adult *pénzzel játszik* 'to play with money')

Four and older

(14) (4;0) *sebzik* 'to wound' (from *seb* 'wound'/adult *vérzik* 'to bleed')

(15) (4;1,14) *lovaz* 'to horse' (from *lo* 'horse'/adult *loval játszik* 'to play with a horse')

(16) (5;4) *lehéjázik* 'to peel' (from *héj* 'peel'/adult *meghámoz* 'to remove skin/peel')

(17) (6;1,28) *bemennyasszonyít* 'to bride' (from *mennyasszony* 'bride'/adult *eljegyez* 'to become engaged')

(18) (6;4,18) *kinyuszizik* 'to bunny' (from *nyuszi* 'bunny'/adult *kirak nyulakkal* 'to fill with rabbits')

(19) (6;6) *betojásozik* 'to egg' (from *tojás* 'egg'/adult *beken tojással* 'to spread egg over')

(20) (6;6,16) *bekulcsol* 'to key' (from *kulcs* 'key'/adult *bezár kulccsal* 'to lock with a key')

(21) (6;8,28) *károl* 'to pity' (from *kár* 'pity'/adult *kárt mond* 'to say "pity"')

Source: MacWhinney 1973.

tivization in children's extensions of conventional verbs (e.g., Bowerman 1974, 1982a, Hochberg 1986). Children's coinages fall into much the same categories as those from adults. In fact, some, recorded earlier this century, have since become conventional for talking about particular activities. For instance, the child verb *homokozik*, meaning 'to play in the sand' (from the noun *homok* 'sand'), recorded in 1928 for a child aged 2;6,19 (Kenyeres 1928; also Ponori 1905), has become established and has replaced the earlier *homokkal játszik* 'to play in the sand.' Child innovations, like adult ones, offer one means of expanding the conventional lexicon.

In Hungarian, children are sensitive early to the productivity of different verbalizing suffixes. They rely primarily on suffixes productive in adult speech. They also show a preference for those that are middle or intransitive, and seem to construct relatively few transitive or causative denominal verbs. Although their verbs from nouns are transparent, they are not necessarily simple in form since they typically have both prefixes (like *le-* or *be-*) and suffixes added to the noun roots.[6]

Hebrew

Hebrew verbs all appear in their basic form in one of the seven verb patterns or *binyanim*. Each pattern marks a syntactic function (causative, passive, reflexive, and so on) and so carries a core of meaning common to many verbs in that pattern (Berman 1978a, 1979). But the meaning relations among established verbs from the same root in different patterns are not always predictable, and only about 2 percent of verb roots appear in all seven patterns (Schwarzwald 1975, 1981). At the same time, recent borrowings and innovations, as well as child errors, suggest that some of the *binyanim* do offer consistent semantic paradigms for new verbs.

Denominal verbs constitute a productive source of new verbs in Modern Hebrew, but this option appears much less productive than in languages like English or Hungarian. The source noun is usually discernible in the verb, but an important consideration with four- and five-consonant root nouns is their pronounceability as verbs. In most *binyanim*, that number of consonants results in unpronounceable clusters, so innovative verbs tend to be limited to certain patterns – *pi'el* (P3) for transitives, *hitpa'el* (P4) for intransitives, and *hif'il* (P5) for causatives. Speakers also show some preference for transparency and keep consonant clusters from source

---

[6] At the same time, one-to-one mappings in Hungarian makes suffixes a simpler option than in synthetic languages where a single affix may carry several meanings at once (Chapter 6).

Table 11–8 *Typical innovative verbs in Hebrew*

Verbs in *pa'al* (P1):
(1)   *ani af paam lo xamarti al xamor* 'I've never donkeyed on a donkey
        before' (from *xamor* 'donkey')
(2)   *mi ze šofer?* 'who's trumpetting?' (from *šofar* 'trumpet')
Verbs in *pi'el* (P3):
(3)   *ima, tešarveli li et ha xulca* 'mummy, sleeve my shirt' (from *šarvul*
        'sleeve,' meaning 'roll up the sleeve')
(4)   *ani mesarex hayom levad et ha na'aláyim* 'I'm lacing my shoes by myself
        today') (from *srox(im)* 'lace(s)')
(5)   *ani a-gafrer lexa et ha nerot* 'I'll match the candles for you' (= light)
        (from *gafrur(im)* 'match(es)')
Verbs in *hitpa'el* (P4):
(6)   Talking about wanting grapes, *le-hitanev* 'to grape' (from *anavim*
        'grapes,' meaning 'to eat grapes')
(7)   Talking about getting stung by a scorpion, *hitakravti* 'I got scorpioned'
        (from *akrav* 'scorpion,' meaning 'got bitten by a scorpion')
(8)   Talking about being like a raisin, *le-hictamek* 'to raisin' (from *cimuk*
        'raisin' 'to be like a raisin')
Verbs in *hif'il* (P5):
(9)   *axšav ta-smixi oti tov tov* 'now blanket me really well' (from *smixa*
        'blanket,' meaning 'cover')
(10)   *carix le hašpic et ha iparon* 'got to sharpen the pencil' (from *špic* 'point,
        sharp end')

Note: These coinages are all from children aged 4;0 to 6;0.
Source: Berman 1982, Berman and Sagi 1981.

nouns intact, so that the source noun remains recognizable. This places
limits on which pattern a new verb can appear in.

   Children produce novel denominal verbs in Hebrew in just the verb
patterns adults favor, namely *pi'el* (P3), *hitpa'el* (P4), and *hif'il* (P5)
(Berman 1981, 1982, 1985, Berman and Sagi 1981, Bolozky 1978, 1982,
Rivka'i 1933, 1938, Walden 1982). The general properties of the denominal
verbs in each pattern also mirror those assigned by adults. Both transitives
and intransitives appear in P3; those in P4 are nearly all intransitive; and
those in P5 causative. Typical examples of children's verbs in each of these
patterns are given in Table 11–8. Children make use of intransitive,
inchoative, and causative verbs in their innovations. Once they begin to
coin denominal verbs in Hebrew, they appear to follow the same course as
adults.

Lastly, just as in Hungarian, some child innovations have since entered the language and become established verbs. Among the innovative verbs noted in the 1930s, for example, were *le-histoded* 'to tell secrets' (from *sod* 'secret') and *le-hitbokses* 'to box' (the sport, from English *box*) (Rivka'i 1933, 1938). Both are now the conventional verbs for those meanings in Modern Hebrew. They filled gaps not only for children but also for adults.

Hebrew-speaking children appear attentive to the same factors as adults in the formation of novel verbs. They attend to transparency of meaning in their new verb-forms. Like adults, they preserve consonant clusters from the source noun (see *smixa* 'blanket' in Table 11–8). They also appear to avoid verb patterns that would result in unpronounceable clusters, perhaps a further effect of simplicity. They are also sensitive to the productivity of different verb-patterns. At the same time, the available studies record few novel verbs for children under age four. This is probably a reflection of the fact that they take time to work out the core meanings associated with each verb pattern or *binyan*. Up to age three, they typically rely on a single non-alternating form for a given verb-root, and only from four on begin to make use of appropriate alternations between patterns to mark transitive or causative, say, versus inchoative or reflexive meaning (Berman 1982, 1993, Walden 1982). Their knowledge about verb patterns, then, is just becoming established around age four, the point at which they apparently begin to coin new verbs.

Summary

Examination of children's innovative verbs across several languages suggests that here too children do rely on transparency, simplicity, and productivity. Transparency of meaning surfaces in the preservation of root forms when children add suffixes. There seems to be a general preference in adults too for keeping the root in its original shape in a derived word. Simplicity of form is also a consideration early on. In languages that allow zero-derivation, children construct new verbs from nouns as early as age two. And where zero-derivation is an option, children do not make use of any suffixal options at all. In agglutinating languages, however, they do add suffixes to form new verbs, and do so from the age of two on. The difficulty here lies in identifying what counts as simple. If children have expectations based on exposure to an agglutinative language, suffixes may be more accessible early on than in a synthetic language like French or Polish. Finally, where children have to place the consonantal root into a specific verb pattern, as in Hebrew, children coin few denominal verbs before age four.

Productivity is also an important factor. Children first make use of productive derivational options, those preferred by adult speakers in their own coinages. Languages differ, of course, in what is productive, and this has consequences for acquisition. In some languages, the zero-derivation of verbs from nouns (high on simplicity and transparency) is very productive. There children make use of such verbs early, e.g., in English and German. In others, the formation of verbs from nouns is possible but not productive, and there children make relatively little use of them, relying less on coining new verbs than, perhaps, on using general-purpose verbs like French *faire*. Within a language, some verb-forming affixes may be more productive than others, and there too children make greater use in their own coinages of the more productive options in adult speech. This reliance on what is productive among the available options will show up more clearly, of course, in languages where several options differ in productivity for adult speakers.

Finally, transparency and productivity go hand-in-hand in children's regularizations of language. Productive forms with an identifiable meaning lend themselves more readily than unproductive forms to the building of paradigms. The more productive a form, the more exemplars with some element of form and meaning in common children will hear, and the more readily accessible such combinations should be in the formation of new verbs.

Children coin new verbs for actions just as they coin new nouns for objects and events. The factors governing their choices of forms to convey their new meanings again seem to be encompassed by transparency of meaning, simplicity of form, and productivity. However, the interaction of these principles is moderated by the typological characteristics of each language. If simplicity and transparency conflict, transparency wins. That is, the elements used in building new words must be known to children or they can't use them. But if there is a transparent form available that is also simple, that will always take priority over less simple transparent forms. Finally, if children have two or more transparent forms to choose from, they base their choice on relative productivity. The more productive of the options for a specific meaning is the one chosen. In order to take one more look at these interactions, I focus in the next chapter on a special case of verb coinage – the formation of verbs for talking about undoing or reversing actions already performed.

12 *Words for undoing actions*

String can be knotted or unknotted. Lights can be turned on or off. Doors can be opened or closed. Among the many actions we can talk about are reversals of actions performed earlier. In English, the notion of undoing or reversal can be expressed in several ways. The most widespread is through use of a productive prefix, *un-*, added to the verb, as in *fold* to *unfold* or *tie* to *untie*. Reversal can also be expressed through use of verb particles such as *off*, as in the shift from *switch on* to *switch off*. Or it can be expressed suppletively by verbs unrelated in form, as in pairs like *bend* and *straighten* or *lose* and *find*. In addition, there are mixed verb cases where one of the pair occurs with a particle but its reversal has *un-*, as in *tuck in* to *untuck*, or where both verb and particle change in the expression of reversal, as in *put on* to *take off*.

Forms for the expression of reversal can take several shapes, and each language typically makes use of more than one means. In English, one uses a prefix on the verb, *un-*, as in *unknot*. Or one might use a particle like *back*, often combined with an adverb like *again*, as in *put X back again*. Or one can make use of verb particles like *out*, *off*, or *down*, as in *get up/get down*. German, however, lacks a productive verbal prefix for expressing reversal and instead generally relies on separable particles with meanings like 'out' or 'off.' These verb–particle combinations, as in English, may be combined with an adverbial like *wieder* 'again.' Romance languages appear to rely primarily on a prefix on the verb, such as French *dé-*. Slavic also makes use of negative prefixes. These prefixes often mark aspect as well as reversal; they may encode notions of 'back' with 'again,' or be closer in meaning to English *un-*. Overall, these languages all rely on morphemes attached to or associated with the verb, in the form of either a prefix or a particle, to express the meaning of reversal.

Are some options simpler than others? Are particles acquired before prefixes because they are transparent to children earlier? And at what point do children begin to choose among possible options on the basis of productivity. In this chapter, I look at children's first expressions of reversal, and then compare the course of acquisition for two closely related languages, English and German. In both languages, I rely on spontaneous and elicited coinages. The elicitation data allow for detailed comparisons of the options children treat as simple, transparent, and productive at different stages in acquisition. I conclude with a brief look at innovative reversal verbs from other languages.

Undoing in English

Talking about reversal, then, exploits a variety of means, one of which is the productive English prefix *un-* (Marchand 1969, 1973). *Un-* has other negative meanings besides reversal, but here I will be concerned only with the notion of reversal of some prior action. Benjamin Whorf argued that verbs that can take *un-* all belong to a cryptotype or covert category in English. They all have a "covering, enclosing, or surface-attaching meaning" (Whorf 1956). Speakers of English can say *uncover, uncoil, undress, unfasten, unlock, unroll, untangle, untie* and *unwind*, but not **unbreak, *undry, *unhang, *unheat, *unlift, *unmelt, *unopen, *unpress*, or **unspill*. (Many of these starred *un-* forms are actually pre-empted by existing verbs in the lexicon, e.g., **unbreak* is pre-empted by *mend, *undry* by *wet, *unheat* by *cool, *unlift* by *drop* or *lower*, and **unopen* by *close* or *shut*.) *Un-*, then, is used for actions of departure from covering, enclosing, or attaching. That is, it marks release from constriction. It is never used, on a novel verb, for example, to encode the meaning of 'cover' or 'enclose,' only for the reversal of such meanings.

Transparency predicts that children should begin by using an option whose meaning is already known to them. They might rely initially on a general verb with the approximate meaning of 'release from constriction.' One obvious candidate in English is the verb *to open*. Other candidates are verb particles like *off, out,* or *down*. Both *off* and *out* carry some sense of release from constriction. That is, children who have not yet analyzed *un-*, nonetheless have some forms at their disposal for talking about reversal. Once children have analyzed *un-*, of course, it too will be as transparent to them as the other options, and therefore just as available for use.

Simplicity predicts that children will use particles before suffixes or prefixes. Particles require no change in the form of the verb root, and they are salient since they typically carry stress. In general, postpositional particles and suffixes are acquired earlier than prefixes or prepositions (Kuczaj 1979, Slobin 1973), but affixes have to be analyzed before they can be attached to verb roots. Early on, therefore, children may prefer particles, or even attend only to particles, for talking about reversal. But simplicity is important only up to the point where children grasp the range of structural types in their language. Once past that point, prefixes should be as simple to make use of as any other device.

Lastly, the most productive device available in English is the prefix *un-*. But *un-* carries other meanings besides reversal. It can mark privative (along with *de-* (*dis-*)) and ablative (removal) meaning on verbs (Marchand 1973); it is also used to mark opposites on certain adjectives in English, e.g., *happy/unhappy*. In addition, many conventional verbs used for reversal come from mixed or irregular subparadigms. Children may therefore take some time before they identify *un-* as the most productive option for expressing reversal.

Open

Children first seem to talk about reversing an action in contexts where that action has denied them access to a place they wish to go to or to some object they wish to have. The verb they typically use in requesting or offering access is *open*. As the data in Table 12–1 show, *open* typically marks the removal of a constraint or obstacle to access. These data are representative of D's uses of *open*.[1] On many occasions, early uses of *open* are complemented by uses of *shut* to indicate the opposite – enclosing, covering, or attaching (see Table 12–1). These uses of *shut* all seem to fit the cryptotype for verbs that allow prefixation of *un-*. *Open* and *shut* offer English-speaking children a first transparent means for talking about the relevant cryptotype actions and their reversals.

Verb particles

As predicted by simplicity, another device children make use of early on is pairs of verb particles (at first without any accompanying verb), as in uses of *on* and *off* for talking about lights, radios, taps, or clothes, or *up* and *down* for displacements of self or of other objects. Like *open*, such particles emerge early, and are often put to use in reversal contexts from around age

---

[1] Similar examples are cited by Griffiths and Atkinson (1978), e.g.:
　(i) P (1;10, trying to take a toy horse out of a tin) *Horse, horse, horse.* (as it got wedged in the opening) *Stuck, stuck.* (trying to get it out) ə *stuck. Open, horse.*
　(ii) J (2;5,5, trying to pull an arm off a plastic monkey): *Open it.* (uses his teeth and succeeds) *Oh* [unintelligible].
　Adult: Poor monkey.
　J (putting arm on floor): *'s open it.*
(See also Bowerman 1978, and, for early uses of Hebrew *délet* 'door,' Berman 1978b.)

Table 12–1 *Typical early uses of* open *and* shut *for D*

Open
(1)   D (1;9,1, trying to open the lip of a milk carton): *I open.*
(2)   D (1;9,29, looking at the snaps on the 'bowl' of his bib): *It open.*
(3)   D (1;10,14, trying to get past the table corner): *Open!*
(4)   D (1;10,15, wanting his chair pulled away from the table so he could climb out): *Open* [ə] *chair.*
(5)   D (1;11,4, as he pulled his Mo's skirt over her knees): *Shut. Not open.*
(6)   D (1;11,17, tilting his bowl with one hand so only one side of the bottom rested on the table): *Damon open* [ə] *bowl.*
(7)   D (1;11,23, taking a big bite out of his toast): *Get* [ə] *open it!*
(8)   D (1;11,28, with his fingers extended): *I open* [ə] *finger.*
(9)   D (2;1,24, pulling up his T-shirt to display his stomach): *I open my T-shirt.*
(10)   D (2;2,2, lifting his plate to show how he'd hidden a piece of paper): *Open it and see.*
(11)   D (2;2,3, wanting a chair moved out from the table so he could climb onto it): *Open that chair.*
(12)   D (2;2,28, wanting a tangerine to be peeled by his Fa): *Herb, open that tangerine. Open that.*
(13)   D (2,4,2, trying to get his rolled-up napkin out of its ring): *You open this?*
(14)   D (2;6,13, playing with his napkin, folding and then unfolding it): *Fold up ... open.*
(15)   D (2;7,19, smoothing a piece of crumpled paper): *I'm opening it.*

Shut
(16)   D (1;8,22, as he tried to push two small tables together): *Table shut, shut.*
(17)   D (1;9,27, reaching for the milk carton to close its lip): *I want get shut.*
(18)   D (1;10,14, cupping four spoons, nested together, in his hand): *Shut.*
(19)   D (1;10,14, pushing his booster chair right against the table): *Shut.*
(20)   D (1;10,18, fixing a lego block to his garbage truck): *I get* [ə] *shut.*
(21)   D (1;10,26, as his Mo closed the air-vent for the heater at the wall): *Eve* [ə] *turn it on shut.*
(22)   D (1;10,27, as he dropped a removeable chair-seat back into its frame): *Chair shut.*
(23)   D (1;11,4, as he pushed his Mo's legs together so he could somersault over them): *Shut.*

Source: Clark, diary data.

two (Choi and Bowerman 1991, Farwell 1977). For example, one finds utterances like D's *Make it sink up* (2;2,6) as a reversal of 'sink down,' *Not standing down* (2;3,29), meaning '[I'm] not lying down' (so a reversal of 'stand up'), *I wanna roll it down* (2;6,2), of a belt he wanted to unroll (a reversal of 'roll up'), *It's already snapped off* (2;6,6), of a snap on his pyjamas that had been undone, or *My buttons are undone. I don't need them buttoned up. I need them buttoned down,* followed by a laugh and a change of topic (2;6,7). Verb particles like *off* and *down,* of course, do occur in conventional expressions for reversal, but their distribution (and what each one gets paired with) is not altogether predictable. A verb like *tuck in* (of blankets or sheets) is conventionally reversed by *untuck* – children typically produce *tuck out* – yet *turn on* (of lights or taps) is reversed by *turn off*. Children have to learn these one by one since particles do not offer a productive way of expressing reversal in English.

Early un-

The first uses children make of *un-* are on established verbs such as *undo* or *untie*. These uses are typically appropriate, and may appear from 2;0 or so onwards, though they may be limited to just one or two verbs in the child's own speech. (They are presumably being exposed to many more instances of *un*-prefixed verbs in the input, perhaps a necessary condition for the identification and analysis of *un-*, even if they themselves produce only one or two established forms.) D, for example, first used a conventional *un*-form in a request for his seat-belt to be undone, *You get my buckle undone?* (2;3,28). Over the next three months, he combined *undone* (for the resultant state) with several other verbs (e.g., *snap, wrap,* and *roll*) on a number of occasions to express reversal. The only other conventional *un*-verb he produced at this time was *untie* (first used at 2;3,30).

Four months later (at 2;8), D began to use *un-* productively, on verbs that he could not have heard used with *un-* by adults. Some typical examples are given in Table 12–2. Although these uses have no adult counterparts, they do fit Whorf's characterization of the kinds of actions for which one can add a reversal *un-* to the verb. They are all reversals of actions of enclosing, attaching, or surface-contact. That is, the actions fit the characterization even though the choice of verb may not. Take example 4 in Table 12–2: *disappear* is not normally a verb of enclosing, but on this occasion it was used to describe the action of enclosing the child's thumbs inside his fists. The subsequent use of *un-* in talking about a possible reversal of that action is then consistent with the semantic type that licenses *un-*.

Children have to learn at least two things in learning how to use *un-*: that this prefix marks reversal, and that it does so only on the verbs for certain kinds of actions. Some grasp both these properties prior to producing

Table 12–2 *Typical innovative uses of English* un- *for D*

(1)	Mo (after D pulled her belt undone): Did someone undo my belt?
	D (2;8,22): *No, no, I unpulled it because it wasn't tied yet.*
(2)	D (2;9,11, opening plug in bidet and letting the water out): *It's unflowing.* [= emptying out]
(3)	D (2;9,24, of a PanAm badge he wanted taken off his shirt): *No, no, I was tighting my badge. I tighted my badge, and you should untight it.* [= loosen]
(4)	D (2;10,20, having hidden his thumbs by closing his fists on them): *They've disappeared.*
	Mo Can you make them appear again?
	D *No, I can't make it undisappear.* [= re-appear]
(5)	D (3;0,4, as a hairpin fell out of Mo's hair): *Oh your hair is unpinning.*
(6)	D (3;1,5, needing to put his blocks in a bag to take upstairs): *First I unbuild it, okay?* [= take apart]
(7)	D (3;4,3, feeling his Christmas stocking): *I don't know what's in my stocking. I'll have to unhang it.* [= take down]
(8)	D (3;4,8, getting things out of his nursery school cubbyhole): *That's a picture and you have to uncrumple it to see what it is.* [= smooth out]
(9)	D (3;5,9, to Mo): *Show me how you uncatch your necklace.* [= undo the catch]
(10)	D (3;8,11, of a block castle he'd just built): *It doesn't have a door.*
	Fa Then how do you get in?
	D *I just have to unmake it and put the people in.*
(11)	D (3;10,5, having put pyjamas on over his clothes, and now proceeding to take them off): *I'm unpyjama-ing.* [= taking off]
(12)	D (4;3,15, of a balloon-replica of a Spitfire belonging to his cousin): *Here's Duncan's airplane. D'you want me to unblow it?* [=deflate]
(13)	D (4;3,17, telling a story) *... he unstrings the worms every day and throws them on the fire.* [= takes off]
(14)	D (4;5,14, speculating about a small knob on the stove, function unknown): *Maybe it's for unlighting the flame ... a faster way.* [= putting out, extinguishing]
(15)	D (4;6,26, of a character in a book) *... but the two big kids didn't know that the* LITTLE *one was unknitting the wool.* [= undoing the knitting]

Source: Clark, diary data.

novel instances of *un-*. Others begin to use the prefix before fully identifying both aspects of the meaning. This is the case, for example, for one child, C, who began to use *un-* productively before having identified the type of verbs that license *un-*. She produced novel uses of reversal *un-* a good year before identifying the relevant semantic class. Among her first novel uses were *uncome* (3;9) to mean 'stop coming out' (of water from holes in a cup), *unstraighten* (4;5) to mean 'bend' (of wire that her mother had been straightening with pliers), and *unhate* (4;7) to mean 'stop hating.' Only from age five on did she restrict *un*- to verbs for covering, enclosing, or attaching to a surface. In contrast, her sister E, like D, acquired both the reversal meaning of *un*- and the relevant semantic category at the same time (from 3;2 onwards). Also, like D, E used *un*- at times on verbs that would not conventionally take *un*-: on those occasions, she was using the verbs for actions belonging to the relevant semantic type (Bowerman 1982b).

In summary, children acquiring English appear to rely, initially, on a verb like *open* to talk about reversal of a prior action. They rely on verb particles like *out*, *off*, or *down* in requesting or observing a reversal. Only after this, and after some use of conventional, unanalyzed *un*- verbs, do children produce novel uses of *un*-. What diary data do not reveal, though, is whether children rely on particles and *un*- at different ages and stages (Clark 1981b). I therefore turn now to some elicitation tasks designed to find out which options children prefer when.

Eliciting particle reversals

To find out how consistently young children rely on particles for talking about reversal, we asked two-, three-, and four-year-olds to request reversals in a game where they did the voice for a Sesame Street puppet, Oscar, who consistently disagreed with whatever had just been done (Clark and Carpenter 1991). The initial, precipitating, action was described with a verb–particle combination where the particle was either positive, as in *turn on*, *tie up*, or *plug in*, or negative, as in *clean off*, *take down*, or *put out*. Having heard an action requested by one of the experimenters, and having seen it carried out, the child-as-Oscar then asked for the action to be reversed. Each child asked for 19 reversals, 12 where the initial action was described with a verb with a positive particle, and 7 where the initial particle was negative.

Overall, children relied on particles for their reversals 65 percent of the time. As Table 12–3 shows, they were more likely to do this in response to negative particles (78 percent) than positive ones (53 percent).[2] Two- and three-year-olds also relied on *open* and, to a lesser extent, conventional *undo*, but only for reversing actions described with positive particles. With

---

[2] Spontaneous uses of *open* (Table 12–1) are also preferred for reversing positive actions.

Table 12–3 *Particles versus other options for reversals*

	Form given	Possible reversal	Age		
			2;10	3;6	4;2
Positive	Verb+	Verb+			
	up/in/on	*down/out/off*	50	56	52
		open	22	11	7
		undo	2	10	5
		un+Verb	8	23	23
		Other	18	0	13
Negative	Verb+	Verb+			
	down/out/off	*up/in/on*	71	79	83
		shut/close	6	0	0
		un+Verb	0	0	0
		Other	24	21	17

Note: The positive percentages for each age group are based on 120 responses, and the negative ones on 70 responses.
Source: Clark and Carpenter 1991.

age, children made less use of *open*, and more of *un*-, up to 23 percent by age four. *Un*- was also more likely to be used when the original action was described with a positive particle (18 percent) than with a negative one (zero percent overall).

When children used a particle, they sometimes retained the original verb. Otherwise, they tended to rely on the particle combined with a general-purpose verb such as *put* or *get*. This overall pattern showed little change with age. Children relied on general-purpose verbs in 46 percent of their responses, and on the original verbs in 29 percent, overall. Although there was little difference between positive and negative actions in children's uses of general-purpose verbs, they were more likely to retain the original verb in the case of positive actions (34 percent) than of negative ones (20 percent). This was paralleled by children's increasing reliance on *un*- as a device for talking about reversal, as shown by the increases with age in the number of verbs retained and the amount of time *un*- was used for reversal. Four-year-olds used *un*- 23 percent of the time on positive actions, and not at all on negative ones (Table 12–3).

A number of the verb–particle combinations used had a conventional reversal form, sometimes with the same verb and a different particle, sometimes with a different verb and different particle, and sometimes with *un-* added to the original verb. When conventional reversal forms were tallied for each action, there was a steady increase from 38 percent for two-year-olds to 55 percent for four-year-olds in the conventional forms used. The prefix *un-* appeared to have become transparent in meaning to several of the four-year-olds who consistently over-used it on verbs that did not conventionally take it. Such over-uses were more likely in the older children, but also appeared in one of the younger children. The age range here coincides with that observed for spontaneous innovative uses of *un-* (see Table 12–2).

These data support the observations of children's spontaneous speech where the earliest general device used for reversals tends to be *open*. Some children also rely from an early stage on *undo*. But for actions encoded with verb–particle constructions, children typically depend heavily on the meaning of the particle, and simply reverse that, by producing its opposite. Knowledge of opposite pairs appears to be acquired relatively early for verb particles and is well established in several semantic domains by age four (Clark 1972, Donaldson and Wales 1970). However, these data also suggest that by age four, and, in one or two instances even earlier, children have analyzed the prefix *un-* as a device for encoding reversal. A few clearly over-used *un-* and produced such reversals as *unclimb* (in place of *climb down*), *unmix* (for suppletive *separate*), and even *unput X in* (for *take X out*).

Eliciting un- reversals

In a second study, using the same technique, we asked children for reversals of actions described either with verbs that could take the prefix *un-*, e.g., *snap, roll,* or with verbs whose reversal was normally expressed with a suppletive form, e.g., *bend, crush,* where adults usually supply *straighten* and *smooth out*. The aim, as before, was to find out when children would use *un-*, and to what extent they did so productively to express reversal. They were also given some actions that were pragmatically irreversible (e.g., *hit, scratch*) to see whether they would over-apply *un-* to those as well, or whether they distinguished between pragmatically reversible and irreversible actions by the time they acquired *un-*. They responded freely with reversal forms for all the reversible actions, but tended to respond with 'Don't know' or with negative imperatives (e.g., *Don't hit*) for pragmatically irreversible ones. The responses to reversible verbs are shown in Table 12–4. Three-year-olds made some use of *open* and

Table 12–4 *Reversals with* open, undo, *suppletion, and* un-

Age	*open*	*undo*	Suppletion	*un-*	Other
3;2	27	11	8	49	5
3;8	15	2	21	51	0
4;4	2	8	4	84	2
4;8	4	7	8	72	9
Mean	12	7	10	64	4

Note: Each percentage is based on 100 responses.
Source: Clark and Carpenter 1991.

undo as well as *un-*. By age four, reliance on general-purpose *open* and *undo* had become negligible.

Use of *un-* rose steadily with age. Children at all ages were more likely to make use of *un-* on a verb requiring *un-* for reversal than on a verb that possessed a suppletive reversal form. This difference is illustrated in Table 12–5 for reversible actions. At the same time, children relied much more heavily on *un-* than on any suppletive forms to ask for reversals. This over-reliance on *un-* offers strong evidence for children's identification of *un-* as the device for indicating reversal. A few even used *un-* on verbs for irreversible actions (3 percent of the responses overall). Such uses, though, were characteristically marked as different from the others by hesitation and laughter, especially among the four-year-olds.

No children in this study relied on particles for reversal. This suggests

Table 12–5 Un- *for verbs reversed with* un- *and verbs reversed with suppletive forms*

	Verbs with *un-*	Verbs with suppletion
3;2	54	44
3;8	70	32
4;4	94	74
4;8	80	64
Mean	74	54

Note: Each percentage is based on 50 responses.
Source: Clark and Carpenter 1991.

that it is an option for reversal favored mainly by younger children. Verb particles are simple compared to a prefix, and children typically know several particle pairs by age two or so, *on/off*, *up/down*, *in/out*. These offer one of the earliest options for expressing reversal. Only later do children analyze the prefix *un-*. They also learn that particle-based paradigms contain many exceptions among conventional pairs (e.g., *tuck in/*tuck out/untuck*). By age four or so, they rely on *un-* as the general means for expressing reversal. In doing so, they over-regularize, using *un-* on such verbs as *bend*, with *unbend* in lieu of *straighten*, or *bury*, with *unbury* in lieu of *dig up* (see also Table 12–2). Conventional pairs that do not fit the *un-* paradigm simply have to be learnt one by one. This takes time.

This sequence of acquisition offers strong support for the roles of transparency and simplicity. If children have already acquired certain particle pairs, in either verbal or locative contexts, such pairings are transparent, and available early, for expressing contrasts of opposites, of just the type required in reversing an action. Particles offer a transparent option early on. Furthermore, particles follow their verbs and bear stress, both characteristics that make linguistic units more accessible. Separate morphemes with the requisite meanings appear to be simpler in form for children to analyze than prefixes attached to verb stems. The latter become available, it seems, only from around age three or later. At the same time, once a prefix does become transparent, it can compete with other available devices. At that point, productivity leads children to opt for *un-* over particles as the regular means for expressing reversal.

Undoing in German

German lacks a prefixal means for expressing the notion of reversal on verbs. Instead, speakers rely on particles, especially with separable verbs, together with a number of existing suppletive forms. Many verbs present mixed cases in that a bare verb is often paired with a verb–particle construction, and vice-versa. And the reversal of a verb–particle form may require a switch in verb root as well as in particle, just as in English *put on/take off*. The option used in novel instances, though, appears to be the particle opposite in meaning to the original, or the addition to the verb of a negative particle, most commonly *auf*, *aus*, or *ab*.

The course of acquisition in German should resemble English-speaking children's treatment of verb–particle forms. That is, early on, children probably rely on verbs like *offen* 'to open' for talking about reversal, or on general-purpose verbs like *machen* 'to make' or *tun* 'to do' combined with a negative particle. As they learn some conventional pairings, they should come to rely on the oppositeness relation between specific pairs of particles and to adopt this as the major option for innovative cases.

To find out what course children follow, a similar elicitation task was carried out for German (Clark and Deutsch 1991). As in English, transparency predicts that children will initially rely on some general means for expressing reversal of any action that constrains, attaches, or encloses an object in some way. The first candidate here is *offen*, probably in the form *offen machen* 'to make open,' but another possible candidate is *los* 'free, loose,' as in *los machen* 'to let go, release.' Or they might use a general reversal form, *aufmachen* 'to undo, unfasten, open.' As they learn particle pairs, e.g., *zu/aus* 'to/from,' *an/ab* 'on/off,' such general means should give way to more specific forms for the expression of reversal.

One difficulty for children acquiring German is the meanings of non-separable verbs (verbs where the particle can't carry stress and remains attached to the left of the verb root). Here, the meaning contributed by the particle is typically not compositional to the same degree as for separable verbs (Asbach-Schnitker 1984, Wunderlich 1983). Children might therefore be more likely to rely on a general-purpose reversal like *offen machen* or *aufmachen* when presented with inseparable prefix verbs than with separable ones. Separable particles should be more transparent in meaning than non-separable ones because they will already be familiar to children in their locative meanings. As in English, many locative pairs are mastered early by German-speaking children (Grimm 1975).

Simplicity also predicts that children should find it easier to use particles than prefixal forms, and so easier to find a reversal form in a separable particle. Finally, productivity favors the option of a specific particle combined with the verb form. Separable verbs therefore offer a better model for reversals than non-separable ones. By combining a locative particle with an inflected verb, they also offer a source of new verb meanings in German (Wunderlich 1983, 1987).

Early particle use

Young German-speaking children spontaneously produce several different negative particles in combination with a variety of verbs to express reversal. As the examples in Table 12–6 show, the commonest appear to be *ab-* and *aus-*. Such expressions of reversal begin to appear before age two and in several instances appear on verbs that are themselves novel

Table 12–6 *Typical early uses of German particles for reversals*

(1)	RN (1;11,22) *abschnuren* 'to un-lace' (from *Schnur* 'lace,'/adult *abbinden* 'to untie (shoes)')
(2)	RN (2;1,15) *forträdeln* 'to wheel-away,' (from *Rad* 'wheel,' meaning 'to leave' of a train)
(3)	TS (2;3) *abzangen* 'to tong off' (from *Zange* 'tongs'/adult *abzwicken*, *mit der Zange* 'to pinch off/nip off, with tongs')
(4)	RN (2;4) *abzangen* 'to tong away' (from *Zange* 'tongs')
(5)	SC (2;11) *abbliemeln* 'to un-flower' (from (dialectal) *bliemeln* 'flower'/adult *abfallen* 'to fall over, wilt')
(6)	SC (3;4) *aussinden* 'to out-light' (from *anzünden* 'to light (a fire)'/adult *auslöschen* 'to put out')
(7)	GS (3;5,15) *austropfen* 'to out-drop' (from *Tropfen* 'drop, tear'/adult *ausspritzen der angefeuchteten Bürste* 'to shake drops off a dampened brush')
(8)	LD (4;6) *abkleben* 'to off-stick' (from *ankleben* 'to stick together')
(9)	SC (5;3) *absensen* 'to off-scythe' (from *Sense* 'scythe'/adult *abmähen* 'to cut (with a scythe)')

Source: Neugebauer-Kostenblut 1914, Stern and Stern 1928.

coinages, e.g., *absensen* 'to scythe off' (from the noun *Sense* 'scythe', for adult *abmähen* 'to cut (away) with a scythe'); or *austropfen* 'to shake drops off (a brush)' (from the noun *Tropfen* 'drop, tear,' for adult *ausspritzen*). However, relatively few such forms have been reported in the diaries, possibly because innovative uses of particles within regular paradigms are not very noticeable.

Elicited reversals

In the elicitation task, as predicted, younger children relied heavily on both *offen machen* or *los machen*. (A few used *weg* rather than *los*.) When these three options – *offen*, *los*, and *weg* – were tallied, they accounted for 43 percent of the responses from three-year-olds. Uses of *aufmachen* contributed a further 32 percent, and other particles 22 percent. By age five, reliance on *offen machen* and the general-purpose *aufmachen* had dropped (to 21 percent and 26 percent of the responses respectively), and other particles now accounted for 34 percent, as shown in Table 12–7.

The general-purpose verb most favored was *machen*, used by all three age groups. (Only one three-year-old consistently used *tun* instead.) But as children got older, they stopped relying on general-purpose *machen* combined with a negative particle. Instead, they retained the inflected verb

Table 12–7 *Reversals with* offen/los/weg machen, aufmachen, *and othe particles in German*

	machen offen/los/weg	machen auf	Other particles	Other
3;7	43	27	18	10
4;4	28	27	32	3
4;10	21	22	28	29

Note: Each percentage is based on 120 responses.
Source: Clark and Deutsch 1991.

used for the initial action, and either changed the particle, or added a negative particle, to encode the notion of reversal.

Because three-year-olds relied more on *machen*, they retained th original verb less often than older children (28 percent for three-year-old compared with 50 percent for four-year-olds). Overall, they were mor likely to retain the original verb if they had heard a separable verb first (4. percent) than if they had heard a non-separable one (27 percent). Lastly they were also more likely to rely on a particle with opposite polarity t express the reversal for separable verbs than for non-separable ones, a shown in Table 12–8.

Finally, when German-speaking children were given pragmaticall irreversible actions and asked to reverse them, they typically either refuse to say anything or used a negative imperative, *nicht machen* 'don't' o

Table 12–8 *Appropriate particle reversals with separable and non-separable verbs*

	Verb type	
	Separable	Non-separable
3;7	50	40
4;4	72	47
4;10	60	40
Mean	61	42

Note: Each percentage is based on 60 responses.
Source: Clark and Deutsch 1991.

'don't do.' They rarely used particles or the general-purpose options they relied on in talking about reversible actions.

These findings suggest that, as in English, children are influenced initially by both transparency of meaning (use known locative particles, in particular the negative members of pairs) and by simplicity of form (rely on particles that are separable). Such particles are the most productive means available in German.[3] Because the productive option for reversal is also the one most easily identifiable, children have little problem in German learning how to express reversal. Their only real difficulty stems from idiosyncratic switches in conventional verb roots and the conventional pairings of some particles, and in the identification of suppletive pairs in the established lexicon.

Dutch

Observations of children acquiring Dutch support the patterns observed for both German and English in the early stages of expressing reversals. Dutch-speaking children, like German ones, pick up first on negative particles like *af* 'off/down' and *uit* 'out,' and apply those to express the undoing of actions (Schaerlaekens 1980, de Vooys 1916). Children express reversals like the following from age two onwards: *afplooien* (2;6) 'to fold off/down' (for adult *ontplooien* 'to unfold [of a newspaper]'); *afplakken* (2;6) 'to stick off' (for adult *lostrekken* 'to pull loose/pull off [of a sticking plaster]'; *uitdekken* (2;10) 'to blanket out' (for adult *de dekens wegdoen* 'to put away the blankets'); *afnaaien* (3;0) 'to sew off,' said of a loose thread the child wanted removed from his pyjamas; *afbouwen* (4;8) 'to build down' (for adult *afbreken* 'to demolish'). In Dutch, children begin by making general use of separable particles like *af* and *uit*.

As they get older, children begin to use the negative prefix *ont-* 'un-' as an option for expressing reversal. Dutch, unlike German, uses the prefix *ont-* on verbs as well as adjectives (much as English does with *un-*). However, until children have analyzed *ont-* as a prefix, it remains less accessible than (negative) separable particles as a means for encoding reversal. Their analysis of *ont-* may be complicated by two factors: first, the existence of an inchoative prefix with the same form, in such verbs as *ontbranden* 'to set on fire,' and second, the existence of a large number of verbs constructed with a non-inchoative, non-negative *ont-*, e.g., *ontmoeten*

---

[3] There is one negative prefix for verbs, namely *ent-*, but this is used only in highly specialized domains and typically on borrowed or non-Germanic verbs (Curme 1964, Marchand 1973). It is not otherwise productive.

'to meet,' *ontwerpen* 'to throw,' and so on. While inchoative *ont-* is no longer productive, these other uses of *ont-* may obscure its negative sense and so delay acquisition.

The Dutch data, then, offer some further evidence that children opt first for the transparent and simple means provided by locative particles, for the expression of reversal. In both Dutch and English, children go on to acquire the productive prefixes (*ont-* and *un-*) that provide the most productive means for expressing the notion of reversal.

Undoing in other languages

While there are no systematic data available from other languages, the records of children's spontaneous innovations in this domain suggest that similar factors govern children's acquisition of whichever device is most widely used for expressing the notion of reversal.

Romance

In French, there is a single form available to express reversal, the prefix *dé-* (*dés-* before vowels). The Romance languages, unlike the Germanic ones, do not make use of verb particles to express directionality, and have no particles for talking about reversal. However, French-speaking children can and do make use of various forms of the verb *ouvrir* 'open' for this purpose. They use *ouvre* from as young as 1;5,18 to request the removal of obstacles and constraints: to open doors, peel fruit, remove lids from boxes, or peas from a peapod, and undo shoelaces (Guillaume 1927). The settings in which *ouvre* gets used are very similar to those where *open* is used in English (Table 12–1). Once past this earliest stage, children acquiring French begin to use the prefix *dé-*, from around age three, and rely on it alone for innovative verbs of reversal from then on. Some typical examples of their uses are listed in Table 12–9.

Other Romance languages also express reversal through a prefix on the verb. In Spanish, *de-* functions much as in French. Children produce innovative uses of *de-*, again from around age three, as in one child's *Artulito se desacostó* (3;7) 'Arthur un-goed to bed' (from *acostarse* 'to go to bed'). Another child commented *El niño está desdormido* (3;9) 'the boy is un-sleeping', meaning 'awake.' And another, talking about braids coming undone, said *Se [d]escordonó* (3;11) 'they un-braided' (Montes Giraldo 1976). Similar examples have been reported for Portuguese. Again, children begin to use the reversal prefix *de(s)-* between age three and five, as in *dezipar* 'to unzip' (from *zipar* 'to zip'); *desabrir* 'to un-

Table 12–9 Typical early innovative uses of French dé- for reversal

1)   LA (2;0) *déconstruire* 'to un-build' (from *construire* 'to build'/adult *démolir* 'to demolish, knock down')

2)   EA (2;6) *dégrandir* 'to un-grow big' (from *grandir* 'to grow, enlarge'/adult *rétrécir* 'to shrink')

3)   GP (3;0) *débagager* 'to un-baggage' (from GP's innovative *bagager la voiture* 'to baggage the car', meaning 'to go on holiday'; said here of unloading the car, meaning 'to come back from the holiday')

4)   VA (3;3) *désendormir* 'to un-fall asleep' (from *endormir* 'to fall asleep'/adult *réveiller* 'to wake up')

5)   VA (3;5) *démonter* 'to un-climb (up)' (from *monter* 'to climb (up)'/adult *descendre* 'to climb down')

6)   VA (3;5) *déchauffer* 'to un-warm up' (from *chauffer* 'to warm'/adult *refroidir* 'to cool down')

7)   SF (3;6) *défroidir* 'to un-cool' (from *froidir* 'to cool, make cold'/adult *rechauffer* 'to warm up (again)')

8)   SF (3;6) *débîmer* 'to un-spoil' (from *abîmer* 'to spoil,' meaning 'to make new again')

9)   VA (3;6) *décoincer* 'to un-wedge' (from *coincer* 'to wedge, stick')

10)   EV (3;6) *déprocher* 'to un-approach' (from *approcher* 'to approach'/adult *éloigner* 'to go away, depart')

11)   VA (3;9) *détourner* 'to un-turn' (from *tourner* 'to turn around,' meaning 'to go back in the opposite direction')

12)   EV (3;10) *débâtir* 'to un-build' (from *bâtir*/adult *démolir* 'to knock down, demolish')

13)   VA (4;0) *désattacher* 'to un-attach' (from *attacher* 'to attach'/adult *détacher* 'to detach')

14)   VA (4;1) *désécarter* 'to un-spread out' (from *écarter* 'to spread out'; of a hand of cards)

15)   VA (4;1) *déprisonner* 'to un-prison' (from *prison* 'prison'/adult *libérer* 'to free')

16)   VA (4;1) *développer* 'to un-wrap up' (from *envelopper* 'to wrap (up)'/adult *ouvrir* 'to open, unwrap')

17)   EV (4;2) *décorder* 'to un-arrange' (from *accorder* 'to arrange, organize'/adult *déranger* 'to disarrange')

18)   VA (4;3) *désescabeauter* 'to un-stool' (from *escabeau* 'stool'; for adult *descendre* 'to get down')

19)   CG (4;3) *dégrasser* 'to un-fat' (from *gras* 'fat'/adult *dégraisser* 'to remove fat (from meat)')

20)   VA (4;6) *désorteiller* 'to un-toe' (from *orteil* 'big toe,' meaning 'to cut toe-nails')

21)   LC (5;3) *désorer* 'to un-like' (from *adorer* 'to like, adore'/adult *détester* 'to dislike')

22)   PM (6;0) *dessoufler* 'to un-blow' (from *souffler* 'to blow'/adult *dégonfler* 'to deflate')

Source: Aimard 1975, Cohen 1969, Decroly 1932, François 1977, Grégoire 1947, Méresse-Polaert 1969, Vinson 1915–16.

open' (from *abrir* 'to open'/adult *fechar* 'to shut'); *desquentar* 'to un
warm up' (from *quentar* 'to warm (up)'/adult *esfriar* 'to cool down')
desenfiar 'to un-put on' (from *enfiar* 'to put on'/adult *tirar* 'to take off')
and *destampar* 'to un-lid' (from *tampar* 'to cover with a lid') – all from
children under 5;0 (Figueira 1977, 1979).

Both the Spanish and Portuguese observations bear a strong resem
blance to the French data (Table 12–9). The negative prefix in both
languages offers the only means for expressing the reversal of an action
And its use emerges, like that of other affixes, between age three and four

Slavic

In Slavic, as in Romance, reversal is typically expressed through some form
of prefix on the verb. In Polish, children seem to rely on such prefixes from
quite an early age. For instance, one two-year-old contrasted the prefix *na*
(an inchoative perfective marker) with the negative *od-* 'un-' in *Nacisnalem
pedal, a teraz odcisnalem* (2;8,15) [I on-pushed-PERF the pedal and now
un-pushed] 'I pressed down on the pedal and then I unpressed.' Another
child, around the same age, also offered an explicit contrast in *przytwierdz
to ... a teraz musze odtwierdzic* (2;9,26) 'Fix it on to ... and now I must un
fix (it)' (meaning 'tear off'). Other prefixes besides *od-* occasionally appear
in such reversals, e.g., from a three-year-old, a contrast between *dod-* 'up'
and *wyd-* 'down' in *dodmucham materac, a teraz wydmucham* (3;0,12) 'I
blew up the mattress, and now I'm blowing it down,' and from a four-year-
old a different negative prefix, *roz-* 'un-' in *zszyj mi, bo mi sie kolderka
rozszyla* (4;0,2) 'Sew that because my blanket has un-sewn' (Chmura-
Klekotowa 1972).

The commonest prefix for reversal in Polish appears to be *od-*. It appears
in a variety of settings with a reversal meaning in coinages from children
aged three to six. Among the reversal forms children produce are *odbić* 'to
un-arrive' (a reversal of *przybić* 'to arrive'), *odboleć* 'to un-hurt', *odchować*
'to un-hide' (from *schować* 'to hide'), *odmęczyć* 'to un-tire,' *odszyć* 'to un-
sew' (from *zaszyć* 'to sew'), *odpić* 'to be un-thirsty' (from *tróchę nadpić* 'to
be a little thirsty'), and *odstawać* 'to un-stand,' meaning 'to stand down'
(from *przstawać* 'to stand up'). The prefix *od-* appears to offer a productive
means for expressing reversal. From about age three on, it is the means
most favored by children.[4]

---

[4] Although Chmura-Klekotowa didn't study this prefix in any detail, other word-formation
devices children favor at this stage tend to be the more productive ones in adult speech
(Chmura-Klekotowa 1970).

Data from other Slavic languages suggest that Polish *od-* and its
cognates there too offer the main device for talking about the reversal of an
action. In Russian, children rely on the prefix *ot-*, which can be glossed in
English as 'away from,' 'from,' or 'un-,' and the innovative uses there
appear very similar to those in Polish. One Russian three-year-old, for
example, contrasted the perfective prefix *za-* with negative *ot-* in *Lampa
ražigoetsja i otžigoetsja. Otožgi svet* (3;5) 'The lamp lights and un-lights.
Un-light the light.' The prefix *ot-* seems to function for children in a
manner analogous to English *un-* (Gvozdev 1961). In Serbo-Croatian,
children also make use of a negative prefix to express reversal, here in the
form *od-* (Savić 1982). However, no studies of Slavic languages appear to
have looked in detail at how children express the general notion of reversal,
or at the range of options that might be available in these languages.

Hungarian

Lastly, Hungarian researchers have reported a few instances of reversals
being formed with the aid of the negative prefix *ki-*. This prefix seems to
emerge quite early, as in one two-year-old's denominal verb *kimorzsál*
2;1,31) 'to un-crumb' (for adult *morzsát kiráz* 'to shake out crumbs').
Similar examples are reported from three-year-olds, as in the denominal
verb *kibojtozik* (3;2) 'to un-tassel' (for adult *kibogoz* 'to untie'), or, from
a six-year-old, another denominal verb, *kiszálkázik* (6;6,2) 'to un-sliver'
for adult *szálkát kivesz* 'to remove a sliver') (Endrei 1913, Kenyeres
928). As in Slavic, there has been little discussion for Hungarian of how
children begin to express the notion of reversal. What is clear from these
few examples is that here too children have recourse to a negative prefix,
and that they make use of it on novel verbs. Whether this is the only option
for expressing reversal is unclear.

Summary

The elicitation data from English and German offer further evidence that
simplicity and transparency together predict early choices, on the part of
children, in novel word-formation. With the notion of reversal, simplicity
leads them to choose particles, while transparency leads them to the same
solution, because they already know the meanings of these forms and can
pick the opposites of *up*, *in*, or *on* to encode the requisite reversal.

Once a verb prefix with reversal meaning in English (or in other
languages) has been analyzed, it is then just as transparent as a particle. By
this time, too, simplicity is less of a consideration. Children acquiring

English at this point could chose either a particle or the prefix *un-* – bo
are transparent – to express reversal meanings. As Table 12–5 shows, th
opt for the prefix, the more productive option of the two in English.

In German, separable particles are the most productive optio
Transparency may lead children initially to rely on a single genera
purpose verb and, often, on a single negative particle such as *auf, los, c*
occasionally, *weg*. Simplicity also favors particles. In German, the
productivity simply confirms choices based on transparency and simplicit

The other languages offer too few data for any evaluation of acquis
tional principles. Where the only available means of encoding reversal is
prefix (as in French or Hungarian, for example), children appear to pick
up fairly early, at least by age three, and by four or so to make extensive u
of it. Where there are two or more prefixes available, the more producti
appears to be mastered first.

3

CONCLUSION

The intolerable wrestle
With words and meanings.

T. S. Eliot, East Coker II

13 *Issues for acquisition*

This investigation into children's acquisition of the lexicon raises a number of issues. Some are clarified by the findings discussed here; others require more investigation before they can be resolved. I begin by summarizing what the research on lexical development and word formation has revealed about acquisitional principles. I then take up three issues pertinent to all research on language use – the relation between production and comprehension, the representation of linguistic knowledge in memory, and the relation between structure and process in theories of language and language acquisition.

Lexical acquisition

Let me summarize what we have learnt: As children acquire words, they make few obvious errors, and they appear not to find the task a taxing one. Children acquiring very different languages appear to go through the same initial steps and rely on the same ontological categories (Chapters 2 and 3). They begin by producing just a few words and add to them slowly for the first few months; they over-extend many early words to other referents with similar properties. From early on, they build up semantic fields, adding further terms to each domain as they elaborate their vocabularies.

Conventionality and contrast

Yet the process of acquisition is a complex one. As children add words to their repertoires, they act as if every new word differs in meaning from those already acquired. They rely on the principle of CONTRAST, that every difference in form marks a difference in meaning. Throughout this early period, they take as their targets words that adults use to them – the conventional word-stock of their language community (Chapters 4 and 5). They do not make up arbitrary words – they do not just put together possible sound sequences and assign them some meaning. They adopt t CONVENTIONAL forms they hear and work at assigning to those forms plausible meaning. What is plausible is what is consistent with the appare meanings being used by adult speakers. Conventionality and contra apply regardless of language and age: Children and adults alike depend them for language to work.

As children build up a vocabulary, they give priority to establish words, allowing them to pre-empt potential synonyms. To do this, the must first find out whether, say, such pairs as *to broom* and *to sweep*, *runned* and *ran*, in fact have exactly the same meaning. If they do, the contrast requires one term to be dropped, and conventionality selects t established one for retention (Chapter 5). Children also rely on contrast their acquisition of register, in working out the differences in meani between *lots of* and *many*, *daddy* and *father*, or *build* and *construct*. Mu of the higher or more formal Latinate vocabulary in English is o acquired from age seven or later. Every language reserves some forms f formal, high, or specialized registers. Learning which words belong different registers is also a part of lexical acquisition, and it depends on t same general principles.

Transparency, simplicity, and productivity

Any other principles proposed for lexical acquisition must likewise robust enough to hold independently of the language being acquired. T test of candidate principles must be cross-linguistic, with data fro different languages and language types. The acquisitional princip examined here (Chapters 6 and 7) were tested in just this way for gene predictions across languages as well as specific predictions within the TRANSPARENCY OF MEANING, SIMPLICITY OF FORM, and PRODUCTIVITY ma predictions about the acquisition of word formation in German Romance, and Slavic languages, as well as in Hungarian (Finno-Ugr and Hebrew (Semitic). The data were drawn from observations spontaneous coinages and systematic elicitation studies (Chapters 8–1 Each principle applies across children and across languages, but each also affected by the structures available, so the patterns for each langua may differ.

These three principles also interact in the acquisition of word formatic First, if a form type is simple, it is also transparent, but the reverse does hold. Words that are transparent in meaning to children are not necessar simple in form. Second, if a word-form type is productive, it is also transparent. Again, not all transparent forms are productive, so productivity selects a subset of the transparent ones. Third, for productivity to apply, children need a choice of form types to choose from, hence their reliance initially just on simplicity and transparency. Although productive forms are available earlier – they are more frequent in input – the full effects of productivity in word formation can only be seen once children have mastered a near-adult repertoire of the relevant form-types and are in a position to choose among them when coining a new word.

This partial ordering of principles goes from transparency (use familiar word roots and elements to build new words) to simplicity (make as few changes as possible in the building blocks used for new words), and from transparency to productivity (where there are several possible forms, choose the options preferred in the speech community). Since children continually add to their word stock as they acquire more words, they simultaneously add to their store of usable roots and affixes. These provide additional material to which they can apply transparency, simplicity, and productivity. These principles, then, capture certain aspects of how children go about acquiring new words. They are all PRINCIPLES OF PROCESSING.

Do these principles apply elsewhere in the acquisition of language? Conventionality and contrast clearly apply to syntax, just as they do to the lexicon. Different constructions carry different meanings and are conventional for the expression of those meanings (e.g., Bolinger 1972, 1977, Borkin 1984). Children's initial hypotheses about the meanings of constructions may be based on an incomplete analysis, much as with complex words. For example, once young children notice initial-position auxiliary verbs, they may pick on just one form and assume it marks questions, as in *Can he wants to come out?* (see Johnson 1981). But as they analyze the construction more fully, they adopt its conventional meaning. Constructions, though, can take a long time to analyze, in large part because they can appear with such a range of lexical items. Moreover, some of those items may have more than one variant, as in the salient *not* versus unstressed *n't*. As elsewhere, children initially treat such variants as contrasting in meaning. For example, their earliest sentential negatives are unanalyzed negative auxiliary forms such as *can't*, *won't*, and *don't*. *Not isn't* acquired until later (Klima and Bellugi 1966).

To what extent might the processing principles from word formation apply to syntactic structures? Take transparency. Since each syntactic construction is instantiated with words, it may make some construction more accessible than others. Those where more of the lexical units are familiar should be easier to acquire than those where they are not. For example, *to*-complements may occur at first only after such verbs as *war* or *like*, as in *I want to climb up*, but not after verbs like *wait* (*They waite to see him*). Few studies of syntactic acquisition, though, have looked at the lexical range in children's production or comprehension of syntactic structures.

Simplicity could apply to syntactic acquisition in several ways. I predicts that constructions with full forms like *not*, *is*, and *will* should be easier to understand than contracted forms like *n't*, *'s* or *'ll* (Slobin 197. 1985a). Constructions with overt marking, as in relative clauses introduce with *that*, should be easier to understand than ones where the relativizer is omitted. In short, overt marking of structural boundaries for clauses an phrases should always be simpler than constructions that omit such marking. This prediction is consistent with available evidence (e.g., Brow 1971). It is less clear how simplicity would affect production since childre may place some premium on brevity. Omitting *that* in a relative clause is production, for example, may be simpler than including it. This too consistent with observations of children's earliest relative clauses. But littl research has focussed on what is simple to produce in syntax.

Lastly, does productivity apply to syntactic acquisition? Some construc tions are more constrained than others. More-constrained forms ar generally identified as idiomatic since their meanings are not a transparer composition of the component words. Consider *pull a fast one, spill th beans, answer the door, all of a sudden, sight unseen*: their meanings are no predictable, and some of them exemplify structures rarely found elsewher in English (e.g., *sight unseen*). In some constructional idioms, every elemer may be fixed, as in *It takes one to know one*. In others, only the ver inflection can vary, as in *trip the light fantastic* where *trip* can be singula or plural, present or past. In others, the construction allows person to vary in *blow one's nose*, one can find *You blow your nose, He blows his nose, an* so on. Others allow an indefinite range of lexical substitutions. For example, the construction *the X-er, the Y-er*, exemplified by such fixe forms as *The bigger they come, the harder they fall*, can also appear wit novel lexical content, e.g., *The more carefully you pack, the easier it will b to carry the bags*. Although use of the definite article here appears uniqu and the two-part structure linking the atypical *the*-phrases doesn't appea among standard syntactic forms in English, this construction is full productive. It allows an indefinite number of instantiations with new lexical material (Fillmore, Kay, and O'Connor 1988). Constructions like this suggest that the present notion of productivity may be applicable to syntax as well as to the lexicon.

In summary, as children accumulate vocabulary, they attach meanings to more and more forms. And they steadily acquire more words and affixes that can be used to construct new words. They readily make use of established words and, when they need to, coin new ones. Their usage offers support for both the general principles of conventionality and contrast, and the more specific processing principles of transparency, simplicity, and productivity. Children must also process syntax, and here too they may rely on the same processing principles as they do in word formation.

Production does not equal comprehension

In conversation, we talk and listen, concerned with the goals of each participant in the conversation. So when we think about adult speakers, it is easy to assume comprehension and production are symmetrical. It is only a small step to assume further that both comprehension and production rely on the identical linguistic information in memory. But both assumptions are unwarranted. Comprehension and production are not symmetrical (Clark and Hecht 1983, Ingram 1974b, Straight 1986). Their differences show up in the earliest stages of language acquisition; they play an essential role in the process of acquisition itself; and they continue to play a general role in the comprehension and production of speech for adults.

Young children can understand forms well before they can produce them. Infants under one year old, for example, understand some words for up to three or four months before they try to produce them; older children understand comparative word-forms, for instance, long before they themselves can produce any; and they also understand novel derived-nouns before they themselves coin any. This asymmetry has been documented in a number of studies (e.g., Clark and Berman 1984, Clark and Hecht 1982, Harris, Yeeles, Chasin, and Oakley 1993, Layton and Stick 1979). Much of the data discussed in this book has been from production only, from early vocabulary acquisition (e.g., Chapter 2) and from later exploitation of word structure in coinages (e.g., Chapter 10). But one's production vocabulary is always smaller than one's comprehension vocabulary. (This holds for adults as well as children.) Production can therefore reveal only part of the picture. If we chart acquisition only from production, we seriously underestimate what children know, both about the lexicon and about language in general.

Logically, comprehension must precede production. How else can speakers know which words to use to convey a particular meaning? They must already have mapped the relevant meanings onto specific forms, and have these units represented in memory, to be accessed on subsequent occasions whenever they hear the relevant forms from others. Without some representation of the form and meaning(s) of a word, speakers would have no way of knowing that it exists and is therefore potentially available. The precedence of comprehension over production is itself critical to the process of acquisition. It allows children to work at leisure on their own production and to perfect it without having to rely directly on adult speakers for examples of the target words. I'll illustrate the differences by looking at word forms.

C-representations and P-representations

The process works as follows: First, assume that children set up C-representations of words they hear in input. These enable them to recognize that they are hearing the same word, *frog* say, on a subsequent occasion. The C-representation must contain information about the auditory form of *frog*: the sound segments and their ordering. This auditory information will be represented here as /frog/. It must also contain whatever meaning children have mapped onto that form, however tentative or uncertain (Chapter 3). Then, when children hear /frog/, they not only recognize the form as one they have heard before, they can also access their C-representation and look up whatever meaning goes with the form. Similarly, for a word like *builder*, children's C-representation would contain the auditory sequence /bɪldər/, plus, eventually, information about the internal structure of the word – the root *build* plus the affix *-er* and any meaning already mapped onto the form.

C-representations for words, then, start from auditory information about forms. This provides the route for looking up words in memory. Without such C-representations, children would not know whether they had heard /frog/ before or not; nor would they be able to track successive uses of the same word-form in order to refine any hypotheses about possible meanings. As children hear more input, they add further C-representations. They must fine-tune their representations as they grasp more details of the sound system (e.g., Jusczyk 1992, Lindblom 1992) and ear the same word-form from a variety of speakers in a variety of contexts. They also add information about the internal structure of words like *builder* or *frog-man*, and they elaborate the semantic information for each form as they hear more uses in more contexts. Once some C-representation for a word has been stored in memory, children can start trying to produce that word. But producing a recognizable word takes time and practice (Chapter 2). Articulatory skills lag far behind auditory ones. And to produce a word, children need to set up production representations – P-representations – that contain all the *articulatory* information necessary for producing that word. They must include information about sound segments, along with their sequencing within a word, their relation to syllable structure, to stress, and to internal morphological structure, as well as about neighboring words. For example, for a word like *frog*, the P-representation must specify that the initial sound is articulated with the lower lip against the upper teeth, with outgoing breath but with no vibration of the glottis, /F/. (P-representations of words will use small capital letters to symbolize articulatory information, as in /FROG/ for the word *frog*.)

The alignment process

When children try to produce a word, they need a target against which to assess their own current efforts. They need some way to check on the adequacy of their P-representation. Is their word recognizable? Can others understand it? That is, children's production of words must eventually be *aligned* with the forms produced in the language community. One source for checking their own productions is adult pronunciations of the target, but adults will not necessarily produce the right word just when children need it (they are not mind-readers). In fact, they often fail to recognize the young child's target (e.g., Scollon 1976).

Another source, always available to children, is their own C-representations for the target words. But since these are designed for recognition, for identifying linguistic units heard in the input, they don't contain any information about the articulatory programs needed for production. They do, however, provide a means for checking on the adequacy of children's P-representations. They can check what they produce against what they have heard and represented from others. This allows them to detect any mismatch between their P-representation and C-representation, e.g., between /FO/ and /frog/. But this assumes further that children, like adults, monitor what they say. Monitoring for adults is an integral part of

production (Levelt 1989). It allows the detection of any mismatch with t
intended target so the speaker can repair the defective production. F
young children, the detection of mismatches is critical to changing a
adjusting their P-representations. In evaluating their own pronunciatio
of words, therefore, children could proceed as follows:

(a)   The child creates a C-representation for a word-form, x.
(b)   The child tries to create a P-representation for x.
(c)   The child executes the P-representation and, monitoring his wo
       form, compares the word heard with his own existing
       representation for x.
(d)   The child then corrects the P-representation for x.

What evidence is there that children do this? First, they make repai
spontaneously, to their own productions from a very early age, and the
repairs typically move them closer to the adult forms (e.g., Clark a:
Andersen 1979, Käsermann and Foppa 1981, Scollon 1976). In the case
pronunciations like *fo* (typical of early attempts at *frog*), they may rep;
their form and produce *fwo*. That is, the P-representation has be
elaborated from /FO/ to /FWO/ to take account of the initial cluster
sounds, *fr-*, at the beginning of *frog*. A little later, when children attem
the final *-g*, they may repair *fwo* to *fwonk* – which includes both voici
(from the nasal) and the right place of articulation for the final consona
(Clark and Bowerman 1986). Here, the P-representation has been revis
from /FWO/ to /FWONK/, but it still has some way to go before it will
fully aligned with the C-representation, /frog/. Further revisions a
needed in the initial cluster, *fr-*, and the final voiced stop, *-g*, befc
children will produce *frog* with adult-like pronunciation.

Additional evidence that C-representations are established ahead of
representations comes from three further sources: the *fis* phenomeno
minimal-pair discrimination, and across-the-board adjustments for new
acquired sounds. For example, in recognition tasks, children consistent
reject other people's pronunciations that imitate their own defecti
productions and accept only adult forms. They prefer *fish* over *fis* ev
though they themselves say *fis*, and the same goes for *shoe* versus *su*, a
merry-go-round versus *mewwy-go-wound* (e.g., Berko and Brown 196
Dodd 1975, Maccoby and Bee 1965, Weir 1966). And, although,
production, they fail to distinguish such pairs as *mouth* and *mouse* (bo
pronounced *mouse*), or *sip* and *ship* (both *sip*), they reliably distingui
them in comprehension (e.g., Smith 1973). Finally, once they master a n

sound in production, for example the initial /s-/ in clusters, they add it only to the appropriate forms: '*top* (halt) goes to *stop*, but *top* (the toy) remains unchanged; '*pider* goes to *spider*, and '*nake* goes to *snake* (e.g., Smith 1973, Weir 1966). Once they can adjust their P-representations for any forms where there was at first some mismatch between their own pronunciation and the target form, they can be said to have aligned their P-representation with their C-representation for the target form (see further Clark and Hecht 1983, Levelt 1983, 1989).

This general model of change in acquisition depends critically on the asymmetry between comprehension and production. Children rely on already established C-representations as a check on their initial P-representations. When they locate mismatches, they try to adjust the P-representations. They may take longer to set up adequate P-representations for some forms than others, so their interim repairs are often only partly successful. But with constant monitoring and repairs, children gradually adjust their P-representations until they produce adult-like versions of the target forms.

Meaning also contributes to the general asymmetry here. When children decide to say something, they create a meaning and then search for the word form associated with just that meaning. But they may fail to find a match with any of the meanings already available in their P-representations. When they hear words, though, they access their C-representations for the word forms and simply take whatever meaning is already there in the C-representation as the meaning intended. There is little or no dislocation of form and meaning in comprehension compared with production (see also Dell and O'Seaghdha 1992, Levelt, Schriefers, Vorberg, Meyer, Pechmann, and Havinga 1991).

Comprehension and production are asymmetric in adults too. People can understand many words they never produce like *e'en, erstwhile, thither, betwixt* or, for example, such crossword rarities as *eleemosynary* or *orison*. They can understand many dialects they cannot produce, for example, Edinburgh, Lancashire, and London English in the UK, or Appalachian, Georgia, and western Pennsylvania English in the US. And they can understand many earlier varieties of their language, for instance, the English of Dickens, Richardson, Pepys, Shakespeare, and Chaucer, again varieties they can't reproduce. To achieve this, they must clearly have many more C-representations than P-representations. This asymmetry is also evident in the learning of another language, where comprehension invariably outstrips production.

Such a range for comprehension is essential. Addressees can't limit or restrict a priori what others will say or how they will say it. People therefore need to store a great deal of information in order to understand most, if not all, of what they hear. As speakers, though, they can confine their production to what they feel confident in producing; they are free to avoid words or constructions they are unsure of. They are in command of how they say what they want to say.[1] In short, production, for adults just as for children, corresponds to a subset of comprehension.

We therefore need a theory of acquisition that will account for both comprehension and production. The few studies that have looked at both processes suggest that there are clear differences between them. For example, three-year-olds appropriately interpret the suffix *-er* on novel nouns as agentive and offer glosses that make this clear. The same children in production, construct new agent-nouns not by adding *-er* to the relevant verb root, but by forming a compound with the head *-man*, as in *wagon man* for 'someone who pulls wagons.' Although these children can interpret novel agent-nouns like *holder, puller,* or *thrower,* they themselves coin forms like *pull-man* and *throw-man* (Clark and Hecht 1982). Yet children never hear forms like *throw-man,* with verb–noun order, for agents.

In another study, children were first given a range of novel compounds to gloss (all of them possible compound-types); they consistently offered appropriate interpretations. They were then asked questions designed to elicit novel compounds formed with both noun and verb roots, e.g., *record holder, writing-shelf, turn-handle.* In production, children under five consistently placed verb roots as heads in the leftmost or initial slot of the compounds. For example, for 'someone who throws balls,' they produce the compound *throw-ball.* But when they were later given a further set of novel compounds to interpret, based on form types in their own production, they took the *rightmost* element as the head. For example, given the novel form *climb-rope,* they interpreted the rightmost element as the head, glossing it as a kind of rope, not a person who climbs ropes. In comprehension, children act like adults, with the rightmost element treated as the head of a compound. In production, they place noun roots in the

---

[1] They must, of course, take account of their addressees in designing their utterances (Clark 1985, in press), but they can nonetheless, for example, avoid verb forms constructions they are uneasy with. Consider, for instance, the past tenses of *tread forbid*; the inversion of auxiliaries for unfulfilled conditions, as in *Had he listened, ...* or form of the tag question after *No-one should leave early, should —* (see further Green 19 Langendoen 1970).

rightmost slot as head (e.g., *snow-hat* for 'a hat you wear in the snow'). But they place verb roots as heads in the leftmost slot (*throw-ball*), as in verb phrases (Clark 1986; also Clark, Hecht, and Mulford 1986).

To conclude, there must be different representations for comprehension and production, so both processes can be taken into account in any theory of acquisition. Accounts based on production alone, or comprehension alone, are necessarily incomplete. This view is incompatible with all accounts that simply take for granted that there is a single set of representations in memory, neutral between comprehension and production, that captures the idealized speaker's linguistic knowledge. This overly simple view ignores both the asymmetry between comprehension and production observable in all speakers, regardless of age, and also the essential differences, for example, between the auditory information in C-representations and the articulatory information in P-representations. In acquisition, the asymmetry between the two types of representation plays a critical role in the alignment process. C-representations, set up first, offer a means for checking and, where necessary, adjusting the products of early P-representations.

Representing linguistic knowledge

What does the mental lexicon look like? How is it organized? One view is that it consists of listings of all the forms and meanings speakers know. They consult a list when they need to interpret an established or novel form; they also consult one when they produce an established or novel form.

Listing in the mental lexicon

But what is the nature of these lists? What units do they contain? And how are the units arranged? Speakers need to be able to find words to express the meanings they wish to convey, so they presumably organize words or lexical entries according to meaning. As addressees, people must also be able to access words through their forms and presumably consult a listing organized according to initial sound segments. And lexical entries could form paradigms with all the inflected forms of a particular root grouped together, as in *eat, eats, eating, ate, eaten*; *she, her, hers*; or *cat, cats, cat's*.

There have been two main proposals about the forms stored in memory: full-listing and root-listing. With full-listing, each inflected form would be represented separately, as a distinct form; with root-listing, each root would be listed, together with a set of procedures, each associated with a

different inflection. For languages with little inflectional morphology, l̲
English, the difference between full-listing and root-listing may be rat̲
small. But for agglutinative languages like Turkish, with highly regu̲
morphology, a full-listing of inflected verb forms alone rapidly reac̲
astronomical proportions, with several hundred or more forms per r̲
(Anderson 1988, Hankamer 1986). Still other languages make complica̲
adjustments to the form of each root and affix combination, adjustme̲
that may change the forms of both, such that full-listing might seem m̲
helpful for comprehension and root-listing for production. For so̲
languages, full-listing appears quite impractical. What is unknown at t̲
point is the extent to which language typology affects and shapes h̲
people access the words in their mental dictionary.[2]

Children give evidence of identifying some roots and affixes fairly ear̲
In English, they first produce uninflected root forms, but these ̲
common in adult speech too. For example, the bare root (*eat*) appears̲
the infinitival and imperative verb (*to eat*; *eat!*), in most present-ter̲
forms (*I/you/we/they eat*), and after some auxiliary verbs (*can/will/*
eat). In languages where the bare root does not occur, children must in̲
its form from what occurs in common across different inflected forms.̲
Spanish, for example, the verb 'to walk' appears in the present-tense for̲
camino, caminas, camina, caminamos, camináis, caminan, all with t̲
sequence *camin-* in common. Children presumably identify this sequen̲
as the verb root.

Children identify word parts in English quite early, and, for instan̲
spontaneously pick out roots from compound forms, e.g., the *run* in *ru̲*
way or the *angel* in *angel-cake* (Chapter 2, Table 2–3). By age three,̲
earlier, they successfully strip all the affixes from roots when they fo̲
compounds, as when they characterize someone who hugs dogs as a *hu̲*
dog. Equally, in Hebrew, by age three to four, children can extract the ro̲
consonants from familiar and unfamiliar word-forms (Berman 198̲
1993). Getting access to roots and affixes is presumably determined ̲
part by transparency and simplicity.

Further evidence that children represent both roots and affixes com̲
from their formation of innovative word-forms, with new combinations̲

---

[2] The data on listing from studies of adult processing are hard to interpret. Some stud̲
offer strong evidence for full-listing being used in spoken-word recognition (e.g., Ty̲
Marslen-Wilson, Rentoul, and Hanney 1988); others suggest people may rely on b̲
root-listing and full-listing (e.g, Meijers and Jarvella 1982). Many studies, though, ha̲
looked only at written, not spoken, words and few have examined on-line speech (̲
further Cutler 1983). Even fewer have looked at different language-types.

roots and affixes (Chapters 8–12). Certain errors in word formation also offer evidence for the units children are using. In French, for example, children often add affixes to the wrong stem in second-conjugation verbs, as in *fineur* (for *finisseur*) from *finir* 'to finish' (Chapter 10). In doing this, they show that they have identified the infinitival stem *fin-*, but not yet realized that each verb has two stems, the infinitival one (*fin-*) and the derivational one (*finiss-*).[3] They must use their knowledge about roots and stems in identifying affixes. And they make no errors in the forms of affixes used in their coinages. That is, they make no segmentation errors, either of extracting part of the root together with the affix or of extracting less than the whole affix (Chapters 8 and 9).[4]

Frequency tallies

Speakers keep tallies of the words they hear and can make accurate judgments about their relative frequencies (Carroll and White 1973a, 1973b). Children also represent information about frequency. They appear sensitive to frequency in acquiring new words, and learn words presented more frequently over those presented less frequently (Schwartz and Terrell 1983). But token frequency is not all: they are sensitive to type frequency too, for example, in adult verb-use (e.g., Guillaume 1927, de Villiers 1985; also Chapter 7). They also take account of type-based frequency in word-formation, as in English-speaking children's *bicycler* for *bicyclist*. The productivity of an affix is reflected in part in its frequency, and again children use this information: first, when they begin to use derivational affixes, they pick up on the most widespread ones first; and second, once they have acquired an adult-like repertoire, they favor more-productive affixes – those used more frequently in innovations by adults – over less-productive ones (e.g., Chapters 7 and 10).[5]

In summary, children appear to store whole words as well as roots and

---

[3] They are presumably delayed in this acquisition by the fact that the two stems are identical for first-conjugation verbs, and the first conjugation contains over 90 percent of verb types in French. Children acquiring other Romance languages encounter a similar problem in identifying the relevant stems for derivation.

[4] In languages where the lines between stem and affix are blurred by complex adjustment rules, children may make some segmentation errors and so mis-identify the forms of some affixes (and roots). I have found no instances, though, in any of the data discussed here.

[5] Notice that even if children instead constructed each new word on the basis of some immediately preceding model in the input, one would still expect to see an effect of frequency, so some models would be more frequent and so more often available than others. However, a number of studies have shown that children do not rely on immediately preceding models in the input, but instead opt for the most productive form for the pertinent meaning (e.g., Clark and Cohen 1984; also MacWhinney 1978).

affixes. In production, for example, they use conventional terms with complex internal structure, but they also coin new words from familiar roots and affixes. This suggests that for production, they must store both full- and root-listings for words. The same presumably applies in comprehension. Children also store information about word frequency for both types and tokens, and draw on it when they choose the building blocks for new words.

Structure versus process

Linguistic theories describe products. For example, theories of syntactic structure have focussed on sentences; they offer accounts of syntactic form, with analyses of forms and the relations among their subparts. But these descriptions of products do not include any metric for describing developmental changes in forms or functions. Linguistic accounts offer *static* models of language. They are assumed to represent what speakers know about syntax, but they offer no account of how such knowledge is exploited in language use.

Theories of acquisition, on the other hand, like theories of language use, are designed to capture *dynamic* properties of language. They are necessarily models of *process*. They deal with change: Children are continually adding to what they know about the lexicon, about morphological modulations, about syntactic structure and function, and about the pragmatics of everyday use. Because their language is continually changing, their representations in memory for what they know are also changing. In addition, as we have seen, their representations for comprehension and production are different. They consistently understand more than they can produce. Static idealizations are therefore bound to fall short as theories of processes, whether in acquisition or in adult usage.

Yet one avowed goal of linguistic theory over the last few decades has been to account for children's acquisition of language. A number of researchers have drawn on linguistic theories to make predictions about the *order* in which children acquire particular syntactic, morphological, or semantic structures. Their general assumption appears to have been the following: linguistic complexity as derived from the linguistic account of the relevant domain is reflected in order of acquisition for words or constructions. The more complex the construction, the earlier it is acquired. In short, they tacitly assume that static theories of products can apply to processes like acquisition.

But which aspects of a static account should be reflected in acquisition

Should children learn first those elements of language that are universal? Should they go through the abstract steps postulated in static linguistic accounts? Should they instantiate 'underlying' forms en route to adult usage? Underlying forms are typically postulated for theory-internal reasons, and there is little reason to assume they form part of the speaker's linguistic representations in memory.[6] In short, when researchers have made predictions about acquisition, they have smuggled in tacit processing assumptions without either spelling them out or articulating their relation to the static linguistic theory itself.

Linguistic theories have, in fact, been the source of two types of prediction in acquisition. First, they have been used to predict what children should acquire early on, on the basis of what is universal across languages. Second, they have been used to make predictions about order of acquisition, according to complexity, with underlying or more basic forms being acquired before surface or adult-like ones.

Universals of language

The rich parallels in structure across languages have led to the postulation that such universals are a reflection of our innate knowledge about language (e.g., Chomsky 1965). While this view contains a tacit processing theory, how one moves from innate structures to universals has never been spelled out. But it has led to the assumption that such parallels should also show up in acquisition. Static theories about products (here, cross-linguistic commonalities in structure) are therefore used to explain dynamic change, tacitly importing a processing account.

There *are* clear parallels between universals and acquisition. Jakobson (1968) pointed out that the inventories of sounds children produce in their first words parallel the simplest inventories possible in the languages of the world, and that children add further sound classes in the order predicted from the patterns found in languages of the world. For example, all languages with fricative consonants also have stop consonants, but not the reverse. And children in general acquire stops before fricatives. And in morphology, for example, suffixing is heavily preferred to prefixing

---

[6] These tacit processing assumptions are reminiscent of the long discredited reliance on theories of cumulative derivational complexity in the 1960s, where the number of transformations in a transformational generative grammar was assumed to be a direct measure of processing complexity in sentence comprehension. The more transformations applied to a neutral base or kernel sentence, the harder it should be to process. But the results from processing studies did not bear this out, and cumulative derivational complexity was abandoned (see Clark and Clark 1977, Fodor, Bever, and Garrett 1974, Olson and Clark 1976, and especially Watt 1970 for an incisive critique).

(Hawkins and Cutler 1988), and children find it easier to learn suffixes than prefixes (e.g., Kuczaj 1979, Slobin 1973). In addition, languages are consistent in adding morphemes to roots or words (rather than subtracting them) to express modulations of meaning (Greenberg 1966). Children too show a preference for adding morphemes to mark modulations, like the plural on nouns (e.g., Anisfeld and Tucker 1968). Languages are also highly consistent in their word-order patterns across construction types (Greenberg 1963, Hawkins 1983). Again, children show certain consistencies in their early word-orders (e.g., Braine 1976, Slobin 1970). In every case, the move in considering such universals has been from a theory about products – the forms observable in a language – to a tacit theory about processes. But while universals often have parallels in early acquisition, it is generally unclear what predictions can be made about detailed orders of acquisition in each domain.

An alternative approach here has been to argue that cross-linguistic universals exist precisely because of processing constraints on language use and language acquisition. For example, the consistencies in word order studied by Greenberg have arisen within languages because they allow for easier processing. Speakers can expect that if one modifier-type follows its head, most others will too, in other constructions in the same language (Clark and Clark 1978). Equally, the general preference across languages for suffixes over prefixes reflects processing needs in that word roots or stems can be more readily identified if they do not first have to be stripped of prefixes. Suffixes, though, do not hinder on-line word recognition. Suffixes before prefixes as a universal is now motivated by a processing consideration – the need to be able to recognize word roots and stems. Ease of processing would also predict, for example, that in languages where bare root forms make up parts of noun or verb paradigms, these should be acquired before inflected forms. In verbs, for example, the root form (used for the present and the imperative in English) is acquired before forms inflected for the past with -*ed* or marked for the future with modal *will* (Brown 1973, Harner 1976). Where added morphemes mark added complexity of meaning in languages, children consistently learn less-complex forms before more-complex ones.

But can these findings be ascribed with certainty only to processing constraints? Can they be distinguished, for example, from the effects of input (Bowerman 1985, Choi and Bowerman 1991)? Children attend to the frequency of the forms and constructions they hear. And the more frequent a form type, the earlier it is acquired (Chapters 7 and 10). The frequency of input forms may also vary with the register being used – whether speakers are addressing intimates or not, being informal or formal, deferential or demanding, and so on. Again, children are sensitive to the distribution of form types in different registers in the input (Andersen 1990). In general, the more frequent a form and the constructions it can appear in, the earlier children learn it. It is therefore difficult to ascribe order of acquisition in any one domain to universals alone.

Order of acquisition

Linguistic theories have often been used to make predictions about the order in which children will acquire structures and the errors they will produce on the way. But can static linguistic theories predict the errors children will produce? Errors of over-regularization reflect children's discovery of patterns or paradigms in the language, where there is systematicity in the form-to-meaning mappings (Chapters 3 and 6). But theories of morphology, for instance, have little to say about regularized forms like *bringed* for *brought*, or *bicycler* for *bicyclist*, or about when in the course of acquisition they should occur. Such forms are *consistent* with major morphological paradigms, but don't resemble underlying forms and so have no direct source in the target language. Linguistic accounts, however sophisticated, just don't contain any *mechanism* to account for over-regularization errors.

Print-out errors, a second major type of error, are those errors that could reflect intermediate, abstract steps in the linguistic derivation of a form prior to its attaining its surface realization (Bowerman 1982a). Such intermediate steps or stages are abstract theoretical constructs, postulated to explain within a particular theory how certain structures are related. For example, within certain semantic theories, causative verbs contain an underlying CAUSE that may surface as English *make* in such child-forms as *I made it dead* (for 'I killed it') or *I made it be on the chair* (for 'I put it on the chair'). Such underlying forms have no surface realizations in the adult language and so do not appear in the input children hear. But as children acquire language, they may give temporary surface realizations to some underlying forms, and can thereby support certain theory-internal claims about form x being related to or derived from form y.

Consider some candidate print-out errors from children's compound formation. Roeper and Siegel (1978) analyzed synthetic compounds of the form [N + V-*er*], as in *wall-builder* (where the first element is a noun root and the second a verb root). They assumed such compounds were derived from phrases of the type 'X Verbs Object-Noun.' So *wall-builder* would b₁ derived from 'X builds walls.' The compound, in their account, is derive₁ first from the terms V + O (*build* + *wall*) being re-ordered to O + V (*wall* + *build*); then the affix -*er* is attached to the whole to form a nominal [*wall* + *build*] + -*er*. Any print-out errors in acquisition, then, could be o₁ the [O + V] (*wall-build*) type in which the two roots are appropriatel₁ ordered but still lack the agentive suffix -*er*. Bowerman argued that print out errors could lend support to a linguistic account, while error incompatible with the underlying forms being postulated would b₁ evidence against that same account.

The acquisition data from compounding lend Roeper and Siegel'₁ account no support. First, children never produce compound nouns lik₁ *wall-build* (correct O + V order without affixation). Instead, they ad₁ affixes before they learn how to order the roots in such compounds, as i₁ *builder-wall* for a person who builds walls (Clark, Hecht, and Mulfor₁ 1986; Chapter 8). Second, counter to prediction, they first add affixes wit₁ the bases in V + O order (*builder-wall*, *puller-wagon*). This error i₁ incompatible with the proposed inversion of V and O prior to adding -*er* i₁ Roeper and Siegel's account. The predictions from underlying forms her₁ suffer from both errors that don't occur and errors that do.

An alternative theory about compound derivation was offered b₁ Selkirk (1982). In her theory, synthetic compounds like *wall-builder* resul₁ from the combination of a derived noun in -*er* and a modifying nou₁ (typically the object of the verb). The underlying structure of the compoun₁ can be represented as [O + [V-*er*]] rather than as [[O + V]-*er*]. But thi₁ analysis is vulnerable to another kind of child error where the affix is adde₁ to the root in second position, with V + O order, e.g., *dry-hairer*. Althoug₁ such errors are rare, they occur in spontaneous speech (Clark *et al.* 1986)₁ This error poses a problem for Roeper and Siegel too since they conside₁ that the roots must be ordered as O + V (*wall* + *build*) before any affixes ca₁ be added. In short, neither account postulates underlying forms that ca₁ predict the errors children make en route to production of the conventiona₁ forms.

In summary, linguistic theories don't translate in any simple way int₁ processing theories. They are theories about products, not theories abou₁ the processes used in producing and understanding utterances. The₁ ignore processing constraints, whether from memory, planning, lineari₁ zation, goals in conversation, coordination between speakers and addres₁ sees, or reliance on mutual knowledge in designing utterances (H. Clark, i₁ press, Levelt 1989). And, like theories of comprehension and production, any theory of acquisition must be a processing theory, a theory of changing performance. Theories of acquisition can usefully draw on linguistic theories for detailed descriptions of linguistic phenomena, but they can't, in principle, use them as the sole source for predictions about performance. Acquisition theories need to take account of what speakers and addressees *do* in talking and listening – whether they are two-year-olds or adults. They must account for the fact that children are *acquiring* language and take time to do this.

Coda

This book has offered an account of how children acquire both established words and the means to coin new words. The principles proposed and the conclusions drawn are based on evidence from a variety of languages and from large numbers of children. This evidence suggests that children take a common approach to the acquisition of words and word structure, and that, in doing so, they are sensitive to the typology of their language and the productivity in adult speech of word-formation patterns. These studies have drawn on acquisition data from a number of languages in the Germanic, Romance, and Slavic groups, as well as from such non-Indo-European languages as Hungarian and Hebrew. We need to add data on the acquisition of word structure from prefixing languages like Mohawk, polysynthetic ones like Greenlandic Eskimo, and isolating ones like Cantonese. But the findings to date strongly suggest that there, too, children will rely on the same principles for acquiring words and for processing word-structure.

The lexicon is basic to language and language use. It provides the content for syntax and the instantiation of syntactic rules, and it is the environment for phonological and morphological patterns. So understanding what it means to learn a word is critical to the construction of a general theory of how children acquire a language.

Bibliography

Abbott, Valerie, Black, John B., and Smith, Edward E. (1985) The representation of scripts in memory. *Journal of Memory and Language* 24, 179–199.

Adams, Valerie (1973) *An introduction to Modern English word-formation*. London: Longman.

Aimard, Paule (1974) *L'enfant et son langage*. Villeurbanne: Simép Editions.

(1975) *Les jeux de mots de l'enfant*. Villeurbanne: Simép Editions.

Aksu-Koç Ayhan A., and Slobin, Dan I. (1985) The acquisition of Turkish. In Dan I. Slobin (ed.), *The crosslinguistic study of language acquisition*, vol. 1. Hillsdale, NJ: Lawrence Erlbaum Associates, pp. 839–878.

Alloni Fainberg, Yaffa (1974) Official Hebrew terms for parts of the car: a study of knowledge, usage, and attitudes. In Joshua A. Fishman (ed.), *Advances in language planning*. The Hague: Mouton, pp. 493–517.

Ammon, Mary Sue (1980) Development in the linguistic expression of causal relations: comprehension of features of lexical and periphrastic causatives. Unpublished doctoral dissertation, University of California, Berkeley.

(1981) Semantic differentiation among expressions of causality by children and adults. *Papers and Reports on Child Language Development* [Stanford University] 20, 25–33.

Andersen, Elaine S. (1990) *Speaking with style: the sociolinguistic skills of children*. London: Routledge.

Anderson, Stephen R. (1985) Typological distinctions in word formation. In Timothy Shopen (ed.), *Language typology and syntactic description*, vol. 3: *Grammatical categories and the lexicon*. Cambridge: Cambridge University Press, pp. 3–56.

(1988) Morphology as a parsing problem. *Linguistics* 26, 521–544.

Anglin, Jeremy M. (1977) *Word, object, and conceptual development*. New York: W. W. Norton and Co.

Anisfeld, Moshe, and Tucker, G. Richard (1968) English pluralization rules of six-year-old children. *Child Development* 28, 1201–1217.

Anshen, Frank, and Aronoff, Mark (1988) Producing morphologically complex words. *Linguistics* 26, 641–655.

Aronoff, Mark (1976) *Word formation in generative grammar*. (Linguistic Inquiry Monograph 1.) Cambridge, MA: MIT Press.

(1980) The relevance of productivity in a synchronic description of word formation. In Jacek Fisiak (ed.), *Historical morphology*. (Trends in Linguistics, Studies and Monographs 17.) The Hague: Mouton, pp. 71–82.

Aronoff, Mark, and Schvaneveldt, Roger (1978) Testing morphological productivity. *Annals of the New York Academy of Sciences* 318, 106–114.

Asbach-Schnitker, Brigitte (1984, February) On the coining of complex verbs in children acquiring German. Paper presented at the 6. Jahrestagung der Deutschen Gesellschaft für Sprachwissenschaft, Bielefeld, Germany.

Au, Terry K.-F. (1990) Children's use of information in word learning. *Journal of Child Language* 17, 393–416.

Au, Terry K.-F., and Glusman, Mariana (1990) The principle of mutual exclusivity: to honor or not to honor? *Child Development* 61, 1474–1490.

Augst, Gerhard (ed.) (1984a) *Kinderwort: der aktive Kinderwortschatz.* (Theorie und Vermittlung der Sprache 1.) Frankfurt am Main: Verlag Peter Lang.

Augst, Gerhard (1984b, August) Pre-school children's actively used vocabulary – first results of a research project. Paper presented at the Meeting of the Association Internationale de Linguistique Appliquée, Bruxelles.

Augst, Gerhard, Bauer, Andrea, and Stein, Anette (1977) *Grundwortschatz und Ideolekt: empirische Untersuchung zur semantischen und lexicalischen Struktur des kindlichen Wortschatzes.* Tübingen: Max Niemeyer.

Baayen, Harald (1989) *A corpus-based approach to morphological productivity.* Amsterdam: Centrum voor Wiskunde en Informatica.

(1991) Quantitative aspects of morphological productivity. In Geert Booij and Jaap van Marle (eds.), *1991 yearbook of morphology.* Amsterdam: Kluwer, pp. 109–149.

Baayen, Harald, and Lieber, Rochelle (1991) Productivity and English derivation: a corpus based study. *Linguistics* 29, 801–843.

Backhouse, A. E. (1981) Japanese verbs of dress. *Journal of Linguistics* 17, 17–29.

Badry, Fatima (1982) The centrality of the root in Semitic lexical derivation: evidence from children's acquisition of Moroccan Arabic. *Papers and Reports on Child Language Development* [Stanford University] 21, 9–15.

(1983) Acquisition of lexical derivational rules in Moroccan Arabic: implications for the development of Standard Arabic as a second language through literacy. Unpublished doctoral dissertation, University of California, Berkeley.

Baker, C. Leroy (1979) Syntactic theory and the projection problem. *Linguistic Inquiry* 10, 533–581.

Balassa, József (1893) A gyermek nyelvének fejlödése [The development of child language]. *Nyelvtudományi Közlemények* 23, 60–73, 129–144.

Baldwin, Dare A. (1989) Priorities in children's expectations about object-label reference: form over color. *Child Development* 60, 1291–1306.

Banigan, Rae L., and Mervis, Carolyn B. (1988) Role of adult input in young children's category evolution: II. An experimental study. *Journal of Child Language* 15, 493–504.

Barcsai, Károly (1921) Adatok a gyermek nyelvének fejlödéséhez [Data on the development of child language]. *Magyar Nyelvõr* 50, 31–32.

Barrett, Martyn D. (1986) Early semantic representations and early word usage. In

Stan A. Kuczaj II and Martyn D. Barrett (eds.), *The development of word meaning: progress in cognitive development research*. Berlin and New York: Springer, pp. 39–67.

Barrett, Martyn, Harris, Margaret, and Chasin, Joan (1991) Early lexical development and maternal speech: a comparison of children's initial and subsequent uses of words. *Journal of Child Language* 18, 21–40.

Barsalou, Lawrence W., and Sewell, Daniel R. (1985) Contrasting the representation of scripts and categories. *Journal of Memory and Language* 24, 646–665.

Bateman, William G. (1914) A child's progress in speech, with detailed vocabularies. *Journal of Educational Psychology* 5, 307–320.

(1915) Two children's progress in speech. *Journal of Educational Psychology* 6, 475–493.

Bates, Elizabeth (1976) *Language and context: the acquisition of pragmatics*. New York: Academic Press.

Bates, Elizabeth, Bretherton, Inge, and Snyder, Lynn S. (1988) *From first words to grammar*. Cambridge: Cambridge University Press.

Baudouin de Courtenay, Jan (1974) *Spostrzeżenia nad językiem dziecka: Wybór i opracowanie* [Observations on child language], edited by Maria Chmura-Klekotowa. Wroclaw: Polska Akademia Nauk, Komitet Językoznawstwa.

Bauer, Laurie (1979) Patterns of productivity in new formations denoting persons using the suffix -*er* in modern English. *Cahiers de Lexicologie* 35, 26–31.

(1983) *English word-formation*. Cambridge: Cambridge University Press.

Behrend, Douglas A. (1990a) The development of verb concepts: children's use of verbs to label familiar and novel events. *Child Development* 61, 681–696.

(1990b) Constraints and development: a reply to Nelson (1988). *Cognitive Development* 5, 313–330.

Bellugi, Ursula, and Brown, Roger (eds.) (1964) *The acquisition of language. Monographs of the Society for Research in Child Development* 29 (Serial No. 92).

Berko, Jean (1958) The child's learning of English morphology. *Word* 14, 150–177.

Berko, Jean, and Brown, Roger (1960) Psycholinguistic research methods. In Paul H. Mussen (ed.), *Handbook of research methods in child development*. New York: John Wiley and Sons, 517–557.

Berlin, Brent, Breedlove, David E., and Raven, Peter H. (1973) General principles of classification and nomenclature in folk biology. *American Anthropologist* 75, 214–242.

Berman, Ruth A. (1978a) *Modern Hebrew structure*. Tel-Aviv: University Publishing.

(1978b) Early verbs: comments on how and why a child uses his first words. *International Journal of Psycholinguistics* 5, 21–39.

(1979) Lexical decomposition and lexical unity in the expression of derived verbal categories in modern Hebrew. *Afroasiatic Linguistics* 6, 117–142.

(1981) Language development and language knowledge: evidence from the acquisition of Hebrew morphophonology. *Journal of Child Language* 8, 609–626.

(1982) Verb-pattern alternation: the interface of morphology, syntax, and semantics in Hebrew child language. *Journal of Child Language* 9, 169–191.

(1985) Acquisition of Hebrew. In Dan I. Slobin (ed.), *The crosslinguistic study of language acquisition*, vol. 1. Hillsdale, NJ: Lawrence Erlbaum Associates, pp. 255–371.

(1987) Productivity in the lexicon: new-word formation in Modern Hebrew. *Folia Linguistica* XXI, 425–461.

(1993) Marking of verb transitivity by Hebrew-speaking children. *Journal of Child Language* 20(3), 641–669.

Berman, Ruth A., and Clark, Eve V. (1989) Learning to use compounds for contrast: data from Hebrew. *First Language* 9, 247–270.

Berman, Ruth A., and Sagi, Yisrael (1981) al darxey tecurat hamilim vexidušan bagil haca'ir [Word-formation processes and lexical innovations of young children]. *Hebrew Computational Linguistics Bulletin* 18, 36–62.

Bernstein-Ratner, Nan (1987) The phonology of parent-child speech. In Keith E. Nelson and Anne Van Kleeck (eds.), *Children's language*, vol. 6. Hillsdale, NJ: Gardner Press, pp. 159–174.

Bessé, Bruno de (1980) Terminology committees in France: balance and perspectives. *International Journal of the Sociology of Language* 23, 43–49.

Bierwisch, Manfred (1967) Some semantic universals of German adjectivals. *Foundations of Language* 5, 153–184.

Blanc, Haim (1957) Hebrew in Israel: trends and problems. *The Middle East Journal*, Autumn, 397–409.

Bloom, Lois (1970) *Language development: form and function in emerging grammars*. Cambridge, MA: MIT Press.

(1973) *One word at a time: the use of single word utterances before syntax*. The Hague: Mouton.

Bloomfield, Leonard (1933) *Language*. New York: Holt.

Bogoyavlenskiy, D. N. (1973) The acquisition of Russian inflections. In Charles A. Ferguson and Dan I. Slobin (eds.), *Studies of child language development*. New York: Holt, Rinehart and Winston, pp. 284–292.

Bohn, William E. (1914) First steps in verbal expression. *Pedagogical Seminary* 21, 578–595.

Bolinger, Dwight (1972) *That's that*. The Hague: Mouton.

(1975) *Aspects of language* (2nd edn). New York: Harcourt Brace Jovanovich.

(1977) *Meaning and form*. London: Longman.

(1980) *Language - the loaded weapon*. London: Longman.

Bolozky, Shmuel (1978) Word formation strategies in the Hebrew verb system: denominative verbs. *Afroasiatic Linguistics* 5, 111–136.

(1982) Strategies of Modern Hebrew verb formation. *Hebrew Annual Review* 6, 69–79.

Booij, Geert E. (1977) *Dutch morphology: a study of word formation in generative grammar*. Lisse: Peter de Ridder Press.

(1979) Semantic regularities in word formation. *Linguistics* 17, 985–1001.

Borkin, Ann (1984) *Problems in form and function*. Norwood, NJ: Ablex.

Bornstein, Marc H. (1981) Two kinds of perceptual organization near the beginning of life. In W. Andrew Collins (ed.), *Minnesota symposium on child psychology*, vol. 14: *Aspects of the development of competence*. Hillsdale, NJ: Lawrence Erlbaum Associates, pp. 39–91.

(1985) Colour-name versus shape-name learning in young children. *Journal of Child Language* 12, 387–393.

Bowerman, Melissa (1973) Structural relationships in children's utterances: syntactic or semantic? In Timothy E. Moore (ed.), *Cognitive development and the acquisition of language*. New York: Academic Press, pp. 197–213.

(1974) Learning the structure of causative verbs: a study in the relationship of cognitive, semantic, and syntactic development. *Papers and Reports on Child Language Development* [Stanford University] 8, 142–179.

(1977) The acquisition of rules governing 'possible lexical items': evidence from spontaneous speech errors. *Papers and Reports on Child Language Development* [Stanford University] 13, 148–156.

(1978) The acquisition of word meaning: an investigation of some current conflicts. In Natalie Waterson and Catherine E. Snow (eds.), *The development of communication*. New York: John Wiley and Sons, pp. 263–287.

(1982a) Evaluating competing linguistic models with language acquisition data: implications of developmental errors with causative verbs. *Quaderni di Semantica* 3, 5–66.

(1982b) Reorganizational processes in lexical and syntactic development. In Eric Wanner and Lila R. Gleitman (eds.), *Language acquisition: the state of the art*. Cambridge: Cambridge University Press, pp. 319–346.

(1985) What shapes children's grammars? In Dan I. Slobin (ed.), *The crosslinguistic study of language acquisition*, vol. 2. Hillsdale, NJ: Lawrence Erlbaum Associates, pp. 1257–1319.

(1987) The 'no negative evidence' problem: how do children avoid constructing an overly general grammar? In John A. Hawkins (ed.), *Explaining language universals*. Oxford: Basil Blackwell, pp. 73–101.

(1989) Learning a semantic system: what role do cognitive dispositions play? In Mabel Rice and Richard L. Schiefelbusch (eds.), *The teachability of language*. Hillsdale, NJ: Lawrence Erlbaum Associates, pp. 133–169.

Boyd, William (1914) The development of a child's vocabulary. *Pedagogical Seminary* 21, 95–124.

Braine, Martin D. S. (1976) *Children's first word combinations. Monographs of the Society for Research in Child Development* 41 (Serial No. 164).

Braine, Martin D. S., Brody, Ruth E., Fisch, Shalom M., Weisberger, Mara J., and Blum, Monica (1990) Can children use a verb without exposure to its argument structure? *Journal of Child Language* 17, 313–342.

Brandenburg, George C. (1915) The language of a three-year-old child. *Pedagogical Seminary* 22, 89–120.

Braun-Lamesch, Marie M. (1962) Le rôle du contexte dans la compréhension du langage chez l'enfant. *Psychologie Française* 7, 180–189.

Braunwald, Susan R. (1978) Context, word and meaning: toward a communicational analysis of lexical acquisition. In Andrew Lock (ed.), *Action, gesture and symbol: the emergence of language*. London: Academic Press, pp. 487–527

Bréal, Michel (1897) *Essai de sémantique*. Paris: Hachette.

Brekle, Herbert E. (1978) Reflections on the conditions for the coining, use and understanding of nominal compounds. In Wolfgang U. Dressler and Wolfgang Meid (eds.), *Proceedings of the Twelfth International Congress of Linguists, Vienna 1977*. Innsbruck: Innsbrucker Beiträge zur Sprachwissenschaft, pp. 68–77.

Brewer, William F., and Stone, J. Brandon (1975) Acquisition of spatial antonym pairs. *Journal of Experimental Child Psychology* 19, 299–307.

Broen, Patricia (1972) *The verbal environment of the language-learning child. Monograph of the American Speech and Hearing Association* 17.

Broselow, Ellen (1977) Language change and theories of the lexicon. In Woodford A. Beach, Samuel E. Fox, and Shulamith Philosoph (eds.) *Proceedings of the thirteenth regional meeting*. Chicago, IL: Chicago Linguistic Society, pp. 58–68.

Brown, H. Douglas (1971) Children's comprehension of relativized English sentences. *Child Development* 42, 1923–1936.

Brown, Roger (1957) Linguistic determinism and the part of speech. *Journal of Abnormal and Social Psychology* 55, 1–5.

(1958) *Words and things*. New York: Free Press.

(1973) *A first language: the early stages*. Cambridge, MA: Harvard University Press.

Brown, Roger, and McNeill, David (1966) The 'tip of the tongue' phenomenon. *Journal of Verbal Learning and Verbal Behavior* 5, 325–337.

Budwig, Nancy (1989) The linguistic marking of agentivity and control in child language. *Journal of Child Language* 16, 263–284.

Burke, Deborah, Worthley, Joan, and Martin, Jennifer (1988) I'll never forget what's-her-name: aging and tip of the tongue experiences in everyday life. In Michael M. Gruneberg, Peter E. Morris, and Robert N. Sykes (eds.), *Practical aspects of memory: current research and issues*, vol. 2. Chichester: John Wiley, pp. 113–118.

Bushnell, Emily W., and Maratsos, Michael P. (1984) *Spooning* and *basketing*: children's dealing with accidental gaps in the lexicon. *Child Development* 55, 893–902.

Bybee, Joan L., and Pardo, Elly (1981) On lexical and morphological conditioning of alternations: a nonce-probe experiment with Spanish verbs. *Linguistics* 19, 937–968.

Bybee, Joan L., and Slobin, Dan I. (1982) Rules and schemas in the development and use of the English past tense. *Language* 58, 265–289.

Caramazza, Alfonso, and Grober, Ellen H. (1976) Polysemy and the structure of the subjective lexicon. In Clea Rameh (ed.), *Semantics: theory and application* (27th Georgetown University Round Table on languages and linguistics). Washington, DC: Georgetown University Press, pp. 181–206.

Carey, Susan (1978) The child as word learner. In Morris Halle, Joan Bresnan, and George A. Miller (eds.), *Linguistic theory and psychological reality*. Cambridge, MA: MIT Press, pp. 264–293.

Carey, Susan, and Bartlett, Elsa J. (1978) Acquiring a single new word. *Papers and Reports on Child Language Development* [Stanford University] 15, 17–29.

Carroll, John B., Davies, Peter, and Richman, Barry (1971) *The American Heritage word frequency book*. New York: American Heritage.

Carroll, John B., and White, Margaret N. (1973a) Word frequency and age of acquisition as determinants of picture-naming latency. *Quarterly Journal of Experimental Psychology* 25, 85–95.

(1973b) Age of acquisition norms for 220 picturable nouns. *Journal of Verbal Learning and Verbal Behavior* 12, 563–576.

Carstairs-McCarthy, Andrew (in press) Uses for junk: a new look at inflection classes. In Wolfgang U. Dressler, Martin Prinzhorn, and John R. Rennison (eds.), *Papers from the 5th international morphology meeting*. Berlin: Mouton de Gruyter.

Cazden, Courtney B. (1968) The acquisition of noun and verb inflections. *Child Development* 39, 433–448.

Cederschiöld, Vilhelm (1944) *Barnspråk*. Stockholm: Wahlström and Widstrand.

Chamberlain, Alexander F., and Chamberlain, Isabel C. (1904) Studies of a child. *Pedagogical Seminary* 11, 264–291.

Chmura-Klekotowa, Maria (1964) Rozwój rozumienia budowy wyrazów i umiejętności tworzenia wyrazów nowych (analogicznych) u dzieci w wieku przedszkolnym [The development of understanding of the internal structure of words and of the capacity to create new (analogic) words in preschool children]. *Psychologia Wychowawcza* 1, 403–418.

(1970) Odbicie tendencji slowotwórczych języka polskiego w neologizmach dzieci [Reflection of derivational trends of the Polish language in children's neologisms]. *Prace Filologiczne* (Warsaw) 20, 153–159.

(1971) Neologizmy slowotwórcze w mowie dzieci [Derivational neologisms in children's speech]. *Prace Filologiczne* (Warsaw) 21, 99–235.

(1972) Slovoobrazovatyelniye neologizmi v detskoy rechi na materialach polskogo i russkogo yazika [Derivational neologisms in children's speech from material in Polish and Russian]. In Karel Ohnesorg (ed.), *Colloquium paedolinguisticum*. The Hague: Mouton, pp. 83–110.

Choi, Soonja, and Bowerman, Melissa (1991) Learning to express motion events in English and Korean: the influence of language-specific lexicalization patterns. *Cognition* 41, 83–121.

Chomsky, Noam (1965) *Aspects of the theory of syntax*. Cambridge, MA: MIT Press.

Chukovskiy, Kornei I. (1966) *Ot dvukh do pyati* (19th edn). Moscow: Gos. Izdat. Detskoy Lit. Min. Prosveshcheniya RSFSR. [Translated by Miriam Morton, *From two to five*. Berkeley and Los Angeles: University of California Press, 1968.]

Church, Joseph (ed.), (1966) *Three babies: biographies of cognitive development*. New York: Random House.

Clark, Eve V. (1971) On the acquisition of the meaning of *before* and *after*. *Journal of Verbal Learning and Verbal Behavior* 10, 266–275.

(1972) On the child's acquisition of antonyms in two semantic fields. *Journal of Verbal Learning and Verbal Behavior* 11, 750–758.

(1973a) What's in a word? On the child's acquisition of semantics in his first language. In Timothy E. Moore (ed.), *Cognitive development and the acquisition of language*. New York: Academic Press, pp. 65–110.

(1973b) Nonlinguistic strategies and the acquisition of word meanings. *Cognition* 2, 161–182.

(1973c) How children describe time and order. In Charles A. Ferguson and Dan I. Slobin (eds.), *Studies of child language development*. New York: Holt Rinehart and Winston, pp. 585–606.

(1977) Strategies and the mapping problem in first language acquisition. In John Macnamara (ed.), *Language learning and thought*. New York: Academic Press, pp. 147–168.

(1978a) Awareness of language: some evidence from what children say and do. In Anne Sinclair, Robert J. Jarvella, and Willem J. M. Levelt (eds.), *The child's conception of language*. Berlin and New York: Springer, pp. 17–43.

(1978b) Discovering what words can do. In Donka Farkas, Wesley M. Jacobsen, and Karol W. Todrys (eds.), *Papers from the parasession on the lexicon*. Chicago, IL: Chicago Linguistic Society, pp. 34–57.

(1978c) Strategies for communicating. *Child Development* 49, 953–959.

(1979) Building a vocabulary: words for objects, actions, and relations. In Paul Fletcher and Michael Garman (eds.), *Language acquisition*. Cambridge: Cambridge University Press, pp. 149–160.

(1980) Here's the *top*: nonlinguistic strategies in the acquisition of orientational terms. *Child Development* 51, 329–338.

(1981a) Lexical innovations: how children learn to create new words. In Werner Deutsch (ed.), *The child's construction of language*. London: Academic Press, pp. 299–328.

(1981b) Negative verbs in children's speech. In Wolfgang Klein and Willem J. M. Levelt (eds.), *Crossing the boundaries in linguistics*. Dordrecht: Reidel, pp. 253–264.

(1982a) The young word-maker: a case study of innovation in the child's lexicon. In Eric Wanner and Lila R. Gleitman (eds.), *Language acquisition: the state of the art*. Cambridge: Cambridge University Press, pp. 390–425.

(1982b) Language change during language acquisition. In Michael E. Lamb and Ann L. Brown (eds.), *Advances in child development*, vol. 2. Hillsdale, NJ: Lawrence Erlbaum Associates, pp. 171–195.

(1983) Meanings and concepts. In John H. Flavell and Ellen M. Markman (eds.), *Handbook of child psychology*, vol. 3: *Cognitive development* (General editor, Paul H. Mussen). New York: John Wiley and Sons, pp. 787–840.

(1985) Acquisition of Romance, with special reference to French. In Dan I. Slobin (ed.), *The crosslinguistic study of language acquisition*, vol. 1. Hillsdale, NJ: Lawrence Erlbaum Associates, pp. 687–782.

(1986, October) What does *acquired* mean? Discrepancies in linguistic knowledge: acquisition and beyond. Paper presented at the 11th annual conference on language development, Boston University, Boston, MA.

(1987) The Principle of Contrast: a constraint on language acquisition. In Brian MacWhinney (ed.), *Mechanisms of language acquisition*. Hillsdale, NJ. Lawrence Erlbaum Associates, pp. 1–33.

(1988) On the logic of Contrast. *Journal of Child Language* 15, 317–335.

(1990) The pragmatics of Contrast. *Journal of Child Language* 17, 417–431.

(1991) Acquisitional principles in lexical development. In Susan A. Gelman and James P. Byrnes (eds.), *Perspectives on thought and language: interrelations in development*. Cambridge: Cambridge University Press, pp. 31–71.

Clark, Eve V., and Andersen, Elaine S. (1979, March) Spontaneous repairs: awareness in the process of acquiring language. Paper presented at the Biennial Meeting of the Society for Research in Child Development, San Francisco, CA.

Clark, Eve V., and Berman, Ruth A. (1984) Structure and use in the acquisition of word-formation. *Language* 60, 547–590.

(1987) Types of linguistic knowledge: interpreting and producing compound nouns. *Journal of Child Language* 14, 547–567.

Clark, Eve V., and Bowerman, Melissa (1986) On the acquisition of final voiced stops. In Joshua A. Fishman (ed.), *The Fergusonian impact*, vol. 1: *From phonology to society*. Berlin and Amsterdam: Mouton/de Gruyter, pp. 51–68.

Clark, Eve V., and Carpenter, Kathie L. (1989a) The notion of source in language acquisition. *Language* 65, 1–32.

(1989b) On children's uses of *from*, *by*, and *with* in oblique noun phrases. *Journal of Child Language* 16, 349–364.

(1991) Undoing actions: acquiring English *un-*. Manuscript, Stanford University.

Clark, Eve V., and Clark, Herbert H. (1979) When nouns surface as verbs. *Language* 55, 767–811.

Clark, Eve V., and Cohen, Sophia R. (1984) Productivity and memory for newly-formed words. *Journal of Child Language* 11, 611–625.

Clark, Eve V., and Deutsch, Werner (1991) More on undoing actions: acquiring negative verbs in German. Manuscript, Stanford University.

Clark, Eve V., Gelman, Susan A., and Lane, Nancy M. (1985) Noun compounds and category structure in young children. *Child Development* 56, 84–94.

Clark, Eve V., and Hecht, Barbara F. (1982) Learning to coin agent and instrument nouns. *Cognition* 12, 1–24.

(1983) Comprehension, production, and language acquisition. *Annual Review of Psychology* 34, 325–349.

Clark, Eve V., Hecht, Barbara F., and Mulford, Randa C. (1986) Acquiring complex compounds: affixes and word order in English. *Linguistics* 24, 7–29.

Clark, Eve V., Neel-Gordon, Amy, and Johnson, Susan (1993, July) Convention and contrast in the acquisition of verbs. Paper presented at the Sixth International Congress for the Study of Child Language, Trieste.

Clark, Eve V., and Svaib, Trisha (1991, March) Speaker perspective and lexical acquisition. Paper presented at the Child Language Seminar, University of Manchester, UK.

Clark, Herbert H. (1983) Making sense of nonce sense. In Giovanni B. Flores d'Arcais and Robert J. Jarvella (eds.), *The process of language understanding*. New York: John Wiley and Sons, pp. 297–331.

(1985) Language use and language users. In Gardner Lindzey and Elliot Aronson (eds.), *Handbook of social psychology*, vol. 2: *Special fields and applications*. New York: Random House, pp. 179–231.

(in press) *Language in action*.

Clark, Herbert H., and Clark, Eve V. (1977) *Psychology and language*. New York: Harcourt Brace Jovanovich.

(1978) Universals, relativity, and language processing. In Joseph H. Greenberg (ed.), *Universals of human language*, vol. 1: *Method and theory*. Stanford, CA: Stanford University Press, pp. 225–277.

Clark, Herbert H., and Gerrig, Richard J. (1983) Understanding old words with new meanings. *Journal of Verbal Learning and Verbal Behavior* 22, 591–608.

Clark, Herbert H., and Marshall, Catherine R. (1981) Definite reference and mutual knowledge. In Aravind K. Joshi, Bonnie L. Webber, and Ivan A. Sag (eds.), *Linguistic structure and discourse setting*. Cambridge: Cambridge University Press, pp. 10–63.

Clark, Herbert H., and Schaefer, Edward F. (1989) Contributing to discourse. *Cognitive Science* 13, 259–294.

Clark, Herbert H., and Wilkes-Gibbs, Deanna (1986) Referring as a collaborative process. *Cognition* 22, 1–39.

Cohen, Leslie B., and Strauss, Mark S. (1979) Concept acquisition in the human infant. *Child Development* 50, 419–424.

Cohen, Marcel (1969) Sur l'étude du langage enfantin. *Enfance* 22, 203–272.

Compayré, Gabriel (1896) *L'évolution intellectuelle et morale de l'enfant* (2nd edn). Paris: Hachette.

Condry, Sandra M. (1979) A developmental study of processes of word derivation in elementary school children and their relation to reading. Unpublished doctoral dissertation, Cornell University.

Corbin, Danielle (1976) Le statut des exceptions dans le lexique. *La Langue Française* 30, 90–110.

Cortelazzo, Manlio, and Cardinale, Ugo (1986) *Dizionario di parole nuove 1964–1984*. Torino: Loescher.

Costa, Sérgio R. (1976) Aprendizagem de alguns aspectos da morfologia portuguesa por crianças brasileiras [The learning of some aspects of Portuguese morphology by Brazilian children]. Unpublished master's thesis, Universidade de Campinas, Brazil.

Croft, William (1991) *Syntactic categories and grammatical relations*. Chicago, IL: University of Chicago Press.

Cruse, D. Alan (1986) *Lexical semantics*. Cambridge: Cambridge University Press.

Csapodi, István (1905) Gyermekek nyelvtudománya [The linguistics of children]. *Magyar Nyelvőr* 34, 464–466.

Curme, George O. (1964) *A grammar of the German language* (2nd rev. edn). New York: Frank Ungar.

Cutler, Anne (1980) Productivity in word formation. In Jody Kreiman and

Almerindo E. Ojeda (eds.), *Papers from the sixteenth regional meeting* Chicago, IL: Chicago Linguistic Society, pp. 45–51.

(1983) Lexical complexity and sentence processing. In Giovanni B. Flore d'Arcais and Robert J. Jarvella (eds.), *The process of language understanding* New York: John Wiley and Sons, pp. 43–79.

Daehler, Marvin W., Lonardo, Rita, and Bukatko, Danuta (1979) Matching and equivalence judgments in very young children. *Child Development* 50, 170–179

Dale, Philip, Bates, Elizabeth, Reznick, J. Steven, and Morisset, Colleen (1989 The validity of a parent report instrument of child language at twenty months *Journal of Child Language* 16, 239–249.

Decroly, Ovide (1932) *Comment l'enfant arrive à parler.* Bruxelles: Cahiers de l Centrale.

Dell, Gary S., and O'Seaghdha, Padraig G. (1992) Stages of lexical access i language production. *Cognition* 42, 287–314.

Derwing, Bruce L. (1976a) Morpheme recognition and the learning of rules fo derivational morphology. *Canadian Journal of Linguistics* 21, 38–66.

(1976b) What kind of rules can children learn? In Walburga von Raffler Enge and Yves Lebrun (eds.), *Baby talk and infant speech. Neurolinguistics* 5, 68–78

Descoeudres, Alice (1922) *Le développement de l'enfant de deux à sept ans* (Collection d'Actualités Pédagogiques.) Neuchâtel: Delachaux et Niestlé.

Deville, Gabriel (1891) Notes sur le développement du langage. *Revue d Linguistique* 24, 10–42.

Devoto, Giacomo, and Oli, Gian C. (1985) *Le nuove parole. Aggiornamento a dizionario della lingua italiana,* edited by Lorenzo Magini. Firenze: L Monnier.

Dewey, John (1894) The psychology of infant language. *Psychological Review* 63–66.

Dockrell, Julie (1981) The child's acquisition of unfamiliar words: an experimenta study. Unpublished doctoral dissertation, University of Stirling, UK.

Dockrell, Julie, and McShane, John (1990) Young children's use of phras structure and inflectional information in form-class assignments of nov nouns and verbs. *First Language* 10, 127–140.

Dodd, Barbara (1975) Children's understanding of their own phonological form Quarterly Journal of Experimental Psychology 27, 165–172.

Donaldson, Bruce C. (1981) *Dutch reference grammar.* The Hague: Martinu Nijhoff.

Donaldson, Margaret, and Wales, Roger J. (1970) On the acquisition of som relational terms. In John Richard Hayes (ed.), *Cognition and the developmer of language.* New York: John Wiley and Sons, pp. 235–268.

Downing, Pamela (1977) On the creation and use of English compound noun Language 53, 810–842.

Dressler, Wolfgang U. (1985) *Morphophonology: the dynamics of derivation.* An Arbor: Karoma Publishers.

Dromi, Esther (1987) *Early lexical development.* Cambridge: Cambridge Universi Press.

Dromi, Esther, and Berman, Ruth A. (1982) A morphemic measure of earl language development: data from Modern Hebrew. *Journal of Child Language* 9, 403–424.

Dromi, Esther, and Fishelzon, Gil-li (1986) Similarity, specificity and contrast: a study of early semantic categories. *Papers and Reports on Child Language Development* [Stanford University] 25, 25–32.

Dubois, Jean (1962) *Etude sur la dérivation suffixale en français moderne et contemporain.* Paris: Librairie Larousse.

Edwards, Derek, and Goodwin, Roger (1986) Action words and pragmatic function in early language. In Stan A. Kuczaj II and Martyn D. Barrett (eds.) *The development of word meaning: progress in cognitive development research.* Berlin and New York: Springer, pp. 257–273.

Egger, Emile (1887) *Observations et réflexions sur le développement de l'intelligence et du langage chez les enfants.* Paris: Picard.

Eilers, Rebecca E., Oller, D. Kimbrough, and Ellington, Judy (1974) The acquisition of word meaning for dimensional adjectives: the long and the short of it. *Journal of Child Language* 1, 195–204.

Einarsson, Stefán (1945) *Icelandic.* Baltimore, MD: The Johns Hopkins Press.

Elbers, Loekie (1988) New names from old words: related aspects of children's metaphors and word compounds. *Journal of Child Language* 15, 591–617.

Elbers, Loekie, and Wijnen, Frank (1992) Effort, production skill, and language learning. In Charles A. Ferguson, Lise Menn, and Carol Stoel-Gammon (eds.), *Phonological development: models, research, implications.* Timonium, MD: York Press, pp. 337–368.

El'konin, Daniil B. (1973) General course of development in the child of the grammatical structure of the Russian language (according to A. N. Gvozdev). In Charles A. Ferguson and Dan I. Slobin (eds.), *Studies of child language development.* New York: Holt, Rinehart and Winston, pp. 565–583.

Endrei, Gerzson (1913) Adalélok a gyermeknyelv fejlõdéséhez [Contributions to the development of child language]. *A Gyermek* 7, 461–466, 524–526.

Ervin-Tripp, Susan (1974) Is second language learning like the first? *TESOL Quarterly* 8, 111–127.

Escalona, Sibylle K. (1973) Basic modes of social interaction: their emergence and patterning during the first two years of life. *Merrill-Palmer Quarterly* 19, 205–232.

Fantini, Alvino E. (1976) *Language acquisition of a bilingual child.* Brattleboro, VT: The Experiment Press.

Farwell, Carol B. (1975) Aspects of early verb semantics – pre-causative development. *Papers and Reports on Child Language Development* [Stanford University] 10, 48–58.

(1977) The primacy of *goal* in the child's description of motion and location. *Papers and Reports on Child Language Development* [Stanford University] 13, 126–133.

Fellbaum, Christiane, and Miller, George A. (1990) Folk psychology or semantic entailment? Comment on Rips and Conrad 1989. *Psychological Review* 97, 565–570.

Ferguson, Charles A., and Farwell, Carol B. (1975) Words and sounds in early language acquisition: English initial consonants in the first 50 wor(*Language* 51, 419–439.

Fernald, Anne (1989) Intonation and communicative intent in mothers' speech infants: is the melody the message? *Developmental Psychology* 60, 1497–151

Figueira, Rosa Attié (1977, October) Aréas de dificuldade na aquisição do léxic exame do 'corpus' de um (1) sujeito (2; 8 a 3; 10) [Difficulties in the acquisiti(of the lexicon: examination of the corpus from one subject, 2; 8 to 3; 10]. Pap presented at II Encontro Nacional de Lingüistas, Rio de Janeiro, Brazil.

(1979) Análise preliminar dos verbos causativos no 'corpus' de um (1) sujei (2; 8 a 5) [Preliminary analysis of causative verbs in the corpus from o1 subject 2; 8 to 5; 0]. Unpublished manuscript, Universidad de Campina Brazil.

(1984) On the development of the expression of causativity: a syntac(hypothesis. *Journal of Child Language* 11, 109–127.

Fillmore, Charles J. (1975) An alternative to checklist theories of meaning. Cathy Cogen, Henry Thompson, Graham Thurgood, Kenneth Whistler, a1 James Wright (eds.), *Proceedings of the first annual meeting of the Berkel(Linguistics Society.* Berkeley, CA: Berkeley Linguistics Society, pp. 123–13

(1978) On the organization of semantic information in the lexicon. In Don] Farkas, Wesley M. Jacobsen, and Karol W. Todrys (eds.), *Papers from t(parasession on the lexicon.* Chicago, IL: Chicago Linguistic Society, p 148–173.

Fillmore, Charles J., Kay, Paul, and O'Connor, M. Catherine (1988) Regulari and idiomaticity in grammatical constructions. *Language* 64, 501–538.

Firth, John R. (1966) *The tongues of men and speech.* Oxford: Oxford Universi Press.

Fisiak, Jan, Lipińska-Grzegorek, Maria, and Zabrocki, Tadeusz (1978) (*introductory Polish-English contrastive grammar.* Warsaw: Państwov Wydawnictwo Naukowe.

Fodor, Jerry J., Bever, Thomas, G., and Garrett, Merrill (1974) *The psychology language.* New York: McGraw-Hill.

Forbes, Nevill (1964) *Russian grammar* (3rd edn revised and enlarged by J. (Dumbreck). Oxford: Oxford University Press.

François, Denise (1977) Du pré-signe au signe. In Frédéric François, Deni François, Emilie Sabeau-Jouannet, and Marc Sourdot, *La syntaxe de l'enf(avant 5 ans.* Paris: Larousse, pp. 53–89.

François, Frédéric, François, Denise, Sabeau-Jouannet, Emilie, and Sourd(Marc (1977) *La syntaxe de l'enfant avant 5 ans.* Paris: Larousse.

Fraser, Bruce (1974) *The verb-particle combination in English.* Tokyo: Taishuk; Publishing Company.

Frauenfelder, Uli H., and Schreuder, Robert (1991) Constraining psycholinguis(models of morphological processing and representation: the role of pr ductivity. In Geert Booij and Jaap van Marle (eds.), *1991 yearbook morphology.* Amsterdam: Kluwer, pp. 163–185.

Friðjónsson, Jón (1978) *A course in Modern Icelandic.* Reykjavík: Tímaritið Ská

Fromkin, Victoria A. (ed.) (1973) *Speech errors as linguistic evidence.* The Hague: Mouton.

Gale, M. C., and Gale, Harlow (1902) The vocabularies of three children in one family at two and three years of age. *Pedagogical Seminary* 9, 422–435.

Garnica, Olga K. (1977) Some prosodic and paralinguistic features of speech to young children. In Catherine E. Snow and Charles A. Ferguson (eds.), *Talking to children: language input and language acquisition.* Cambridge: Cambridge University Press, pp. 63–88.

Gaskill, William H. (1980) Correction in native speaker / non-native speaker conversation. In Diane Larsen-Freeman (ed.), *Discourse analysis in second language research.* Rowley, MA: Newbury House, pp. 125–137.

Gelman, Rochel, Bullock, Merry, and Meck, Elizabeth (1980) Preschoolers' understanding of simple object transformations. *Child Development* 51, 691–699.

Gelman, Susan A., and Taylor, Marjorie (1984) How two-year-old children interpret proper and common names for unfamiliar objects. *Child Development* 55, 1535–1540.

Gelman, Susan A., Wilcox, Sharon A., and Clark, Eve V. (1989) Conceptual and lexical hierarchies in young children. *Cognitive Development* 4, 309–326.

Gentner, Dedre (1978) On relational meaning: the acquisition of verb meaning. *Child Development* 49, 988–998.

(1982) Why nouns are learned before verbs: linguistics relativity versus natural partitioning. In Stan A. Kuczaj II (ed.), *Language development*, vol. 2: *Language, culture, and cognition.* Hillsdale, NJ: Lawrence Erlbaum Associates, pp. 301–334.

Gerhardt, Julie (1988) From discourse to semantics: the development of verb morphology and forms of self-reference in the speech of a 2-year-old. *Journal of Child Language* 15, 337–393.

Gerrig, Richard J. (1989) The time course of sense creation. *Memory and Cognition* 17, 194–207.

Gibson, Eleanor J., and Spelke, Elizabeth S. (1983) The development of perception. In John H. Flavell and Ellen M. Markman (eds.), *Handbook of child psychology*, vol. 3: *Cognitive development* (General editor, Paul H. Mussen). New York: John Wiley and Sons, pp. 1–76.

Giles, Howard (ed.) (1984) The dynamics of speech accommodation. *International Journal of the Sociology of Language* 46.

Giles, Howard, Mulac, Anthony, Bradac, James J., and Johnson, P. (1987) Speech accommodation theory: the first decade and beyond. In Margaret L. McLaughlin (ed.), *Communication yearbook 10.* Beverly Hills, CA: Sage, pp. 13–48.

Gleitman, Lila R. (1990) The structural sources of verb meanings. *Language Acquisition* 1, 3–55.

Gleitman, Lila R., and Gleitman, Henry (1992) A picture is worth a thousand words, but that's the problem: the role of syntax in vocabulary acquisition. *Current Directions in Psychological Science* 1, 31–35.

Goldfield, Beverly A., and Reznick, J. Steven (1990) Early lexical acquisition:

rate, content, and the vocabulary spurt. *Journal of Child Language* 17, 171–183.

Goldin-Meadow, Susan, Seligman, Martin E. P., and Gelman, Rochel (1976) Language in the two-year-old. *Cognition* 4, 189–202.

Golinkoff, Roberta M., Hirsh-Pasek, Kathy, Baduini, Carol, and Lavallee, April (1985, October) What's in a word? The young child's predisposition to use lexical contrast. Paper presented at the 10th annual conference on language development, Boston University, Boston, MA.

Golinkoff, Roberta M., Hirsh-Pasek, Kathy, Bailey, Leslie M., and Wenger, Neill R. (1992) Young children and adults use lexical principles to learn new nouns. *Developmental Psychology* 28, 99–108.

Goodwin, Marjorie H., and Goodwin, Charles (1986) Gesture and coparticipation in the activity of searching for a word. *Semiotica* 62, 51–75.

Gopnik, Alison (1988) Three types of early word: the emergence of social words, names, and cognitive-relational words in the one-word stage and their relation to cognitive development. *First Language* 8, 49–70.

Gopnik, Alison, and Meltzoff, Andrew N. (1986) Words, plans, and locations: interactions between semantic and cognitive development in the one-word stage. In Stan A. Kuczaj II and Martyn D. Barrett (eds.), *The development of word meaning: progress in cognitive development research.* Berlin and New York: Springer, pp. 199–223.

Gordon, Peter (1985) Evaluating the semantic categories hypothesis: the case of the count/mass distinction. *Cognition* 20, 209–242.

Gougenheim, Georges (1971) L'action de l'homonymie sur le lexique. *Bulletin de la Société de Linguistique de Paris* 66, 299–302.

Grant, James R. (1915) A child's vocabulary and its growth. *Pedagogical Seminary* 22, 183–203.

Green, Georgia M. (1989) *Pragmatics and natural language understanding.* Hillsdale, NJ: Lawrence Erlbaum Associates.

Greenberg, Joseph H. (ed.), (1963) *Universals of language.* Cambridge, MA: MIT Press.

(1966) *Language universals.* The Hague: Mouton.

Greenfield, Patricia M., and Smith, Joshua H. (1976) *The structure of communication in early language development.* New York: Academic Press.

Grégoire, Antoine (1939, 1947) *L'apprentissage du langage* (2 vols.). Paris and Liège: Librairie Droz.

(1948) L'apprentissage du langage. *Lingua* 1, 162–174.

Grevisse, Maurice (1964) *Le bon usage: grammaire française avec des remarques sur la langue française d'aujourd'hui* (8th edn). Paris: Hatier.

Grey, Pamela (1925) *The sayings of the children.* New York: Frederick A. Stokes

Grice, H. Paul (1957) Meaning. *Philosophical Review* 66, 377–388.

(1975) Logic and conversation. In Peter Cole and Jerry L. Morgan (eds.), *Syntax and semantics*, vol. 3: *Speech acts.* New York: Academic Press, pp. 41–58.

Griffiths, Patrick, and Atkinson, Martin (1978) A 'door' to verbs. In Natalie Waterson and Catherine E. Snow (eds.), *The development of communication* London: John Wiley and Sons, pp. 311–319.

Grimm, Hannelore (1975) On the child's acquisition of semantic structure underlying the wordfield of prepositions. *Language and Speech* 18, 75–119.

Grimshaw, Jane (1981) Form, function, and the language acquisition device. In C. Leroy Baker and John J. McCarthy (eds.), *The logical problem of language acquisition.* Cambridge, MA: MIT, pp. 165–182.

Gruber, Jeffrey S. (1976) *Lexical structures in syntax and semantics.* (North-Holland Linguistic Series 25.) Amsterdam: North-Holland Publishing Company.

Guilbert, Louis (1965) *La formation du vocabulaire de l'aviation.* Paris: Librairie Larousse.

(1971) De la formation des unités lexicales. *Grand Larousse de la langue française,* vol. 1. Paris: Larousse, pp. 9–81.

(1975) *La créativité lexicale.* Paris: Librairie Larousse.

Guillaume, Paul (1927) Le développement des éléments formels dans le langage de l'enfant. *Journal de Psychologie* 24, 203–229.

Gustafsson, Anne (1979) Treåringars språkliga kreativitet [The linguistic creativity of three-year-olds]. Child Language Research Institute, Stockholm University, Paper No. 2.

Gvozdev, Alexandr N. (1961) *Voprosy izucheniya detskoy rechi* [The development of language in children]. Moscow: Akademii Pedagogicheskikh Nauk RSFSR.

Haiman, John (1980) The iconicity of grammar. *Language* 56, 515–540.

Hankamer, Jorge (1986) Finite state morphology and left to right phonology. *Proceedings of the fifth West Coast conference on formal linguistics,* pp. 41–52. Stanford, CA: CSLI.

Harner, Lorraine (1976) Children's understanding of linguistic reference to past and future. *Journal of Psycholinguistic Research* 5, 65–84.

Harris, Margaret, Yeeles, Caroline, Chasin, Joan, and Oakley, Yvonne (1993) Symmetries and asymmetries in early lexical comprehension and production. Manuscript, Birkbeck College.

Hawkins, John A. (1983) *Word order universals.* New York: Academic Press.

Hawkins, John A., and Cutler, Anne (1988) Psycholinguistic factors in morphological asymmetry. In John A. Hawkins (ed.), *Explaining language universals.* Oxford: Blackwell, pp. 280–317.

Heibeck, Tracy H., and Markman, Ellen M. (1987) Word learning in children: an examination of fast mapping. *Child Development* 58, 1021–1034.

Hochberg, Judith G. (1986) Children's judgments of transitivity errors. *Journal of Child Language* 13, 317–334.

Hofmann, Thomas R. (1982) Lexical blocking. *Journal of the Faculty of Humanities* [Toyama University] 5, 239–250.

(1983) Lexical blocking, II. *Journal of the Faculty of Humanities* [Toyama University] 6, 119–145.

(1984) A restatement of lexical blocking. *Journal of the Faculty of Humanities* [Toyama University] 8, 257–268.

Horn, Laurence R. (1989) *A natural history of negation.* Chicago, IL: University of Chicago Press.

276   *Bibliography*

Houwer, Annick de (1990) *Two at a time: an exploration of how children acquire two languages from birth.* Cambridge: Cambridge University Press.

Humboldt, Wilhelm von (1836/1971) *Linguistic variability and intellectual development* [translated by George C. Buck and Frithjof A. Raven]. (Miami Linguistic Series No. 9.) Coral Gables, FL: University of Miami Press [Originally published in 1836, *Über die Verschiedenheit des menschlichen Sprachbaues und ihren Einfluss auf die geistige Entwicklung des Menschengeschlects.*]

Huttenlocher, Janellen, Haight, Wendy, Bryk, Anthony, Seltzer, Michael, and Lyons, Thomas (1991) Early vocabulary growth: relation to language input and gender. *Developmental Psychology* 27, 236–248.

Huttenlocher, Janellen, and Smiley, Patricia (1987) Early word meanings: the case of object names. *Cognitive Psychology* 19, 63–89.

Huttenlocher, Janellen, Smiley, Patricia, and Charney, Rosalind (1983) Emergence of action categories in the child: evidence from verb meanings. *Psychological Review* 90, 72–93.

Ingram, David (1974a) Phonological rules in young children. *Journal of Child Language* 1, 49–64.

(1974b) The relationship between comprehension and production. In Richard L. Schiefelbusch and Lyle L. Lloyd (eds.), *Language perspectives – acquisition retardation, and intervention.* Baltimore, MD: University Park Press, pp. 313–334.

Jackendoff, Ray S. (1975) Morphological and semantic regularities in the lexicon. *Language* 51, 639–671.

Jaeger, Jeri J. (1984) Assessing the psychological status of the vowel shift rule. *Journal of Psycholinguistic Research* 13, 13–36.

Jakobson, Roman (1968) *Child language, aphasia, and phonological universals.* The Hague: Mouton.

Jefferson, Gail (1974) Error correction as an interactional resource. *Language Society* 2, 181–199.

Jespersen, Otto (1942) *A Modern English grammar on historical principles, Part VI Morphology.* Copenhagen: Ejnar Munksgaard.

John, Oliver (1985) Actions, verbs, and the role of context: differences between categories of objects and those of actions and events. Unpublished manuscript, University of Oregon and Oregon Research Institute, Eugene, OR.

Johnson, Carolyn E. (1981) Children's questions and the discovery of interrogative syntax. Unpublished doctoral dissertation, Stanford University.

Jusczyk, Peter W. (1992) Developing phonological categories from the speech signal. In Charles A. Ferguson, Lise Menn, and Carol Stoel-Gammon (eds.), *Phonological development: theories, research, implications.* Timonium, MD: York Press, pp. 17–64.

Kameyama, Megumi (1983) Acquiring clothing verbs in Japanese. *Papers and Reports on Child Language Development* [Stanford University] 22, 66–73.

Kaper, Willem (1959) *Kindersprachforschung mit Hilfe des Kindes.* Groningen: Wolters.

Karcevski, Serge (1932) Autour d'un problème de morphologie. *Annales Academiae Scientiarum Fennicae* B27, 84–91.

Kardos, Albert (1896) Szárazház, utcaház [Child neologisms]. *Magyar Nyelvõr* 25, 466.

Käsermann, Marie-Louise, and Foppa, Klaus (1981) Some determinants of self-correction. In Werner Deutsch (ed.), *The child's construction of language*. London: Academic Press, pp. 77–104.

Kastovsky, Dieter (1986) The problem of productivity in word formation. *Linguistics* 24, 585–600.

Katz, Nancy, Baker, Erica, and Macnamara, John (1974) What's in a name? A study of how children learn common and proper names. *Child Development* 45, 469–473.

Kay, Deborah A., and Anglin, Jeremy M. (1982) Overextension and under-extension in the child's expressive and receptive speech. *Journal of Child Language* 9, 83–98.

Kay, Paul (1971) Taxonomy and semantic contrast. *Language* 47, 866–887.

Keil, Frank (1979) The development of the young child's ability to anticipate the outcomes of simple causal events. *Child Development* 50, 455–462.

Kelly, Edward F., and Stone, Philip J. (1975) *Computer recognition of English word senses*. Amsterdam: North-Holland.

Kent, Ray D. (1992) The biology of phonological development. In Charles A. Ferguson, Lise Menn, and Carol Stoel-Gammon (eds.), *Phonological development: theories, research, implications*. Timonium, MD: York Press, pp. 65–90.

Kenyeres, Elmér (1928) *A gyermek beszédének fejlodése* [Child speech development]. Budapest: Stadium.

Kernan, Keith, and Blount, Ben (1968) The acquisition of Spanish grammar by Mexican children. *Anthropological Linguistics* 8, 1–14.

Kiefer, Ferenc (1970) *Swedish morphology*. Stockholm: Skriptor.

Kiparsky, Paul (1982) From cyclic phonology to lexical phonology. In Harry van der Hulst and Norval Smith (eds.), *The structure of phonological representations* (part 1). Dordrecht: Foris, pp. 131–175.

(1983) Word-formation and the lexicon. In Frances Ingemann (ed.), *Proceedings of the 1982 mid-American linguistic conference*. Lawrence, KS: University of Kansas, Department of Linguistics, pp. 3–29.

Klatzky, Roberta L., Clark, Eve V., and Macken, Marlys M. (1973) Asymmetries in the acquisition of polar adjectives: linguistic or conceptual? *Journal of Experimental Child Psychology* 16, 32–46.

Klima, Edward S., and Bellugi, Ursula (1966) Syntactic regularities in the speech of children. In John Lyons and Roger J. Wales (eds.), *Psycholinguistics papers*. Edinburgh: Edinburgh University Press, pp. 183–208.

Kohn, Susan E., Wingfield, Arthur, Menn, Lise, Goodglass, Harold, Berko Gleason, Jean, and Hyde, Mary (1987) Lexical retrieval: the tip-of-the-tongue phenomenon. *Applied Psycholinguistics* 8, 245–266.

Kučera, Henry, and Francis, W. Nelson (1967) *Computational analysis of present-day American English*. Providence, RI: Brown University Press.

Kuczaj, Stan A., II (1977) The acquisition of regular and irregular past tense forms *Journal of Verbal Learning and Verbal Behavior* 16, 589–600.

(1978) Children's judgments of grammatical and ungrammatical irregular pas tense verbs. *Child Development* 49, 319–326.

(1979) Evidence for a language learning strategy: on the relative ease c acquisition of prefixes and suffixes. *Child Development* 50, 1–13.

(1983) *Crib speech and language play*. New York and Berlin: Springer.

Kutscher, Eduard Y. (1982) *A history of the Hebrew language*, edited by Raphae Kutscher. Jerusalem: Magnes Press/Leiden: Brill.

Lakoff, George, and Johnson, Mark (1980) *Metaphors we live by*. Chicago, IL University of Chicago Press.

Lakoff, Robin (1973) The logic of politeness; or, Minding your P's and Q's. I Claudia Corum, T. Cedric Smith-Stark, and Ann Weiser (eds.), *Papers fro the ninth regional meeting*. Chicago, IL: Chicago Linguistic Society, p 292–305.

Landau, Barbara, Smith, Linda B., and Jones, Susan S. (1988) The importance shape in early lexical learning. *Cognitive Development* 3, 299–321.

(1992) Syntactic context and the shape bias in children's and adults' lexic learning strategies. *Journal of Memory and Language* 31, 807–825.

Landau, Barbara, and Stecker, Deanna S. (1990) Objects and places: geometr and syntactic representations in early lexical learning. *Cognitive Developme 5, 287–312.

Langenbeck, Mildred (1915) A study of a five year old. *Pedagogical Seminary 2 65–88.

Langendoen, D. Terence (1970) *Essentials of English grammar*. New York: Ho Rinehart and Winston.

Lanza, Elizabeth (1990) Language mixing in infant bilingualism: a sociolinguis perspective. Unpublished doctoral dissertation, Georgetown Universit Washington, DC.

Layton, Thomas L., and Stick, Sheldon L. (1979) Comprehension and producti of comparatives and superlatives. *Journal of Child Language* 6, 511–527.

Lehrer, Adrienne (1974) *Semantic fields and lexical structure*. (North-Holla Linguistic Series, 11.) Amsterdam: North-Holland Publishing Company.

Leonard, Laurence B., Fey, Marc E., and Neuhoff, Marilyn (1981) Phonologic considerations in children's early imitative and spontaneous speech. *Journal Psycholinguistic Research* 10, 123–133.

Leonard, Laurence B., Schwartz, Richard G., Folger, M. Karen, and Wilcox, I Jeanne (1978) Some aspects of child phonology in imitative and spontaneo speech. *Journal of Child Language* 5, 403–417.

Leopold, Werner F. (1939–1949) *Speech development of a bilingual child* (4 vols Evanston, IL: Northwestern University Press.

(1948) Semantic learning in infant language. *Word* 4, 173–180.

Leslie, Alan (1982) The perception of causality in infants. *Perception* 11, 173–1

(1984) Infant perception of a manual pick-up event. *British Journal Developmental Psychology* 2, 19–32.

Levelt, Willem J. M. (1983) Monitoring and self-repair in speech. *Cognition* 14, 41–104.

(1989) *Speaking: from intention to articulation.* Cambridge, MA: MIT/Bradford.

Levelt, Willem J. M., Schriefers, Herbert, Vorberg, Dirk, Meyer, Antje S., Pechmann, Thomas, and Havinga, Jaap (1991) The time course of lexical access in speech production: a study of picture naming. *Psychological Review* 98, 122–1142.

Lewis, David K. (1969) *Convention: a philosophical study.* Cambridge, MA: Harvard University Press.

Lewis, Morris M. (1951) *Infant speech* (2nd edn). London: Routledge and Kegan Paul.

Lewis, Pamela F., and Strauss, Mark S. (1986) Infant concept development. In Grover T. Whitehurst (ed.), *Annals of Child Development,* vol. 3. Greenwich, CT: JAI Press, pp. 99–143.

Lindblom, Bjorn (1992) Phonological units as adaptive emergents of lexical development. In Charles A. Ferguson, Lise Menn, and Carol Stoel-Gammon (eds.), *Phonological development: theories, research, implications.* Timonium, MD: York Press, pp. 131–163.

Lindner, Gustav (1898) *Aus dem Naturgarten der Kindersprache: ein Beitrag zur kindlichen Sprach- und Geistentwicklung in den ersten vier Lebensjahren.* Leipzig: Grieben.

Ljung, Magnus (1974) *A frequency dictionary of English morphemes.* Stockholm: AWE/Gebers.

Lodge, R. Anthony (1991) Authority, prescriptivism and the French standard language. *Journal of French Language Studies* 1, 93–111.

Lo Duca, Maria G. (1990) *Creatività e regole: studio sull'acquisizione della morfologia derivativa dell'italiano* [Creativity and rules: study of the acquisition of derivational morphology in Italian]. Bologna: Il Mulino.

Lord, Carol (1979) 'Don't you fall me down': children's generalizations regarding cause and transitivity. *Papers and Reports on Child Language Development* [Stanford University] 17, 81–89.

Lyamina, G. M. 1960. Razvitie ponimaniya rechi u detei vtorogo goda zhizni [Development of speech comprehension in children in the second year of life]. *Voprosy Psikhologii* 3, 106–121.

Lyons, John (1963) *Structural semantics: an analysis of part of the vocabulary of Plato.* (Publications of the Philological Society XX.) Oxford: Basil Blackwell.

(1966) Towards a 'notional' theory of the 'parts of speech.' *Journal of Linguistics* 2, 209–236.

(1977) *Semantics* (2 vols.). Cambridge: Cambridge University Press.

McCune, Lorraine (1992) First words: a dynamic systems view. In Charles A. Ferguson, Lise Menn, and Carol Stoel-Gammon (eds.), *Phonological development: models, research, implications.* Timonium, MD: York Press, pp. 313–336.

Maccoby, Eleanor E., and Bee, Helen L. (1965) Some speculations concerning the lag between perceiving and performing. *Child Development* 36, 367–377.

Macnamara, John (1982) *Names for things: a study of human learning.* Cambridge, MA: MIT/Bradford.

MacWhinney, Brian J. (1973) How Hungarian children learn to speak. Unpublished doctoral dissertation, University of California, Berkeley.

(1976) Hungarian research on the acquisition of morphology and syntax. *Journal of Child Language* 3, 397–410.

(1978) *The acquisition of morphophonology. Monograph of the Society for Research in Child Development* 43 (Serial No. 174).

(1985) Hungarian language acquisition as an exemplification of a general model of grammatical development. In Dan I. Slobin (ed.), *The crosslinguistic study of language acquisition*, vol. 2. Hillsdale, NJ: Lawrence Erlbaum Associates, pp. 1069–1155.

Major, Diana R. (1906) *First steps in mental growth.* New York: Macmillan Co.

Mandler, Jean M. (1983) Representation. In John H. Flavell and Ellen M. Markman (eds.), *Handbook of child psychology*, vol. 3: *Cognitive development* (General editor, Paul H. Mussen). New York: John Wiley and Sons, pp. 420–494.

Maratsos, Michael P. (1990) Are actions to verbs as objects are to nouns? On the differential semantic bases of form, class, category. *Linguistics* 28, 1351–1379.

Maratsos, Michael P., Gudeman, Roxane, Gerard-Ngo, Poldi, and DeHart, Ganie (1987) A study in novel word learning: the productivity of the causative. In Brian MacWhinney (ed.), *Mechanisms of language acquisition.* Hillsdale, NJ: Lawrence Erlbaum Associates, pp. 89–113.

Marchand, Hans (1969) *English word-formation* (2nd rev. edn). München: C. H. Beck.

(1973) Reversative, ablative, and privative verbs in English, French, and German. In Braj B. Kachru, Robert B. Lees, Yakov Malkiel, Angelina Pietrangeli, and Sol Saporta (eds.), *Issues in linguistics: papers in honor of Henry and Renée Kahane.* Urbana, IL: University of Illinois Press, pp. 636–643.

Marcus, Gary F., Ullman, Michael, Pinker, Steven, Hollander, Michelle, Rosen, T. John, and Xu, Fei (1992) *Overregularization. Monographs of the Society for Research in Child Development* 57 (Serial No. 228).

Markman, Ellen M. (1984) The acquisition and hierarchical organization of categories by children. In Catherine Sophian (ed.), *Origins of cognitive skills: the 18th Annual Carnegie Symposium on Cognition.* Hillsdale, NJ: Lawrence Erlbaum Associates, pp. 371–406.

(1987) How children constrain the possible meanings of words. In Ulric Neisser (ed.) *Concepts and conceptual development: ecological and intellectual factors in categorization.* Cambridge: Cambridge University Press, pp. 255–287.

(1989) *Categorization and naming in children: problems of induction.* Cambridge, MA: MIT/Bradford.

Markman, Ellen M., and Hutchinson, Jean E. (1984) Children's sensitivity to constraints on word meaning: taxonomic vs thematic relations. *Cognitive Psychology* 16, 1–27.

Markman, Ellen M., and Wachtel, Gwyn F. (1988) Children's use of mutua exclusivity to constrain the meanings of words. *Cognitive Psychology* 20, 121–157.

Marle, Jaap van (1983) Some notes on the paradigmatic dimensions of morphological productivity. In Shiro Hattori and Kazuko Inoue (eds.), *Proceedings of the Thirteenth International Congress of Linguists*, Tokyo, Japan 1982. Tokyo, pp. 576–581.

(1985) *On the paradigmatic dimension of morphological productivity*. (Publications in Language Sciences 18.) Dordrecht: Foris.

(1986) The domain hypothesis: the study of rival morphological processes. *Linguistics* 24, 601–627.

(1988) On the role of semantics in productivity change. In Geert Booij and Jaap van Marle (eds.), *1988 yearbook of morphology*. Dordrecht: Foris, pp. 139–154.

Mateer, Florence (1908) The vocabulary of a four-year-old boy. *Pedagogical Seminary* 15, 63–74.

Mediano, Zelia D. (1976) Preliminary studies in the acquisition of Portuguese morphology by Brazilian children. Unpublished doctoral dissertation, University of New Mexico.

Meijers, Guust, and Jarvella, Robert J. (1982) La perception des racines et des réflexions verbales en langue parlée. *Bulletin de Psychologie* XXXV (No. 356), 587–599.

Menn, Lise (1976) Pattern, control, and contrast in beginning speech: a case study in the development of word form and word function. Unpublished doctoral dissertation, University of Illinois, Champaign-Urbana, IL.

Méresse-Polaert, Janine (1969) *Etude sur le langage des enfants de six ans*. Neuchâtel: Delachaux and Niestlé.

Mervis, Carolyn B. (1987) Child-basic object categories and early lexical development. In Ulric Neisser (ed.), *Concepts and conceptual development: ecological and intellectual factors in categorization*. Cambridge: Cambridge University Press, pp. 201–233.

Mervis, Carolyn B., and Long, Laurel M. (1987, April) Words refer to whole objects: young children's interpretation of the referent of a novel word. Paper presented at the biennial meeting of the Society for Research in Child Development, Baltimore, MD.

Mervis, Carolyn B., and Mervis, Cynthia A. (1982) Leopards are kitty-cats: object labeling by mothers for their 13-month-olds. *Child Development* 53, 267–273.

Mikeš, Melanie (1967) Acquisition des catégories grammaticales dans le langage de l'enfant. *Enfance* 20, 289–298.

(1990) Some issues of lexical development in early bi- and trilinguals. In Gina Conti-Ramsden and Catherine E. Snow (eds.), *Children's language*, vol. 7. Hillsdale, NJ: Lawrence Erlbaum Associates, pp. 103–120.

Miller, George A. (1972) English verbs of motion: a case study in semantics and lexical memory. In Arthur W. Melton and Edwin Martin (eds.), *Coding processes in human memory*. Washington, DC: V. H. Winston and Sons, pp. 335–372.

(1978) Semantic relations among words. In Morris Halle, Joan Bresnan, and

George A. Miller (eds.), *Linguistic theory and psychological reality*. Cambridge, MA: MIT Press, pp. 60–118.

Mithun, Marianne (1989) The acquisition of polysynthesis. *Journal of Child Language* 16, 285–312.

Montes Giraldo, José J. (1976) El sistema, la norma y el aprendizaje de la lengua. *Thesaurus: Boletín del Instituto Caro y Cuervo* 31, 14–40.

Moore, Kathleen C. (1896) The mental development of a child. *Psychological Review, Monograph Supplement* 1 (3).

Morag, Shelomo (1959) Planned and unplanned development in Modern Hebrew. *Lingua* 8, 247–263.

Moskowitz, Breyne A. (1973) On the status of vowel shift in English. In Timothy E. Moore (ed.), *Cognitive development and the acquisition of language*. New York: Academic Press, pp. 223–260.

Moss, Norman (1986) *British/American language dictionary*. Lincolnwood, IL: Passport Books.

Mulford, Randa C. (1980) Lexical innovation in modern Icelandic. Unpublished manuscript, Stanford University.

(1983) On the acquisition of derivational morphology in Icelandic: learning about *-ari*. *Íslenskt mál og almenn málfræði* 5, 105–125.

Myerson, Rosemary F. (1978) Children's knowledge of selected aspects of Sound patterns of English. In Robin N. Campbell and Philip T. Smith (eds.), *Recent advances in the psychology of language: formal and experimental approaches*. New York: Plenum, pp. 377–402.

Nagy, William E., and Anderson, Richard C. (1984) The number of words in printed school English. *Reading Research Quarterly* 19, 304–330.

Nagy, William E., and Herman, Patricia A. (1987) Breadth and depth of vocabulary knowledge: implications for acquisition and instruction. In Margaret G. McKeown and Mary E. Curtis (eds.), *The nature of vocabulary acquisition*. Hillsdale, NJ: Lawrence Erlbaum Associates, pp. 19–35.

Naigles, Letitia G. (1990) Children use syntax to learn verb meanings. *Journal of Child Language* 17, 357–374.

Nash, David, and Simpson, Jane (1981) 'No name' in Central Australia. In Carrie S. Masek, Roberta A. Hendrick, and Mary F. Miller (eds.), *Parasession on language and behavior*. Chicago, IL: Chicago Linguistic Society, pp. 165–177.

Nelson, Katherine (1973) *Structure and strategy in learning to talk. Monographs of the Society for Research in Child Development* 38 (Serial No. 149).

Neugebauer-Kostenblut, Hanna (1914) Sprachliche Eigenbildungen meines Sohnes. *Zeitschrift für Kinderforschung* 19, 174–181, 242–246, 362–370.

(1916) Die ersten Wortbedeutungen, die Entwicklung der Wortarten und des Satzes bei meinem Sohn Rafael. *Zeitschrift für Kinderforschung* 21, 158–165.

(1917) Wie sich mein Sohn bis zum Alter von 3 1/2 Jahren zu den Dingen, Tieren und Pflanzen der Umwelt stellte. *Zeitschrift für Kinderforschung* 22, 65–92.

Nice, Margaret M. (1915) The development of a child's vocabulary in relation to environment. *Pedagogical Seminary* 22, 35–64.

(1919) A child's imagination. *Pedagogical Seminary* 26, 173–201.

Nida, Eugene A. (1948) *Morphology: a descriptive analysis of words*. Ann Arbor, MI: University of Michigan Press.

Nir, Raphael (1978) New trends of word formation in modern Hebrew. In Wolfgang U. Dressler and Wolfgang Meid (eds.), *Proceedings of the Twelfth International Congress of Linguists*, Vienna 1977. Innsbruck: Innsbrucker Beiträge zur Sprachwissenschaft, pp. 447–450.

(1982) hashkifut haleshonit shel xidushey ha'akademiya lalashon ha'ivrit [Linguistic transparency of neologisms coined by the Academy of the Hebrew Language]. *Hebrew Computational Linguistics* 19, 20–33.

Norman, Donald A., and Rumelhart, David E. (1983) Studies of typing from the LNR research group. In William E. Cooper (ed.), *Cognitive aspects of skilled typewriting*. New York: Springer, pp. 45–65.

Nunberg, Geoffrey (1978) Slang, usage conditions, and l'arbitraire du signe. In Donka Farkas, Wesley M. Jacobsen, and Karol W. Todrys (eds.), *Papers from the parasession on the lexicon*. Chicago, IL: Chicago Linguistic Society, pp. 301–311.

(1979) The non-uniqueness of semantic solutions: polysemy. *Linguistics and Philosophy* 3, 143–184.

Olson, Gary M., and Clark, Herbert H. (1976) Research methods in psycholinguistics. In Edward C. Carterette and Morton P. Friedman (eds.), *Handbook of perception*, vol. 7: *Language and speech*. New York: Academic Press, pp. 25–74.

Orr, John (1962) *Three studies on homonymics*. Edinburgh: Edinburgh University Press.

Orwell, George (1950) Politics and the English language. In *Shooting an elephant*. New York: Harcourt Brace, pp. 84–101.

O'Shea, Michael V. (1907) *Linguistic development and education*. New York: Macmillan.

Pačesová, Jaroslava (1976) Some notes on developmental universals in Czech-speaking children. In Walburga von Raffler Engel and Yves Lebrun (eds.), *Baby talk and infant speech. Neurolinguistics* 5, 192–198.

Palmer, Frank R. (1981) *Semantics* (2nd edn). Cambridge: Cambridge University Press.

Panagl, Oswald (1977) Aspekte der kindersprachlichen Wortbildung. In Gaberell Drachman (ed.), *Salzburger Beiträge zur Linguistik: Akten der 3. Salzburger Jahrestagung für Linguistik*. Salzburg: Neugebauer, pp. 79–101.

Paul, Hermann (1898) *Principien der Sprachgeschichte* (3rd edn). Halle: Max Niemeyer.

Pavlovitch, Milivoie (1920) *Le langage enfantin: acquisition du serbe et du français par un enfant serbe*. Paris: Champion.

Pelsma, John R. (1910) A child's vocabulary and its development. *Pedagogical Seminary* 17, 328–369.

Peters, Ann M. (1983) *The units of language acquisition*. Cambridge: Cambridge University Press.

(1985) Language segmentation: operating principles for the perception and analysis of language. In Dan I. Slobin (ed.), *The crosslinguistic study of language acquisition*, vol. 2. Hillsdale, NJ: Lawrence Erlbaum Associates, pp. 1029–1067.

Peters, Ann M., and Menn, Lise (1993) False starts and filler syllables: ways to learn grammatical morphemes. *Language* 69, 742–777.

Piaget, Jean (1951) *Play, dreams, and imitation in childhood* (Translation of *La formation du symbole chez l'enfant.*) New York: W. W. Norton.

Pieraut-Le Bonniec, Gilberte (1985) From visual-motor anticipation to conceptualization: reaction to solid and hollow objects and knowledge of the function of containment. *Infant Behavior and Development* 8, 413–424.

Pinker, Steven (1984) *Language learnability and language development*. Cambridge, MA: Harvard University Press.

(1986) Productivity and conservatism in language acquisition. In William Demopoulos and Ausonio Marras (eds.), *Language learning and concept acquisition*. Norwood, NJ: Ablex, pp. 54–79.

(1989) *Learnability and cognition*. Cambridge, MA: MIT/Bradford.

Plank, Frans (1976) Morphological aspects of nominal compounding in German and certain other languages: what to acquire in language acquisition in case the rules fail? In Gaberell Drachman (ed.), *Salzburger Beiträge zur Linguistik*: *Akten der 2. Salzburger Jahrestagung für Linguistik*. Tübingen: Gunter Narr, pp. 201–219.

Ponori Thewrewk, Emil (1905) Gyermeknyelv és gyermeklélek [Child language and the child's soul]. *Magyar Nyelvõr* 1, 392–399, 433–436.

Poulisse, Wijnanda M. (1989) The use of compensatory strategies by Dutch learners of English. PhD dissertation, Katholiek Universiteit te Nijmegen, The Netherlands.

Pustejovsky, James (1991) The syntax of event structure. *Cognition* 41, 47–81.

Quay, Suzanne (1993, January) Bilingual evidence against the principle of contrast. Paper presented at the 67th Annual Meeting of the Linguistic Society of America, Los Angeles, CA.

Quirk, Randolph, Greenbaum, Sidney, Leech, Geoffrey, and Svartvik, Jan (1972) *A grammar of contemporary English*. New York: Seminar Press.

Rabin, Chaim (1983) The sociology of normativism in Israeli Hebrew. *International Journal of the Sociology of Language* 41, 41–56.

Rainer, Franz (1988) Towards a theory of blocking: the case of Italian and German quality nouns. In Geert Booij and Jaap van Marle (eds.) *1988 yearbook of morphology*. Dordrecht: Foris, pp. 155–185.

Ravid, Dorit (1978) Word-formation processes in modern Hebrew nouns and adjectives. Unpublished MA thesis, Tel Aviv University.

Reich, Peter A. (1976) The early acquisition of word meaning. *Journal of Child Language* 3, 117–123.

Rescorla, Leslie (1980) Overextension in early language development. *Journal of Child Language* 7, 321–335.

Reznick. J. Steven, and Goldsmith, Lynn (1989) A multiple form word production checklist to assess early language. *Journal of Child Language* 17, 171–183.

Riddle, Elizabeth M. (1985) A historical perspective on the productivity of the suffixes -*ness* and -*ity*. In Jacek Fisiak (ed.), *Historical semantics/historical word-formation*. The Hague: Mouton, pp. 435–461.

Rifkin, Anthony (1985) Evidence for a basic-level in event taxonomies. *Memory and Cognition* 13, 538–556.

Rijpma, E., and Schuringa, Frans G. (1969) *Nederlandse spraakkunst* (21st edn, revised by Jan van Bakel). Groningen: Wolters-Noordhoff.

Rips, Lance J., and Conrad, Frederick G. (1990) Parts of activities: reply to Fellbaum and Miller (1990). *Psychological Review* 97, 571–575.

Rivka'i, Yisrael (1933) al haspecifiyut halšonit befiy yladeynu be'erec yisra'el [On the linguistic specificity of the language of our children in Eretz Israel]. *Leshonenu* 4, 279–294; (1934) 5, 73–77, 231–242.

(1938) *al sfat yeladeynu ba'arec* [The language of our children in this land]. Tel Aviv: Mefiz Hasefer.

Roberts, Kenneth (1988) Retrieval of a basic-level category in prelinguistic infants. *Developmental Psychology* 24, 21–27.

Robertson, Duncan McL. (1910) *A history of the French Academy*. New York: Dillingham.

Roeper, Thomas, and Siegel, Muffy (1978) A lexical transformation for verbal compounds. *Linguistic Inquiry* 9, 199–240.

Romaine, Suzanne (1980) Variability in word formation patterns and productivity in the history of English. In Jan Fisiak (ed.), *Papers from the 16th international conference on historical linguistics*. Amsterdam: John Benjamins, pp. 451–465.

(1983) On the productivity of word formation rules and the limits of variability in the lexicon. *Australian Journal of Linguistics* 3, 176–200.

Rosch, Eleanor (1973) On the internal structure of perceptual and semantic categories. In Timothy E. Moore (ed.), *Cognitive development and the acquisition of language*. New York: Academic Press, pp. 111–144.

(1978) Principles of categorization. In Eleanor Rosch and Barbara Lloyd (eds.), *Cognition and categorization*. Hillsdale, NJ: Lawrence Erlbaum Associates, pp. 27–48.

Rosch, Eleanor, and Mervis, Carolyn B. (1975) Family resemblances: studies in the internal structure of categories. *Cognitive Psychology* 7, 573–605.

Rosenblum, Tamar, and Pinker, Steven A. (1983) Word magic revisited: monolingual and bilingual children's understanding of the word-object relationship. *Child Development* 54, 773–780.

Ross, Gail S. (1979) Categorization in 1- and 2-year-olds. *Developmental Psychology* 16, 391–396.

Rumelhart, David E., and Norman, Donald A. (1982) Simulating a skilled typist: a study of skilled cognitive-motor performance. *Cognitive Science* 6, 1–36.

Saussure, Ferdinand de (1916/1968) *Cours de linguistique générale*, publié par Charles Bally et Albert Sechehaye, avec la collaboration de Albert Riedlinger. Paris: Payot.

Sauvageot, Aurélien (1951) *Esquisse de la langue hongroise*. Paris: Klincksieck.

(1971) *L'édification de la langue hongroise*. Paris: Klincksieck.

Savić, Svenka (1982, September) Universal and particular in lexical innovations of preschool children: a pilot study. Paper presented at the annual meeting of the European Society of Linguists, Athens.

Scalise, Sergio, Ceresa, Marco, Drigo, Marina, Gottardo, Maria, and Zannier, Irene (1983) Sulla nozione di *Blocking* in morfologia derivazionale. *Lingua e Stile* XVIII, 243–269.

Schaerlakens, Anne M. (1980) *De taalontwikkeling van het kind* (2nd edn). Groningen: Wolters-Noordhoff.

Schegloff, Emmanuel A., Jefferson, Gail, and Sacks, Harvey (1977) The preference for self-correction in the organization of repair in conversation. *Language* 53, 361–382.

Schenker, Alexander M. (1967) *Polish declension*. The Hague: Mouton.

(1973) *Beginning Polish*. New Haven, CT: Yale University Press.

Schieffelin, Bambi B. (1985) The acquisition of Kaluli. In Dan I. Slobin (ed.), *The crosslinguistic study of language acquisition*, vol. 1. Hillsdale, NJ: Lawrence Erlbaum Associates, pp. 525–593.

Schlieben-Lange, Brigitte (1971) Les grammaires normatives des langues romanes: principes et fondements. *Actes du 13ème congrès international de linguistique et de philologie romanes*, pp. 127–135.

Schultink, Henk (1961) Produktiviteit als morfologisch fenomeen. *Forum der Letteren* (Leiden) 2, 110–125.

Schupbach, Richard D. (1973) The limits of Russian derivation. *Lingua* 28, 301–328.

(1984) *Lexical specialization in Russian*. Columbus, OH: Slavica Publishers.

Schwartz, Joan (1980) The negotiation for meaning: repair in conversations between second language learners of English. In Diane Larsen-Freeman (ed.), *Discourse analysis in second language research*. Rowley, MA: Newbury House, pp. 138–153.

Schwartz, Richard G., and Leonard, Laurence B. (1982) Do children pick and choose? An examination of phonological selection and avoidance in early lexical acquisition. *Journal of Child Language* 9, 319–336.

Schwartz, Richard G., and Terrell, Brenda Y. (1983) The role of input frequency in lexical acquisition. *Journal of Child Language* 10, 57–64.

Schwarzwald, Ora R. (1975) More about the relationship between root and pattern in the Hebrew lexicon. *Hebrew Computational Linguistics* 9, 47–59.

(1981) *diqduq umeci'ut bapo'al ha'ivri* [Grammar and reality in the Hebrew verb]. Ramat-Gan: Bar-Ilan University Press.

Scollon, Ronald (1976) *Conversations with a one-year-old: a case study of the developmental foundation of syntax*. Honolulu, HA: University Press of Hawaii.

Seidler, Sabine (1988) Untersuchung zum Erwerb von Wortbildungsregeln Deverbativa Nomina (Agens und Instrument) im Französischen. Unpublished MA thesis, Universität Hamburg.

Selander, Einar (1980) Language for professional use from the Swedish point of view. *International Journal of the Sociology of Language* 23, 17–28.

Selkirk, Elisabeth O. (1982) *The syntax of words*. (Linguistic Inquiry Monograph 7.) Cambridge, MA: MIT Press.

Shibatani, Masayoshi (1976) The grammar of causative expressions. In Masayoshi Shibatani (ed.), *Syntax and semantics*, vol. 6: *The grammar of causative constructions*. New York: Academic Press, pp. 1–40.

Shipley, Elizabeth F., and Kuhn, Ivy F. (1983) A constraint on comparisons: equally detailed alternatives. *Journal of Experimental Child Psychology* 35, 195–222.

Simonyi, Zsigmond (1881) Az analógia hatásairól [The effects of analogy]. *Értekezések a Nyelv- és Széptudoományok köreből*. Budapest.

(1906) Két gyermek nyelvéről [From the language of two children]. *Magyar Nyelvőr* 35, 317–323.

Slobin, Dan I. (1966) The acquisition of Russian as a native language. In Frank Smith and George A. Miller (eds.), *The genesis of language: a psycholinguistic approach*. Cambridge, MA: MIT Press, pp. 129–148.

(1970) Universals of grammatical development in children. In Giovanni B. Flores d'Arcais and Willem J. M. Levelt (eds.), *Advances in psycholinguistics*. Amsterdam: North-Holland, pp. 174–186.

(1973) Cognitive prerequisites for the acquisition of grammar. In Charles A. Ferguson and Dan I. Slobin (eds.), *Studies of child language development*. New York: Holt, Rinehart and Winston, pp. 173–208.

(1978) A case study of early language awareness. In Anne Sinclair, Robert J. Jarvella, and Willem J. M. Levelt (eds.), *The child's conception of language*. New York: Springer, pp. 45–54.

(1981) The origins of grammatical encoding of events. In Werner Deutsch (ed.), *The child's construction of language*. London/New York: Academic Press, pp. 187–199.

(1985a) Crosslinguistic evidence for the Language-Making Capacity. In Dan I. Slobin (ed.), *The crosslinguistic study of language acquisition*, vol. 2. Hillsdale, NJ: Lawrence Erlbaum Associates, pp. 1157–1249.

Slobin, Dan I., (ed.), (1985b) *The crosslinguistic study of language acquisition* (2 vols.). Hillsdale, NJ: Lawrence Erlbaum Associates.

Slobin, Dan I. (1985c) Developmental paths between form and meaning: crosslinguistic and diachronic perspectives. Keynote Address, 10th annual conference on language development, Boston University, Boston, MA.

Slobin, Dan I., (ed.), (1992) *The crosslinguistic study of language acquisition*, vol. 3. Hillsdale, NJ: Lawrence Erlbaum Associates.

(1993) *The crosslinguistic study of language acquisition*, vol. 4. Hillsdale, NJ: Lawrence Erlbaum Associates.

Slobin, Dan I., and Bever, Thomas G. (1982) Children use canonical sentence schemes: a cross-linguistic study of word order and inflections. *Cognition* 12, 229–265.

Smedts, Willy (1979) Lexicale morphologie: de beheersing van de woordvorming door vlaamse 'brugklassers' [Lexical morphology: control of word formation by Flemish middle-school children]. Unpublished doctoral dissertation, Herent, Belgium.

Smith, Edward E., and Medin, Douglas L. (1981) *Categories and concepts*. Cambridge, MA: Harvard University Press.

Smith, Neilson V. (1973) *The acquisition of phonology: a case study.* Cambridge: Cambridge University Press.

Smoczyńska, Magdalena (1985) The acquisition of Polish. In Dan I. Slobin (ed.), *The crosslinguistic study of language acquisition*, vol. 1. Hillsdale, NJ: Lawrence Erlbaum Associates, pp. 595–686.

Snow, Catherine E., and Ferguson, Charles A. (eds.), (1977) *Talking to children: language input and acquisition.* Cambridge: Cambridge University Press.

Snyder, Alice D. (1914) Notes on the talk of a two-and-a-half year old boy. *Pedagogical Seminary* 21, 412–424.

Söderbergh, Ragnhild (1968) *Svensk Ordbildning.* Stockholm: Läromedelsförlagen.

(1979) Barnets språkliga kreativitet belyst av exempal från ordböjning och ordbilding [The linguistic creativity of children: word-inflection and word-formation]. *Språkform och Språknorm* 67, 236–245.

Soja, Nancy N. (1992) Inferences about the meanings of nouns: the relationship between perception and syntax. *Cognitive Development* 7, 29–45.

Soja, Nancy N., Carey, Susan, and Spelke, Elizabeth S. (1991) Ontological categories guide young children's inductions of word meaning: object terms and substance terms. *Cognition* 38, 179–211.

Spelke, Elizabeth S. (1990) Principles of object perception. *Cognitive Science* 14, 29–56.

Starkey, David (1979) The origins of concept formation: object sorting and object preference in early infancy. *Child Development* 52, 489–497.

Steinberg, Danny D., and Krohn, R. K. (1975) The psychological validity of Chomsky and Halle's vowel shift rule. In E. Koerner (ed.), *The transformational paradigm and modern linguistic theory.* Amsterdam: John Benjamins, pp. 233–259.

Sterling, Christopher M. (1983) The psychological productivity of inflectional and derivational morphemes. In Don Rogers and John A. Sloboda (eds.), *The acquisition of symbolic skills.* London: Plenum Press, pp. 179–185.

Stern, Clara, and Stern, William (1928) *Die Kindersprache: eine psychologische und sprachtheoretische Untersuchung* (4th rev. edn). Leipzig: Barth.

Stern, William (1924) *Psychology of early childhood* [translated from the 3rd rev. edn by Anna Barwell]. New York: Holt.

Sternberg, Saul, Monsell, Stephen, Knoll, Ronald L., and Wright, Charles E. (1980) The latency and duration of rapid movement sequences: comparisons of speech and typewriting. In Ronald A. Cole (ed.), *Perception and production of fluent speech.* Hillsdale, NJ: Lawrence Erlbaum Associates, pp. 469–505.

Sternberg, Saul, Wright, Charles E., Knoll, Ronald L., and Monsell, Stephen (1980) Motor programs in rapid speech: additional evidence. In Ronald A. Cole (ed.), *Perception and production of fluent speech.* Hillsdale, NJ: Lawrence Erlbaum Associates, pp. 507–534.

Straight, H. Stephen (1986) The importance and irreducibility of the comprehension/production dialectic. In Graham McGregor (ed.), *Language for hearers.* New York: Pergamon Press, pp. 69–90.

Strauss, Mark S. (1979) Abstraction of prototypical information by adults and 10-month-old infants. *Journal of Experimental Psychology* 5, 618–632.

Sully, James (1896) *Studies of childhood.* New York: Appleton.

Svartvik, Jan, and Quirk, Randolph (eds.), (1980) *A corpus of English conversation.* Lund: C. W. K. Gleerup.

Szuman, Stefan (1968) *O rozwoyu jezyka i myslenia dziecka* [On the development of language and thought in children]. Warsaw: Panstwowe Wydawnictwo Naukowe.

Taeschner, Traute (1983) *The sun is feminine.* Berlin and New York: Springer.

Talmy, Leonard (1985) Lexicalization patterns: semantic structure in lexical forms. In Timothy E. Shopen (ed.), *Language typology and syntactic description*, vol. 3: *Grammatical categories and the lexicon.* Cambridge: Cambridge University Press, pp. 57–149.

Taulelle, Dominique (1984) *L'enfant à la rencontre du langage.* Bruxelles: Pierre Mardaga.

Taylor, Marjorie, and Gelman, Susan A. (1988) Adjectives and nouns: children's strategies for learning new words. *Child Development* 59, 411–419.

(1989) Incorporating new words into the lexicon: preliminary evidence for language hierarchies in two-year-old children. *Child Development* 60, 625–636.

Templin, Mildred C. (1957) *Certain language skills in children: their development and interrelationships. Institute of Child Welfare Monograph* 26. Minneapolis, MN: University of Minnesota Press.

Thomson, Jean R., and Chapman, Robin S. (1977) Who is 'Daddy' revisited: the status of two-year-olds' over-extended words in use and comprehension. *Journal of Child Language* 4, 359–375.

Thompson, Sandra (1975) On the issue of productivity in the lexikon [sic]. *Kritikon Litterarum* 4, 332–349.

Thorell, Olof (1981) *Svensk ordbildningslära* [Swedish word formation]. Stockholm: Norstedts.

Thorndike, Edward L., and Lorge, Irving (1944) *A teacher's word book of thirty thousand words.* New York, NY: Teachers College, Columbia University.

Tinbergen, Dirk C. (1919) Kinderpraat. *De Nieuwe Taalgids* 13, 1–16, 65–86.

Toivainen, Jorma (1980) *Inflectional affixes used by Finnish-speaking children aged 1–3 years.* Helsinki: Suomalaisen Kirjallisuuden Seura.

Toivainen, Jorma (1993) Acquisition of Finnish as a first language. In Dan I. Slobin (ed.), *The crosslinguistic study of language acquisition*, vol. 4. Hillsdale, NJ: Lawrence Erlbaum Associates.

Tomasello, Michael (1992) *First verbs: a case study of early grammatical development.* Cambridge: Cambridge University Press.

Tomasello, Michael, Mannle, Sara, and Werdenschlag, Lori (1988) The effect of previously learned words on the child's acquisition of words for similar referents. *Journal of Child Language* 15, 505–515.

Toorn, Maarten C. van den (1976) *Nederlandse grammatica.* Groningen: Tjeenk Willink.

Trier, Jost (1934) Das sprachliche Feld. Eine Auseinandersetzung. *Neue Jahrbücher für Wissenschaft und Jugendbildung* 10, 428–449.

Tversky, Barbara, and Hemenway, Katherine (1984) Objects, parts, and categories. *Journal of Experimental Psychology: General* 113, 169–193.

Tyler, Lorraine K., Marslen-Wilson, William, Rentoul, James, and Hanney, Peter (1988) Continuous and discontinuous access in spoken word-recognition: the role of derivational prefixes. *Journal of Memory and Language* 27, 368–381.

Uhlenbeck, E. M. (1977) The concepts of productivity and potentiality in morphological description and their psycholinguistic reality. In Gabere Drachman (ed.), *Salzburger Beiträge zur Linguistik: Akten der 3. Salzburge Jahrestagung für Linguistik*. Salzburg: Neugebauer, pp. 379–392.

Ullmann, Stephen (1962) *Semantics*. New York: Barnes and Noble.

Unbegaun, Boris O. (1957) *Russian grammar*. Oxford: Oxford University Press.

Ushakova, Tatiana N. (1969) O mekhanizmakh detskogo slovotvorchestva [On mechanisms in children's word creation]. *Voprosy Psikhologii* 15, 62–74.

(1970) O prichinakh detskogo slovotvorchestva [On causes of children's word creation]. *Voprosy Psikhologii* 16, 114–127.

(1976) Children's word creation. In Jan Průcha (ed.), *Soviet studies in languag and language behavior*. (North-Holland Linguistic Series 24.) Amsterdam North-Holland Publishing, pp. 165–175.

Valentine, Charles W. (1942) *The psychology of early childhood*. London: Methuen

Velten, H. V. (1943) The growth of phonemic and lexical patterns in infant language. *Language* 19, 281–292.

Vihman, Marilyn M. (1985) Language differentiation by the bilingual infant *Journal of Child Language* 12, 297–324.

Villiers, Jill G. de (1985) Learning how to use verbs: lexical coding and the influence of input. *Journal of Child Language* 12, 587–595.

Vincent-Smith, Lisbeth, Bricker, Diane D., and Bricker, William (1974) Acquisition of receptive vocabulary in the child. *Child Development* 45, 189–193.

Vinson, Julien (1915–1916) Observations sur le développement du langage che l'enfant. *Revue de Linguistique* 48, 1–39.

Vogel, Irene (1975) One system or two: an analysis of a two-year-old Romanian English bilingual's phonology. *Papers and Reports on Child Languag Development* [Stanford University] 9, 43–62.

Vooys, Cornelis G. N. de (1916) Iets over woordvorming en woordbeteekenis in kindertaal. *De Nieuwe Taalgids* 10, 93–100, 128–141.

Walden, Zvia P. (1982) The root of roots: children's construction of word formation processes in Hebrew. Unpublished doctoral dissertation, Harvard University, Cambridge, MA.

Waldron, R. A. (1979) *Sense and sense development* (2nd rev. edn). London: Andre Deutsch.

Wales, Roger J., and Campbell, Robin N. (1970) On the development o comparison and the comparison of development. In Giovanni Flores d'Arcai and Willem J. M. Levelt (eds), *Advances in psycholinguistics*. Amsterdam North-Holland, pp. 373–396.

Walker, John (1936) *Walker's rhyming dictionary* (revised and enlarged by L. H Dawson). New York: Dutton.

Walmsley, Jane (1987) *Brit-think, Ameri-think*. London: Penguin.

Wartburg, Walther von (1963) *Problèmes et méthodes de la linguistique.* Paris: Presses Universitaires de France.

Wasow, Thomas, Sag, Ivan A., and Nunberg, Geoffrey (1983) Idioms: an interim report. In Shiro Hattori and Kazuko Inoue (eds.), *Proceedings of the XIIIth International Congress of Linguists,* August 19-September 4, 1982, Tokyo. Published under the auspices of the CIPL (The Hague), pp. 102–115.

Watt, William C. (1970) On two hypotheses concerning psycholinguistics. In John R. Hayes (ed.), *Cognition and the development of language.* New York: John Wiley and Sons, pp. 137–220.

Waxman, Sandra R., and Gelman, Rochel (1986) Preschoolers' use of superordinate relations in classification. *Cognitive Development* 1, 139–156.

Waxman, Sandra R., and Hatch, Thomas (1992) Beyond the basics: preschool children label objects flexibly at multiple hierarchical levels. *Journal of Child Language* 19, 153–166.

Weir, Ruth H. (1962) *Language in the crib.* The Hague: Mouton.

(1966) Some questions in the child's learning of phonology. In Frank Smith and George A. Miller (eds.), *The genesis of language.* Cambridge, MA: MIT Press, pp. 153–168.

Werner, Heinz, and Kaplan, Edith (1952) *The acquisition of word meanings: a developmental study. Monographs of the Society for Research in Child Development* 15 (Serial No. 51).

Whorf, Benjamin L. (1956) *Language, thought, and reality: selected writings of Benjamin Lee Whorf* (edited and with an introduction by John B. Carroll). Cambridge, MA: MIT. Press.

Woodward, Amanda L. (1992) The role of the whole object assumption in early word learning. Unpublished doctoral dissertation, Stanford University.

Woodward, Amanda L., and Markman, Ellen M. (1991) Constraints on learning as default assumptions: comments on Merriman and Bowman's 'The mutual exclusivity bias in children's word learning.' *Developmental Review* 11, 137–163.

Wunderlich, Dieter (1983) On the compositionality of German prefix verbs. In Rainer Bäuerle, Christoph Schwarze, and Arnim von Stechow (eds.), *Meaning, use, and interpretation of language.* Berlin: Walter de Gruyter, pp. 452–465.

(1987) An investigation of lexical composition: the case of German *be-* verbs. *Linguistics* 25, 283–331.

Younger, Barbara A. (1985) The segregation of items into categories by ten-month-old infants. *Child Development* 56, 1574–1583.

Younger, Barbara A., and Gotlieb, Sharon (1988) Development of categorization skills: changes in the nature or structure of infant form categories? *Developmental Psychology* 24, 611–619.

Zakharova, A. (1973) Acquisition of forms of grammatical case by preschool children. In Charles A. Ferguson and Dan I. Slobin (eds.), *Studies of child language development.* New York: Holt, Rinehart and Winston, pp. 281–284.

Zimmer, Karl E. (1964) *Affixal negation in English and other languages: an investigation of restricted productivity.* Supplement to *Word* 20, Monograph No. 5.

Zsidó, Vince (1928) Germeknyelv [Child language]. *Magyar Nyelvõr* 46, 243–2
Zsidó, Vince (1931) Adatok a gyermeknyelvhez [Data on child language]. *Mag
    Nyelvõr* 60, 92.
Zwanenburg, Wiecher (1981) Le principe du blocage dans la morpholᴇ
    dérivationnelle. In Saskia Daalder and Marinel Gerritsen (eds.), *Linguistic
    the Netherlands 1981.* Amsterdam: North-Holland, pp. 65–72.
    (1984) Word formation and meaning. *Quaderni di Semantica* 5, 130–142.

Index of names

Index of subjects